# Urban Revolution

AF216071

During the Great Leap Forward (1958–62), the collectivization of the Chinese countryside had catastrophic results, but how did this short-lived political experiment reshape urban life? In the first English history of urban collectivization, Fabio Lanza explores the most radical attempts to remake cities under Mao. Examining the universalization of production, the collectivization of life, including communal canteens and nurseries, and women's liberation, intended to transform modern urban life along socialist lines, he shows how many residents, and women in particular, struggled to enact a radical change in their every-day lives. He argues that the daily reality of millions of city residents proved the limitations of an effort that tied emancipation to industrial labor and substituted subjugation to the assembly line for subjugation to the stove, confronting some of the crucial contradictions of the socialist revolution.

Fabio Lanza is Professor of History and East Asian Studies at the University of Arizona.

# CAMBRIDGE STUDIES IN THE HISTORY OF THE PEOPLE'S REPUBLIC OF CHINA

*Series Editors*

Jennifer Altehenger, Jacob Eyferth, Daniel Leese, Michael Schoenhals, Aminda Smith

Cambridge Studies in the History of the People's Republic of China is a major series of ambitious works in the social, political, and cultural history of socialist China. Aided by a wealth of new sources, recent research pays close attention to regional differences, to perspectives from the social and geographical margins, and to the unintended consequences of Communist Party rule. Books in the series contribute to this historical re-evaluation by presenting the most stimulating and rigorously researched works in the field to a broad audience. The series invites submissions from a variety of disciplines and approaches, based on written, material or oral sources. Particularly welcome are those works that bridge the 1949 and 1978 divides, and those that seek to understand China in an international or global context.

A full list of titles in the series can be found at:
www.cambridge.org/HPRC

# Urban Revolution

*People's Communes in Beijing*

Fabio Lanza

*University of Arizona*

Shaftesbury Road, Cambridge CB2 8EA, United Kingdom

One Liberty Plaza, 20th Floor, New York, NY 10006, USA

477 Williamstown Road, Port Melbourne, VIC 3207, Australia

314–321, 3rd Floor, Plot 3, Splendor Forum, Jasola District Centre,
New Delhi – 110025, India

Cambridge University Press is part of Cambridge University Press & Assessment,
a department of the University of Cambridge.

We share the University's mission to contribute to society through the pursuit of
education, learning and research at the highest international levels of excellence.

www.cambridge.org
Information on this title: www.cambridge.org/9781009682435

DOI: 10.1017/9781009682459

First published 2026

*A catalogue record for this publication is available from the British Library*

*A Cataloging-in-Publication data record for this book is available from the Library
of Congress*

ISBN 978-1-009-68243-5 Hardback
ISBN 978-1-009-68247-3 Paperback

Cambridge University Press & Assessment has no responsibility for the persistence
or accuracy of URLs for external or third-party internet websites referred to in this
publication and does not guarantee that any content on such websites is, or will
remain, accurate or appropriate.

For EU product safety concerns, contact us at Calle de José Abascal, 56, 1°,
28003 Madrid, Spain, or email eugpsr@cambridge.org

To Mindy and our walks in Beijing

# Contents

# Maps

# Acknowledgments

The idea of a research project that took seriously the attempt to build a "Maoist everyday" emerged when I was in graduate school, and it followed me for over twenty years. As it always happens, this book carries very little resemblance to the one I originally set out to write: Its focus shifted, its articulation changed, and new questions grew out of old ones. There were archival brick walls I could not get past and intellectual turns I needed and wanted to follow. However, two elements remained steady throughout the years: my stubborn concern to try to understand Maoism as a "revolution in the quotidian" and a certain *political* commitment, which I hope comes through in the pages that follow.

I could not have made it to this point without the support, help, and criticism of friends and comrades. Rebecca Karl and Tani Barlow, both comrades *extraordinaires*, bravely slogged through an earlier draft of this manuscript and offered invaluable suggestions. Many others read portions of my work in progress and were instrumental in defining its directions: Jennifer Altehenger, Angie Baecker, Harlan Chambers, Chris Cheng, Susan Crane, Puck Engmann, Jacob Eyferth, Sean Forner, Cindy Gao, Diego Gullotta, Paola Iovene, Steve Johnstone, Benjamin Kindler, Covell Meyskens, Aaron Moore, Michael Schoenhals, Lewis Siegelbaum, Malcolm Thompson, and Yiching Wu. I am sure I am forgetting many others. The two readers at Cambridge University Press were the best kind of readers an author can wish for: critical yet supportive, thorough, and helpful. My former graduate student (and now professor in her own merit), Xuefei Ma, provided priceless help with some of the most unreadable archival documents. Jie Xiang came to the rescue when I needed to find some last-minute references. Over the years I presented sections of this work at conferences, workshops, and invited talks. I am sincerely thankful to all those – too many to mention here – who offered criticism, volunteered suggestions, and asked probing questions. There are those with whom I have shared intellectual paths, if not a direct research topic, and that common journey has made both my life and my research better: Federico Marcon, Claudia

Pozzana, Massimo Raveri, Alessandro Russo, Anna Shields, Kevin Yang, Angela Zito, and the comrades in both Critical China Scholars and positions politics.

Gail Hershatter has been an encouraging, wise, and generous presence throughout my entire academic career. Harriet Evans kindly shared archival documents (and good company in London). I am fortunate enough to work in two very friendly departments, with incredibly supportive chairs and colleagues. Sara Marchetta and Edoardo Chiamenti gave me a home in Beijing, while Harvey Maskvitys offered one in Tucson (with fresh eggs and Meyer lemons).

The archival research for this manuscript was funded by a three-year grant from Capital Normal University in Beijing, a one-year American Council of Learned Societies (ACLS) fellowship, and two grants from the Social and Behavioral Sciences Research Initiatives at the University of Arizona. A residency at the Institute for Advanced Studies in Princeton provided much-needed time as well as the perfect conditions for writing. I am very thankful to the archivists at Beijing Municipal and district archives; they were at times stern and unbending in their adherence to the rules, but always very sympathetic and helpful.

I wrote this book with Cambridge University Press and its series "Studies in the History of the People's Republic of China" in mind. I could not have asked for a better editor than Lucy Rhymer, who shepherded this project from the very first steps, and a better series director than Jennifer Altehenger.

Friends and family provided comfort and sanity in between the lonely writing hours: here's to Ani, Karrin, and Mickey in Lansing; Stacy in Tucson; Roger, Alain, Roberta, and Gian Luca in Venice. And to my mother and to Roberto, to brother Mauro, to Hannah, and to Caspar, whom I don't see often enough, alas. It's been a joy to witness Ashima Seth grow into a funny, clever, and beautiful person. Last but definitely not least, Aminda (Mindy) Smith has been an intellectual partner, a travel companion, and a true comrade, in all possible ways. This book is dedicated to her.

# Abbreviations

| | | |
|---|---|---|
| ACFTU | 中华全国总工会 | All-China Federation of Trade Unions |
| ACWF | 中华全国妇女联合会 | All-China Women's Federation |
| BMA | 北京市档案馆 | Beijing Municipal Archives |
| CCP | 中国共产党 | Chinese Communist Party |
| CYL | 中国共产主义青年团 | Communist Youth League |
| FFYP | 一五计划 | First Five-Year Plan |
| HDA | 海淀区档案馆 | Haidian District Archives |
| NPC | 全国人民代表大会 | National People's Congress |
| PRC | 中华人民共和国 | People's Republic of China |
| QMSYZ | 全民所有制 | Ownership by the whole people |
| *RMRB* | 人民日报 | *People's Daily* |
| SOE | 国营企业 | State-owned enterprise |
| XDN | 西城区档案馆 (北) | Xicheng District Archives (North) |
| XDS | 西城区档案馆 (南) | Xicheng District Archives (South) |

# Introduction

## I.1    Revolution in the Everyday

The research project behind this book began, as it often happens, with a question. It was a question that French theorist Henri Lefebvre posed, almost in passing, in his *The Production of Space*: "Has state socialism produced a space of its own? The question is not unimportant. A revolution that does not produce a new space has not realized its full potential; indeed it has failed in that it has not changed life itself, but has merely changed ideological superstructures, institutions or political apparatuses."[1] Since my first encounter with Lefebvre's work, in graduate school, this question has stayed with me. In 1974, Lefebvre was probably thinking primarily of the Soviet Union, and he refrained from providing any definitive, or even tentative answer – I suspect he was quite pessimistic in that regard. But then, what about Communist China? Did the Maoist revolution change life itself, did it produce new spaces, new social relations, a new quotidian, distinct and alternative to the one of capitalist societies? These were also the questions that, with much more practical urgency, (some) Chinese revolutionaries repeatedly asked of their own enterprise. They understood that Marxism was not simply an explanatory device to understand the world, but that it had to be, as Marx himself noted, the revolutionary praxis that changes it. That was even more the case for the particular form of Marxism that had animated the Chinese revolution and that stood as the ideological underpinning of the People's Republic of China. Mao Zedong thought (Maoism) was organized around the dialectical and necessary integration of theory and practice – it was a theory whose truth could only be expressed and universalized as a practice [2] – and, as such, its correctness could only

---

[1]  Henri Lefebvre, *The Production of Space*, translated by Donald Nicholson-Smith (Oxford: Blackwell, 1991): 55.

[2]  Christopher Leigh Connery, "Introduction: Worlded Pedagogy in Santa Cruz," in Rob Wilson and Christopher Leigh Connery, eds., *The Worlding Project: Doing Cultural Studies in the Era of Globalization* (Santa Cruz, CA: New Pacific Press, 2007): 97.

1

be manifested in its capacity to change the lives of "ordinary" people. For Mao and for others in the Chinese Communist Party (CCP), the measure of the revolution's success and failure then rested on the "new life" the socialist state could create and on which percentage of the people in China had access to that promised life.

Coherently, throughout the Maoist period, the Communist state displayed a stubborn insistence on changing lived practices, ranging from the foundational to the seemingly mundane. I argue that this was not the result of authoritarian obsession; rather, it reflected a specific understanding of the goal of Marxism, which is not, to cite Lefebvre again, "simply a matter of intensifying production, of cultivating new spaces, of industrializing agriculture, of building giant factories, of changing the State and then finishing once and for all with that monster, 'of all cold monsters the coldest.' These are merely means to an end. And what is that end? *It is the transformation of life in its smallest, most everyday detail.*"[3] Only such a transformation could prove and guarantee the success of the revolution.

For Lefebvre, "everyday life" is "a collection of things and activities that are repetitive and banal,"[4] the "humble and sordid side" of life and social practice, "the realm of the trivial."[5] Yet it is also and simultaneously "the time and the place where the human either fulfils itself or fails, since it is a place and a time which fragmented, specialized and divided activity cannot completely grasp, no matter how great and worthy that activity may be."[6] Everyday life is both the mediating element and the field of realization of any social transformation, in that "[w]hatever is produced or constructed in the superior realms of social practice must demonstrate its reality in the everyday, whether it be art, philosophy or politics … It is everyday life which measures and embodies the changes which take place 'somewhere else', in the 'higher realms.'"[7] Therefore, Lefebvre argued, everyday life is constituted by and constitutive of "the dialectical interaction that is the inevitable starting point for the realization of the possible."[8] Similarly, for Mao and his comrades, who had no connection to Lefebvre but shared his deep roots in Marxism and dialectical materialism, the critique of the social had to start from the

---

[3] Henri Lefebvre, *Critique of Everyday Life, vol. 1: Introduction*, translated by John Moore (London: Verso, 1991): 226. Emphasis mine.
[4] Rob Shields, *Lefebvre Love & Struggle: Spatial Dialectics* (Routledge, 1999): 69.
[5] Shields, *Lefebvre Love & Struggle*: 65.
[6] Henri Lefebvre, *Critique of Everyday Life, vol. 2: Foundations for a Sociology of the Everyday*, translated by John Moore (London: Verso, 2002): 19.
[7] Lefebvre, *Critique of Everyday Life*, vol. 2: 45.
[8] Henri Lefebvre, *Everyday Life in the Modern World* (New York: Transaction, 1984): 14.

minute and the ordinary, and, more specifically, the *trivial* – we will see in the following pages how the "trivial" character of housework was central to their analysis and approach. Therefore, politics was everyday life in Maoism. It focused on the space of the quotidian, where the encounter and the confrontation between the state, revolutionary movements, and the lives of "ordinary" people took place.

If everyday life is where the possibilities of revolutionary change are instantiated and verified, then no political praxis can exist apart from it. The tendency inherent in the political to separate itself from the everyday and to be identified with privileged moments or locations (the party, specific political figures, elections) must therefore be continuously fought against.[9] The history of Maoism is also the history of this seemingly relentless fight against politics as a separate activity, and of a collective attempt to address the everyday, or "social space" – which was how Lefebvre later reframed the concept of everyday life – as the site of political change. Because "social space" is "at once result and cause, product and producer; it is also a *stake*, the locus of projects and actions deployed as part of specific strategies, and hence also the object of *wagers* on the future."[10] This was particularly evident and urgent in the case of the Maoist China. The transition between one mode of production (capitalism) and another (communism) entailed the production of a new social space, characterized and defined by new social relations and new patterns of human interactions. Socialism was the transitional stage between these two modes of production and two spaces, but which social practices were more appropriate to produce the new relationships of the future remained a very much open question. In the perspective of Maoist politicians and thinkers, the space of the socialist city was therefore a specifically *transitional* space, the result of a transitional mode of production, embodying in its trivial details and in its minute functioning the promises of a communist future, the constraints of a resource-limited present, and the lingering threat of a reactionary and backward slippage into capitalism.

To examine this space, whose archival traces are fragmented, scattered, and elusive, I have chosen one specific instance of Maoist political experimentation, the urban commune movement in Beijing during the Great Leap Forward (1958–1963). Urban collectivization largely paralleled the establishment of communes in the countryside and followed

---

[9] Lefebvre, *Critique of Everyday Life*, vol. 1: 92. "Thus the critique of everyday life involves a critique of political life, in that everyday life already contains and constitutes such a critique: in that it is that critique."

[10] Lefebvre, *The Production of Space*: 142–143. Emphasis in the original.

similar strategies and principles, but urban communes were meant to tackle issues specific to the socialist city space. Unlike their rural counterpart, they developed at a slower and more cautious pace, they lasted only a few years, and the Great Leap did not produce in the cities the tragic outcomes it did in the countryside.[11] Urban collectivization embodied the promises and some of the methods of the Maoist project of social revolution. It was presented as a way to radically transform the very texture of modern urban life, to create new cities, new citizens, new forms of collective relationships. It centered on the involvement of supposedly idle female "dependents" (*jiashu* 家属) – primarily the spouses, but also other relatives of male workers[12] – in industrial production and on the concomitant expansion, at the neighborhood level, of collective welfare services to compensate for that now displaced domestic labor, such as communal canteens, nurseries, and service centers.[13] It combined three major goals, interconnected and interdependent: universalization of production, collectivization of life, and women's liberation.[14]

The choice of the Great Leap as a case study for the Maoist revolution in social relationships and everyday practices might sound a bit far-fetched. Most accounts of the Great Leap – generally focused on the rural side – depict it as a utopian daydream by Mao and a few other radicals centered on the *economic* sphere, with the goal of achieving previously unthinkable levels of productivity and overall industrial output by forcing Chinese workers and citizens to deploy almost superhuman amounts of physical labor. It was this productivist hubris, the irrational desire to jump over stages of economic development, the simplistic voluntarism that ignored the basic functions of remuneration and

---

[11] Felix Wemhauer, *Famine Politics in Maoist China and the Soviet Union* (New Haven, CT: Yale University Press, 2014); Gail Hershatter, *The Gender of Memory: Rural Women and China's Collective Past* (Berkeley: University of California Press, 2011).

[12] On the changing meaning of *jiashu*, see Yige Dong, "'Red Housekeeping' in a Socialist Factory: *Jiashu* and Transforming Reproductive Labor in Urban China (1949–1962)," *International Review of Social History* (January 18, 2024): 1–24, https://doi.org/10.1017/S0020859023000706. See also Song Shaopeng, "The State Discourse on Housewives and Housework in the 1950s in China," in Mechthild Leutner, ed., *Rethinking China in the 1950s* (Münster: LIT Verlag, 2007): 49–63.

[13] Janet Salaff, "The Urban Communes and Anti-City Experiment in Communist China," *China Quarterly*, no. 29 (January–March 1967): 82–110; Shih Ch'eng-chih, *Urban Commune Experiments in Communist China*, Communist China Problem Research Series (Hong Kong: Union Research Institute, 1962); D. E. T. Luard, "The Urban Communes," *China Quarterly*, no. 3 (July–September 1960): 74–79.

[14] Li Duanxiang 李端祥, *Chengshi renmin gongshe yundong janjiu* 城市人民公社运动研究 [Studies on the urban people's commune movement] (Changsha: Hunan Renmin Chubanshe, 2006).

incentivization, and the illogical effort to ground new relationships of production on underdeveloped productive forces that led to the disruption of the economy and the disastrous famine. The emphasis on steel production and the infamous practice of backyard furnaces are often cited as evidence of the foolishness of the project. This is not necessarily a completely wrong depiction in factual terms, but it is partial and very selective. It is also grounded on a historically and theoretically inappropriate understanding of what the Maoist (and Marxist) concept of "the economy" was and, more broadly, of what the stakes of political change were in the Mao era.

First, viewed from our present situation where the world is reduced to a stage for the triumph of global capitalism and history to the unavoidable advance of neoliberal homologation, the experience of socialism, and especially Maoism, can only appear incomprehensible. If we assume that "human behavior and experience of the world is always-already economic, in the classical political-economistic sense,"[15] the display of massive collective, self-sacrificing efforts to achieve radical transformations that went declaredly against that behavior can only be regarded as pathological. This is because, as Rebecca Karl has pointed out, socialism must be understood as presenting – potentially and perhaps always incompletely – a challenge to any capitalist teleology.[16] Thus, when we talk about the "socialist economy," we should consider it as programmatically exceeding and even subverting the capitalist sphere of "the economic." Maoist economics did, of course, include a central and crucial aspiration toward modernization, meant as development of modern industrial production – and the Great Leap is a primary example of that. But, following Marx, Maoist political economy was always defined by and based on a rejection of the economy as "an ontologically separate sphere of society governed by its own distinctive 'economic' logic or rationality." Rather the economy was a set of social relations.[17] Therefore the "economic" revolution that the Great Leap was supposed to produce directly implied the radical transformation of social relations, cultural distinctions, and everyday practices toward a more equal system, often *against* what would be classic economic rationality, that is, an economistic conception of the economy. One of the major flaws of several existing accounts of the debates and intra-Party maneuvers

---

[15] Rebecca E. Karl, *The Magic of Concepts: History and the Economic in Twentieth-Century China* (Durham, NC: Duke University Press, 2017): 23.
[16] Karl, *The Magic of Concepts*: 22.
[17] Søren Mau, *Mute Compulsion: A Marxist Theory of the Economic Power of Capital* (London: Verso, 2023): 21.

leading to the Great Leap is that, no matter if they center the semi-dictatorial role of Mao or point at other more structural causes, they all start from the assumption that "the economy" belongs to a separate and largely non-ideological sphere, with its own unchanging rationality. This is also the assumption underlying the CCP's own 1981 assessment of the Leap, a mistake attributed to the "inadequate understanding of the laws of economic development."[18] If one embraces that perspective, then the Maoist principle that different economic policies reflect ideological differences and that economic decisions do not belong to a sphere separate from political beliefs can only appear perverse and absurd.[19]

Second, even in the context of Maoist political experimentation, the Great Leap Forward stands out. Coming after a sustained period of industrial growth and the establishment of a socialist economy and socialist relationships, the Great Leap challenged the political meanings of that recently achieved configuration.[20] Following the main tenets of Maoism, this challenge took place in two closely intertwined but distinct venues: at a theoretical level, in a wide-ranging debate on the socialist economy and law of value,[21] and, in practice, through a nation-wide campaign aimed at inducing radical, far-reaching social and political

[18] "Resolution on Certain Questions in the History of Our Party since the Founding of the People's Republic of China" (1981), available at https://digitalarchive.wilsoncenter.org/document/resolution-certain-questions-history-our-party-founding-peoples-republic-china. See also William A. Joseph, "A Tragedy of Good Intentions: Post-Mao Views of the Great Leap Forward," *Modern China* 12:4 (October 1986): 419–457.

[19] See, for example, Alfred L. Chan, *Mao's Crusade: Politics and Policy Implementation in China's Great Leap Forward* (New York: Oxford University Press, 2001); Frederick C. Teiwes and Warren Sun, *China's Road to Disaster: Mao, Central Politicians and Provincial Leaders in the Great Leap Forward, 1955–59* (Armonk, NY: M. E. Sharpe, 1999). For an institutional analysis of the origins of the Leap, see David Bachman, *Bureaucracy, Economy, and Leadership in China: The Institutional Origins of the Great Leap Forward* (Cambridge: Cambridge University Press, 1991).

[20] While there seems to be widespread agreement about the overall growth in industrial production during the First Five-Year Plan, the assessment of the coeval process of agricultural collectivization is more varied. State investment disproportionally favored the industrial sector, but the generalized assumption that collectivization "failed to energize agricultural growth" (Yang) has been challenged by more recent scholarship. Yuan Gao, for example, has shown that, in certain areas, collectivization had very positive effects and led to steady growth. Yuan Gao, "Peasant Cooperation and Agricultural Growth in Historical Perspective: Southeastern Shanxi in the 1950s," *Modern China* 45:5 (2019): 537–563. For the more negative assessment, see Dali L. Yang, *Calamity and Reform in China: State, Rural Society, and Institutional Change since the Great Leap Famine* (Stanford, CA: Stanford University Press, 1996): 23.

[21] Michael Schoenhals, "Saltationist Socialism: Mao Zedong and the Great Leap Forward 1958," doctoral dissertation, University of Stockholm, 1987; Zhuoyuan Zhang, ed., *Historical Perspectives on Chinese Economics (1949–2011)*, translated by Xiaotong Zhang (Singapore: China Social Sciences Press/Springer, 2020).

changes in every aspect of the urban everyday *through mass participation in industrial work*.

The Great Leap – and specifically urban collectivization – can therefore best be understood as the first instance since the founding of the People's Republic of China (PRC) in which Chinese Marxists tried to tackle, directly and *through a mass campaign*, issues that had been left largely unsolved in the Soviet Union and about which only scant references could be found in the canonical texts by Marx and Lenin. These were also issues that had emerged starkly to the fore with the implementation of the First Five-Year Plan (FFYP), which, following the Soviet model, had led to the development of a sizable (urban) industrial base and industrial proletariat, but also to new forms of economic inequalities and social differences, seemingly incompatible with the egalitarian promise and revolutionary practice of Maoism. With the declared achievement of socialism in 1956 and with the contradictions of the FFYP in full display, the overarching concern of the late 1950s was how the vaunted transition from socialism to communism could be achieved, how quickly it should happen, what methods could be deployed to accelerate it, and how the progress of that transition could be measured and evaluated. The answers to these questions had huge and practical implications for the organization of the socialist planned economy, its structure of capital accumulation and distribution, but also for the kind of labor people were required to perform, for how they were going to be remunerated for that labor, and even for whom was actually included in the category of "worker." Intimately connected to that were the specific issues determining women's labor and women's liberation, meaning from what kind of labor women had to be liberated, through what kind of labor this liberation would happen, and how newly restructured socialist gender relationships would alter the structure of the family and society as a whole.

The task that Chinese Maoists set for themselves with the Great Leap was an ambitious one indeed, as these were issues that had loomed large in the history of the socialist revolution worldwide. Urban communes did produce changes in the everyday lives of urban residents; they provided responses to actual needs and yet generated new burdens. For example, communes freed women from the family, but the women later lamented the way they were tied to mind-numbing labor. When communes disappeared, opinions were divided, and the disappearance was neither universally decried nor universally welcomed. Yet – and this is why I argue that this experience was and remains important – collectivization, as a political quest, included a shift in national policy, a radical mass movement, and daily sacrifices by millions of people, and through that experiential process, new and old contradictions within the project of socialist revolution were unearthed, disputed, and experimented on. Once again, this did not simply happen at the level of intellectual debate and political discussion, but those contradictions – between productivity and equality, social reproduction and production – became the lived experience of millions of urban denizens.

The end of the Great Leap in the aftermath of the famine did not necessarily mark the end of the discussion and experimentation on the issues it had helped highlight. The debate on the socialist economy and the law of value continued, after a pause, during the Cultural Revolution – when Mao famously incited people to study "a little political economy"[22] – and there were several attempts to shape alternative models of labor organization and relationships of production in the workplace.[23] But those experiments never reached the level of mass mobilization and mass participation of the Great Leap. Similarly, as Wang Zheng has argued, questions related to women's liberation and social reproduction were summarily foreclosed after 1960, and while the issue of gender equality never disappeared, especially thanks to the often behind-the-scenes work of the All-China Women's Federation (ACWF), it never acquired again the defining role it had during the Great Leap.[24]

Then, contrary to what still is the prevalent opinion in English- and Chinese-language scholarship, which dismisses the project of the Great Leap as pure hubris and reduces it to the playing out of intricate intra-Party games or to its tragic ending, the years of the Great Leap constituted an attempt to challenge crucial issues concerning the socialist economy, socialist relations of production, and social reproduction. These are all issues that, to this day, are highly relevant to anyone who is either interested in the history of the socialist experiment or invested in the future of radically progressive politics.

## I.2    Problems of Socialism

By the second half of the 1950s, it had become evident, at least to some among the CCP leadership, that while Soviet-style industrialization under the First Five-Year Plan had brought undeniable and substantial

---

[22] Peer Moller Christensen and Jorgen Delman, "A Theory of Transitional Society: Mao Zedong and the Shanghai School," *Bulletin of Concerned Asian Scholars* 13:2 (1981): 2–15.

[23] Andrea Piazzaroli Longobardi, "What Does a Socialist Factory Produce? Workers in the Chinese Cultural Revolution," *PRC History Review* 6:1 (February 2021): 1–13, https://networks.h-net.org/volume-6-number-1-february-2021.

[24] Wang Zheng, *Finding Women in the State: A Socialist Feminist Revolution in the People's Republic of China, 1949–1964* (Berkeley: University of California Press, 2016).

results in terms of production and capital accumulation,[25] that process had also led to a rapid increase in old and new socioeconomic inequalities and to other social phenomena that seemed incompatible with the political goals of socialism. The development of Chinese industry had been achieved through a system that relied heavily on strict labor discipline – Taylorist methods having been refined in the USSR and then transferred to the PRC – centered on "one-man management," and where productivity was enforced through material incentives and marked wage differences. By 1956, wage points were eliminated and substituted almost universally with piece-rate salaries, which were supposed to better reflect the principle of "remuneration according to labor" and more actively spur individual workers' productivity.[26] Not only did the First Five-Year Plan exacerbate and enshrine preexisting differences between urban and rural residents,[27] as it was capital extraction from agriculture that financed urban industries, but it also created quite marked differences among employees of the industrial sectors; between managers, technicians, and workers; and among the urban proletariat themselves.

These new inequities within the working class were at the same time balanced and made starker by the establishment of the system of the urban work unit (*danwei* 单位), which marked the emergence of what one might consider as the "new normal" of Maoist urban life, embodied by the workers in state-owned enterprises (SOEs), the proud masters of the country. For them, the imposition of labor discipline and the experience of wage differences were mitigated by the guarantee of lifetime employment and an expansive set of (nonmonetary) welfare provisions (*fuli* 福利), ranging from childcare to healthcare, from housing to leisure opportunities.[28] Yet the life of those workers was, in Li Huaiyin's

---

[25] Between 1952 and 1957, Chinese industry grew at an annual rate of 16–18 percent. Urban industrial employment also increased, from approximately 6 million to 10 million workers. Maurice Meisner, *Mao's China and After: A History of the People's Republic*, 3rd ed. (New York: Free Press, 1999): 113.

[26] Charles Hoffmann, "Work Incentive Policy in Communist China," *China Quarterly*, 17 (January–March 1964): 95–96; "Quanguo zonggonghui zhishi gonghui geji zuzhi fadong qunzhong canjia he jiandu gongzi gaige gongzuo" 全国总工会指示工会各级组织 发动群众参加和监督工资改革工作" [The All-China Federation of Trade Unions instructs trade union organizations at all levels to mobilize the masses to participate in and supervise the wage reform process], *RMRB*, July 6, 1956.

[27] "During the First Five-Year Plan (1953–57), even though the rural sector produced more than half of the income and employed more than 80 percent of the labor force, it received less than 8 percent of the total state investment, in contrast to more than 52 percent for industry." Yang, *Calamity and Reform in China*: 22.

[28] On the history of the *danwei*, see David Bray, *Social Space and Governance in Urban China: The Danwei System from Origins to Reform* (Stanford, CA: Stanford University Press, 2005).

summation, a "closed ecosystem," whose members were "entitled to a full range of rights and privileges unavailable to the working population outside the system."[29] The normativity of the *danwei* worker remained at best aspirational and at worst a mirage, not only for the overwhelming majority of the population in rural areas but also for large swaths of urban residents: workers in collectively owned enterprises, temporary employees, peddlers, small shop owners, and the unemployed. By the late 1950s, when the *danwei* form became fully established, the city "was structured through a dual administrative system consisting of the urban neighborhood and work unit system."[30] The work unit controlled and provided for those who were formally employed (full-fledged "workers"), while neighborhood organizations strove to integrate people who labored in small stores, workshops, or family businesses, as well as those who technically did not participate in social productive labor (housewives, old and young people, the sick).[31] Obviously, the benefits and services provided to these two groups of urban residents were vastly unequal.

Mao was among those who had grown worried of these socioeconomic developments, and he intervened directly in the debate with his famous speech "On the Ten Major Relationships" in April 1956, when he directly tackled the new inequalities Soviet-style industrialization had produced. He singled out, among other issues, the preference for heavy industry over both light industry (objects of everyday use) and agriculture, the geographical unbalance of its distribution, and the tension between capital accumulation and the improvement of workers' conditions. On this latter issue, Mao did not simply make the "economist" argument that, with the increase of productivity and the growth of the economy as a whole, wages should also increase. Rather, his was a distinctly political intervention, in which he refused the supposed separateness of the economic sphere and stressed that reducing wage and income inequalities as well as improving the everyday life of the masses was a crucial component of the CCP's revolutionary mission and one of the main reasons for the existence of the PRC state.[32] Less than a year later, Mao returned to these themes in his "Contradictions" speech. There he highlighted again the unabated tension between accumulation and consumption in the socialist economy, but he also hinted at a

---

[29] Li Huaiyin, *The Master in Bondage: Factory Workers in China, 1949–2019* (Stanford, CA: Stanford University Press, 2023): 23.
[30] Lu Duanfang, *Remaking Chinese Urban Form: Modernity, Scarcity and Space, 1949–2005* (London: Routledge, 2006): 49.
[31] Lu, *Remaking Chinese Urban Form*: 50.
[32] Mao Zedong, "On the Ten Major Relationships" (April 25, 1956), www.marxists.org/reference/archive/mao/selected-works/volume-5/mswv5_51.htm.

critique of the supposed primacy of "the development of the productive forces" as the motor of historical transformation, which was then dominant among CCP leaders and theoreticians. Mao complained that, despite the rapid development of productive forces under socialism, socialist relationships of production had not been transformed, and contradictions, he stated, continued to exist not only between workers and other classes but among workers themselves, as well as between workers and the state, that socialist state of which the workers were the putative masters.[33]

By the mid 1950s, Mao was therefore starting to elaborate a criticism of – and searching for ways to move past – the developmental experience of the Soviet Union, as well as some basic assumptions of vulgar Marxism. None of the contradictions and tensions that had materialized in China in coincidence with the Five-Year Plan were particularly new, as pretty much the very same issues had emerged in the USSR at least thirty years earlier. Yet the Soviet experience offered little guidance to Chinese leaders and no solace to their preoccupations. Marx and Engels had written little about the overarching question of what to do after the victory of the proletarian revolution, that is, how to structure a state, an economy, and a set of social relationships in ways most conducive to achieve the transition from capitalism through socialism and into communism.[34] It rested on the people who conducted the first successful socialist revolution to come up with some answers.

In 1918, Lenin insisted that the foremost priority for Soviet industry was to raise the productivity of labor, and for that, he promoted the adoption of Taylorist rules in the factories, "*iron* discipline" and "*unquestioning obedience*" among workers, wages pegged to skill grades and output, "the strictest and universal accounting," and "one-man management." He wrote: "We must raise the question of piece-work and apply and test it in practice; we must raise the question of applying much of what is scientific and progressive in the Taylor system; we must make wages correspond to the total amount of goods turned out, or to the amount of work done by the railways, the water transport system, etc., etc."[35] A year later, Lenin went even further and argued that what really made socialism

---

[33] Mao Zedong, "On the Correct Handling of Contradictions among the People" (February 27, 1957), www.marxists.org/reference/archive/mao/selected-works/volume-5/mswv5_58.htm.

[34] There were only a few passages in Marx's *Critique of the Gotha Program* and in Engels's *Anti-Dühring*. See Chapter 2.

[35] V.I. Lenin, "The Immediate Tasks of the Soviet Government" (March–April 1918), in *Collected Works*, 4th English ed., vol. 27 (Moscow: Progress Publishers, 1972): 235–277, www.marxists.org/archive/lenin/works/1918/mar/x03.htm. Emphasis in the original. I am thankful to Lewis Siegelbaum for his help on these issues; see his "Soviet Inflection Points – A Play in Three Acts," unpublished.

superior to capitalism and what would guarantee the victory of the new social system was the higher productivity of labor under that system. As capitalism had vanquished feudalism by creating a productivity of labor heretofore unknown, so socialism too will vanquish capitalism by "creating a new and much higher productivity of labor." As Lenin repeated, this was to be achieved by "voluntary, class-conscious and united workers employing advanced techniques," thus through a form of labor radically different from that of capitalism. Of course, Lenin was speaking within the historical constraints and under the political urgency of the civil war. Yet his identification of communism with "the higher productivity of labor" – rather than, for example, the elimination of inequalities – remains a stark and significant choice.[36]

In the 1920s, some of those Soviet "voluntary, class-conscious and united workers" organized themselves in urban communes, with the goal of achieving both increasing productivity through the rational and scientific self-discipline of their own labor and the radical transformation of the daily life of the past into a more equal, collective, and revolutionary everyday. These communes were different in organization, overall scope, goals, and historical conditions from those in the PRC thirty years later, and the Chinese case does not seem to have drawn any inspiration from the Soviet one. Yet there were similarities: Both constituted a radical, collective reaction to what were perceived as socioeconomic problems created by state policies (the New Economic Policy in Russia, Soviet-style industrialization in China); both focused on the everyday as the location of revolutionary change; and both were defined by a tendency toward egalitarianism, as the prefiguration of the universal equality to come.[37]

The experience of the Soviet urban communes reached its end in the early 1930s, with the affirmation of Stalin's "managerial turn." In 1931, he condemned wage equalization as a "leftist practice," which prevented differentiating between skilled and unskilled labor or heavy and light work, dampened enthusiasm, and led to "fluidity of manpower." Against that he reaffirmed the need for precise business accounting, strict labor discipline, wage scales based on actual labor output, and the personal responsibility of each and every worker for their own

---

[36] V.I. Lenin, "A Great Beginning: Heroism of the Workers in the Rear 'Communist Subbotniks'" (June 28, 1919), in *Collected Works*, vol. 29: 408–434, www.marxists.org/archive/lenin/works/1919/jun/19.htm.

[37] Andy Willimott, *Living the Revolution: Urban Communes & Soviet Socialism, 1917–1932* (Oxford University Press, 2017); Lewis H. Siegelbaum, "Production Collectives and Communes and the 'Imperatives' of Soviet Industrialization, 1929–1931," *Slavic Review* 45:1 (Spring 1986): 65–84.

work.[38] In 1934, Stalin reasserted these principles in his report to the Party. In that report, however, he also added a sharp criticism of those who wanted to push toward a "supply system," with direct provision of goods and consequent abolition or restriction of the role of commerce and of money. He directly attacked the experience of urban communards, "[l]eftist blockheads, who at one time idealised the agricultural communes to such an extent that they even tried to set up communes in mills and factories, where skilled and unskilled workers, each working at his trade, had to pool their wages in a common fund, which was then shared out equally." He concluded, "You know what harm these infantile equalitarian exercises of the 'Left' blockheads caused our industry." [39] It was this Stalinist economic orthodoxy that made its way to the PRC and shaped not only the first Five-Year Plan but much economic thinking in 1950s China. Industrialization was centered on "one-man management," with professional managers mostly drawn from the pre-1949 intelligentsia, under which workers were subject to "increasingly strict codes of labor discipline," with "increasing wage and status differentials" within their ranks.[40]

## I.3     Expanding the New Normal

By the second half of the 1950s, Mao had become quite wary of both the theoretical tenets and the practical implications of that orthodoxy. As early as 1956, he encouraged the Party at the Eighth National Congress to criticize the Soviet Union and to identify error where there was error: "The slogan we have advocated all along is to draw on the advanced Soviet experience. Who told you to pick up its backward experience? Some people are so undiscriminating that they say a Russian fart is fragrant. That too is subjectivism. The Russians themselves say it stinks. Therefore, we should be analytical." [41] Two years later, the Great Leap Forward represented the moment in which that critique merged into a collective search for alternative models and for solutions to the inequalities and contradictions that were plaguing

---

[38] J. V. Stalin, "New Conditions – New Tasks in Economic Construction" (June 23, 1931), www.marxists.org/reference/archive/stalin/works/1931/06/23.htm.

[39] J. V. Stalin, "Report to the Seventeenth Party Congress on the Work of the Central Committee of the C.P.S.U.(B.)" (January 26, 1934), www.marxists.org/reference/archive/stalin/works/1934/01/26.htm.

[40] Meisner, *Mao's China and After.* 117.

[41] Mao Zedong, "Strengthen Party Unity and Carry Forward Party Traditions" (August 30, 1956), www.marxists.org/reference/archive/mao/selected-works/volume-5/mswv5_53.htm.

Chinese industrialization – as they had plagued Soviet industrialization before. Urban collectivization was the form this search took for residents in Chinese cities.

As mentioned earlier, the First Five-Year Plan had created new patterns of socioeconomic inequalities in urban centers, and primary among them was one that split the urban working class itself: on the one hand, the "new" urban proletariat, employed in SOEs or state agencies or institutions, such as schools or hospitals, and, on the other, the rest of the urban population, who toiled under different and less protected arrangements. Under the FFYP, state investment flowed directly to specific projects and to the relevant *danwei*, thus making work units financially and administratively independent of the surrounding city. As David Bray argues, the result of that investment structure was that work units were "generally much better funded and thereby able to provide a higher standard of facilities and services for their employees than were available to urban residents in the collective-owned sector or who didn't belong to a *danwei*."[42] This division among urban workers was also reflected in the Beijing urban space. Because resources had flowed from the top into each large organization (factories, schools, institutions), that in turn led to a "scattered" pattern of urban development, with an inefficient and often autarchic use of land. Beijing expanded massively by the mid 1950s, but that growth was heavily skewed toward government offices, schools, and factories (which doubled in terms of built surface), while housing and services enjoyed comparatively less significant growth (around 40 percent). In the 1950s, Beijing suffered from a chronic lack of residential space as well as a haphazard distribution in terms of stores and services. And while SOEs could provide for their workers in situ, the rest of the urban population often had to traverse the city in search of accessible services.[43] Beijing in a sense stands as the opposite case to that of Daqing, which Hou Li has analyzed: While Daqing was thoroughly and uniformly planned as an oil town, in Beijing the interaction between the plan and the existing physical/social structure created radical differences and a massive unbalance in the very configuration of the city and the lives of residents.[44] Urban communes were supposed to provide a (partial) solution to that unbalance.

[42] Bray, *Social Space and Governance in Urban China*: 143.
[43] Fabio Lanza, "A City of Workers, a City for Workers? Remaking Beijing Urban Space in the Early PRC," in Ding Yannan, Maurizio Marinelli, and Zhang Ziaohong, eds., *China: A Historical Geography of the Urban* (London: Palgrave Macmillan, 2018): 41–66.
[44] Hou Li, *Building for Oil: Daqing and the Formation of the Chinese Socialist State* (Cambridge, MA: Harvard University Press, 2018).

Nationally, urban communes were organized according to three distinct forms: They could be centered around a government institution, an agency, or a school; they could be constructed around a large factory; or they could be based on the bottom-up development of neighborhood enterprises.[45] In Beijing, SOE *danwei* had been established primarily in the suburban areas, so the people who remained programmatically excluded from that life and its set of privileges tended to reside in the downtown area, within the perimeters of the old city walls (*chengqu* 城区).[46] They occupied the physical space defined by the networks of tiny alleys (*hutong* 胡同), the now mostly gone neighborhoods whose later history Harriet Evans has vividly depicted.[47] Most of the communes I analyze in the following pages were located in this space, and not by chance. Like their rural counterparts, urban communes aimed at expanding at least some of the features of the aspirational normativity of the SOE work unit to the rest of the population, thus offering a remedy to some of the ingrained inequalities in socialist urban space and a glimpse into a potential, more equal future. The overwhelming majority of urban communes in Beijing, then, belonged to the third kind; that is, they were grounded in neighborhood production. And while in other cities communes could vary substantially in terms of the size of their administrative area (some being as large as an entire city district), in Beijing, urban communes coincided with preexisting subdistrict offices, thus largely avoiding administrative overlaps and confusion.

Urban communes could not solve the more entrenched problems of urban distribution in the capital city. Housing scarcity remained a huge issue, and the following chapters provide examples of communes scrambling to find room for workshops, canteens, and kindergartens in the overpopulated downtown. Urban collectivization did not attempt to promote communal housing or break down the one-family home. Yet communes, while they could not radically alter the physical structure of the city, affected the urban everyday of the capital in ways that were otherwise profound. To those people excluded from the *danwei* system, participation in urban communes offered a series of benefits through a set of newly established collective services: prepared meals at communal canteens; childcare at nurseries, kindergarten, and crèches; personal care at barbers and bathhouses; plus tool repairs, house cleaning, washing and

---

[45] Li, *Chengshi renmin gongshe yundong janjiu*: 9.
[46] The term 城区 refers to the districts that were originally within the city walls. I translate it as "inner city" or "downtown."
[47] Harriet Evans, *Beijing from Below: Stories of Marginal Lives in the Capital's Center* (Durham, NC: Duke University Press, 2020).

mending clothes, and even sometimes forms of intimate care, like visiting the elderly and the sick, or helping with weddings, funerals, and so on. The introduction of these services and of industrial workshops in the downtown areas strengthened the "mixed land-use pattern" of the old city.[48] Because these services were, at least programmatically, reserved for members of the communes – that is, they were made possible by and in exchange for work in commune enterprises – they configured an embryonic form of the supply system that existed in the SOE *danwei*, where salaries constituted only a part of the workers' remuneration. In a reversal of the Stalinist doxa, the communes thus were also expanding the scope of relationships of production not entirely based on wages and monetary exchange. And indeed, urban collectivization coincided with a theoretical critique of rigid salary scales and of the system of wages in general, which was reflected in an overall reduction of the more exploitative and disciplinary forms of remuneration, in what were later disparagingly labeled the "egalitarian" or "communist" winds of 1958–1959. The initial development of urban communes marked the temporary but widespread elimination of piece-rate wages, the wholesale adoption of nonmaterial incentives, and the overall compression of salary scales, with the goal of reducing socioeconomic differences.

## I.4    Liberation through Production

Key to collectivization was a massive expansion of the urban labor force and its deployment in commune enterprises, which were supposed to recruit and organize almost anybody who could perform some kind of work: the young, the old, the weak, the disabled, but first and foremost women. Formerly unproductive "housewives" (*jiating funü* 家庭妇女) or "dependents" (*jiashu*) left their homes to create neighborhood factories from scratch, mostly devoted to finishing work for larger SOEs and to manufacture of objects of everyday use. Production in commune factories, created not through a top-down dispersal of capital but through a bottom-up deployment of (female) labor, was supposed to lead to a rapid increase in overall industrial output, but it also had other, more radical implications. These factories were supposed to be centered on light industry and everyday products, thus redressing the unbalance toward heavy industry of the Five-Year Plan; it was through their capital accumulation that collectivized services were going to be financed; and finally, it was through women's participation in (productive) labor and

---

[48] Lu, *Remaking Chinese Urban Form*: 121.

the correlated socialization of domestic work that the old patriarchal family life was supposed to be radically transformed, leading to the "complete liberation of women."

In making women's liberation strictly dependent on – or at least inextricably linked to – their participation in industrial labor, Chinese Maoists were following what was then considered the orthodox Marxist path. And in this case, unlike in their critique of Stalinist economics, they did not significantly diverge from it, at least in the initial arguments for the campaign. Marx had never extensively addressed women's oppression and their liberation, so the canonical reference, often cited in Great Leap–era debates, was Engels, who in *The Origin of the Family, Private Property and the State* had argued that the oppression of women under capitalism was due to their being confined to domestic labor, isolated in the home, and denied participation in social productive labor. That situation, Engels argued, could only be amended through the expansion of modern industry and the concurrent socialization of domestic labor:

The emancipation of woman will only be possible when woman can take part in production on a large, social scale, and domestic work no longer claims anything but an insignificant amount of her time. And only now has that become possible through modern large-scale industry, which does not merely permit of the employment of female labor over a wide range, but positively demands it, while it also tends towards ending private domestic labor by changing it more and more into a public industry.[49]

In 1921, Lenin similarly celebrated the abolition of the private ownership of land and factories as one of the most important steps toward women's equality, as it had opened the way for their liberation from "household bondage" through the transition from petty individual housekeeping to large-scale socialized domestic services.[50] To Engels's assessment, Lenin added the determination that women were further oppressed because domestic work was "backward, little rationalized by machines, and stultifyingly repetitive."[51] In the same 1919 text in which he singled out higher productivity as the hallmark of communism, Lenin also elaborated on the slavery of housework and women's emancipation:

Notwithstanding all the laws emancipating woman, she continues to be a domestic slave, because petty housework crushes, strangles, stultifies and

[49] Frederick Engels, *The Origin of the Family, Private Property and the State* (1884), www .marxists.org/archive/marx/works/1884/origin-family/index.htm.
[50] V. I. Lenin, "International Working Women's Day" (March 4, 1921), www.marxists .org/archive/lenin/works/1921/mar/04.htm.
[51] Diemut Elisabet Bubeck, *Care, Gender, and Justice* (Oxford: Oxford University Press, 1995): 48.

degrades her, chains her to the kitchen and the nursery, and she wastes her labour on barbarously unproductive, petty, nerve-racking, stultifying and crushing drudgery. The real emancipation of women, real communism, will begin only where and when an all-out struggle begins (led by the proletariat wielding the state power) against this petty housekeeping, or rather when its wholesale transformation into a large-scale socialist economy begins.[52]

In the early days of the PRC, the pursuit of women's liberation was framed in terms close to those of Engels and Lenin. For example, in 1949, as historian Wang Zheng recounts, the Shanghai Women's Federation declared that the long-term goal of organizing housewives was "to liberate them from subordinate positions and to engage them in social production," thus creating a "reserve labor force" that would be progressively integrated into industrial work.[53] This meant, as Song Shaopeng has highlighted, that, because "the state ideology maintained that only productive work created history," only women participating in social production *outside the home* could claim the same worker identity as their male counterparts.[54] "What went on in the home was not labor, but domestic tasks (*jiawu huo*),"[55] and housewives were at times described as "political parasites."[56] So, while CCP policies toward "woman-work" were theoretically grounded on the principle of equal rights enshrined in the marriage law, "the official approach to gender equality (*nannü pingdeng*) did not include a focus on the gender arrangements of family and domestic life."[57] By the mid 1950s, however, the ACWF pushed forth a reevaluation of domestic work as essential, providing an "indirect contribution to socialism," and encouraged the *jiashu* to perform the "five goods": "Maintain good harmony in the family and neighborhood and give mutual assistance, organize a good domestic life, give children a good education, encourage their dear ones to do good work and study well, and push themselves to obtain good results in their studies."[58] While this form of "red housekeeping" was officially celebrated, it remained conceptually and practically subsidiary to "productive work," and "women continued to be viewed as secondary workers and primary caregivers."[59]

Delia Davin pointed out the contradiction between a theory according to which "women were to liberate themselves through participation in

[52] Lenin, "A Great Beginning."    [53] Wang, *Finding Women in the State*: 31.
[54] Song, "The State Discourse on Housewives and Housework in the 1950s in China": 50.
[55] Hershatter, *The Gender of Memory*: 186.
[56] Song, "The State Discourse on Housewives and Housework in the 1950s in China": 50.
[57] Harriet Evans, *The Subject of Gender: Daughters and Mothers in Urban China* (Lanham, MD: Rowman and Littlefield, 2007): 12.
[58] Song, "The State Discourse on Housewives and Housework in the 1950s in China": 53.
[59] Dong, "Red Housekeeping": 6.

productive labour" and a reality where "urban women were often unable to get jobs."[60] As of 1953, only 6 percent of the entire female population was employed in state- owned industrial enterprises, [61] and even those, Davin recounts, continued to be solely responsible for childcare, washing clothes, food preparation, and domestic work in general.[62] Most urban women in the 1950s were still "housewives."[63] In the early 1950s, these unemployed women were often organized in "dependents' associations" whose "basic purpose was to help the dependants of workers to under-stand and assist their men folk and to provide a harmonious home atmosphere so that they might give their whole attention to their jobs." These associations did work that benefited female urban residents, yet they implicitly and explicitly endorsed the principle that certain women "should make their contribution to society not as independent producers, but as the wives and mothers of productive workers, the limelight heroes of the new society."[64] This subordinate position was reinforced in 1957, when at the Third National Women's Congress, the ACWF adopted the new agenda of "diligently, frugally build the country, and diligently, frugally manage the family" (qinjian jianguo, qinjian chijia 勤俭建国, 勤俭持家), the so-called two diligences. As of July 1958, this policy was slated to last for ten or twenty years, drastically postponing any plan to socialize housework and to radically reform social relations within the family.[65] Yet, just a few weeks later, with the inception of the Great Leap, that policy was reversed, and the project of women's liberation was once again connected with social production and productive labor *outside the home*.

Sources from the urban commune campaign reproduced Engels's and Lenin's language to articulate the central junction in the economic/social/political revolution that the Great Leap was supposed to achieve. Women's mass participation in commune industrial labor would fuel massive production increase, and it would also turn them from housewives, toiling unproductively in isolation, into truly socialized, productive workers; it would free them from the dull, trivial, and repetitive tasks of housework and move them into the world of modern and (eventually) mechanized production, whose profits would allow in turn for the

---

[60] Delia Davin, *Woman Work: Women and the Party in Revolutionary China* (Oxford: Oxford University Press, 1976): 59.
[61] Dong, "Red Housekeeping": 11.
[62] Davin, *Woman Work*: 182. In one case mentioned in Davin's book, the husband initially helped with housework, but "when his fellow workers laughed at him and said that he was 'unmanly' and 'henpecked' he became embarrassed and stopped."
[63] Song, "The State Discourse on Housewives and Housework in the 1950s in China": 49.
[64] Davin, *Woman Work*: 60.      [65] Wang, *Finding Women in the State*: 74.

socialization of food preparation, laundry, and childrearing through the establishment of more efficient communal services. In Yige Dong's trenchant summation, "the collectivization of reproduction in the urban commune was not only meant to free up more labor to enter production, but it was also to turn social reproduction itself into a site of 'mass production,' latently following the same logic of concentration and centralization that dictates modern industrial production."[66]

However, despite the backbreaking efforts of thousands of urban residents, urban collectivization did not fulfil these promises. In the cities, as in the countryside, the Great Leap did not work. In fact, it probably never could have worked, given how brief this experiment was and how it was always hampered by practical limitations. Urban communes were first created in 1958, at the same time as the rural ones; the campaign was temporarily slowed down at the end of the year, only to restart with full force in 1960, but by 1961 most of commune social services were being dismantled and those communal enterprises that were still deemed productive were transferred to the control of other administrative units. By 1962, most urban communes had ceased to function.

That failure, like the overall failure of the Great Leap, has been explained (or rather explained away) through the lens of classic economics, that is, as irrational economic hubris. Commune factories, while they produced objects of daily use that were sorely needed, were in general poorly equipped and relied on simple and low-skill manufacturing processes. Productivity was low, and quality of output was often far from optimal. That explanation, however, does not hold, especially in the case of urban collectivization. As I show in the following pages, urban communes' industrial production fulfilled a necessary role in the urban economy, and many of those factories remained profitable and active after the end of the campaign. In that sense, the Great Leap did provide a massive stimulus to women's employment outside the home so that, "[b]y the end of the Mao era, there were about twenty million women working in manufacturing, of which 8.48 million (or 42 percent) were employed in 'collectives' that were largely developed from urban neighborhood industry."[67] More stubborn problems affected the other aspects of the project, first and foremost collectivized services. As Nara Dillon has argued, the Chinese state did not have the resources to provide welfare to all the urban residents *as welfare*, that is, at a cost for the

---

[66] Dong, "Red Housekeeping": 23.
[67] Lu Hanchao, *Shanghai Tai Chi: The Art of Being Ruled in Mao's China* (Cambridge: Cambridge University Press, 2023): 140.

state.[68] The communes were an attempt to solve this conundrum by tying welfare services to increased production by overburdened laborers, and while that was probably unsustainable, communes did not have the time to improve those services, as any further experimentation was foreclosed in the Thermidorean reaction that followed the first phase of the Great Leap. More importantly, it is hugely reductive to analyze the problems that afflicted urban collectivization only through the lens of narrowly understood economic rationality. Because, as I mentioned earlier, while centered on production, the Great Leap was a revolutionary *political* campaign, and in that it aimed to propose and substantiate a very different understanding of "the economic." And according to that understanding, there was nothing irrational in mass collectivization.

## I.5      The Leap as Politics

In the following pages, I follow that understanding of the economics and examine the process of urban collectivization by focusing on the profound social tensions and political contradictions it both engendered and brought to light, which were what made that experience both politically creative and ultimately untenable. This book highlights two closely intertwined sets of issues. The first concerns the political economy under Maoism. Socialism was, by definition, a transitory stage, from a system in which every member of society received goods and remuneration "according to their labor" to the promised land of communism, where everybody's needs would be finally satisfied. Yet how that transition would happen, how it could be measured, how it could be made to happen faster remained largely unanswered questions. In their search for viable answers to those questions, urban residents ended up unearthing further layers of complexity and faced new practical and theoretical conflicts, all central to the revolutionary socialist project. For example, social services were indispensable to substitute for the now displaced domestic labor of housewives-turned-workers, and they were also implicitly promised to those workers as part of their remuneration, mirroring the *fuli* dispersal or SOE units. In that context, what kind and amount of services workers should be receiving, whether they should pay (in part or in full) for those services, whether those services could be open to non-commune members for a fee, and whether they had to be profitable in a strictly monetary sense were not simply "practical" organizational questions. Rather, they impinged on one of the defining political conflicts of

---

[68] Nara Dillon, *Radical Inequalities: China's Revolutionary Welfare State in Comparative Perspective* (Cambridge, MA: Harvard University Press, 2015).

socialist transitional society, that between maximizing capital accumulation versus changing lives and livelihood.

Another, closely connected issue that emerged starkly during the movement, conjointly in the mass practice and the theoretical debate, was that of wages and the disciplining of labor. Urban communes were programmatically established through a bottom-up effort, and the release of women's pent-up desire to participate in productive labor was elicited mostly through nonmaterial (ideological) incentives. Then the problem became how to regulate that effort, how to maintain intense levels of productivity, and how to organize production in general. Throughout the campaign's short duration, commune members experimented with more egalitarian forms of remuneration, relying on voluntary self-disciplining and revolutionary commitment, which stood always in an unresolved tension with the Stalinist economic orthodoxy adopted by many leaders and cadres and with the desire to maximize profit extraction to spur industrial modernization. In the concurrent political debate, this experimentation was reflected and reframed as part of an attempt to eliminate "bourgeois right," meaning those capitalist relations and structures that continued to be reproduced under socialism and threatened its existence. By 1960, many CCP leaders turned against the "excessively egalitarian" tendencies of the Great Leap and reimposed forms of increasingly differentiated remuneration, wage scales, and stricter disciplining of labor and accounting of resources. The debate on bourgeois right was also, if only temporarily, foreclosed. In the experience of urban collectivization, we see another manifestation of the crucial unresolved contradiction on how to achieve and measure the transition to communism, and specifically whether that transition hinged on the development of the productive forces or on the transformation of social relationships. This was a contradiction that split the CCP leadership and the socialist movement globally. For Mao, as Rebecca Karl has argued, "the very point of the revolution in its own terms was to challenge the primacy of forces of production through the insistent transformation of productive relations so as to place the leading classes (the peasant-proletariat alliance) in charge of the productive forces themselves."[69] In the early phase of the Great Leap Forward, during the debate on bourgeois right, Mao and his allies on the left of the CCP rightly pointed out that forms directly derived from capitalism still organized a large part of the social relationships under socialism. People received wages in exchange of labor, transactions were measured by money, commodities still circulated, the

---

[69] Karl, *The Magic of Concepts*: 134–135.

law of value remained essential, and that permanence not only hindered the possibilities of any transition toward communism but left open the door for a restoration of capitalism. And indeed, the Soviet example had showed that the development of productive forces did not automatically create a radically more egalitarian society. The Great Leap was grounded on the awareness that relations of production had not radically been transformed and that those relations shaped all other aspects of social life "by virtue of their absolutely fundamental role in the reproduction of the very existence of social life."[70] By challenging the separation between production (and the relationships it establishes) and the rest of "life," the Great Leap constituted the most radical attempt to date "to shatter the stability of the everyday and the obscure resistance it puts up through the structures it re-establishes at times of important change."[71] Collectivization configured a direct intervention in the minute articulation of all social relationships with the goal of accelerating that transition and of replacing the bourgeois features that Soviet-style "development" continued to reproduce in the socialist everyday.

That intervention was also aimed at tackling another major, structural, and much older inequality: It promised to achieve *complete women's liberation*. The lived experience of the urban communes and their forced dissolution then point to deeper and more fundamental contradictions intrinsic to the Maoist/socialist conception of gendered labor and the Marxist process of liberation, and this is the second major focus of this book. The far-reaching transformations that collectivization was supposed to achieve all hinged on a massively expanded participation by female urban residents in "productive" labor, and that raises the obvious question of which kinds of labor can be considered productive, and which ones cannot. Following Engels and Lenin, the praxis and theory of urban communes took domestic work as by definition unproductive and, as a consequence, the complex and necessary tasks of social reproduction could only be recognized as such – and only partially and temporarily – at the moment of being socialized through collective services. They became valued, that is, only when they were rendered in exchange for some form of remuneration or required some measure of state expense, and that did not necessarily lead to a reconsideration of how domestic labor and affective care took place within the home. In that, not only did the Great Leap continue to enforce the separation between the spheres of production and social reproduction, always centering the former, but it also maintained the gendering of labor, which

---

[70] Mau, *Mute Compulsion*: 130.     [71] Lefebvre, *Critique of Everyday Life*, vol. 2: 35.

associated women with untrained, unpaid, and unproductive domestic labor. Because of that, even when women joined industrial production, they could never escape the gendered characterization of their work, which in turn relegated them mostly to underpaid, under-skilled, monotonous labor. Despite the promise of advancement through education and the acquisition of technical skills, female workers in commune factories were often confined to mind-numbing, repetitive tasks, which were considered too boring for skilled male workers. The Leninist assumption that domestic work was by nature dull and stultifying was the implicit and often explicit justification for the kind of "productive" labor to which women were relegated in urban communes, their presupposed lack of skills a rationalization for their always postponed transformation into full-fledged workers, a process that, in another context, Maria Mies has called "housewifization."[72] Coherently, in the sources, these new female laborers, even after they joined production, continued to be almost uniformly labeled "housewives" – or more rarely *jiashu*, "dependents"[73] – thus maintaining even lexically their separation from actual, real, male workers. This was also reflected in the distinction among those female workers who joined commune factories and those who were employed in canteens, nurseries, and service centers. While both were programmatically paid less than their male counterparts, *fuli* work, which was obviously a replacement for housework and therefore carried with it the negative connotations of domestic labor, was considered to be inferior and was remunerated accordingly. In the following pages, when I make direct or indirect reference to the original sources, I use the term "housewife" or "housewives" to translate the Chinese *jiating funü*; in my own discussion of collectivization and women's labor, I tend to refer to women employed in collective factories and services as "women who worked (or used to work) as housewives." While this is clunky in terms of writing, I want to make clear the distinction between what in the sources becomes almost an identitarian status, which is attached to these women even after they leave the space of the home and the family, and what the actual labor of social reproduction is, a labor whose systematic undervaluing (or, rather, un-valuing) is at the center of this discussion.

Maoism never produced a serious and coherent rethinking of the centrality of social reproduction and of the productive features of

---

[72] Maria Mies, *Patriarchy and Accumulation on a World Scale: Women in the International Division of Labour* (London: Bloomsbury Academic; reprint edition: 2022).

[73] While in imperial China the term referred to both male and female family relations, by the twentieth century *jiashu* was restricted to indicate female family members. See Dong, "Red Housekeeping."

domestic labor, and without that, it was impossible to even formulate an analysis of the gendered structure of labor and social relationships. However, women involved in urban collectivization spoke about those issues themselves, and those issues were highlighted in their collectivized practices. Commune workers embraced the chance offered by the communes to significantly transform their everyday: They chose "slavery to the assembly line" over "slavery to a kitchen sink,"[74] seeing in the former the potential for a new role, for a new identity, and for reframed social relationships, all embodied in the shift from "housewife" to "worker." They protested, often vocally, against the conditions of their labor, the insufficient social services, the permanence of gender disparities, and their never completed liberation. In their experience, then, we find echoes and anticipations, albeit still inchoate, of the critiques of the socialist project of women's liberation that Marxist feminists and social reproduction theorists would wage starting in the 1960s, often deploying references to the Chinese case. In the following chapters, I make references to those critiques in an effort to highlight and unpack both the contradictions and the possibilities that emerged within the Maoist experiment of urban collectivization.

I take both the contradictions and the possibilities embedded in the project of urban collectivization seriously, in large part because my historical actors did so, and they invested energy, time, labor, and political commitment in that venture. I follow the path traced by scholars such as Gail Hershatter and Kimberley Manning, who have centered the experiences and politics of rural women, and I distance myself from those who have instead focused on the supposed economic "irrationality" of the Great Leap Forward. We need to rethink the political stakes and the political potential of the Great Leap, of course without forgetting or dismissing the tragic toll it took in the countryside. Precisely because of the campaign's disastrous consequences, we need to fully understand the logics that drove these radical policies. When viewed from the perspective of urban collectivization, a limited experiment that did not produce either major successes or disastrous failures, the political logic of the Great Leap does not appear foolish – perhaps utopian, but only in the sense that not surrendering to the ineluctability of capitalist development and the reproduction of the existent has now become "utopian." Deploying the only resource that China had in abundance at the time –

---

[74] Mariarosa Dalla Costa, "Women and the Subversion of the Community," in Mariarosa Dalla Costa and Selma James, *The Power of Women and the Subversion of the Community* (1972), https://libcom.org/library/power-women-subversion-community-della-costa-selma-james.

labor – was not irrational, and neither was the desire to diminish the role of the commodity, wages, and other capitalist "remnants" in the socialist economy. If anything, the capitalist reversal after 1978 proves how absolutely correct and rational that desire was, from a socialist point of view. Rather, the story of collectivization points to how the urban politics of the Great Leap Forward was perhaps *not radical enough*, in the sense that, despite the mass collective effort and the intense ideological debate, crucial issues affecting social reproduction, the socialist economy, workplace democracy, and the very structure of the everyday could not be overcome, and in some cases, were systematically left out. Thus, I join a small group of my colleagues in arguing that the disasters of the Mao era, like the disasters elsewhere in the twentieth century, have as much to do with capitalism as they do with communism.

## I.6    Some Methodological and Historiographical Questions

The book follows the founding, development, and demise of urban communes in Beijing between 1958 and 1963. Some fundamental issues recur at different moments of this relatively brief history, as actors at all levels, from Mao to neighborhood workers, from municipal authorities to local cadres, identified them, sometimes with uncanny foresight, while remaining incapable of solving them – or while being prevented from even trying. For example, the issue of how welfare could be provided to larger sectors of the population at no cost to the state or without reducing capital accumulation; the programmatically low-tech character of commune labor, which remained profitable as long as it remained "simple," thus making the promise of mechanization and technological advancement moot; the contradiction inherent in the impulse to shape a more egalitarian society through distribution of services while differences in socioeconomic status were exactly what made those services profitable; the endless return to material incentives as the only way to guarantee productivity, leading to a unsustainable level of labor extraction; and, crucially, the inescapably gendered character of female commune laborers, which made them relentlessly revert to their status as "housewives." All these issues were vividly manifested in the lived experience of urban communes, where ordinary residents, women laborers, cadres, and their families toiled in makeshift factories, built nurseries and canteens, and struggled to create what they believed were the foundations for a potential future of revolutionary abundance and satisfied needs. In that struggle, they continuously faced not only the practical limitations of material scarcity but also the contradictions intrinsic to the socialist economy.

By looking at how these contradictions were explored at the level of both political debate and lived praxis, I also plan to offer a more historically grounded alternative to recent approaches that encapsulate the entire Maoist period under the label of "capitalism" or "state capitalism," sanctioning the communist revolution's inability to produce a true socialist economy.[75] Socialism was indeed "aspirational" and always "in progress," but more importantly, socialism in China took the form of mass efforts and experiments, which did affect lived practices and quotidian experience; those transformations were not univocal, nor evenly felt, yet they affected the lives of millions. In addition, precisely in their unevenness and complexity, those experiments brought to light some of the fundamental issues that marred and defined the Maoist project and the communist revolutionary project at large. Rather than arguing whether Maoist China was inescapably trapped in the vise-like grip of capitalism, I suggest instead that by investigating the very real efforts by Chinese people to create a socialist life, we might clarify the extent and the limitations of change under Maoism.

While this is a study of the Great Leap Forward, it has a specific and localized focus. I am interested in the Great Leap as *politics*, and I engage with the theoretical debates it sparked, be they on the law of value, the transitional political economy of socialism, or the permanence of the commodity form. I take these debates as inseparable from the *praxis* of urban collectivization, and most of the following pages are devoted to the experience of people in Beijing neighborhoods and streets. I don't devote much space to either the intra-party conflicts or the decisional patterns that led to the shifting policies of the period (and their disastrous consequences). Similarly, this is an urban story, and in that, it is complementary to the vast majority of the historical literature on the Great Leap, which has rightly focused on the disastrous famine that it provoked and that led to millions of deaths in the countryside. This book is not a revisionist take on that tragic history, and the evolution of Great Leap policies in China's urban centers cannot be separated from the horrific events in the countryside, as the relative safety of cities relied on the continuing exploitation of the peasantry. The implicit background of this story, which sometimes filters through the official sources, is the sacrifice of rural lives "at the altar of urban industrial development."[76] Yet the

---

[75] Karl Gerth, *Unending Capitalism: State Consumerism and the Negation of the Chinese Socialist Revolution* (Cambridge: Cambridge University Press, 2020). See also the debate on this book in the *PRC History Review*, https://netwcrks.h-net.org/volume-5-number-1-october-2020.

[76] Jeremy Brown, *City versus Countryside in Mao's China: Negotiating the Divide* (Cambridge: Cambridge University Press, 2012): 12.

story of the Great Leap in cities, and especially in the capital, is very different from the story of the Great Leap in the countryside, and I argue that by looking at that much less tragic experience, we can try to understand this moment as a radical yet not illogical or irrational political choice.

This story takes place in Beijing, which not only was one of the first major cities to establish urban communes, but in that city these organizations also lasted longer than elsewhere. Officially, collectivization in Beijing spanned six years, from August 1958 to October 1964, and some Beijing commune production centers perdured up until the eve of the Cultural Revolution.[77] The longer duration and slower decline of this experiment in the capital allows for a closer and more detailed perspective, especially on its forced dissolution.

The sources that I use to ground my analysis are all from archives in the capital: first and foremost, the Beijing Municipal Archive, but also three district archives, two in Xicheng (North and South), and one in Haidian.[78] These are all "official" documents – surveys, petitions, statutes, requests for approval, responses and commentaries from superiors – produced at various levels of the Communist state, from the Central Committee down to neighborhood cadres. Without going into the debate of whether we can actually recover "the voices of the people" from such documents, these texts show how cadres at different levels reported and navigated the changing patterns of residents' involvement in the movement as well as the practical and political concerns it generated among them. Against an old established view in the field that saw the Maoist state as a monolithic juggernaut imposing its will over "society," I follow more recent trends in PRC history that highlight fractures and differentiation among various levels of "the state," as well the continuous imbrication and integration of the people and the government, at a granular level. Many of these documents are internal communications within different parts of the government, including an abundance of surveys of local experiences – a commune or even specific organizations within a commune, such as a nursery or a mess hall. They include directives from

---

[77] Guo Xiuping 郭秀平, "Woguo chengshi renmin gongshehua yundong wei gaocheng juda zainan de yuanyin" 我国城市人民公社化运动未造成巨大灾难的原因 [Reasons why the urban commune movement did not produce a huge catastrophe], *Dangshi yanjiu yu jiaoxue* 党史研究与教学 [Research and Teaching in Party History], 3 (2006): 46.

[78] These sources have not been extensively used, even in Chinese accounts of the campaign. I was quite surprised that they were labeled as "open" (*kaifang*) and fairly accessible in the municipal archives. Xuanwu district, which originally occupied the southwestern quadrant of the inner city, was merged into Xicheng district in 2010; its archives are now labeled "Xicheng South."

district or municipal committees, requests from the neighborhood level, and reports documenting the effects of policy shifts. The local cadres who wrote them often had a direct role and a personal investment in the practice of collectivization.

My research relies almost exclusively on these official sources. I did not make use of any "garbage" sources (archives discarded by sectors of the states and then purchased by historians in secondhand markets or online), but not for lack of trying. I simply did not find any. However, I here stake a different position from the "garbologists" and from some promoters of what has been called "grassroots history." As I argued elsewhere, [79] this is not because I embrace Elizabeth Perry's criticism of that approach as a "janitorial" task, grubbing "for diversity in the dustbins of grassroots society."[80] My criticism is rather that, in their theoretical stances way more than in their historical practice, self-declared grassroots historians argue they can recover the "reality" of everyday life under Maoism, that is, how people *actually* lived and what they *actually* did.[81] Yet that empiricist approach, besides being strangely positivist, also reduces "everyday life" to "an analytical frame through which we can view the real content of the Mao period underneath the thin veneer of Maoist high politics and its categories." As Alexander Day has lucidly pointed out, "[t]reating it as such would reinscribe the state-society dichotomy, with everyday life standing in for society, where real people, individuals, say and do things that do not clearly follow the dictates of the Party-state. And the Party-state in turn would stand outside of the real content of everyday life – a sphere of propaganda, unrealistic policies, faked figures." I share Day's concern as well as his call to view everyday life as "historical, produced in different ways under different material conditions, structured and shaped by social forms in motion."[82] This is why this book begins with Lefebvre, for whom everyday life was never the repository of some empirical reality, of separated

[79] Fabio Lanza, "Introduction: The Politics of (Maoist) History," *positions: asia critique* 29:4 (2021): 675–688.

[80] Elizabeth J. Perry, "The Promise of PRC History," *Journal of Modern Chinese History* 10:1 (2016): 113–117.

[81] Jeremy Brown and Matthew D. Johnson, "Introduction," in Jeremy Brown and Matthew D. Johnson, eds., *Maoism at the Grassroots: Everyday Life in China's Era of High Socialism* (Cambridge, MA: Harvard University Press, 2015): 1–15. I want to stress how both Brown and Johnson are extremely nuanced and sophisticated when it comes to analyzing social relationships in their own historical scholarship.

[82] Alexander F. Day, "Breaking with the Family Form: Historical Categories, Social Reproduction, and Everyday Life in Late 1950s Rural China," *positions: asia critique* 29:4 (2021): 870.

"true" life, but rather the very space the revolution would have to annihilate and reorganize "until it is as good as new."[83]


## I.7    Chapter Outline

The manuscript comprises five chapters, plus this Introduction and a short Epilogue: Chapters 1, 3, and 5 follow the evolution of the campaign in the capital chronologically, from its inception to its demise, while Chapters 2 and 4 focus on two related but specific cases. Chapter 1, "A New Page in the History of Daily Life," is devoted to the initial phase of the movement, the second half of 1958, and I investigate both Party official rhetoric and archival sources from the early communes in Beijing to show how early models of collectivization were presented as "prescriptive descriptions" to be followed, but also how contradictions between the different goals of this mass movement surfaced almost immediately and framed the praxis of activists and workers at the street level.

The urban and rural collectivization campaign of the Great Leap coincided with a nation-wide debate on the law of value, bourgeois right, and the socialist economy. Chapter 2, "Politics for a Transitional Age," demonstrates how what appeared to be an abstruse discussion among economists, social scientists, and party theoreticians was in fact intimately connected with and relevant to the praxis of urban collectivization. This was neither the case of a theoretical position or an ideological argument at the top fueling a policy change at the bottom, nor that of a political experiment at the street level that needed to be justified and rearticulated at the level of Marxist theory. Rather, the two aspects – as is often the case for Marxist politics – were interdependent, co-determined, and yet always in a state of profound tension. It is my contention that to understand the Great Leap Forward requires insights into both theoretical abstraction and the world of quotidian praxis.

The debate was foreclosed by early 1959 at the same time when, faced with the famine taking hold of the countryside, the CCP leadership reined in the more radical aspects of the Great Leap. Yet despite the disastrous famine and the theoretical retreat, urban collectivization continued. Chapter 3, "The Gender of Labor," explores urban experiments in Beijing between 1959 and 1960, when, in a moment of political uncertainty, workers, activists, and cadres in various neighborhoods strove to define the confines of what was possible. In particular, they tried to figure out what the promised transformation from "housewives"

---

[83] Lefebvre, *Everyday Life in the Modern World*: 37.

to (female) "workers" meant, both practically and politically, and what kind of activities should be considered under the category of "productive labor." I set this search in a wider context by showing how it echoes the debates and discussions in Marxist feminism and social reproduction theory.

The collectivization of one profession, hairstyling, is the focus of Chapter 4, "The Barbers of Beijing." Barbershops, with bathhouses and photographers, were considered an essential service for city residents, and they were therefore part of those benefits that had to be provided under the commune umbrella. Yet during the Great Leap not only did hairstyling fashions and a correspondent hierarchy of hairdressers persist, but they were recognized and actively fostered by local and state authorities. The case of hairdressers and barbers in Great Leap Beijing then shows the attentiveness some cadres paid to the minute aspects of the quotidian but also the resilience of subtle (and not so subtle) social differences in the midst of what was supposed to be one of the "egalitarian" moments in the Maoist era.

Chapter 5, "Foreclosing on Liberation," examines the demise of urban collectivization after 1961. While the production side of urban communes had its problems, it remained economically profitable; it was communal welfare services (canteens, childcare, etc.) that were deemed to be wasteful and dysfunctional and were eventually disbanded, and that could not but have disastrous consequences for female labor and the project of female liberation. Many workers, newly subjected to the double disciplining of industrial labor and family chores, protested these closures, and archival sources convey their dismay and their vocal criticism, which highlighted the continued devaluation of female workers and of their labor, both in the home and in the factory. The Epilogue goes back to the initial questions I borrowed from Lefebvre and offers a final brief assessment of both the radical nature and the ultimate failure of the experiment of urban collectivization. I also trace the contested legacies of that experiment in the rest of the Mao period and in the early Reform era, up to the recent (and quite strange) treatment of those events in the PRC historical literature in the twenty-first century.

# 1    A New Page in the History of Daily Life

## 1.1    Early Models

On August 18, 1958, the *People's Daily* published a short, first-person article, penned by a Beijing resident named Wang Zhijie. "I used to be a housewife" (*wo yuanlai shi ge jiating funü* 我原来是个家庭妇女), she emphatically began. "During the high tide of people-run industries, I stepped out of the family home (*zouchu jiating* 走出家庭) and joined a production group set up by the neighborhood committee." With two salary earners in the family, life had improved, but prepping meals for her four children quickly became an issue. Initially, she would rush home at lunchtime and in the evening to cook for the kids. Yet not only did she find it impossible to provide meals at regular times, but the double workload was too tiring, and her productivity at the factory suffered. As she was not the only one facing such an issue, all newly recruited female workers got together and decided to establish a collective canteen within the production group. "We all put together the furniture, selected a cook, and, without spending one dime, the canteen was set up. Now, no less than sixty or seventy people come here to eat every day, and the eleven members of the group eat here with their whole families. Since there is a collective canteen," Wang concluded, "my children and I can have meals at regular hours, and I also have more time for some house chores. I feel very happy, and my productivity is improving day after day."[1]

In this brief, anecdotal, and seemingly matter-of-fact piece, Wang Zhijie described an eventful transformation. Wang's decision to get out of the home and step into a factory had significant economic consequences, as it provided her family with a much needed second income, but also, and more importantly, it meant a radical shift in her own identity. "I *used to* be a housewife"; now she was something else, a member of a collective, and maybe, potentially, a fully recognized

---

[1] Wang Zhijie 王慧洁, "Jiti shitang zhen jiejue wenti" 集体食堂真解决问题 [Collective canteens really solve problems], *RMRB*, August 18, 1958.

"worker." That practical, political, and subjective revolution also implicitly singled out her previous identity of "housewife" as one that
belonged to a pre-socialist or pre-communist past, an old persona that
she had to shed away in the progress toward a new life. Joining a
production group, however, was revealed to be by itself insufficient for
Wang to complete that vaunted transformation, as the tasks of domestic
labor continued to weigh on her even after she stopped being defined
solely by her role within the family. Individual liberation from the
shackles of domesticity could only come through a collective effort to
remake the entire organization of the everyday, down to the daily task of
food preparation, an effort that Wang pointedly depicted as self-
organized, bottom-up, and accomplished "without spending one dime."

Wang's simple account then encapsulates some of the crucial elements
that framed, in the Party's rhetoric but also in the actual practice of
workers and residents, the process of urban collectivization at the beginning of the Great Leap, leading to the formation of people's communes
in the cities. As the "old" urban life that collectivization promised to
reform hinged on the family, domestic labor and the very identity of
those women who worked as housewives stood out as the essential issues
to be tackled. As those women moved out of the home and into the
factory, the tasks of social reproduction became detached from the
sphere of the family and turned into a collective responsibility through
a series of communal services. And while these services were created to
allow for increased participation in industrial work, the purpose of production itself was also supposed to be transformed as part of this revolutionary process. Production was no longer just for economic gains or
increased outputs, although those remained essential. Society was not
being mobilized as a means to achieve the end of further production;[2]
rather, productive labor was instead to be the fulcrum of a revolution in
the everyday, participation in factory work being the necessary element
for a wider reform of social reproduction, social relationships, and life
itself. Individual happiness, as Wang pointed out in the last line of her
piece, could only be realized as one joined a collective and productive
endeavor. However, at the very end the text also hinted at potential limits
in that transformation, as Wang remarked how she was still responsible
for some domestic chores: "housewife" was an identity that could not be
that easily left behind.

Wang was an early herald, as her piece predates by a few days the
official founding of the first urban commune in the nation, the Red Flag

---

[2] Mårten Björk, "Embracing Failure," *Sidecar – New Left Review* (August 25, 2023), https://
newleftreview.org/sidecar/posts/embracing-failure.

commune in Zhengzhou, Henan (August 15, 1958). On August 21, the commune adopted a draft statute, modeled on the famous Satellite (rural) People's Commune in Suiping county, also in Henan. The commune, it stated, "is the basic social organization under the guide of the CCP and the People's government. It is the organizational form best suited to reform the old city and build the new socialist city, and to gradually advance toward a communist society. It merges political and economic governance, aiming to further abolish private ownership and fully unleash productive forces, especially women's productive force."[3] By September 1958, Henan reported a total of 482 people's communes in nine cities, 63 of them neighborhood-based, 218 in the factories and mines, 118 in universities, 42 in government agencies, and 41 in the suburbs.[4]

The Henan communes, both rural and urban, were celebrated as pioneering the radical transformations promised by the Great Leap Forward. Vice Chairman Liu Shaoqi visited Henan and specifically Zhengzhou in September 1958, and during his tour he highlighted some cardinal principles of the local model of collectivization. First, he stated that everyone should take part in productive labor, and specifically manual labor. The communes were founded on the notion that participation in (physical) labor was not only necessary, but ultimately liberating, as it was the required condition for the transition to communism. Organizations of collective welfare, such as canteens and nurseries, were necessary to allow this massive expansion of the productive forces. Then, Liu continued, by restructuring the production process and changing patterns of daily life, the communes would allow for more general improvements in technical skills and cultural levels.[5]

While they were inspired by their rural counterparts, urban communes were designed to deal with the specific issues that had lingered on or had emerged anew in China's cities with the implementation the first Five-Year Plan (FFYP). First among them was the much decried division and disparity between cities and countryside, which had increased and become entrenched in the previous five years. The Plan had intentionally focused on (heavy) industry at the expense of agriculture, with only 8.6

---

[3] Li Duanxiang, *Chengshi renmin gongshe yundong yanjiu*: 3.
[4] Liu Zhenqing 刘振清, "Chengshi renmin gongshe shulun" 城市人民公社述论 [A discussion of urban people's communes], *Changbai xuekan* 长白学刊 [Changbai journal] (February 10, 2006): 96.
[5] "Guoshe dao gongchanzhuyi de jige tiaojian: Shaoqi tongzhi zai Henan shichashi juti chanshu" 过渡到共产主义的几个条件: 少奇同志在河南视察时具体阐述 [Some conditions for the transition to communism: Comrade Liu Shaoqi's concrete suggestions during his inspection tour of Henan], *RMRB*, September 24, 1958.

percent of the total capital investment going to agriculture between 1952 and 1958 (compared with 51.1 percent to industry).[6] The FFYP strategy of heavy industrialization also had the characteristic of fostering higher industrial output without creating massive employment growth, and thus it "further reduced cities' ability to offer jobs to rural migrants." That strategy "was thus not designed to induce massive urbanization because capital-intensive heavy industries did not raise the labor-absorption capacity of cities and therefore failed to help relieve rural surplus labor pressure."[7] In a complete reversal, the Great Leap aimed instead at reducing the urban/rural divide, first by decentralizing industries to the countryside, but also by making cities into sites of food production (through ventures such as raising chickens and urban farming). The further expansion of productive capacity in neighborhood factories would also have allowed cities to finally absorb surplus rural labor.[8]

As for the city itself, with the achievement of "socialism," celebrated with fanfare in 1956, private ownership of the means of (industrial) production had been formally eliminated, but non-socialist forms of property and economic activity persisted, especially in the densely crowded space of old urban centers, where peddlers still roamed the streets and small handicraft or family businesses still eked out a living. While big industrial work units created during the plan, with their generous welfare provisions, offered their employees a prefiguration of what a "socialist life" could be, large sectors of the population were still excluded from those benefits and services. Cadres and leaders lamented the continuing influence of bourgeois thought and petit-bourgeois habits among city denizens. For those residents, the development of urban space around work units, with amenities confined behind the *danwei* walls and reserved for their employees, had also meant a reduction of access to essential services, which were often unevenly distributed across the city. Historian Lu Duanfang cites a 1956 report, according to which "some workers in Beijing had to get up at four o'clock in the morning and walk two miles to buy groceries. To go shopping or take in a movie, one had to travel across the city to Wangfujing, the old commercial district of

---

[6] Chuang, "Sorghum and Steel: The Socialist Developmental State and the Forging of China," *Chuang*, no. 1 (2016), https://chuangcn.org/journal/one/sorghum-and-steel/.

[7] Kevin H. Zhang, "The Evolution of China's Urban Transformation: 1949–2000," in Chen Aimin, Gordon G. Liu, and Kevin H. Zhang, eds., *Urban Transformation in China* (London: Routledge, 2016), Kindle edition: location 1037.

[8] For a detailed analysis of urban-rural relations in the Mao era, see Brown, *City versus Countryside.*

Beijing. In some areas, children walked for more than two hours to attend school."[9]

However, the question was not simply how to include more and more people in the *danwei* system. The problem was deeper and more structural and inherent to the very path of socialism, as Soviet-style modernization had proven incapable of fundamentally transforming old social relationships and relationships of production; rather, it had contributed to entrench them or to create new ones, similarly unequal. This was true in the workplace, where "capitalist" features, such as the wage form, rigid salary scales, strict labor discipline, and "one-man management," were constitutive parts of Stalinist industrialization. But it was also and perhaps more evident in the still private space of the home: While the marriage law had established "love marriage" and formal parity between men and women, gender roles had not changed, women's domestic labor had not improved, and what a socialist (or a communist) family should be and how it should differ from a bourgeois one remained unsolved and endlessly postponed issues. Despite the massive economic and social changes produced by the FFYP, urban life itself had not yet been radically transformed; a new socialist set of relationships had not yet emerged. Historian and Marxist theorist Hu Sheng, in an important contribution at the very beginning of the Great Leap, highlighted how the permanence of that "individualistic way of life" not only was a waste of labor and stood in opposition to socialist production, but was "also an impediment to the improvement of standards of living and the development of a socialist and communist ideology." If in the old society the content of everyday life (*shenghuo de jingchang nei* 生活的经常内) of the oppressed masses was limited to the basic necessities (work, clothes, food, reproduction), that "narrow, basic life" could not be acceptable under socialism, when people needed "medicines and hygiene, culture and education, decent and high-level entertainment." And such a demand could not be satisfied within the narrow confines of one's family – it required a new, collective organization of life.[10] Socializing domestic labor was a crucial step toward such a reorganization.

Under those historical circumstances, urban communes were viewed not only as the culmination of a decade-long process of transformation of the economic structure of the cities but also as the political and organizational form finally capable of changing the very conditions for social and

---

[9] Lu, *Remaking Chinese Urban Form*: 84.
[10] Hu Sheng 胡绳, "Jiawu laodong de jitihua, shehuihua" 家务劳动的集体化、社会化 [The collectivization and socialization of household labor], *Hongqi* 红旗 [Red flag], no. 7 (July 1958): 27.

personal life. By bringing (almost) every able-bodied individual (male or female) within a system that integrated production, collective services, and education, the commune would finally and completely revolutionize social relationships in the city. Commune membership held the promise of a transformative change of identity, leaving behind the status of "dependent" (*jiashu*) or "idle street resident" (*jiedao naosan jumin* 街道 闲散居民) to assume that of "worker in socialist construction" (*shehuiz-huyi jianshe de laodongzhe* 社会主义建设的劳动者). And as historian Wang Xianming has noted, this identitarian shift was not simply a question of status and social attributes, but also had practical consequences, as it implied "the institutionalized support and protection of social welfare."[11]

As the sixth session of the eighth plenum of the National People's Congress (NPC) sanctioned, echoing the statute of the Red Flag commune, "urban communes ... will become the tool to remake the old city into the new socialist city, they will be the organization under which we can incorporate production, exchange, distribution, and people's welfare."[12] Through mass participation in industrial labor, cities would turn from centers of consumption to centers of production. Services such as nurseries and communal canteens would replace housework, not only expanding the benefits of welfare to the entire urban population, but also changing the scattered, individualized way of life into a new, socialist, collective way of life. By combining small-sized or family enterprises (small stores, peddlers, etc.) under a collective umbrella and by merging small cooperatives and production groups into larger ones, the communes were also supposed to rapidly change the form of ownership, from individual and collective ownership to "ownership by the whole people" (*quanminsuoyouzhi* 全民所有制, hereafter QMSYZ), which Mao had defined as the primary standard for the construction of socialism.[13] In historian Li Duanxiang's summation,

---

[11] Wang Xianming 王先明, "Cong jumin dao sheyuan: chengshi renmin gongshe chengyuan de shenfen renting – Yi Tianjin chengshi renmin gongshe wei li" 从居民到 社员:城市人民公社成员的身份认同 – 以天津城市人民公社为例 [From residents to members: The identity of urban people's commune members – The case of Tianjin urban people's commune], *Shehui kexue yanjiu* 社会科学研究 [Social sciences research], no. 4 (2020): 145.

[12] "Guanyu renmin gongshe ruogan wenti de jueyi. Zhongguo gongchandang dibajie Zhongyang weiyuanhui diliuci quanti huiyi tongguo" 关于人民公社若干问题的决议 中 国共产党第八届中央委员会第六次全体会议通过 [Resolution on several issues concerning the people's communes adopted at the Sixth Plenary Session of the Eighth Central Committee of the Communist Party of China], *RMRB*, December 19, 1958.

[13] Li Duanxiang, *Chengshi renmin gongshe yundong yanjiu*: 10. More on this topic in Chapter 2.

the urban communes had three main crucial and interdependent goals: (1) complete universalization of production ("everybody is involved in production, every family is free of troublesome people" *reren nao shengchan, jiajia wu naoren* 人人闹生产,家家无闹人); (2) collectivization of life, socialization of domestic labor (*shenghuo jitihua, jiawu laodong shehuihua* 生活集体化,家务劳动社会化); and (3) women's liberation.[14]

Urban collectivization was indeed touted by CCP leaders as the way to break down the family form, which they viewed as still defined by its feudal and bourgeois legacies. In September 1958, Mao reassured female cadres in Hefei (Anhui), telling them that once they established communes, women and young people would receive a salary and benefits as individuals, freeing them from the economic control of the pater familias. This in turn would lead to the elimination of the patriarchy and the collapse of the ideology of bourgeois right.[15] Similarly, in his Henan trip, Liu Shaoqi encouraged the establishment of communal childcare centers specifically as the way to reduce the relevance of the education children received at home (family education) and to promote its replacement with "social education."[16]

Yet the street-level practices of urban collectivization did not seem to match the lofty revolutionary goals by which they were inspired, either in scale or in the amount of resources deployed by state or local authorities. I argue that this disparity between the transformative goals assigned to the urban communes and the seemingly scrappy means by which collectivization was pursued was, however, a cardinal and defining feature of this process, and it reflected both a set of practical limitations and a specific Maoist understanding of how social and political change can and should be effected. The radical transformation of daily life, down to the level of interpersonal relations, individual attitudes, and everyday practices that the communes promised was to be achieved basically without any deployment of resources, money, or equipment at any level of the state apparatus. It came instead through a reorganization of the labor force and an intervention at the level of the street, the neighborhood, and the family. It was therefore a social and economic revolution that could and should be accomplished not through an expansion of state intervention, but through the willful change of micro-practices by local

---

[14] Li Duanxiang, *Chengshi renmin gongshe yundong yanjiu*: 52.

[15] *Jianguo yilai Mao Zedong wengao* 建国以来毛泽东文稿 (Mao Zedong's writing since the founding of the country), vol. 13 (Beijing: Zhongyang wenxian chubanshe, 2024): 98. Mao's speech had been published originally in the *Anhui Ribao*, September 29, 1958. On bourgeois right, see Chapter 2.

[16] "Guoshe dao gongchanzhuyi de jige tiaojian: Shaoqi tongzhi zai Henan shichashi juti chanshu."

activists; not through a further development of productive forces, as many in the CCP argued, following the Stalinist doxa, but through a revolution in social relationships in the neighborhood.

Lu Duanfang has rightly argued how the new socialist economic system, "privileging production over consumption, and extracting surplus value from agriculture," had created, in the cities as well as in the countryside, the historical conditions of real and perceived scarcity of social provisions.[17] The bottom-up, labor-intensive strategy of urban collectivization, however, was not only the reflection of a pragmatic understanding of what was possible in the situation of relative scarcity of the late 1950s. Rather, that revolutionary "change in people's long-established habits of life," affecting both the political economy of the socialist state and the individualized social relationships of the family, could happen only through a collective movement, through "the conscious and voluntary efforts of the masses,"[18] a cardinal principle of Maoist revolutionary praxis. As I show in this chapter, the process of collectivization described in archival documents embodied crucial elements of that praxis. In that process, the realms of the economic, the social, and the political remained inseparable; individual ideological transformation and the restructuring of economic relations were crucial to participation in collective revolutionary practice; and revolutionary practice was the only way in which social contradictions and tensions could be tackled. But that practice, in a dialectical manner, also always produced new contradictions, which in turn required continuous political rethinking and renewed praxes.

This principle is already evident in the early models singled out for praise in the official media. The Red Flag commune in Zhengzhou, while first in the nation, was not as widely celebrated as its rural counterparts. The urban experiment that received the most public accolades, including enthusiastic coverage in the *People's Daily*, took place in a small neighborhood in Tianjin, Hongshunli, an alley (*hutong*) with only forty-two households, mostly workers and employees of government agencies. Even if only twenty-seven "housewives" were available to be mobilized for productive labor, in August 1958, they formed first a production group, and eventually a commune. As described in the *People's Daily*, every morning at 8 am, at the ring of a bell, seventeen young women moved out of their houses, carrying their spinning wheels and a bundle of electric copper wire; they gathered at a corner of the alley, in a makeshift workshop under a canopy, where they quickly proceeded to spool the

---

[17] Lu, *Remaking Chinese Urban Form*: 9.
[18] Hu Sheng, "Jiawu laodong de jitihua, shehuihua": 28.

copper wire onto a wooden axle. This was then delivered to the nearby Hengda electric wire factory.[19] Among the new workers was twenty-eight-year-old Huang Shuqin, who, due to her family's economic circumstances, had been forced to get married at sixteen. "All day long is this bowl or that pot, wash this or brush that. I have grown tired of it long ago," she lamented, envious of those unmarried women who could participate in "productive" labor. When the chance finally came for her, with collectivization, another problem arose: "To whom do I entrust my four children?"

The answer to that question lay in the creation of institutions of social welfare, which the *People's Daily* described once again as a strictly spontaneous process, shaped solely by the local initiative and voluntary participation of the neighborhood's housewives. Faced with the problem of childcare and housework, the newly mobilized female workers started planning to establish a series of collective services. In order to elicit mass participation in these initiatives, activists prompted a debate on supporting production and a new, socialist life, pushing people to shape a new form of "big family." Soon Hongshunli had a communal canteen, a childcare center, a washing and sewing station, a library, a savings service center, and a store selling articles of daily use.[20] Now, the *People's Daily* reporter wrote, "moms can feel at ease and produce" (*mamamen ye keyi anxin shengchan* 妈妈们也可以安心生产了).[21] The canteen provided three meals a day for only one jiao (¥0.1), while saving on the overall consumption of coal, grain, and water; the commune store at the entrance of the alley was stocked with over 300 kinds of products, and the tailor quickly and efficiently made clothes for those female workers who now did not have time to do their own sewing. Participation in production and service was on a voluntary basis, and people either volunteered or were elected to take on specific tasks, formally transferring the largely hidden domestic labor of many *jiashu* to the public

[19] "Jiedao gongzuozhong de yimian hongqi – ji Tianjin shi Hongshunli zuzhi qilai hou de xin qixiang" 街道工作中的一面红旗－记天津市鸿顺里组织起来后的新气象 [A red flag in neighborhood work – Remembering the new atmosphere after the reorganization of Hongshunli in Tianjin], *RMRB*, August 19, 1958.
[20] "Renren canjia shehui laodong, jiajia dou guo jitishenghuo. Hongshunli jumin shenghuo dageming. Chengli shengchan fusu hezuoshe, shuli le wo wei renren, renren weiwo de xinfengge" 人人参加社会劳动 家家都过集体生活 鸿顺里居民生活大革命 成立生产服务合作社，树立了我为人人、人人为我的新风格 [Everyone participates in social work, and every family lives collectively. A revolution in the life of the residents of Hongshunli. The establishment of production and service cooperatives has created a new style of "I for everyone and everyone for me."] *RMRB*, August 19, 1958.
[21] "Jiedao gongzuozhong de yimian hongqi – ji Tianjin shi Hongshunli zuzhi qilai hou de xin qixiang."

sphere, turning it into visible social labor.[22] Old woman Gu was an excellent cook and agreed to work in the canteen, while granny Yang, who was patient with kids, was chosen for the childcare center. Another older woman owned a sewing machine, so she naturally ended up at the tailoring station; two men, one sixty-nine, one over seventy, who had some experience with trade, went to work at the store; Wang Junting, who could read and do basic math, became the accountant.[23] As a result of all these efforts, the average monthly income went up by ¥20.8, and that in turn led to a drastic reduction in the number of people needing social assistance.[24]

In August 1958, the *People's Daily* celebrated these achievements by remarking how "collective life really is like a big crucible, it can mold people's ideology, and it can take old social relationships and cast them into new relationships."[25] Accordingly, the newspaper listened poignant examples of such ideological change and improved relations. Zong Bingzhen, the head of the production group, owned the two rooms now turned into the canteen and the storehouse for the factory. Before collectivization, she had not trusted other people with them, locking the doors even when she went out to buy groceries, and refusing to rent them even short-term, but after she got involved in production and heard about the commune's need, she offered those spaces for public use.[26] She also made peace with her neighbor, Liu Yuzhen, with whom she had not exchanged a word for nine years. Now, they worked together, helping each other, learning new skills, living proof of the transformative power of productive labor.[27]

Reports such as those in the *People's Daily* were not supposed simply to provide a *description* of the process of collectivization in a small Tianjin alley; it is largely irrelevant whether the details about elderly volunteers and overenthusiastic mothers are amusing notes of color, obvious exaggerations, or pure fabrications for propaganda's sake (although I very much doubt they were the latter). As the small community at Hongshunli was being heralded as a model, these reports were instead *prescriptive* of

---

[22] Dong, "Red Housekeeping": 15.

[23] "Jiedao gongzuozhong de yimian hongqi – ji Tianjin shi Hongshunli zuzhi qilai hou de xin qixiang."

[24] Li Duanxiang 李端祥, Wang Qianzhen 汪前珍,(2014) "Chengshi renmin gongshe yu funü jiefang" 城市人民公社与妇女解放 [Urban people's commune and women's liberation], *Dangshi yanjiu yu jiaoxue* 党史研究与教学 [Research and teaching of Party history], 3 (2014): 83.

[25] "Renren canjia shehui laodong, jiajia dou guo jitishenghuo."

[26] "Jiedao gongzuozhong de yimian hongqi – ji Tianjin shi Hongshunli zuzhi qilai hou de xin qixiang."

[27] "Renren canjia shehui laodong, jiajia dou guo jitishenghuo."

how collectivization should be implemented, of the political priorities that inspired it, and of the economic logic that framed it. If the model behavior of the forty-two families at Hongshunli were to be replicated everywhere, the revolutionary promises of the Great Leap would be realized.[28] While the early publicized reports highlighted the discursive elements of the Great Leap project and gave cadres and activists the language to recount their own local experiments, they also identified the main vectors along which this transformation was supposed to be moving as well as the needs that animated it (at the level of the state, the collective, and the individual), and they hinted at early ambiguities and inconsistencies. Reports on collectivization were therefore not simply a prefab depiction of reality; rather, they were political interventions, often framed as exchanges between parts of the state (or the people and the state), continuously engaged in a redefinition of the practices at the bottom. As in other cases, the language of Maoism did not simply provide a rhetorical tool to produce the desired understandings of social and political relations, or even a way to express legitimate concerns in an acceptable manner; it also revealed existing sociopolitical fissures and created new ones. It was prescriptive, dialectical, and hermeneutical.

More importantly, these documents provide early indications of the tensions and the contradictions that emerged in the project of collectivization, at all levels, starting from the relation between its constitutive elements – production, social reorganization, ideological reform. Production came first, with the mobilization of women who worked as housewives providing the solution for the perceived lack of labor force. This was supposed to be a form of production for which little or no capital or financial support was needed, a true "Operation Bootstraps," as Phyllis Andors aptly called it:[29] Female workers would indeed be building their own workshop out of scraps and bringing their own tools from home. Communal welfare services were then necessary to allow for this participation in production but were likewise created and staffed with no external financial help, producing a seemingly endless virtuous cycle of increasing profits and reduced expenses or consumption of resources. The *Beijing Ribao* described the creation of communal services almost as a "natural" and effortless consequence of production (*shui dao qucheng, guashu diluo* 水到渠成，瓜熟蒂落, "when the water comes a channel is

[28] Hongshunli's pioneering example was quickly followed in the entire city of Tianjin, which mobilized 245,000 urban residents into commune membership in less than two months. Wang Xianming, "Cong jumin dao sheyuan": 144.
[29] Phyllis Andors, "Social Revolution and Woman's Emancipation: China during the Great Leap Forward," *Bulletin of Concerned Asian Scholars* 7:1 (1975): 39.

naturally formed; when a melon is ripe, it falls").[30] The logical and chronological primacy of production in the process of collectivization was not simply based on a universally accepted practical requirement. Rather, it embodied a political split among CCP leaders, theoreticians, and eventually activists. For some, this process followed a specific and quite rigid understanding of Marxism: The expansion of the forces of production through the inclusion of large numbers of women was the necessary prerequisite for a parallel change in relations of production, and social relationships in general, in this case, through the socialization of domestic work. Economic and social transformations would in turn lead to a new ideological awareness and a new "culture" – a new super-structure. For others, Mao included, collectivization was instead going to revolutionize the *social relations* of production, which in turn not only would generate both increased outputs and a new ideological conscious-ness, but would also herald a radical transformation of the entire social organization, down to the structure of remuneration and commodity exchange.[31]

Different understandings of the primacy of production and its mean-ing were also reflected in other tensions within the project of collectiviza-tion, which became visible in the praxis of urban communes. If the expansion of productive forces was the main immediate goal, that meant privileging accumulation (to be reinvested in further expansion, i.e., simple reproduction) over anything else, therefore curtailing any other endeavor that could subtract from that accumulation. This, as I show in the next pages, had an immediate effect over those collective services that socialized domestic tasks – child rearing, food prep, and so on. What happened when those services could not be sustained simply through extraction of fees from users, but required financial support from the commune, leading to a decrease in capital accumulation? Finally, the primacy of "production" also implied the primacy of "productive" fac-tory labor over other forms of collectivized labor, and that distinction was reflected in terms of pay, work condition, and status. The praxis of gendered labor in the commune continuously posed the question of

---

[30] "Shoudu de diyige chengshi renmin gongshe – Shijingshan Zhongsu youhaorenmin gongshe diaocha baogao" 首都的第一个城市人民公社 – 石景山中苏友好人民公社调查报告 [Survey report on the first urban people's commune in the capital – The Shijingshan Sino-Soviet Friendship people's commune], *Beijing Ribao* 北京日报, April 9, 1960. Cited in Li Duanxiang 李端祥, "Duiyu Beijing chengshi renmin gongshe lishi de kaocha" 对于北京城市人民公社历史的考察 [An examination of the history of the urban people's commune in Beijing], in Li Duanxiang, ed., *Chengshi renmin gongshe yanjiu ziliao xuanbian* 城市人民公社研究资料选编 [Selected research materials on urban people's communes] (人民出版社, 2021), vol. 1: 17.
[31] I will explore this division and the debate it engendered in Chapter 2.

who was really and fully a "worker," and of what kind of labor entitled one to that identity.

In the rest of chapter, I outline the process by which the first people's communes were established in Beijing, highlighting both the political logic behind this process and the tensions that emerged in the early phase. In Section 1.3 I will discuss the primacy of production and its relationship with the social services necessary to allow for the mobilization of women. Section 1.4 deals with the transformation of commerce and finance under the new organization, and Section 1.5 introduces how early collectivization affected social relationships and ideological attitudes.

## 1.2    Building Communes in Beijing

The people and the Party leaders in the capital did not want to lag behind in the collectivization effort, and Beijing soon emerged as a pioneer in the urban commune campaign. On August 4, 1958, the Party committee secretary, Peng Zhen, and vice-mayor Zhang Youyu presided over the meeting of the "Socialist Construction Leap Forward General Meeting of All Beijing Neighborhood Residents," where about 90,000 city dwellers were organized in a series of new collective enterprises, including over seventy kinds of services and factories,

such as tailor shops, barber shops, shower-bath houses, mess halls, shoe, trunk and box factories, a spinning mill and a packing plant. The street nursery took care of over 170,000 children. They also set up twenty-three street mess halls.... In Hsuanwu [Xuanwu] district alone, five "Red and Expert" schools were set up and 12,000 inhabitants were organized to participate in learning how to read newspapers. They also set up spare-time middle schools, primary schools and "sweep away illiteracy" organizations.[32]

Collective eating in canteens was supposed to reduce the consumption of basic resources, like coal or rice, while collective rearing of children exposed them more easily and more fully to socialist education, and Liu Shaoqi himself had emphasized boarding schools in October 1958.[33] But the movement was declaredly aimed at revolutionizing potentially every aspect of the everyday, reaching into every corner of urban space, be it public or private. The goals of the campaign were summarized with the usual pithy (and numbered) slogans. Urban collectivization was meant to achieve the "five transformations" (transform

---

[32] Shih Ch'eng-chih, *Urban Commune Experiments in Communist China*, Communist China Problem Research Series (Hong Kong: Union Research Institute, 1962): 53.
[33] Roderick MacFarquhar, *The Origins of the Cultural Revolution, vol. 2: The Great Leap Forward 1958–1960* (New York: Columbia University Press, 1983): 105.

the streets into workshops, transform waste into treasure, transform the poor families into well-to-do families, transform laziness into labor, transform individuals into collectives) and the "three changes" (change household work into collective work, change security and sanitation into everyday practices, change the streets by planting green trees and making everything beautiful). There were "five nos" (no idle people in any household, no waste in any family, no extravagance by anybody, no poverty in any group, no disturbance in any place) and "ten everybody has a job to do" (every family has savings, every person has cultural training, every person has a special ability, tailoring and laundry each has its organization, every group has its dining hall, every child has a place to be taken care of in, every deformed or aged person has a place to settle down, everybody has a newspaper to read every day, everybody has a morning drill every day).[34] What we have listed here are, once again, the elements of a totalizing transformation. The campaign would affect the physical space of Beijing streets by planting trees and improving hygiene; it would improve the economic conditions of neighborhood residents and reduce overall class inequalities, through the elimination of both poverty and excessive consumption ("extravagances"); it would restructure the organization of reproductive labor and care work; and it would improve the cultural life of each individual through schooling. Collectivization promised a better, greener, cleaner city, a more equal and affluent society, and, more importantly, the complete remaking of social relationships, including within the family. The list also explicitly points to how this revolutionary change could be achieved, that is, through the voluntary deployment of each and every person's labor into an organized collective effort. As any ounce of waste had to be recovered and transformed into a resource, so the abilities and the labor of each resident had to be deployed in a disciplined and ordered way (a drill every morning, no disturbance anywhere). Yet that discipline, at least in the ideal prefiguration of the campaign, was not to be imposed from above as a form of authoritarian regimentation; it could only be the result of the voluntary renunciation of individual interest in the name of a collective mission. It could only be achieved through self-discipline, as that transformation did not rely solely on backbreaking and endless work, but on the ideological remolding of each member of the collective through their participation in revolutionary praxis.

Beijing was among the first major cities to establish urban communes, and these early examples often acquired national fame for their

---

[34] Shih, *Urban Commune Experiments in Communist China*: 56–57.

pioneering efforts. The first was the Sino-Soviet Friendship Commune in the suburban district of Shijingshan, a mixed urban-rural commune that encompassed four villages, four residential committees, and one urban residential area. It was founded in August 1958 after a visit by Liu Shaoqi.[35] After Shijingshan, the other communes were all located within the old city walls, in the downtown area: Chunshu in Xuanwu district (September 29, 1958), Tiyuguanlu in Chongwen (autumn 1958), Beixinqiao in Dongcheng (autumn 1958), and Erlonglu in Xicheng (September 28, 1958).[36] This was the portion of the capital least touched by modern development, and even the construction of the Ten Great Buildings in 1959, which included the restructuring of Tiananmen Square into its current form,[37] affected only a relatively small portion of this area. Central Beijing remained defined by the intricate network of *hutong*, by old, often dilapidated one- or two-story residential buildings, and by historical commercial and entertainment areas (e.g., Dashilar, Tianqiao). Residents differed widely in terms of class, income, and education, with poor peddlers living close to famed Beijing opera actors and wealthy "capitalists."[38]

As in previous cases, Beijing communes are also described as being produced by popular initiative, through an impressive display of bottom-up frugality and devotion. Reports from the Chunshu commune convey images of unrelenting voluntarism and dazzling speed. In August, before the commune was even established, the Xuanwu district conducted a survey on the campaign, and out of 101 families, the most pressing requests for further collectivization came from forty-eight "dependents," who were either from poor families relying on little income or from high-income families with "high socialist consciousness." As an example of the latter, the report mentions a Mrs. Lu, wife of a worker, who, despite a family income of ¥100 a month, was still eager to join production and publicly castigated a neighbor, the wife of a capitalist, who refused to

---

[35] BMA 002-020-00983-1, Shijingshan renmin gongshe qingkuang baogao 石景山人民公社情况报告 [Report on the situation of the Shijingshan people's commune], September 12, 1958.

[36] Li Duanxiang, *Chengshi renmin gongshe yundong yanjiu*: 89.

[37] On the Ten Great Buildings and the transformation of Tiananmen, see Micheal Dutton, Hsiu-ju Stacy Lo, and Dong Dong Wu, *Beijing Time* (Cambridge, MA: Harvard University Press, 2008); Wu Hung, *Remaking Beijing: Tiananmen Square and the Creation of a Political Space* (Chicago: University of Chicago Press, 2005).

[38] Aminda Smith has explored the history of the CCP's thought reform of beggars and prostitutes who were concentrated in this area: Aminda M. Smith, *Thought Reform and China's Dangerous Classes: Reeducation, Resistance, and the People* (Lanham, MD: Rowman and Littlefield, 2012). For a description of old Beijing in the Republican era, see Madeleine Yue Dong, *Republican Beijing: The City and Its Histories* (Berkeley: University of California Press, 2003).

participate in manual labor: "You have plenty of food and plenty of clothes, what do you do then? You have no children, so what do you have to look forward to? We all should do our best to build socialism, not for ourselves but for others."[39] Consequently, the founding of the Chunshu commune was celebrated primarily as an endeavor *by housewives* and as the fulfillment of a promise *to housewives*. As Yuan Xiuchun, wife of a worker, summarized, "the day we establish a commune is also the day when the complete liberation of housewives arrived. In the five years since my first child was born, I did not see one single movie. This is the sentence that the 'family tribunal' issued me. The founding of the commune is truly a happy event for us housewives. I want to send my kids to childcare, I want to eat in the canteen, I will do whatever the commune wants me to do, I will take any assignment."[40] The acceptance, or rather the voluntary embrace, of collective labor under the commune was grounded on the promise not so much (or solely) of a monetary reward but of an actual liberation, a liberation whose effects could be measured even by the simple fact that women who used to work as housewives could now enjoy time and leisure outside the home.

After months of educational work, the commune reported widespread support in the area (about 80 percent); students, teachers, and employees of local businesses all contributed. Elderly people offered silver dollars and jewelry from their wedding dowry to the commune fund. Mrs. Wang, the wife of an old (over fifty) worker, dug her entire dowry – a gold-plated bracelet, a necklace, a kitchen cabinet, and other items – out of her wedding casket and wrote a moving letter to the CCP district committee, saying she was going to donate it all to the commune, and these were objects that she had steadily refused to sell even during the tough pre-liberation days.[41] Even some capitalists agreed to give up the dividends from the enterprises they had formerly owned and bought machinery for the factories.[42] Under such favorable conditions, productions and services developed quickly. It took them two days to create a childcare center, with service workers bringing all the necessary materials

---

[39] XDS, 1-1-295-3 Guanyu Chunshu hutong zuzhi jumin hezuoshe de qingkuang baogao 关于椿树胡同组织居民合作社的情况报告 [Report on the organization of residents' cooperatives in Chunshu *hutong*], August 14, 1958.

[40] XDS, 1-1-295-12 Chunshu renmin gongshe diaocha baogao (caogao) 椿树人民公社调查报告(草稿) [Report on a survey of the Chunshu people's commune (draft)], November 1958.

[41] XDS, 15-1-2-11 Zhonggong Xuanwuqu Chunshu dangwei 中共宣武区椿树党委 [Xuanwu District Chunshu CCP Committee], Xuanwuqu Chunshu renmin gongshe jianli qianhou de qingkuang 宣武区椿树人民公社建立前后的情况 [Before and after the establishment of the Chunshu people's commune in Xuanwu District], October 4, 1958.

[42] XDS, 1-1-295-12 Chunshu renmin gongshe diaocha baogao (caogao).

from their individual homes and setting it up next to the workshop. A rhyming clappertalk celebrated the endeavor: "Mom is involved in production, what about the kids? We work hard overnight and for another half day, and here we have a kindergarten. It's not difficult to do everything from scratch, from now on, mom produces while the kids have this new playground."[43]

At Taipingqiao, even before the creation of the commune in late September, the rate of participation in collective work was already quite high (68.49 percent in a population of around 50,000), and women were particularly vocal in calling for expansion of collective services: "Move quickly to solve the problem of childcare, then tell me what to do and I will do it."[44] When the commune was founded, people who joined it (after paying a nominal fee of one yuan) surrendered their property to the collective but were supposed to be repaid by the commune for what was used for services and production. Housing remained the individual's responsibility, but the commune administration had "eminent domain" powers in case of need. The duties of commune members included participation not only in production but in all other forms of "work" – political, theory, technical learning, and social work.[45]

Documents from the Erlonglu commune portray a similar situation but are more detailed about the kind of "productive labor" required. Following rural models, they adopted the motto, "Housewives do whatever they can to help with building socialism. If residents want to open a factory, then what they do it is to work and work some more, and in a

---

[43] "*Mama gao shengchan, haizi zenme ban? Kuzhan yiye lingbantian, chengliqi you'erban, baishou qijia bingbunan, congci mama de shengchan, haizi youle xin leyuan* 妈妈搞生产，孩子怎么办？苦战一夜另半天，成立起幼儿班，白手起家并不难，从此妈妈得生产，孩子有了新乐园." XDS, 1-1-295-3 Guanyu Chunshu hutong zuzhi jumin hezuoshe de qingkuang baogao. In an article in the *Beijing Ribao*, Liu Yong, the secretary of the Chunshu commune committee, wrote that, when it came to building a factory, they had nothing (*liangshou kongkong* 两手空空 "both hands were empty"); they lacked technical facilities and capital, and could rely only on the enthusiasm of the "housewives." Liu Yong 刘勇, "Cong zuzhi shengchan rushou, shengchan shenghuo yiqi zhua" 从组织生产入手，生产生活一起抓 [Start from organizing production, grasp production and life together], *Beijing Ribao* (April 18, 1960), reprinted in Li, ed., *Chengshi renmin gongshe yanjiu ziliao xuanbian*, vol. 7: 95–97.

[44] "*Kuaidian ba haizi gei jiejuele ba, jiaowo gan shenme wo gan shenme* 快点把孩子给解决了吧，叫我干什么我干什么." BMA 002-020-01000-1 Guanyu Tiapingqiao banshichu guanjie shijian renmin gongshe de chubu yijian 关于在太平桥办事处管界试建人民公社的初步意见 [Preliminary views on trying to establish a people's commune in the Taipingqiao jurisdiction], September 12, 1958.

[45] BMA 002-020-01000-2 Beijing Xichengqu Taipingqiao renmin gongshe shixing zhangcheng (cao'an) 北京市西城区太平桥人民公社试行章程(草案) [Beijing Xicheng District Taipingqiao people's commune draft charter (draft)].

month there will be a factory."[46] Female workers built their own work-shops and small factories, deploying labor as a substitute for actual means of production, creating everything from scratch – "working hard and with little resources, starting with nothing" (*qionggan kugan, baishou qijia* 穷干苦干, 白手起家). They collected waste materials, made their own tools, built the barracks, and got some of the small business owners and retired workers to teach them some basic skills. If there was some-thing missing in the factory, they would bring it from home; if they lacked tools or machinery, they would look in the garbage; if they had no raw material, they would use discarded scraps.[47] The initial capital came from the district administration, some "capitalists," small business owners, and from residents' contributions; property donated by wealth-ier residents was going to be repaid and turned into the commune's property.[48] More astonishingly, the newly recruited female workers labored without pay for three months, to quickly return the capital invested. They reached that goal by November, but even when they started receiving normal salaries, they selflessly asked for their pay to be kept low (¥15 on average), so as to increase capital accumulation and reinvestment in commune production.[49]

Following one of the Great Leap Forward cardinal principles, deploy-ment of diligent and frugal labor was used as a substitute for lack of capital investment, yet there were quite obvious limitations to the kind of

---

[46] "*Jiating funü wei jianshe shehuizhuyi tianzhuan tianwa, juminban gongchang, banfa dajia xiang laogan jia kugan, yuenei chu gongchang* 家庭妇女为建设社会主义添砖添瓦, 居民办工厂, 办法大家想劳干加苦干, 月内出工厂." BMA 002-020-0113-2 Fujian yi: Xichengqu Erlonglu renmin gongshe jiedao gongchang de dianxing cailiao 附件一: 西城区二龙路人民公社街道工厂的典型材料 [Appendix 1: Representative material about the neighborhood factories in the Erlonglu People's Commune, Xicheng district].

[47] BMA 101-001-00782-7 Yong zuikuai de bufa jianshe shehuizhuyi xin xhengshi: Beijing shi Erlonglu renmin gongshe diaocha 用最快的步伐建设社会主义新城市: 北京市二龙路人民公社调查 [Building a new socialist city at the fastest pace: A survey of the Erlonglu People's Commune in Beijing]; XDN 7-1-211-1 Erlonglu renmin gongshe shidian qingkuang de baogao (Erlonglu jiedao dangwei) 二龙路人民公社试点情况的报告 (二龙街道党委) [Report on the situation at the pilot test of Erlonglu people's commune (Erlonglu neighborhood party committee)]. A *Beijing Ribao* report from the Guangwai commune in 1960 describes the construction of the local carbon powder factory, with female workers making walls out of clay and using bamboo mats for the roof. Shen Lizhu 沈丽珠, "Guangwai gongshe guanche zhixing qinjian fangzhen" 广外公社贯彻执行勤俭方针 [The Guangwai Commune carries out the policy of diligence and thrift], *Beijing Ribao* (August 10, 1960), reprinted in Li, ed., *Chengshi renmin gongshe yanjiu ziliao xuanbian*, vol. 7: 105–106.

[48] BMA 002-020-0113-2 Fujian yi: Xichengqu Erlonglu renmin gongshe jiedao gongchang de dianxing cailiao.

[49] BMA 002-020-0113-2 Fujian yi: Xichengqu Erlonglu renmin gongshe jiedao gongchang de dianxing cailiao; BMA 101-001-00782-7 Yong zuikuai de bufa jianshe shehuizhuyi xin xhengshi.

production these hastily assembled factories and workshops could engage in. Over a year after the founding of the Erlonglu commune, reports admitted that they were still very much relying on handicraft and that technical skills and equipment were sorely lacking. Of the 3,000 female workers, only thirty-one were skilled, and on average they reached only half the productivity level of a (male) SOE worker.[50] That, however, did not necessarily make those factories unproductive or unprofitable. Take the case of the General Factory (*Zonghe gongchang* 综合工厂) at Erlonglu: It had started with ten housewives, four craftsmen, two and half rooms of space, one table, two wooden benches, and a borrowed capital of just over ¥140. After a year, it had grown to 425 workers, 32 machine tools of all kinds, and 92 rooms, and the average daily output had risen from ¥2,300 in January 1959 to ¥27,000 in December.[51] In the same period, the commune had established fifteen factories and nineteen production teams overall, with over 5,000 workers; in the fourth quarter of 1959, production rose to 14.2 times what it had been in the same period in 1958.

The economic worth of commune production would become the object of critique and contention later in the campaign, but direct profitability was neither the main purpose nor the central meaning of collectivized production and commune labor. The overwhelming share of capital accumulation was usually not transferred to the upper echelons of the state, but remained in loco, to finance further development and services, and commune industries were supposed to concentrate on the manufacture of objects of everyday use. It was a form of production directly related to the provision of everyday necessities to city residents, a crucial element in the promised overall improvement of their livelihood and in the transformation of scarcity into socialist abundance through the increasing availability of products to be distributed – not commodities to be sold. In a similar way, while women moved from the home to the factory, from a form of labor that was deemed domestic, unproductive, and unpaid (more on that assessment later) to one that was collective, productive, and waged, that labor was not supposed to become commodified, as the perhaps idealized depictions of female workers voluntarily toiling for little or no pay illustrate. In the following months, tensions would arise about how to evaluate commune production, but at least at the beginning of the Great Leap Forward, the value of industrial labor was therefore not primarily in the economic profit it could accrue, either for the individual or the state. It lay in the much wider revolution that hinged on it.

---

[50] BMA 101-001-00782-7 Yong zuikuai de bufa jianshe shehuizhuyi xin xhengshi.
[51] BMA 101-001-00782-7 Yong zuikuai de bufa jianshe shehuizhuyi xin xhengshi.

## 1.3    Production and Its Consequences

As fittingly noted in a report from the Chunshu commune, urban communes were transforming the relations of production, and that in turn would produce a change in the habits of daily life, "an inevitable trend in the development from socialism to communism."[52] This was usually summarized as "the three transformations," meaning the collectivization of production (*shengchan jitihua* 生产集体化), the canteen-ization of eating (*chifan shitanghua* 吃饭食堂化), and the nursery-fication of childcare (*ertong tuo'erhua* 儿童托儿化).[53] To put it differently, this meant the collectivization of both production and social reproduction (or at least the most obvious aspects of the latter), which could not have but radical consequences for family structure and social relationships. Yet while the social reach of collectivization was deep, production remained the prime motor and the ultimate justification of the other transformations, and that had major, if largely unforeseen, effects. As exemplified in the cases of the first urban communes, industrialization had the logical and chronological priority, as it was participation in industrial work that would then spur women to push for services – and specifically for those services that would aid their presence in the factory. In turn, new services would further foster participation in industrial labor. Therefore, a report from the Chunshu commune recommended that "we must start from production, and we cannot unilaterally emphasize canteens and childcare centers."[54] The guiding principle was: "As long as we manage production well, we will be able to develop and consolidate the neighborhood welfare and every other kind of service. If we place production at the center, then a great leap in services of all kinds will follow."[55] It was the Great Leap's liberation of the productive forces that would further advance the people's collective consciousness (*jiti guan'nian*集体观念), and that in turn would create the conditions for revolutionizing the areas of production, exchange, distribution, and consumption.[56]

This assessment of the primacy of production reflected a specific understanding of socialist economics (explored in Chapter 2), but it also

---

[52] XDS 15-1-2-3 Guanyu jianli chengshi renmin gongshe hou gaige shangye guanli tizhi de zongjie (caogao) 关于建立城市人民公社后改革商业管理体制的总结 (草稿) [Summary on the reform of commercial management system after the establishment of urban people's communes (draft)], October 28, 1958.

[53] XDS 1-1-295-12 Chunshu renmin gongshe diaocha baogao (caogao).

[54] XDS 1-1-295-12 Chunshu renmin gongshe diaocha baogao (caogao).

[55] XDN 7-1-211-1 Erlonglu renmin gongshe shidian qingkuang de baogao (Erlonglu jiedao dangwei).

[56] XDS 15-1-2-3 Guanyu jianli chengshi renmin gongshe hou gaige shangye guanli tizhi de zongjie (caogao).

had practical effects on how the communes were structured and how problems – which emerged almost immediately – were tackled. Setting up an urban commune in downtown Beijing presented a set of specific issues: Unlike in the countryside, there was no preexisting system of cooperatives upon which to build a larger organization; the population was often diverse in term of class, occupation, and income, as was the case in Chunshu; and many residents worked or studied in other districts. The material conditions for production, in term of both resources and quality of the labor force, were very limited, and that affected output as well as salaries.[57] In the first months of the Chunshu commune's existence, salaries for female workers were extremely low, ranging on average between ¥5 and ¥10 a month, with few workers reaching ¥20.[58] At those rates, it was difficult for workers to pay for the vaunted new social services, such as canteens and childcare. Yet, faced with this contradiction, commune authorities could only revert to production as the ultimate solution: They called for increased outputs, which in turn were supposed to imply bigger salaries for female workers, and therefore more widespread access to welfare.[59] We see here in a nutshell a crucial tension that will come to bear heavily on the development of the communes in the following years.

The communes did indeed provide a series of communal services to a population that had been largely excluded from the *fuli* granted to *danwei* employees,[60] and which was recorded and celebrated in reports. In the first Beijing commune, Shijingshan, mess halls and kindergartens were considered "an essential measure to mobilize the broad masses of women to engage in production," and the commune used a portion of its public welfare fund (¥230,000) "to subsidize the wages of all canteen and

---

[57] XDS 1-1-295-13 Dui Xuanwuqu Chunshu renmin gongshe caizheng shuiqu wenti de chubu yijian 对宣武区椿树人民公社财政税取问题的初步意见 [Preliminary views on the issue of financial taxes in the Chunshu people's commune in Xuanwu District] (November 7, 1958).

[58] For comparison's sake, the average annual (monetary) wage for workers in Beijing in 1958 was ¥867 (¥72.5 monthly) for collective enterprises and ¥705 (¥58.75 monthly) for SOEs. *Xin Zhongguo liushinian Tongji ziliao huibian* 新中国六十年统计资料汇编 [China compendium of statistics 1949–2008], compiled by the Department of Comprehensive Statistics of the National Bureau of Statistics (Beijing: China Statistics Press, 2009): 89. Nationally, the annual monetary wage was ¥470 (¥39.1) for collective enterprises and ¥550 (¥45.8) for SOEs. Guojia tongjiju shehui tongjisi bian 国家统计局社会统计司编, *Zhongguo laodong gongzi tongji ziliao* 中国劳动工资统计资料1949–1985 [China's labor wage statistics 1949–1985] (Beijing: China Statistic Press, 1987): 152. I am thankful to Lili Lin for helping with this data.

[59] XDS 1-1-295-12 Chunshu renmin gongshe diaocha baogao (caogao).

[60] Joel Andreas, *Disenfranchised: The Rise and Fall of Industrial Citizenship in China* (Oxford: Oxford University Press, 2019); Evans, *Beijing from Below*.

nursery staff and to purchase equipment." Nursery fees ranged from only
¥0.5 to ¥1.5 yuan,[61] and eating in the canteens cost "no more than
preparing meals at home." Mrs. Chen, a former "dependent" turned
worked from Pingguoyuan, praised the new situation: "I earn ¥22 from
work, and with three children in the nursery, including meals, I pay ¥18.
My income alone is enough – how could life not improve?"[62]

At Erlonglu, in just one year, the commune had established thirteen
kindergartens, seventeen communal canteens, fourteen service centers,
two stores, and even an old people's home and a neighborhood hospital,
with 579 people employed in the new service sector. There were only
nineteen "advanced work units" (xianjin danwei 先进单位) in the commune service sector as of August 1958, but by the end of the year, they
had risen to forty-one. Communal canteens had expanded from the
original four makeshift sheds to twenty-five buildings, with a capacity
of over 1,000 patrons; they had electric machines for kneading and
cutting dough as well as for chopping vegetables, and they even set up
a steam boiler that could cook mantou (steamed bread) for 240 people in
ten minutes. Three original childcare groups from 1958 had been combined into the Xitiejiang hutong kindergarten, which was awarded the
"red banner unit" distinction in August 1959; it had never registered
even a single case of infectious disease and was approximating the level of
city-run childcare centers.[63]

Xicheng district had 125 canteens (and 540 employees) by December
1958, which were praised, with a somewhat Taylorist precision, for
saving labor power and resources. Assuming the average housewife spent
four hours per day buying groceries and prepping meals, the district
Party Committee calculated that the canteens were saving the equivalent
of 2,358 labor hours. The canteens were also credited with reducing coal
consumption. They did not conform to one specific model: The large
majority were very small, created at the neighborhood level with local
resources and "managed by housewives"; they were convenient; and the
food tasted "just like at home," yet the wealthier district residents

---

[61] While the document does not specify, in these kinds of reports service fees are usually
assessed per month.
[62] "Wo canjia gongzuo zheng ershier yuan, sange xiaohai ru tuoersuo lianhuo shijiao shiba yuan,
zhi wo yigeren de shouru jiubuwan, shenghuo zenme bu tigao? 我参加工作挣二十二元,三个
小孩入托儿所连伙食交十八元,只我一个人的收入就不完,生活怎么不提高." BMA 101-
001-00782-5 Zhigong jiashu chengle shehui caifu de chuangzaozhe: Shijingshan
Zhongsu youhao renmin gongshe jieshao 职工家属成了社会财富的创造者: 石景山中苏
友好人民公社介绍 [The families of the workers have become the creators of social
wealth: Introduction to the Shijingshan Sino-Soviet Friendship People's Commune].
[63] BMA 101-001-00782-7 Yong zuikuai de bufa jianshe shehuizhuyi xin xhengshi: Beijing
shi Erlonglu renmin gongshe diaocha.

complained that the quality was not up to the more sophisticated standards they were used to. Other canteens were managed by the commune in collaboration with work units, taking advantage of existing facilities with few attendees. Some *danwei* simply opened their canteens to commune members.[64]

Just south of Xicheng district, the Chunshu commune boasted a registration for canteens up to 96 percent, with an actual attendance of 80 percent of the commune members. They served mostly the newly recruited housewives-turned-workers, students, and some local cadres. Patrons still needed to hand in a grain ration (*liang piao* 粮票) and they had to pay a monthly fee, ranging between ¥8–9 and ¥14–15, for two meals a day, with no breakfast or late-night service. The commune also set up over 100 crèches and kindergartens, with over 200 childcare nurses. The large majority were daytime-only, with a few boarding nurseries. Fees for boarding nursery were normally around ¥14–15 per month, but they could go as high as ¥17–18, and even ¥24. The daytime ones were ¥2 or ¥2.5 per month (extra ¥0.3 for dinner). The half-day ones were between ¥0.6 and ¥1.[65] The district conducted a series of early surveys, which highlighted the issues that needed to be ironed out but also some resistance among certain sectors of the populace. Despite the wide range in pricing, these services often remained still too expensive for poor families, while they were not considered refined enough for wealthier people. The latter did not want to send children to the communal kindergarten, and even when they did, they waited outside the door after their child went in, and if the child cried, they would rush in and refuse to leave. Likewise, they complained that the canteen food was not as good as what they were used to at home, and called the canteens unhygienic and unfree (*buziyou* 不自由, probably meaning that they felt pressured to attend). People who regularly attended were, according to

---

[64] BMA 002-020-01001-13 Zhonggong Xicheng quwei guanyu banhao jiedao shitang de yijian 中共西城区委关于办好街道食堂的意见 [Opinions of the CCP Xicheng District Committee on running good neighborhood canteens] (December 2, 1958).

[65] For comparison, at the rural/urban commune of Shijingshan, the fee for the childcare center was about ¥6 per month per child, including meals. At the canteen, you could buy ten *jiaozi* (dumplings) for ¥0.09, a dish of *baicai* (cabbage) for ¥0.05, cabbage soup for ¥0.01, and a meat dish for ¥0.1. BMA 001-006-01493-7 Shijingshan Zhongsu youhao renmin gongshe zuzhi zhigong jiashu canjia shengchan laodong qude jingyan 石景山中苏友好人民公社组织职工家属参加生产劳动取得经验 [Shijingshan Sino-Soviet Friendship People's Commune gained experience in organizing the families of workers to participate in production work]. At Xicheng, childcare full board ranged from ¥8 to ¥14. Daycare (with food) from ¥7 to ¥12, without food from ¥2 to ¥8, BMA 002-020-01001-12 Zhonggong Xicheng quwei guanyu banhao jiedao tuo'er zuzhi gongzuo de yijian 中共西城区委关于办好街道托儿组织工作的意见 [Opinions of the Xicheng District Committee of the CCP on running good neighborhood childcare organizations], December 2, 1958.

the survey, residents with good political consciousness, and then there were those who followed the trend of the moment but did not really believe in the project. They would eat at the canteens for a few days, then stop, "buying the food, but not buying the equality" (*guang maifan bu mai pingdeng* 光买饭不买平等).[66]

In the surveyors' assessment, these were temporary issues that could be tackled by improving quality and by educating commune members, and, given that these organizations were only months old, one would assume that this was indeed the case. Yet another problem, which became apparent almost since the founding of the first Beijing communes, seemed not only more stubborn but also more foundational: These new services were not accessible to every commune member. At Chunshu, as early as August, people complained that the childcare centers, makeshift as they were, were too expensive and that while "one could scrounge up a simple meal at home, it cost actual money to eat at the canteen" (*zai jia yi couhe jiushi yidun, yaochi shitang yijiazi yidun de haojimao* 在家一凑合就是一顿,要吃食堂一家子一顿得好几毛).[67] In Xicheng district, facing low attendance in the commune canteens, a survey revealed that the only regular patrons were better-off residents with no family members who would cook for them at home. Residents with older relatives who needed care, had many children, or were otherwise in dire straits did not avail themselves of the new collective services. They cited the case of a mother with five children and a family monthly income of ¥100, of which ¥40 was needed for basic expenses; eating at home cost ¥46.9, while taking the family to the canteen amounted to ¥56.4.[68] The survey did not produce a discussion of these complaints, but here we have one of the first clear indications of what happened when the unvalued and unpaid labor of social reproduction was transferred to collective service and performed by waged employees. Services that had been provided by housewives in the hidden space of domesticity suddenly acquired an exchange value; their cost had to be estimated and they had to be assigned a price. Who should shoulder that cost and pay that price remained an open issue, however, and while this issue was discussed in practical terms and was central to the experiential practice of the commune residents, urban collectivization did not spur an in-depth debate over the hidden costs of social reproduction. When that cost fell back onto the family to be paid with the income from the former housewife, now a salaried worker, the obvious "economic" solution was for

[66] XDS 1-1-295-12 Chunshu renmin gongshe diaocha baogao (caogao).
[67] XDS 1-1-295-3 Guanyu Chunshu hutong zuzhi jumin hezuoshe de qingkuang baogao.
[68] BMA 002-020-01001-13 Zhonggong Xicheng quwei guanyu banhao jiedao shitang de yijian.

families to return those services to the unvalued – and therefore apparently "free" – sphere of gendered domestic labor, thus placing the burden of both domestic and factory labor on the female workers.

While the problem was universally recognized, the solutions proposed were far from univocal, anticipating the heated discussions of the following years. At Shijingshan, for example, the local cadres called for subsidizing service fees, arguing that the commune made ¥530,000 from the labor of the new female workers, so it should invest that money in keeping the fees low and providing facilities.[69] At Xicheng, however, the CCP district committee reverted once again to production as the fulcrum of the entire project: They called for getting more of the "unused labor force" into communal factories, so as to increase revenue, and thus raise workers' salaries while reducing fees and prices.[70]

These issues of costs were, in some cases, compounded by lapses in the quality of the services provided. That was not overly surprising, given the speed with which communal canteens and kindergartens had been created and the largely bottom-up nature of that effort. As was often the case, reports laid at least part of the blame on the political background of the new (female) service employees, who were singled out as the main reason for recurring instances of mistreatment of children, excessive corporal punishment, and embezzlement. In Xicheng district, 123 (out of 540) employees were labeled as politically suspicious, including a woman who had been married to a KMT officer and was still in touch with him even after their divorce. Another one had worked as a translator for the Japanese and was described as "sexually promiscuous" (luangao nannü guanxi 乱搞男女关系).[71] The head of one childcare center, Mrs. Zhang, was the wife of a rightist, an opium smoker, and had reportedly engaged in extramarital affairs. She was accused of pinching the children's cheeks so hard that they turned blue. Another service worker, the wife of a collaborationist police chief, stole the children's milk and meat from the kitchen by hiding them in her pants. In one childcare center, three out of six educators had been labeled counterrevolutionaries; they served children cold food, and if a child was defecating regularly, they gave them less food; if they urinated a lot, they gave them less water.[72]

[69] BMA 001-006-01493-7 Shijingshan Zhongsu youhao renmin gongshe zuzhi zhigong jiashu canjia shengchan laodong qude jingyan.
[70] BMA 002-020-01001-13 Zhonggong Xicheng quwei guanyu banhao jiedao shitang de yijian.
[71] BMA 002-020-01001-13 Zhonggong Xicheng quwei guanyu banhao jiedao shitang de yijian.
[72] BMA 002-020-01001-12 Zhonggong Xicheng quwei guanyu banhao jiedao tuo'er zuzhi gongzuo de yijian.

However, political background was seemingly not the only and probably not the most serious issue affecting the quality of the commune personnel. At Erlonglu, out of 138 childcare employees tested, three had tuberculosis, eighteen trichomoniasis, two syphilis, and five had severe trachoma.[73] In general, sounding a refrain that will be repeated over and over in the discussion of the communes, reports complained that the housewives staffing canteens and kindergarten were, in the end, "just housewives": They needed pedagogical training, had no experience in management and accounting, and often lacked even rudimentary knowledge of hygiene. There were reports of children having to share the same basin, towel, and spoon, and in one nursery, at Beichang jie 北长街 (just west of the Forbidden City), they registered twenty-five cases of cold and cough and two of pneumonia among the twenty-eight children in just one quarter.[74] While these numbers might indeed be indicative of a troubling situation in communal childcare, first, they were colored by ingrained prejudices toward women who worked as housewives, and, second, it was the very establishment of collective nurseries and kindergartens that allowed for the collection of such data. For both children and mothers, it was their participation in childcare organizations that made their health, probably for the first time, into an object of statistical relevance. In that sense, these numbers might tell us more about the overall well-being of the residents of some Beijing districts than about the specific situation after the founding of communes.[75]

What seems indeed to be the case was that early childcare ventures were plagued by a chronic lack of resources. Most of the new centers in Xicheng were overcrowded and poorly equipped, lacking basic facilities, including beds, chairs, tables, and toys. One Xicheng nursery hosted over twenty infants but had only two little beds,[76] while Chunshu communal kindergarten units could not afford coal for heating in the winter and had to resort to asking families to provide for it.[77] The Chunshu canteens suffered from similar failures in hygiene and cleanliness as well as from lack of experience and funds. The equipment was often

[73] BMA 002-020-01001-12 Zhonggong Xicheng quwei guanyu banhao jiedao tuo'er zuzhi gongzuo de yijian.
[74] BMA 002-020-01001-12 Zhonggong Xicheng quwei guanyu banhao jiedao tuo'er zuzhi gongzuo de yijian.
[75] See Aminda Smith and Fabio Lanza, "Anatomy of a Woman Worker: Collectivization and Labour during the Great Leap Forward," in Ivan Franceschini and Christian Sorace, eds., *Proletarian China: A Century of Chinese Labour* (London: Verso, 2022): 108–117.
[76] BMA 002-020-01001-12 Zhonggong Xicheng quwei guanyu banhao jiedao tuo'er zuzhi gongzuo de yijian.
[77] XDS 1-1-295-12 Chunshu renmin gongshe diaocha baogao (caogao).

rudimentary, cooking skills were poor, ingredients were simple, labor was badly distributed and organized, and space was cramped; this led to huge discrepancies in prices and profits among canteens and a lack of variety in the menu.[78] These limitations made the services less convenient and less responsive to "the needs of the masses." People complained that canteens were not being flexible with opening and closing times. Female workers in Xicheng who had to drop off children at childcare ended up being late for work, while centers often closed around 5 or 5:30 pm, when parents were still working in the factories. One day, a worker who could not get home until 8 pm found her two children asleep on the doorstep.[79]

These issues were compounded, and their solution was made even more difficult by the perception that service workers in commune enterprises were unfairly treated. In general, all (female) commune employees received lower salaries and much inferior benefits than their (male) counterparts in SOEs, and that was a structural and foundational characteristic of collectivized female labor. Despite the very real effects that participating in communal labor had, female workers in commune enterprises were often still identified with their supposedly discarded identity of "housewives" or "dependents." While that was obviously not a class label, such as "poor peasant" or "capitalist," and theoretically depended solely on one's specific role within the process of social reproduction (what a woman does, not what a woman is), that identity proved to be a difficult one to divest oneself of. As I will examine in detail later, negative connotations associated with domestic work – unskilled, unvalued, repetitive – remained attached to women who worked as housewives even when they left those chores behind and devoted themselves to "productive" tasks; their labor, even industrial labor, was systematically devalued because of who was performing it, because it was done by "housewives." The situation was even worse for service employees, whose work was practically and theoretically subsidiary to the "real" productive work of the factories, and whose labor directly substituted for family care and domestic work. As a consequence, they were on average paid less than their counterparts involved in communes' industrial production. Childcare workers in Xicheng made between ¥2 and ¥15 per month (¥10 on average), but as of December 1958, five months into the collectivization drive, several of them had not been paid at all. Out of 345 employees at Fengsheng (丰盛) and Erlonglu, 107 (31

[78] XDS 1-1-295-12 Chunshu renmin gongshe diaocha baogao (caogao).
[79] BMA 002-020-01001-12 Zhonggong Xicheng quwei guanyu banhao jiedao tuo'er zuzhi gongzuo de yijian.

percent) did not receive a fixed salary, despite what was considered a pretty heavy workload.[80] Communal canteens in the district faced similar issues of huge salary differences and unpaid labor: Thirty-nine out of eighty employees at Fusuijing (福绥境 in Xicheng district) had yet to be paid in December. The Xicheng district committee cited the case of a canteen employee at the Zaolin compound (*Zaolin dayuan* 枣林大院), married to a worker, with two kids, so poor that the children were still wearing unlined garments; she had worked for months and had not yet been paid. Finally, she exploded, "I worked hard for three months, when does it end? Does anybody care if my children's feet are cold?"[81] This situation reinforced the conviction among commune members that working in the communal service sector was for "inferior people" (*diren* 低人). It was a job with no future, a dead-end position, as former house-wives continued to perform "womanly" tasks like cooking and tending children, rather than being involved in industrial production, where one could potentially learn new, useful skills and even perhaps achieve the vaunted status of fully recognized "worker." Prejudice toward service work was indeed cited as one of the main reasons for women leaving collective labor just after a few months.[82] This also exemplifies how quickly and easily, under specific ideological conditions, the voluntary deployment of labor for a collective enterprise by politically motivated workers could be turned into systematically unpaid or underpaid toil.

## 1.4    Reforming Commerce

Production, distribution, exchange, and consumption, Marx argued in the *Grundrisse*, "all form the members of a totality, distinctions within a unity," among which production predominates. Marx was not arguing here for the primacy of the "forces of production" as the motor of historical change; rather, he was describing and analyzing an integrated system of social relations (a totality) within which a certain aspect, production and relations of production, had a determinative importance. It was therefore logical to think that such a radical change in the size,

[80] BMA 002-020-01001-12 Zhonggong Xicheng quwei guanyu banhao jiedao tuo'er zuzhi gongzuo de yijian. The workload for each employee was four to seven infants aged between fifty-four days and one year, seven to ten between one and three years, and twenty to thirty-five between three and seven years.
[81] "Kuzhan sangeyue, haiyou getou meiyou? Wo haizi de jiao dongle sheiguan! 苦战三个月,还有个头没有？ 我孩子的脚冻了谁管!" BMA 002-020-01001-13 Zhonggong Xicheng quwei guanyu banhao jiedao shitang de yijian.
[82] XDS 1-1-295-12 Chunshu renmin gongshe diaocha baogao (caogao); XDS 15-1-2-3 Guanyu jianli chengshi renmin gongshe hou gaige shangye guanli tizhi de zongjie (caogao).

organization, and structure of production as the one prefigured by the Great Leap would also significantly affect all the other areas of the totality.[83] This echoed CCP leaders' desire to deeply alter the organization of distribution and consumption in the cities. In their view, that organization still preserved too many capitalist or "traditional" characteristics, which in turn prevented further developments. Since their inception, then, Beijing urban communes also constituted an experiment on what socialist commerce could be or, rather, what it should become.

Development during the FFYP had been overwhelmingly focused on heavy industry, which absorbed about 85 percent of the total investment.[84] While this investment led to a noticeable expansion of both the industrial sector and a new proletariat, little was done to supplant or modernize traditional urban handicraft and small-scale enterprises, which continued to produce much-needed everyday commodities and provide indispensable services for city residents. According to one estimate, non-agricultural Chinese handicraft employment in 1957 was around 10 million, compared with only 5.9 million in factories and mining.[85] These handicraft enterprises ranged widely in size and resources, from collectively owned small factories to family shops and itinerant peddlers, with little or no capital and only a few tools. This also meant that, while a portion of the urban population (those employed in large *danwei* and their "dependents") enjoyed an expanding offering of guaranteed goods and services, distributed gratis through the state network, a large share of the city residents was still buying commodities and services "in the market," paying for them with currency. "Socialist commerce" in the late 1950s included a large sector of goods, materials, and services that were part of the national plan, and therefore produced and distributed (or exchanged) under direct state control, but also others that were not, and whose connection to the planned economy was always problematic and subject to continued negotiation.

Communal factory production, while it was a bottom-up and frugal operation, was supposed to eventually reach a scale big enough to be integrated within the national plan. The same went for communes' purchase and distribution. The socialization of domestic work under the commune not only allowed for housewives' participation in

---

[83] Karl Marx, *Grundrisse: Foundations of the Critique of Political Economy* (London: Penguin Books, 1973). Also available at www.marxists.org/archive/marx/works/1857/grundrisse/index.htm.

[84] Nai-Ruenn Chen, *The Chinese Economy under Maoism: The Early Years, 1949–1969* (London: Routledge, 2017): 39.

[85] Chen, *The Chinese Economy under Maoism*: 40.

productive labor but was also supposed to substitute the fragmented, individualized purchase of food and other products by each individual family with their collective acquisition and distribution. Such an expansion of collective purchase and distribution of goods under the commune was a crucial element in a process aimed at reducing the role and importance of those functions of the socialist economy that seemed to perpetuate capitalist features, first and foremost, the commodity form. If the communes were able to continuously increase the amount and kinds of products that were acquired collectively and then given to members of the commune as basic life necessities – instead of being purchased by individuals as commodities – they would significantly contribute to pushing forward the transformation toward the communist ideal of "to each according to its needs." The promised abundance of soon-to-be-achieved communism would then be one of "products," not of "commodities." Consequently, the restriction of the role of the commodity form as part of the transition to communism, in which the commune was supposed to function as the "bridge," could not but come with a related limitation of the use of money, which Marx had described as "the absolutely alienable commodity, because it is all other commodities divested of their shape, the product of their universal alienation."[86] This required, among other changes, a remaking of the commercial and banking sectors as well as a rethinking of the distribution networks. It was not an easy process of integration.

In Xicheng district, it quickly became evident that the old district-level structure of the commerce bureau and service bureau did not fit the newly created communes. With the establishment of communal welfare, the provision of food had been centralized, so while overall consumption remained pretty much the same, canteens, childcare, and service centers all purchased wholesale, negatively affecting the retail sector. Reportedly, both the rate of customer visits to the district stores and the overall number of individual commercial exchanges (*jiaoyi cishu* 交易次数) had drastically diminished. Similarly, communal industrial production created new tasks for the commercial sector, which was now supposed to carry goods and materials that were not usually part of state allocation, while also being entrusted with selling the products of commune factories. In agreement with the district committee, the Erlonglu commune authorities decided to transfer (*xiafang*) the ninety-six stores (and their 682 employees) in its territory under commune control, and to establish a centralized commission store (*daixiaodian* 代销店) together with a main

---

[86] Karl Marx, *Capital, Volume 1*, translated by Ben Fowkes (London: Penguin, 1990): 205.

store (*zhongxindian* 中心店), the latter to be the supervisory agency for the entire commercial and service sector. The stated goal of such a transformation was to maintain a stable revenue for the country, while avoiding pure profit-seeking methods.[87]

The Chunshu commune started discussing how to reform its commercial sector as early as September 1958. The commune encompassed ninety-eight businesses with a total of 682 employees, mostly small stores, except for the Caishikou market, with its sixty-seven employees. Worried that moving all these en masse under commune jurisdiction would be too chaotic, the neighborhood CCP committee decided to transfer only the smaller ones on September 24, eighty-two of them, equaling 83.7 percent of the total number of stores, 38 percent of the capital, 20.3 percent of the monthly revenues, and 61.4 percent of the personnel.[88] Later reports provide different numbers, up to over 100 stores and 1,590 employees or 170 units and 765 employees (I suspect the discrepancies have to do with the inclusion of peddlers, itinerant sellers, and some service enterprises), but they all describe the same orderly process and the same goals. The businesses first moved under commune control were relatively small, low-skilled, serving a relative restricted area, with simple products, and mostly located in alleys (*hutong*). They were either state or collectively owned, and the former remained "ownership by the whole people," while control over personnel, finance, and management (*renquan* 人权, *caiquan* 财权, *guanliquan* 管理权) was transferred to the commune.[89] The process was supposed to follow a simple set of principles. First, stores that sold products that were directly "of service to the people" or had a close relationship to people's lives were to be immediately transferred to the commune. Other stores could wait. Second, the commerce sector under commune jurisdiction should continue to fulfill the national plan, pay taxes, turn profits over to the state, and assure national economic accumulation (*guojia de jingji jilei*

---

[87] XDN 7-7-133 Zhonggong Beijingshi Xicheng quwei caimaobu, Xicheng quwei 1958 nian caimaobu guanyu renmin gongshe jianli hou shangye, fuwuye guanli tizhi he jigou shezhi de chubu yijian 中共北京市西城区委财贸部, 西城区委1958年财贸部关于人民公社建立后商业、服务业管理体制和机构设置的初步意见 [Department of finance and trade of the Xicheng District Committee of the CCP, "Preliminary opinions of the department of finance and trade of the Xicheng District Committee in 1958 on the management system and organizational structure for the commerce and service sector after the establishment of the people's commune"], October 20, 1958.

[88] XDS 1-1-295-6 Zhonggong Xuanwuqu Chunshu hutong dangweihui, Guanyu jianli renmin gongshe shangye xiafang youguan jige wenti de yijian 中共宣武区椿树胡同党委会, 关于建立人民公社商业下放有关几个问题的意见 [Xuanwu District Chunshu hutong party committee, "Opinions on several issues related to the decentralization of the commercial sector in the people's communes"], September 22, 1958.

[89] XDS 1-1-295-12 Chunshu renmin gongshe diaocha baogao (caogao).

国家的经济积累). Third, under the new jurisdiction, expenses should continue to decrease and the quality to increase.[90] The method for reallocation was well regulated: first small units and then big ones, first family enterprises and then joint private-public companies or SOEs, first transfer control over management and then control over finances. This was accompanied by intense political work among the commerce and service sector employees. Apparently, some older employees rejoiced at the news, believing this was a step closer to achieved communism, a promise that was indeed a central theme in the rhetorical push behind collectivization. A barber at Chunshu, named Tan Wang 谭旺 , chimed in, "In the past I believed that communism was indeed good, but I am over fifty now, and I thought I would never live long enough to achieve it; but now communism is not that far, and I might make it." There were doubters, of course, especially among private owners, who wondered what would happen to their stakes in the business or the building in which it was located. A photographer who rented out twelve rooms for a monthly income of ¥60 worried about those financial losses. Some older clerks and shop owners were concerned about the possibility of being sent to the countryside to do manual labor, unlike their younger colleagues, who could still acquire skills and find work in a factory.[91]

The process was geared toward avoiding the "two major mistakes" (concerning the *xiafang* of commercial sector and the supply of business services) and the "three big mess-ups" (messing up the consciousness of employees, professional work, and finances).[92] The method was synthesized in another pithy enumeration: the three transfers, the four unifies, and the five guarantees (*sanfang, sitong, wubaozheng de banfa* 三放, 四统, 五保证的方法). The first referred to the transfer of the three basic rights, over personnel, finances, and management: Cadres from the supply and marketing service bureau and all shop employees would be transferred and with them the responsibility for their salaries, welfare, education, and so on; the capital of the relocated units would go to the commune; selling, buying, hygiene, service, and so on remained the responsibility of each enterprise under the guidance of the commune and the district commercial bureau. "The four unifies" referred to those tasks that remained under the district's jurisdiction, such as the management of market prices, policies concerning welfare or personnel transfer, and the

---

[90] XDS 15-1-2-3 Guanyu jianli chengshi renmin gongshe hou gaige shangye guanli tizhi de zongjie (caogao).
[91] XDS 1-1-295-12 Chunshu renmin gongshe diaocha baogao (caogao).
[92] XDS 15-1-2-3 Guanyu jianli chengshi renmin gongshe hou gaige shangye guanli tizhi de zongjie (caogao).

distribution of essential or scarce products. The new organization had to guarantee the completion of the national plan, national accumulation (taxes and profit), improvement in management, convenience and high-quality service, and the continuous reduction of the cost of circulation. The bottom line is that these enterprises had both to maintain the same levels of national capital accumulation (through taxes and direct transfer) and to provide revenue for the commune.[93] Operating under the principle of "integration of government administration and commune management, and of administration and enterprise" (*zhengshe heyi, xingzheng yu qiye heyi* 政社合一、行政与企业合一), the commune established a supply, marketing, and service bureau (*gongxiao fuwubu* 供销服务部) to function as the management unit for the commercial and the food service sectors.[94]

The reallocation of most commercial services under the commune was meant to make the circulation of goods fit the new collective life and to guarantee a more efficient and more plentiful supply of everyday products so as to fully satisfy all the people's needs. At Chunshu, collectivization led to a substantial increase of collective purchase – the share of collective procurement of staples went from 5 percent to 38 percent, foodstuff from 1.5 percent to 10 percent, coal from 0 to 20 percent – and it seemed then possible they could quickly move to the wholesale purchase and distribution of certain goods. The fragmented, specialized stores were suited to the "one-family one-household life of the past," while the new collective life should be centered instead around the new communal service. Accordingly, the Chunshu commune planned to transfer basic products like food and coal completely under collective purchase; some stores (liquor, miscellaneous) were to be established next to the canteens and would keep the same opening hours, while multi-function stores should be set up for people who could not yet attend the canteens.[95]

The reorganization of the commerce sector also aimed at eliminating other "vestiges of capitalism," meaning all of the small, privately owned stores and family enterprises that were still operating even after the declared achievement of socialism in 1956. Accordingly, Beijing communes proceeded to earnestly "reform" the many peddlers and tradespeople in their jurisdictions. In 1958, Erlonglu had 228 small stores and peddlers, for a total of 446 workers, some doing fairly well, some very

---

[93] XDS 15-1-2-3 Guanyu jianli chengshi renmin gongshe hou gaige shangye guanli tizhi de zongjie (caogao).
[94] XDS 1-1-295-12 Chunshu renmin gongshe diaocha baogao (caogao).
[95] XDS 15-1-2-3 Guanyu jianli chengshi renmin gongshe hou gaige shangye guanli tizhi de zongjie (caogao).

poorly. While some performed services that were useful and needed by the masses, the commune valued their physical labor more than the commercial services they presently offered.[96] Chunshu had 139 such enterprises with 309 workers, the majority of whom (65.1 percent) were over forty-six years old; many were sick, and few were young. Most of these businesses were labeled "unnecessary" and were therefore slated for elimination, but the issue was how to involve these people in "productive labor" and how to provide for their livelihood.[97] The decision was to send the younger ones to either farming or industrial work. The older ones who could still work would be employed in the commercial sector of the commune, while those who were either too old or too feeble and did not have other sources of income would be assigned to very light labor or provided support by the commune. Finally, the old and sick who had no labor power but had children who could support them would be entrusted to the care of their rural-based extended families.[98] In the end, 102 peddlers from Chunshu (33 percent of the total) were sent to the countryside either to do farm labor or to return to their families. Between June and November, about 300 women had been moved to work in the commercial sector of the commune, to replace those employees who had been transferred or retired.[99]

Finally, the reform of the commercial sector was logically and practically connected to the ongoing transformation of the local financial and banking organizations. Chunshu hosted a branch office of the People's Bank at Caishikou, which provided accounting services for remittances, deposits, and loans for all the agencies at all levels as well as for the local enterprises. There were also eight savings offices (*chuxusuo* 储蓄所), which took care of individuals' savings, but also collected taxes, rent, and bills, and provided cashier services for some work units. In order to adapt the financial sector to the new commune system, the CCP committee decided to create a new office, the Chunshu local branch of the Xuanwu district office of the China People's Bank (*Zhongguo Renmin Yinhang Beijingshi Xuanwuqu banshichu Chunshu fenlichu* 中国人民银行北京市宣武区办事处春树分理处), which opened on November 1, 1958.

[96] XDN 7-7-133 Xicheng quwei 1958 nian caimaobu guanyu renmin gongshe jianli hou shangye, fuwuye guanli tizhi he jigou shezhi de chubu yijian.
[97] XDS 1-1-295-6 Zhonggong Xuanwuqu Chunshu hutong dangweihui, "Guanyu jianli renmin gongshe shangye xiafang youguan jige wenti de yijian."
[98] XDS 1-1-295-8 Zhonggong Chunshu hutong dangweihui, Guanyu jianli renmin gongshe hou dui si gaizao jige wenti de yijian 中共椿树胡同党委会，关于建立人民公社后对私改造几个问题的意见 [Party committee of Chunshu hutong, "Opinions on several issues concerning the transformation of private ownerships after the establishment of the people's commune], October 3, 1958.
[99] XDS 1-1-295-12 Chunshu renmin gongshe diaocha baogao (caogao).

It took over responsibility for accounting, deposits, loans, and remittances for all the businesses, schools, and enterprises either recently
moved under the commune jurisdiction or created by the commune.
Five of the eight savings offices were also placed under its control. This
was supposed to be the first step in a more comprehensive plan to
transfer the management of all the financial institutions and the bank
credit system under the commune. With the collectivization of the commerce sectors, much of what used to be currency exchange had now
taken the form of account transfers, meaning non-currency exchanges
had increased. Simultaneously, hundreds of housewives had shifted from
consumers to producers, their income had increased, and the hope was
they could soon be placed under a half-rationing/half-salary system (*ban
gongjizhi ban gongzizhi* 半供给制半工资制), in which the commune
would provide basic goods and services so that their entire salary could
be saved (or, theoretically, be used as disposable income). In turn, this
created a new crucial task for the financial system: to gather currency
through savings and deposits and thus guarantee the amount needed
for the circulation of goods and for production. With that prospect in
mind, the Chunshu Commune Working Group on Banks (*Chunshu
renmin gongshe yinhang gongzuozu* 椿树人民公社银行工作组) proposed
to change the name of the bank to the Chunshu commune business
office of China's People Bank (*Zhongguo Renmin Yinhang Beijingshi
Xuanwuqu Chunshu renmin gongshe yingyesuo* 中国人民银行北京市宣武区
椿树人民公社营业所), which would function at the same time as the
bank's local branch and the commune's finance department. Among its
various tasks were to collect currency from the various units, help regulate
the currency circulation, and satisfy the currency needs of production and
circulation; to lead the saving banks to incentivize saving deposits; and to
manage the cash reserves of the various *danwei* and the non-currency
exchanges between units and between the commune and the outside.
It also had control over credit funds. The working group stressed how
one of the primary goals of such a reform was to reduce the number and
overall percentage of currency exchange within the commune, that is, to
reduce the relevance of money in the economy by increasing instead
the provision of goods under a planned system and decreasing those
of commodities purchased in the marketplace.[100] It was an essential

---

[100] XDS 1-1-295-14 Chunshu renmin gongshe yinhang gongzuozu, Guanyu zai Chunshu
renmin gongshe shixing gaijin jinrong tizhi de yijian 椿树人民公社银行工作组，关于在
椿树人民公社试行改进金融体制的意见 [Bank working group of the Chunshu people's
commune, "Opinions on improving the financial system on a trial basis at Chunshu
people's commune"], November 21, 1958. Alfred Chan reports that in mid-September,
"some central leaders drafted a document that specified that food should be free in the

element in transforming those social relationships that were still organized under capitalist forms, such as moneyed exchange.

Early assessments of the collectivization of the commerce sector were overwhelmingly positive. At Chunshu, they celebrated the close relationship that was immediately forged between female service employees and customers, all now commune members. People were reported praising the new arrangements, stressing how now problems were easier to solve because there was collaboration between shop clerks and the people. They cited the case of a store that had overstocked watermelons (200 *jin*, about 100 kilos): They were going to rot in the rain, so the residents' committee intervened and helped sell them, going door to door. At the opposite end of the circulation spectrum, the reformed commercial sector was apparently also more capable to quickly solve the problem of those products that were scarce and in high demand, such as coal. The new clerks were described as more caring, happy to do home deliveries to the old, the sick, and the pregnant. "The appearance of commerce in the commune" had changed, and it had not come at the expense of revenue: The Xicaochang market went from registering losses to a ¥400 profit, while the food store at Tiemen increased its sales by 20 percent after it went under commune management. The ability to distribute the labor force commune-wide increased what they called "communist big cooperation" (*gongchanzhuyi de daxiezuo* 共产主义的大协作) and raised work efficiency. Before 1958, commerce was organized vertically (*tiaotiao* 条条) and there was no coordination, so some stores were incredibly busy, while others were idle, yet there was no way of moving people around. After the reform, they switched to a "leadership by block" (*ankuai lingdao* 按块领导, meaning organized by region or area) so that, in a moment of high demand, the neighborhood CCP committee was able to relocate fourteen housewives and agencies to move over seventy people to work in food stores. The new system was also supposed to be more profitable and economical: Savings came from salaries, as the housewives were systematically and purposedly underpaid, but also through a general concerted effort of all people to reduce expenses. Finally, this reform was also aimed at producing changes in the lives and thoughts of the employees. Commune-side cross-trade alliances that were aimed at solving issues of personnel also helped turn each employee into a "multifaceted person"

---

communes, and the wages of the members should be deposited with the communes without interest. Their needs would be met by purchases by the communes, or members could use their deposits as exchange for goods. These cash-free transactions would then reduce the scope of currency circulation and eventually abolish capitalism." Chan, *Mao's Crusade*: 82.

(*duomianshou* 多面手) striding across the borders of professions and work units.[101]

## 1.5    A New Life and Its Enemies

"The spirit of the working people has risen, women have made another step toward liberation, the idle now earn their own living, some among the scum of society have started to reform through labor under the people's supervision, and a residential district devoted to pure consumption has turned into one devoted to productive labor."[102] As this report from Chunshu reminds us, Great Leap collectivization did not simply promise increased productivity, efficiency, and greater availability of goods. To those who for the first time participated in "productive labor," it promised nothing less than complete "liberation." That was perhaps the aspect that was more enthusiastically celebrated in early official documents and reports. However, it was specifically around the question of liberation that the process of urban collectivization both unearthed and generated the most obdurate contradictions and tensions. First, the establishment of urban communes made evident that there were different notions of what women's liberation would entail and how it could be achieved, and those notions were not necessarily complementary or compatible. In one view, liberation was centered on economic independence through participation in waged labor, and, even if that personal independence was supposed to have wider consequences for the structure of relationships of production, it was ultimately measured and viewed at the level of the individual. Yet the process of collectivization pointed at the potential for a much more radical and collective transformation, one that could invest the structure of gendered social and family relations as well as the very notion of waged labor. Second, as "liberation" also meant liberation from housework, the process of socializing domestic labor revealed theoretical limitations in how the various tasks of social reproduction were enumerated and understood but also generated new major tensions concerning how the value of those tasks was accounted for.

It was not just that communist leaders and activists were, like other men, blinded by ingrained, gendered prejudice. Rather, the CCP, like

[101]  XDS 15-1-2-3 Guanyu jianli chengshi renmin gongshe hou gaige shangye guanli tizhi de zongjie (caogao).
[102]  BMA 101-001-00782-6 Shunhu renqing, hehu chaoliu: Beijingshi Xuanwuqu Chunshu renmin gongshe diaocha 顺乎人情，合乎潮流：北京市宣武区椿树人民公社调查 [In keeping with people's emotion, in line with the trend: A survey of the Chunshu people's commune in Xuanwu District, Beijing].

the various socialist experiments that preceded it, had not produced an exhaustive analysis of the political economy of domestic labor and social reproduction, and this was one of the reasons why they were largely incapable of dealing with the contradictions that the praxis of collectivization highlighted and created, especially given how radical and intense that praxis was. This was also why, after the Great Leap Forward waned, it was relatively easy for many of its leaders to return to (or in some cases never to depart from) the status quo of calling women to be diligent and frugal housewives.[103] Documents and surveys in the initial phase of the campaign tend to be more effusive in praising the successes of urban collectivization, but signs of emerging tensions started to appear quite early.

As mentioned, in 1958 Mao himself had indicated how women's liberation would come first and foremost through an individual salary and increased income, and reports from Beijing followed suit. A survey of the Erlonglu commune noted how, thanks to their new revenue from labor, women had "changed their dependent economic position and established new egalitarian and harmonious family relationships, making a further step on the road to complete female liberation." One year after the founding of the commune, monthly family income had increased on average by ¥25, and women's salaries now constituted 38.9 percent of family revenues.[104] At Shijingshan, reports singled out as exemplary the case of one family, with three children: The husband's salary was ¥40, and now the wife, who was a particularly good worker and often received bonuses, made an additional ¥40. They could finally afford new clothes and bedding, and even bought a radio and an alarm clock.[105]

Yet even for those local officers who reported on street-level collectivization, individual financial improvement was not the most important measure of success. It was at the level of raising awareness and social relationships that the transformation was both more evident and more enthusiastically celebrated. The same report from Shijingshan noted that, after the 1953 movement to implement the marriage law, while most husbands had learned the correct attitude toward their wives, the wives still had no culture, no real experience, and no life outside the home, leaving the couple with nothing to talk about. They had successfully achieved ideological change, but the structural problems at the economic level prevented social and family practices from changing.

[103] Wang, *Finding Women in the State*.
[104] BMA 101-001-00782-7 Yong zuikuai de bufa jianshe shehuizhuyi xin xhengshi: Beijing shi Erlonglu renmin gongshe diaocha.
[105] BMA 001-006-01493-7 Shijingshan Zhongsu youhao renmin gongshe zuzhi zhigong jiashu canjia shengchan laodong qude jingyan.

The commune allowed for that further step. Mrs. Cui, manager of a communal canteen at Shijingshan, did not have a bad life: Her husband made over ¥110 monthly, was a CCP member, and always treated her respectfully, entrusting all the money to her to manage. But, she remarked, "I used to see all those people 'going to work,' and I felt sad, I lacked a sense of independence; now I work too, I make some money, and now when I go home I sometimes buy something for my children, I tell them 'it's mama who bought it,' and I feel extremely happy."[106] At Erlonglu, "Women dare to do and dare to think, they leave household chores to become workers, beaming with joy they earn their own living." Participation in labor freed urban residents from spending all day obsessing only about the "small world" of their family's interest, and made them realize the connection between their life and the cause of socialist construction; it elicited their interest in politics, shaped their collective attitude, and thus radically transformed the spiritual outlook of the neighborhood.[107] Women who used to work as housewives reportedly praised being freed from the stress of worrying about daily necessities and getting lost in the minutiae of childcare and household chores; collectivization of services allowed them a chance to become "skillful ladies" (*qiao guniang* 巧姑娘), modern-day Mu Guiying, who could do whatever they set their mind to.[108]

The transformation was particularly impressive at the Chunshu commune, which covered an area with no major factory, no government agency, and no school. It was a residential neighborhood, with a lot of old *huiguan* (regional guild halls), and it was home to several famous (and rich) actors, performers, and politicians. Not the ideal place to establish one of the first communes in Beijing, yet the reported effects in terms of social mores were surprising: Gossip and fights decreased drastically, and everybody developed a spirit of communal work.[109] After joining production, women, in particular, stopped bad-mouthing this or that family, and instead focused their attention on issues of production and national events.[110] As a consequence, civil litigations declined: Between January and September 1958, there had been 178 civil cases, among which were

---

[106] BMA 001-006-01493-7 Shijingshan Zhongsu youhao renmin gongshe zuzhi zhigong jiashu canjia shengchan laodong qude jingyan.

[107] BMA 101-001-00782-7 Yong zuikuai de bufa jianshe shehuizhuyi xin xhengshi: Beijing shi Erlonglu renmin gongshe diaocha.

[108] XDS 15-1-2-11 Xuanwuqu Chunshu renmin gongshe jianli qianhou de qingkuang. Mu Guiying was a legendary heroine from the Song Dynasty.

[109] BMA 101-001-00782-6 Shunhu renqing, hehu chaoliu: Beijingshi Xuanwuqu Chunshu renmin gongshe diaocha.

[110] XDS 15-1-2-11 Xuanwuqu Chunshu renmin gongshe jianli qianhou de qingkuang.

12 alimony cases, 52 divorces, and 64 residential disputes. In the twenty days after the commune was created, there were only two cases altogether. As for criminal cases, there had been 490 pre-commune, and only nine in the twenty days since (this was probably connected to the decline in fights and quarrels).[111]

There was also a certain amount of generalized resistance to collectivization, grounded in mundane concerns. Not everybody was enthusiastic about the commune, not even after the fairly prolonged work of propaganda and political education. At Chunshu, about 20 percent of the residents had doubts, and among them, the most stubborn were capitalists, landlords, and those people belonging to high-end artistic and cultural circles. Landlords were afraid that the commune would take away their apartments, turning them into factories, canteens, or childcare centers; some tried to sell them in advance, others spread rumors, and others simply refused to give them up. There were reports of capitalists selling their furniture, afraid it might be collectivized. One woman, the day she heard about the commune, immediately sold two writing desks, one cupboard, and one dresser.[112] A former Guomindang district committee member similarly sold his metal bed, a table, and chairs and was then spending all his time hidden behind his "American door curtains," eating and drinking; he even had three or four big hams in the pantry.[113] One resident committee found out that seven families were selling their sewing machines, while some "bad elements" withdrew their savings from the banks before their due date. Between August 31 and September 27, 195 accounts were closed, for a total ¥66,200. One person withdrew ¥5,000, saying it was for a funeral.[114] According to a report published in the *Neibucankao* [Internal reference], a daily digest of news reserved for the political elite, the rich people's fear also fueled the investment in luxury goods: Prices of watches skyrocketed and yet the famed Wangfujing watch store could not keep up with the demand. Bicycles, radios, and jewelry were also selling like hotcakes: Customers allegedly just came in and bought them, without even asking about the price. One jeweler's revenue was reported to have doubled each month.[115] The richer residents at Chunshu were afraid that, if forced

---

[111] XDS, 1-1-295-12 Chunshu renmin gongshe diaocha baogao (caogao).
[112] XDS, 15-1-2-11 Xuanwuqu Chunshu renmin gongshe jianli qianhou de qingkuang.
[113] XDS 1-1-295-12 Chunshu renmin gongshe diaocha baogao (caogao).
[114] XDS, 15-1-2-11 Xuanwuqu Chunshu renmin gongshe jianli qianhou de qingkuang. Fear of property confiscation and the abolition of money led to bank runs and panic buying in Shanghai as well. See Chan, *Mao's Crusade*: 88.
[115] "Beijing zibenjia dui chengshi jianli renmin gongshe dichu qingxu hen da" 北京资本家对城市建立人民公社抵触情绪很大 [Beijing capitalists are very resistant to the

to join the commune, their income would decrease; a doctor who made about ¥400 a month worried about his salary under the new system. Accordingly, many did not want to participate in either industrial or service labor. A Mrs. Li was quoted scoffing at that idea: "My husband makes over ¥100 and that's plenty for me to spend, why the hell would I do work for the commune, *you* go labor!"[116]

It was the communal services that seemingly elicited the most resistance and scorn from the wealthier residents. Family members ("dependents") of artists and intellectuals (*wenyijia jiashu* 文艺家家属) refused to eat at the communal canteens. The daughter-in-law of famed Beijing opera star Jiang Miaoxiang[117] complained that they never served enough food at the canteen, and besides, they usually came back from the theater past midnight, so what use could they have for the canteen? In order to alleviate political pressure, Wang Yalan, wife of star *xiangsheng* performer Hou Baolin,[118] together with another rich housewife, decided to open a high-end canteen for the wealthy at Haibei Temple, calling it the "satisfy cravings canteen" (*jiechan shitang* 解馋食堂).[119]

The most common reactions among "bad elements" were refusing to work, slacking off, and, of course, spreading rumors. Food figured prominently, and in this case the rumors were probably much less unfounded. A former "puppet army" soldier who steadily refused to join the commune mocked the quality of their food: "You say the commune is a bridge, and communism is paradise. I see that the commune is just *wowotou* (窝窝头 steamed corn bread)."[120] There were also rumors that children being gathered in kindergarten would be sent to the Soviet Union or forcefully separated from their parents, and that the commune

---

establishment of people's communes in the city], *Neibucankao* (October 20, 1958): 23–27. On the *NBCK*, see Michael Schoenhals, "Elite Information in China," *Problems of Communism* 34 (September–October 1985): 65–71.

[116] XDS 1-1-295-12 Chunshu renmin gongshe diaocha baogao (caogao).

[117] Jiang Miaoxiang 姜妙香 (1890–1972) was a Beijing opera actor who worked with Mei Lanfang for half a century. Originally trained as a *qingyi* (female role), he later switched to *xiaosheng* (young male role) and excelled in portraying refined, scholarly characters.

[118] Hou Baolin 侯宝林 (1917–1993) was one of the most popular *xiangsheng* performers of his generation. *Xiangsheng*, crosstalk or comic dialogue, is a traditional form of performance, usually a dialogue between two actors.

[119] XDS 1-1-295-12 Chunshu renmin gongshe diaocha baogao (caogao) and XDS, 15-1-2-11 Xuanwuqu Chunshu renmin gongshe jianli qianhou de qingkuang.

[120] "Beijing gequdi fufanhuaiyoufenzi dui renmin gongshe sanbu henduo yaoyan" 北京各区地富反坏右分子对人民公社散步很多谣言 [Many rumors are spread about the people's commune by the rich, the counterrevolutionaries, the bad elements, and the rightists in various districts of Beijing] (October 10, 1958), *NBCK*: 11–13; XDS 1-1-295-12 Chunshu renmin gongshe diaocha baogao (caogao). "Puppet army" refers to the military forces of the collaborationist Chinese government during the Japanese invasion of China.

would institute communal wives and widows would be forced to live with ruffians. At Xicheng, a rumor spread about Muslims and Han being forced to eat the same food, breaking religious codes.[121] Some people renamed the commune (*renmin gongshe*) the *renmin gongmu* (人民公墓), the people's common grave.[122]

More interestingly, sources also registered the opposition of some poorer residents, who were afraid of the three transformations and thought they wouldn't be able to achieve them (*huabuqi* 化不起). Some of them had elders at home who could look after children and cook food, and realized that going to the canteen was not economically profitable, while others had night shifts and could not even access that opportunity.[123] Young employees of the commercial sector were reportedly – and perhaps justifiably – afraid of being replaced by women and sent to the countryside.[124] The committee chair of the trade council of barbers and bathhouse employees lamented that this transformation was too fast, and if not even the USSR could have moved this quickly, how could China do it?[125]

The frenetic speed with which Great Leap collectivization was pushed forward was indeed one of the main reasons for the disastrous failure of the campaign in the countryside, where the distribution of resources and coordination of production were severely disrupted, with tragic results. In the much more limited experience of the cities, haste was one of the reasons for inefficiencies and problems, but it was not the main factor behind the eventual crisis of collectivization. In the urban context, we can perhaps see more clearly (without the pall of the massive human toll that the Great Leap Forward induced in the countryside) how the process of urban collectivization ended up highlighting deeper fissures and contradictions within the socialist political economy. Glimpses of these tensions manifested early in the first months of the urban communal experiments.

By the end of 1958, these problems became quite evident, and that led to the first campaign aimed at strengthening and reorganizing the urban communes in 1959. The establishment of further communes was also halted in the five largest cities in China, including of course the capital (the others were Tianjin, Shanghai, Guangzhou, and Wuhan). This coincided with and was in part motivated by a much larger retrenchment of Great Leap policies. By October 1958, Mao was already receiving feedback on the worsening situation in the countryside; a report from

---

[121] "Beijing gequdi fufanhuaiyoufenzi dui renmin gongshe sanbu henduo yaoyan."
[122] XDS, 15-1-2-11 Xuanwuqu Chunshu renmin gongshe jianli qianhou de qingkuang.
[123] XDS, 15-1-2-11 Xuanwuqu Chunshu renmin gongshe jianli qianhou de qingkuang.
[124] XDS 1-1-295-12 Chunshu renmin gongshe diaocha baogao (caogao).
[125] "Beijing zibenjia dui chengshi jianli renmin gongshe dichu qingxu hen da."

Yunnan that reached him in November "described serious deaths by oedema, diarrhea, and measles in the spring/summer of 1958 as a result of cadre coercion," while twenty-one counties in Hebei had been affected by "an unprecedented wave of typhoid, dysentery, and gastro-enteritis, caused by the unhygienic canteens, lack of rest, hot food, and heat."[126] Mao then became the first CCP leader to address openly the significant problems produced by Great Leap Forward policies.[127] According to Teiwes and Sun, "From the time of the first Zhengzhou conference in early November to the eve of the July–August 1959 Lushan conference the Chairman repeatedly addressed the excesses of the Leap and called for greater realism."[128] The effect of this retrenchment and the implementation of commune reorganization in Beijing will be the subject of Chapter 3. First, I will introduce the fundamental theoretical debate in the sphere of political economy that accompanied, justified, and interacted with the experience of collectivization during the Great Leap Forward.

---

[126] Chan, *Mao's Crusade*: 88.     [127] Yang, *Calamity and Reform in China*: 44.
[128] Teiwes and Sun, *China's Road to Disaster*: 238.

# 2 Politics for a Transitional Age
## The Debate on the Socialist Economy

## 2.1    Are We There Yet?

The urban and rural collectivization campaign of the Great Leap coincided with a nation-wide debate on the law of value, bourgeois right, and the socialist economy in general. This was a wide-ranging discussion that involved economists, social scientists, and party theorists (including Mao himself), and was reflected in a massive production of essays and articles, in both scholarly journals and newspapers. It tackled crucial issues in Marxist political economy and the very structure of socialist society, issues that had been largely left open or had been very unsatisfactorily dealt with in the Soviet Union. The debate exploded in full force in 1958, was initially foreclosed in November of that same year, and formally (if only temporarily) terminated in the spring of 1959, with a symposium on commodity production and the law of value under socialism, held in Shanghai in April.[1] This timeline largely mirrors the political ebbs and flows of Great Leap policies. The initial push for mass collectivization and the creation of communes in the summer of 1958 was followed by an ideological retrenchment and a policy shift at the end of the year, which took the form of a campaign for "commune rectification" and an official redefinition of the movement goals.[2] Mao seemed to support much more moderate positions in the spring of 1959, and while the Great Leap was relaunched after the Lushan conference in the summer of 1959, the post-Lushan period was a "time of confusion," with "leaders pursuing contradictory policies."[3] That confusion is also revealed in the praxis of urban collectivization: Formation of urban communes had been halted in the

---

[1] Zhongguo kexueyuan jingji yanjiusuo bian 中国科学院经济研究所编, *Guanyu shehuizhuyi zhiduxia shangpin shengchan he jiazhi guilüwenti. 1959 nian 4 yue taolunhui lunwen* 关于社会主义制度下商品生产和价值规律问题。1959 年4月讨论会论文、资料汇编 [A compilation of papers and materials from the April 1959 conference on commodity production and the law of value under the socialist system] (科学出版社, 1959).

[2] MacFarquhar, *The Origins of the Cultural Revolution*: 136; "Guanyu renmin gongshe ruogan wenti de jueyi."

[3] MacFarquhar, *The Origins of the Cultural Revolution*, 318.

five major metropolitan centers in 1958, but that was reversed in 1960, at the same time when, in the midst of the disaster of the famine, the rural side of the Great Leap was being de facto abandoned. It is not clear why the campaign was relaunched in earnest in 1960, given the policy shift and the massive human toll in the countryside. I would argue that collective production, centered on objects of everyday use, and especially collective services responded to the actual needs of a sizable part of the urban population. And the multiple promises and goals of the project of urban collectivization – social welfare, direct distribution of products, but also reformed social relations and women's liberation – were shared by many city residents, who continued to join and toil in commune and neighborhood organizations. Even during the mandated pause in commune formation throughout 1959, local activists in Beijing and other major cities had eagerly continued to establish new neighborhood enterprises and organizations such as childcare centers and canteens. Finally, and it's a grim reminder, cities found it possible to continue to experiment with collectivization because they were sheltered from the worst of the famine, whose toll fell solely and squarely on the countryside. The influx of rural migrants into urban areas that had started in 1958 was reversed in the following years, unloading even more starving people on already starving villages.[4]

Juxtaposing the praxis of urban collectivization with the coeval theoretical debate will help make clear that, while the communes were envisioned as a way to solve lingering problems in the socialist revolutionary process, the experience of urban collectivization brought to the fore, in very practical terms, new ideological contradictions and political issues within socialist society. It was a central tenet of Maoism that Marxist theory and political experimentation were intimately intertwined, codependent, and always in a dialectical and mutually generative relation. A correct and complete perspective on the political economy of socialist society – and here "political economy" indicates a field separate and different from the dominant understanding of "the economic" and economics – was deemed indispensable to comprehend the changing and transitional forms of production and circulation, not simply in their technical, economic function, but as productive of specific social relations. The debate followed an understanding of Marxism as a *critique of political economy*, "not an economic theory intended to produce quantifiable concepts which can be operationalized in empirical economic

---

[4] Over ten million workers workers recruited for factory work from rural areas in 1958 were ordered back to the countryside to reduce urban demand for food. Yang, *Calamity and Reform in China*: 46.

analysis but a qualitative theory of social forms aimed at uncovering and criticizing the social relations" underlying a specific mode of production.[5] In an experiment such as the Great Leap Forward, which aimed at not only a massive increase in production, but also a radical transformation of social relations, the political economy could not but be a crucial field of debate and intervention. This chapter explores some of the main issues at play in that debate and points at how they connected to the experience of urban collectivization, as only by understanding the overall theoretical stakes of that experience we can fully evaluate the political significance of that experiment.

The fundamental assumption behind the whole debate – and the Great Leap in general – was that socialism was a *transitional* stage. The ultimate goal of the revolutionary state was to achieve the ascension into communism, an era where everybody would contribute according to their ability and receive according to their needs. Postulating a particular social formation as transitional raises a series of questions, concerning primarily how to identify the best path to realize that transition, which social and economic indicators can best provide evidence that the transition is indeed moving along, and how long that transition is supposed to take. If the communes were indeed a bridge to heaven, how long was that bridge supposed to be, and how could we tell whether we were getting closer or not?[6] If workers, peasants, and cadres were requested to toil to the limits of their human abilities (as they were through the 1950s) for the sake of building socialism and eventually reaching communism, the stage at which their toil was supposed to finally end, it was quite obvious for them to ask, "Are we there yet?"

The complete elimination of private ownership of the means of production in 1956 had been declared to represent the achievement of socialism; this in turn made questions related to transition at the same time more urgent and more complicated, because how one answered them determined fundamental political choices by the socialist state. Some participants in the debate assumed that, once the conditions of newly achieved socialism were solidly put in place, the task of the state in a transitional temporality was mainly to assure that the forces of production could continue to develop, while preventing any exogenous adverse intervention. Others, including Mao, believed instead that, even under these new favorable conditions, there were both factors internal to

---

[5] Mau, *Mute Compulsion*: 64.
[6] "Communism is heaven, the people's communes are the bridge (to heaven)" (共产主义是天堂，人民公社是桥梁). According to MacFarquhar, the ditty was attributed to Kang Sheng. MacFarquhar, *The Origins of the Cultural Revolution*: 103.

socialist society that could hamper the transition and political-economic levers that could be pulled to hasten it, and they therefore configured a much different role for the state. Mao specifically attacked the assumption of the primacy of the development of productive forces, arguing instead that it was necessary to overthrow the existing superstructure, to disrupt old production relations, and to create new ones in order to clear the way for "the development of new social productive forces."[7] It is not by chance that the debate focused, first, on how to evaluate the persistence under socialism of some structural elements usually associated with capitalism – the law of value, remuneration according to labor, the commodity form, and money itself, among others – and, second, on the state itself as "one of the primary arenas of transitionary struggle."[8]

Analyzing the Great Leap debate on the socialist economy might also provide a different perspective on and clarify the political stakes of the recent discussion on "state capitalism," meaning the historical proposition that all forms of "actually existing socialism" were in the end just slight variations on capitalism, with the state playing the role of the capitalists. This argument was first put forward by historians of the Soviet Union but more recently has been expanded to include the PRC, whose seemingly abrupt transition to market economy in the Deng era appears less problematic if China is presumed to have been always and already capitalist, even under Mao. The case for China's "unending capitalism" has been made more prominently by historian Karl Gerth, who has tried to demonstrate how the Maoist state not only failed to curb capitalism but ended up actively promoting it. Gerth's argument, however, rests on a very problematic identification of "capitalism" with "consumption," "consumerism," and even "desire." But consumption (very much like markets or money) existed way before the emergence of the capitalist economy, and phenomena of conspicuous consumption and even consumerist crazes were recorded in precapitalist societies. And that makes Gerth's point both historically and theoretically flimsy.[9] Marx himself started his analysis of capital by looking at the commodity form, not as an object of consumption but as the embodiment of labor, as "congealed labor time," that is, as the embodiment of those social relationships that were mediated by process of (capitalist) production.[10]

---

[7] Mao Tsetung [Zedong], *A Critique of the Soviet Economics*, translated by Moss Roberts, annotated by Richard Levy, with an introduction by James Peck (New York: Monthly Review Press, 1977): 51.
[8] Karl, *The Magic of Concepts*: 132.    [9] Gerth, *Unending Capitalism*.
[10] Marx, *Capital, Volume 1*.

More theoretically sound and coherent arguments for Maoist China as "state capitalism" have indeed been grounded on an expanded version of Marx's analysis of capitalist production, such as that provided by theorist Moishe Postone, who viewed "modern industrial society itself as capitalist" and conceptualized socialism "in terms of the possible abolition of the proletariat and of the organization of production based on proletarian labor."[11] In Postone's perspective, given that the Maoist state never succeeded (or perhaps never even attempted) to eliminate proletarian labor and the exploitation always presumed to exist in industrial production itself, then it never abandoned capitalism.[12] This is an intellectually and theoretically cogent – if, in my opinion, politically hopeless – argument, but, as I believe the analysis of the 1958 debate in the following pages will show, it is also historically unhelpful because it glosses over the differences in political positions at the time or the political stakes of those involved, be they Mao or a local commune activist. It ends up eliding them as futile or meaningless.

In the "state capitalist" model, the state functions in lieu of the capitalists; it preserves the seemingly unavoidable and insuppressible functions of capital, even under declared socialism; it owns the means of production, organizes labor, secures accumulation, and guarantees the expansion of production. In this model, the state then functions as a pure technocratic apparatus, securing the transhistorical operations of capital as if they were completely separated from the sphere of politics. Yet that was not at all how revolutionaries – Maoist revolutionaries in this case – saw the state. Rather, the state was a historically located site of struggle; it was, especially in the transitory temporality of socialism, an object and one of the major stakes of political struggle, because the state could intervene and affect that temporality. And of course, how and how much the state should intervene were also major issues of debate and confrontation.

I will give here just one example of how the discourse of state capitalism tends to obscure the complexities within the socialist state itself. In a recently published essay, Kim Yong-uk makes the case that "China under Mao was capitalist" by showing how between 1949 and 1962,

---

[11] Moishe Postone, "Rethinking Marx in a Postmarxist World," in Charles Camic, ed., *Reclaiming the Sociological Classics* (Cambridge, MA: Blackwell, 1998): 71. For a critique of Postone's argument see Mau, *Mute Compulsion*, chapter 8.

[12] See the essays by Jake Werner and Joyce C. H. Liu in Joyce C. H. Liu and Viren Murthy, eds., *East-Asian Marxisms and Their Trajectories* (London: Routledge, 2017). For a critique of the state capitalism framework, see Covell F. Meyskens, "Rethinking the Political Economy of Development in Mao's China," *positions: asia critique* 29:4 (November 2021): 809–834.

the CCP, in order to maximize accumulation, willfully maintained and actually increased labor flexibility, creating a class of "free wage laborers" and what was de facto a labor market.[13] Kim rightly points out the massive disparity of treatment not only between urban and rural labor, but also between long-term and temporary workers; he highlights instances in which the central government pursued labor flexibility, and singles out the Great Leap, when large numbers of rural workers moved into cities, as the moment when that flexibility was "closest to the ideal type of 'market capitalism.'"[14] While the historical data Kim musters is well sourced, the overall argument that the CCP pursed either willingly or unwittingly a process of "proletarianization" of its working class is quite problematic.[15] How do we know that there were significant differences in how workers were paid and treated, or that "surplus labor" was especially exploited, or that unauthorized cross-sector and cross-enterprise movement continued despite prohibitions? We gather all that from CCP official sources, and specifically sources denouncing such practices or singling out those issues as needing urgent attention. Aminda Smith has pointedly argued how historians selectively picked exemplary stories critical of the PRC state directly from the records produced by that state, and how, in most cases, those examples are not analyzed nearly as critically as other evidence from the same state discourse.[16] Thus, when CCP sources report on the persistence or reemergence of features of capitalism within socialist society, the tendency is to take them uncritically as evidence of the ultimate failure of the socialist project, which is even more problematic given that these sources were produced by people who were worried about that possibility and were actively trying to prevent it by pushing for even more radical social transformations. What CCP sources usually convey is a conversation, an often contradictory and cacophonic debate within different parts of the state itself – or between the state and other elements of the social. And that debate is usually about what the state could do, how it could intervene to fix specific problems, why it had not solved them already, why it had not prevented them from resurfacing. Unlike the state of "state capitalism," flattened in its acceptance of always already existing capitalism, the socialist state was always an unstable and contingent site of political contention.

---

[13] Kim Yong-uk, "Workers in Mao's China: Labour and Capital under Chinese State Capitalism, 1949–62," in Owen Miller, ed., *State Capitalism and Development in East Asia since 1945* (Leiden: Brill, 2023): 84.
[14] Kim, "Workers in Mao's China": 123.    [15] Kim, "Workers in Mao's China": 89.
[16] Aminda Smith, "Long Live the Mass Line! Errant Cadres and Post-Disillusionment PRC History," *positions: asia critique* 29:4 (November 2021): 783–807.

We should not of course believe triumphalist assertions in the PRC state propaganda (or of any state propaganda). But the very fact that so many CCP intellectuals and leaders were so worried about the possibility of the persistence of capitalism and of its restoration should make us think more carefully and critically about how we evaluate claims about that transitory temporality. Any blank statement that flattens it into the inevitability of capitalism (state or otherwise) elides not only that intense discussion but also the practice of millions who strove toward a revolutionary alternative.

## 2.2 The First Five-Year Plan and Its Discontent

The year 1956 was defined by concerns over the second Five-Year Plan. While "planners, policy makers, and academic economists ... aimed at avoiding a repetition of the sectoral disproportions, material bottlenecks and a general lack of co-ordination in plan execution that had characterized the First FYP,"[17] others were dissatisfied with the results of Soviet-style industrialization at a more profound and more disturbing level. The massive effort of the FFYP had generated impressive results, especially in terms of industrial production (which grew at an annual rate of over 15 percent), but there had been clearly adverse consequences, especially in terms of rising social and economic inequalities, something that seemed (and was) at odds with the progress into socialism and the eventual passage into communism.

Workers were subject to strict labor discipline, not much different from that determining life in the Taylorist factory,[18] and they were organized according to a rigid hierarchy of wages; SOE employees received benefits that were not granted to other urban workers, let alone the large mass of rural dwellers; and industrialization had been financed largely through extraction of surplus from the countryside, making the rural/urban divide even starker. These were not simply "empirical" problems, temporary distortions in the economic realm that could be fixed with some tinkering. Rather, there emerged among CCP leaders the need to search "for an alternative to the Soviet economic model which, by late 1955, was recognized as less than totally suited to Chinese conditions," and definitely not conducive to a transition into

---

[17] Cyril Chihren Lin, "The Reinstatement of Economics in China Today," *China Quarterly* 1 (1981): 7.

[18] Industrial management in the early PRC was modeled on the USSR's, which had been heavily influence by Taylorism. See Franz Schurmann, *Ideology and Organization in Communist China*, 2nd ed. (Berkeley: University of California Press, 1968).

communism.[19] Mao himself pointed this out in his famous speech "On the Ten Major Relationships," which constituted his first major political intervention on the subject, opening the debate that would fully explode in 1958. He singled out, among other phenomena, the lopsided emphasis on heavy industry versus agriculture and light industry and the Soviet Union's excessive "squeezing" of peasants.[20] More importantly, in that text, Mao started to propose how relations of production and social relationships could be rearticulated in ways different from the Soviet Union.[21] Mao also suggested that any such rearticulation could only be achieved through the basic policy of mobilizing all the positive factors, and he identified the workers and peasants as the "basic force." Such a radical transformation could only come via the politics of mass mobilization.[22]

The topic of debate, then, was not simply, as Cyril Lin has remarked, "[p]roblems concerning basic economic laws during the transition period."[23] As Mao had already outlined in the "Ten Major Relationships" and would further stress in his later "Contradictions" speech, "economic" laws, and specifically the law of value and commodity exchange, were operating as part of a system of relations in which politics, economics, and culture were intimately fused, "both as a matter of principle and as a matter of social practice."[24] Economic laws and economic categories were not the organizing principles of a sphere ontologically (or even practically) separated from the rest of society – the economic – rather, they embodied and expressed, albeit in a hidden manner, social relations.[25] However, how those laws and social relations functioned and how they related to each other under socialism remained a major problem. This was a subject on which, unfortunately, Marx himself had written very little, and theorists on different sides of the debate quibbled endlessly over the interpretations of a few lines from the *Critique of the Gotha Program* and Engels's *Anti-Dühring*. In the *Critique*, Marx had famously argued that socialist society, as it emerges from capitalism, is "in every respect, economically, morally, and intellectually, still stamped with the birthmarks of the old society." Hence, the commodity form and exchange for equal labor must continue to exist in

[19] Teiwes and Sun, *China's Road to Disaster*: 119.
[20] Mao, "On the Ten Major Relationships."
[21] Rebecca E. Karl, "Culture, Revolution, and the Times of History: Mao and 20th-Century China," *China Quarterly*, no. 187 (September 2006): 697–698.
[22] Mao, "On the Ten Major Relationships."
[23] Lin, "The Reinstatement of Economics in China Today": 8.
[24] Karl, "Culture, Revolution, and the Times of History": 698.
[25] Mau, *Mute Compulsion*: 17.

the earlier stage of socialism, but only as leftovers, remnants, or vestiges of capitalist society.[26] Yet, in China, after the massive transformation produced by the FFYP, it was becoming increasingly difficult to consider social relationships that had been shaped and, in some instances, directly created by that specific developmental path as "leftovers." French Marxist theorist Charles Bettelheim, in his reflections on the transitional economy, which was partly inspired by the Great Leap Forward, put it clearly:

> What we will for the moment call "survivals" (an expression which makes one think of some legacy from a past which history has not had the time to wipe out) represent, in fact, the products of the structures in which these alleged "impurities" are not "survivals," because they are not alien to the real structures in which they exist. On the contrary, they are the result of the totality of the relations which make up these structures, that is to say, of the particular level of development of the productive forces, of the unevennesses of development which characterize these forces, and of the relations of production linked with these unevennesses of development. If we think of these "impurities" as being "survivals" this is because we have not grasped thoroughly enough the interconnexions of the structures that produce them.[27]

In the late 1950s debate over the socialist economy in the PRC, both the "left" and the "right" moved quickly beyond the idea of "capitalist leftovers," but for radically different reasons and with different political objectives. On the "right," famed economists such as Sun Yefang and Xue Muqiao, deploying a nuanced and painstaking analysis of Marxist texts, argued that not only capitalist forms such as the commodity and the law of value continued to exist and operate under socialism, but that, far from being just "leftovers," these forms had been divested of all their negative influences and therefore could and should play a crucial organizing function in socialist economic planning and in fostering the path toward communism. In 1956, Xue Muqiao argued in the *People's Daily* that, with the expansion of the planned economy, the role of the law of value would progressively diminish. But in the same year, Sun Yefang postulated instead that the law would continue to operate not only under socialism but also under communism, and that even then it should constitute the very foundation of planning.[28]

---

[26] Karl Marx, *Critique of the Gotha Program* (1875), www.marxists.org/archive/marx/works/1875/gotha/.

[27] Charles Bettelheim, *The Transition to Socialist Economy*, translated from the French by Brian Pearce (Sussex: Harvester Press, 1975): 16.

[28] Zhang, ed., *Historical Perspectives on Chinese Economics*: 14; Sun Yefang 孙冶方, "Ba jihua he tongji fangzai jiazhi guilü de jichushang" 把计划和统计放在价值规律的基础上 [Place planning and statistical work on the basis of the law of value], *Jingji Yanjiu* 经济研究 [Economic research], no. 6 (1956): 30–38.

Those on the "left" (and I am simplifying here the complex positions
within the debate) focused instead on the fact that these forms clearly
were not remnants of the past but were being continuously reproduced
by socialist development itself. They were fostering the expansion of the
socialist economy but were always dangerously pushing it toward capitalism, and therefore radical and progressive actions were needed to
reduce their role. I want to highlight here the significance of the fact that
"economists" did not and perhaps could not recognize the persistence of
capitalist forms as an issue – they could only turn them, with an impressive
sleight of hand, into useful economic tools – because those forms were part
and parcel of their understanding of "the economic" as a set of ahistorical
concepts. But in Marxism, none of these categories ever exists as purely or
"only" economic; rather, Marxist analysis forces us to reflect on how these
categories and concepts are produced under specific historical conditions
and organizations of social relations, how they are embedded in localized
everyday practices, and how in turn they affect those practices and those
relations. To paraphrase Rebecca Karl, taking these categories simply as
"economic" means eliding the complex dialectics between history, concepts, and the political possibilities of the present and future.[29] Ultimately,
the always potentially dangerous character of the commodity form, wages,
and so on could not be fully comprehended within the discipline of
economics – as mentioned, Marx's entire oeuvre was a *critique* of the
political economy – and these elements appeared as fundamentally problematic only if viewed from an explicitly political standpoint. And as such,
they required a political intervention.

The debate on the socialist economy and the law of value had profound implications that were not simply limited to the field of "Marxist
theory," and not just for the obvious reason that "theoretical views
published in the process of the discussion on the issue of the relationship
between planning and market exerted important influence on China's
practice in socialist construction."[30] One of Marx's crucial discoveries is
that what appears, under capitalism, in the form of a relation between
things (the circulation and exchange of commodities) is actually a relation between people. The Soviet economist I. I. Rubin, in his analysis of
Marx's theory of value, pushed this argument further, by arguing that
"[t]he circulation of things – to the extent that they acquire the specific
social properties of value and money – does not only express production

[29] Karl, *The Magic of Concepts*: 12.
[30] Zhang, ed., *Historical Perspectives on Chinese Economics*: 12.

relations among men, but *it creates* them."[31] Things, material objects have determinate properties that make them useful as consumer goods or means of production (they have a use value), and through that they perform a *technical function* in production, but they also always perform "the *social function* of connecting people."[32] Things acquire specific properties within the commodity economy (value, price, etc.) not because of some intrinsic qualities, but by being connected to social relationships of production. Therefore, Rubin concluded, "social production relations are not only 'symbolized' by things, but are realized through things."[33] And this leads to the central role of the political economy under socialism. If, as Rubin points out, political economy "is not a science of the relations of *things to things*, as was thought by vulgar economists, nor of the relations of *people to things*, as was asserted by the theory of marginal utility, but it was instead a science of the relations of *people to people* in the process of production,"[34] then the transformation of society, the radical re-creation of social relations cannot but require revolutionaries to "learn some political economy," as Mao famously would urge during the Cultural Revolution. Far from being abstract or academic, the heated discussions on the law of value and the commodity form were tackling issues that affected the destiny of the revolutionary transformation itself and the everyday practices of the people living in that temporality.

## 2.3    Stalin and the Question of Ownership

The background of this debate was the publication of the Chinese translation of a new Soviet textbook on socialist political economy and of Stalin's treatises that accompanied it, conferring upon it a supreme imprimatur.[35] In his analysis, Stalin, following the principle that "the relations of production *must necessarily conform* with the character of the productive forces," argued that, even in the relatively advanced Soviet Union, while capitalism had been eliminated, commodity production and exchange not only continued to exist but should actively be preserved. This was because two different forms of ownership still persisted in the USSR: state ownership, which included the modern industrial

---

[31] I. I. Rubin, *Essays on Marx's Theory of Value* (Montreal: Black Rose Books, 1973): 10–11. Emphasis mine.
[32] Rubin, *Essays on Marx's Theory of Value*: 21–22. Emphasis in the original.
[33] Rubin, *Essays on Marx's Theory of Value*: 11.
[34] Rubin, *Essays on Marx's Theory of Value*: 3.
[35] J. V. Stalin, *Economic Problems of Socialism in the U.S.S.R.* (Peking: Foreign Language Press, 1972).

sector, of whose products the Soviet state could fully dispose; and collective ownership, which comprised the entire rural sector, whose products could only enter into circulation in the form of commodities. Hence, Stalin concluded, a commodity economy, operating under the law of value, with a system of purchase and sale regulated by accounting, currency, productivity, and efficiency, would continue to exist under socialism as long as there was collective ownership. Stalin was notably evasive on how any further evolution could occur, and what specific, active measures would help pave the way, let alone hasten the transition, toward communism. He argued that commodity production under socialism radically differed from commodity production under capitalism, as it was "commodity production without capitalists," confined to "items of personal consumption." As such, there was no risk that this kind of commodity production could revert back into capitalist production; rather, it was designed "to serve the development and consolidation of socialist production."[36] Under those conditions, the law of value continued to influence production, and enterprises could not, and should not, "function without taking the law of value into account," for such things "as cost accounting and profitableness, production costs, prices, etc."[37] There is a tension in Stalin's analysis, as he seems to argue that the law of value not only continued to operate in the USSR between different forms of ownership, but also remained fundamental for measuring, pricing, planning, and accounting in the state-owned industrial sector, the one supposedly fully extricated from capitalism. It seems therefore logical to assume that, in Stalin's perspective, the law of value would continue to operate when, with the full development of the productive forces, collective ownership had finally been eliminated or even after communism had been finally achieved. If one follows Stalin, then one must accept the seemingly paradoxical situation in which under socialism – and potentially under communism – value could not be assessed, resources could not be distributed, and prices could not be fixed without relying on the very same categories and laws that were intrinsic to and definitional of capitalism.

Historian Peter Caldwell describes a similar tension in the case of East Germany, which also went through a debate on the socialist economy in the "transitional period." For economists in the German Democratic Republic, as for Stalin, the socialist economy, on the one hand, "relied on the value-based categories and institutions of capitalism, from wage labor and profit to banks and accountants." On the other, the meaning of

---

[36] Stalin, *Economic Problems*: 16–17.    [37] Stalin, *Economic Problems*: 19.

those categories and institutions was supposed to have shifted "as they became instruments of the plan."[38] Economies in socialist countries were therefore suspended "between two contradictory models of economic organization, between a model aiming to replace the market with the plan, and a model stressing the continued importance of the law of value as a key organizing principle in transitional economies while remaining unable to measure value in a reliable fashion without market relations."[39] East German economists could not figure out a way to square the circle of that contradiction, nor could they provide a way to define, articulate, and possibly accelerate the socialist transition.[40]

In the USSR, the question of the transition to communism had been picked up again "in a more forthcoming manner by Khrushchev at the 20th Congress in early 1956." Khrushchev "made the transition (albeit 'gradual') to communism a current task," and claimed that the Soviet Union's five-year plan would make "a big new step forward in building up a … basis for communist society."[41] However, by the end of the 1950s, Mao and others in the CCP had started to express deep concerns about the process, pace, and even the possibility of that transition. As mentioned in the previous chapter, in China, as in the USSR, the state-owned sectors were under "ownership by the whole people" (*quanmin suoyouzhi*), which implied full integration in the planned economy, including distribution of goods, resources, and welfare, as well as regulated salaries and prices. All forms of rural co-ops were instead under a different form of ownership system, "collective ownership" (*jiti suoyouzhi*), and therefore they were solely and fully responsible for their profits and losses, and could provide to the overall welfare of their members only on the basis of their own available resources. The economic and social transformations produced by the Great Leap, including the creation of large communes, were believed to accelerate the transition of the entire economy into "ownership by the whole people." Mao expressed his dissatisfaction with Stalin's seemingly static assessment at both the Beidahe and the Zhengzhou conferences (in August and November 1958, respectively). In Zhengzhou, he chastised the Soviets for bragging about entering communism, "but you only hear a noise on

---

[38] Peter C. Caldwell, *Dictatorship, State Planning, and Social Theory in the German Democratic Republic* (Cambridge: Cambridge University Press, 2003): 15.

[39] Caldwell, *Dictatorship, State Planning, and Social Theory*: 55.

[40] In the Soviet Union, during the Khrushchev years, Soviet mathematics and cybernetics were invested in the search for a way to measure the entirety of the economy and make it completely malleable to planning. Francis Spufford recounts this story brilliantly in his novel *Red Plenty*.

[41] Teiwes and Sun, *China's Road to Disaster*: 136.

the staircase, you don't see anyone coming down." Stalin, according to Mao, "did not promote the elements of communism at all"; therefore, the transition to communism was hardly possible.[42] Mao contrasted Soviet stasis and inaction against the initial achievements of the Great Leap, which was bringing forth two major transitions, one concerning ownership, one concerning distribution. He toyed with the timeline for moving communes into "the system of communist ownership – almost the same as in factories – that is, public ownership of all eating, clothing, and housing."[43] "Three, four, five, six years or a bit more – isn't it a bit short? Or is it too long?" Mao mused in Zhengzhou. At Beidahe, he had gone so far as to speculate that the transition would take one to three years.[44] He was not alone in this, as Liu Shaoqi "had already been quoted in the *People's Daily* as urging people to 'go right ahead to realise communism. Now we must not think that communism will only be realised very slowly. So long as we work properly, it will be *very soon* when we shall realise communism.'"[45]

Mao also called for the creation of communes in the cities, as a way to push forward the second transition, from exchange of commodities to allocation of products and services, from currency remuneration to a "total supply system." Mao was very keen about that issue and had visited the Xushui commune in Hebei (with Chen Boda and Zhang Chunqiao) "to find out how it could be instituted."[46] At Zhengzhou, he stated, "What is of decisive importance here is whether things can be allocated. Things that cannot be allocated by the state cannot count as being owned by the whole people. [Things] allocated under ownership by the whole people are not 'commodities' any more as defined in political economy."[47] Here Mao takes a decisive step away from Stalin, who had argued for the continuing operation of commodity categories and the law of value even within the state-owned sector.[48] Within the planned economy, instead, Mao depicts a system resembling the

---

[42] "Talk at the First Zhengzhou Conference" (November 6–10, 1958), in Roderick MacFarquhar, Timothy Cheek, and Eugene Wu, eds., *The Secret Speeches of Chairman Mao: From the Hundred Flowers to the Great Leap Forward* (Cambridge, MA: Harvard University Press, 1989): 448.

[43] "Talks at the Beidahe Conference (Draft Transcript)" (August 17–30, 1958), in MacFarquhar et al., eds., *The Secret Speeches of Chairman Mao*: 431.

[44] "Talks at the Beidahe Conference": 431.

[45] MacFarquhar, *The Origins of the Cultural Revolution*: 88. Emphasis by MacFarquhar. Liu's comments were originally published in *RMRB*, July 30, 1958.

[46] MacFarquhar, *The Origins of the Cultural Revolution*: 104.

[47] "Talk at the First Zhengzhou Conference": 451.

[48] Charles Bettelheim pointed out how Stalin's explanation – that this was done for purposes of calculation and accounting – was not satisfactory: "*for the real question is, precisely, why calculations have to be made by means of commodity categories* and why they are

organization of labor within one enterprise (technical division of labor), where – and here I follow Rubin again – "[t]he production relations among people are organized in advance for the purpose of the material production of things, and not by means of things."[49] Products move – between different sectors of the same enterprise or between a regulated system of production – without creating relations of production, that is, without exchange of commodities, because those relations are determined in advance. In this system, then, relationships between people would not be mediated and expressed by relations among things.

One of the goals of the rural communes was precisely to increase the proportion of services and goods that were directly provided by the collective, thus making life in the countryside more like that of the SOE urban work unit but also progressively inserting ever-expanding sectors of the economy under planning, that is, under a system of social relationships potentially not defined by commodity exchange. As the theorist Guan Feng 关锋 highlighted in the *People's Daily*, by the end of September 1958, 70 percent of the pioneering rural communes in Henan adopted a combination of monthly salaries/bonuses and rationing. The latter could include allocation of grain and rice, eating at the commune, which was completely free, or even the provision of basic necessities (food, clothing, lodging, education, medical care, and expenses for marriages and funerals).[50] While everyone, including Mao, agreed that the rural communes remained, at the time, firmly within the realm of collective ownership, they were supposed to incrementally integrate more and more elements of "ownership by all the people," thus embodying a clearly *transitional* form of life.

Urban communes were deemed to be at a further stage of revolutionary transformation than their rural counterparts, but the question of what kind of ownership system they belonged to was more uncertain and open to debate. The position one took within that debate had very important consequences in terms of collective praxis and daily life. For example, in July 1960, the city of Xiamen held a conference over the form of ownership more appropriate to the urban communes, and the diverging assessments came with very different policy prescriptions. Those who argued

---

not made directly in terms of *labour-time*." Bettelheim, *The Transition to Socialist Economy*: 38.

[49] Rubin, *Essays on Marx's Theory of Value*: 14.

[50] Guan Feng 关锋, "Xiang gongchanzhuyi guoshe de zuihao de fenpei xingzshi. Shilun bufen gongji he bufen gongzi xiangjiehe de fenpei zhidu" 向共产主义过渡的最好的分配形式 试论部分供给和部分工资相结合的分配制度 [The best form of distribution for the transition to communism. Experimenting with a distribution system combining supply and wages], *RMRB*, October 22, 1958.

for "ownership of the whole people" pointed at the close connection between commune production and state planning. In Xiamen, the commune industrial production had already "basically been integrated into the national plan." If they performed contract work for larger factories, commune enterprises functioned as subsidiary branches of an SOE; if they produced small objects of everyday use, they followed a production plan mandated monthly by the top, received materials through the state-owned commercial sector, and sold finished products through the same path. "Factories were not allowed to sell [their products] themselves."[51] They were therefore very close to reaching the desired stage of "ownership by the whole people." Other contributors stressed how prices of commune products were regulated and how, unlike rural communes, salaries did not rely on work points but were generally based on hourly wages[52] and were largely independent of the enterprise's profits and losses ("there is basically no direct link between members' income and the enterprise's profits or losses").[53] In Beijing, a report by the bureau of industry (*gongyeju* 工业局) reiterated similar points: the urban communes' factories had been created with resources provided by the state or by SOEs; they often worked as subsidiaries of the SOEs; and, like SOE employees, commune workers were paid salaries. This placed the commune enterprises straight under "socialist ownership by the whole people" (*shehuizhuyi de quanmin suoyouzhi* 社会主义的全民所有制). However, the author urged, it was advisable not to spread this piece of information to commune workers, who could then start demanding welfare, salary, services, and conditions comparable to those of SOE workers.[54]

---

[51] Li Chengzong 李成宗, "Wo dui chengshi renmin gongshe suoyouzhi xingzhi de kanfa" 我对城市人民公社所有制性质的看法 [My opinion on the nature of the ownership system in urban people's communes], *Zhongguo jingji wenti* 中国经济问题 [Economic issues in China], no. 8 (1960): 12–14. The assumption that products of urban commune factories were not to be sold on the market was not, however, followed in other localities, such as Beijing, for example.

[52] Chu Hongdao 初宏道, "Cong sheban gongye de gongchanxiao qingkuang kanlai, sheban qiye shi shu quanminsuoyouzhi xingzhide" 从社办工业的供产销情况看来, 社办企业是属全民所有制性质的 [On the basis of the supply, production and marketing of commune industries, they belong to the form of ownership by the whole people], *Zhongguo jingji wenti* 中国经济问题 [Economic issues in China], no. 8 (1960): 14.

[53] Su Shucheng 苏树澄, "Guanyu chengshi renmin gongshe suoyouzhi xingzhi wenti de shangque" 关于城市人民公社所有制性质問题的商榷 [A discussion of the issue of the ownership form of urban communes], 中国经济问题 [Economic issues in China], no. 8 (1960): 14–17; Lei Yaoling 雷尧玲, "Chengshi renmin gongshe suoyouzhi jibenshang shi quanmin xingzhide" 城市人民公社所有制基本上是全民性质的 [The ownership of urban people's communes is essentially universal in nature], *Zhongguo jingji wenti* 中国经济问题 [Economic issues in China], no. 8 (1960): 11.

[54] BMA 112-001-00782-1 Guanyu chengshi jiedao renmin gongshe dangqian jige zhengze wenti de yijian (er gao) 关于城市街道人民公社当前几个政策问题的意见 (二稿)

Leaving aside for a moment this last, quite revealing caveat, these examples were once again meant to have both a descriptive and a pre-scriptive power. As we have seen, the experience of urban communes was far from uniform across cities, and highlighting specific cases in which integration with the state sector and other characteristics made these often makeshift enterprises more similar to SOEs had strategic policy implications for the present and the near future, a future that was defined by the aspiring normativity of the SOE work-unit employee, with his (the aspiration was largely gendered as male) salaries and his set of benefits. In terms of welfare, while it was recognized that (female) workers in urban commune factories and services did not and should not yet have benefits equal to their (male) SOE counterparts, this was assumed to be only a transitory situation (even if the timeline of that transition remained undetermined), one to be overcome via economic development and further expansion of the supply system.[55] Another implication of these arguments was that urban commune enterprises did not constitute an alternative model of production, but just a stage in the process of devel-opment leading to the SOE format and to their complete absorption into the planned economy.[56] Stressing that commune enterprises were closer to the SOE model also had less obvious – and possibly more ominous – consequences for workplace governance and workers' rights: If they were under ownership by the whole people (*quanmin suoyouzhi*), commune factories were not supposed to be democratically managed by an assem-bly of workers – as was the case for cooperatives and collective enterprise. Potential inscription in the state ownership system also meant the exten-sion of a system of control and labor management.[57]

Collectivization had produced radical changes in the very structure of the system of property relations and in the economy as a whole. Those changes, as the secretary of the Chongqing municipal committee stated, would in turn lead to "the establishment of a completely new relationship between people, based on a noble communist style and communist moral qualities."[58] The expansion of the productive forces under

[Opinions on several policy issues regarding the people's commune in urban neighborhoods (second draft)], March 17, 1961.
[55] Li Chengzong, "Wo dui chengshi renmin gongshe suoyouzhi xingzhi de kanfa."
[56] BMA 112-001-00782-1 Guanyu chengshi jiedao renmin gongshe dangqian jige zhengze wenti de yijian (er gao).
[57] Li Chengzong, "Wo dui chengshi renmin gongshe suoyouzhi xingzhi de kanfa."
[58] Ren Baige 任白戈, "Zuzhi chengshi renmin de jingji shenghuo shi jianshe shehuizhuyi xin chengshi de yige zhongyao fangmian" 组织城市人民的经济生活是建设社会主义新城市的一个重要方面 [Organizing the economic life of urban people is an important aspect of building new socialist cities], *Hongqi* 红旗 5 (1960), reprinted in Li, ed., *Chengshi renmin gongshe yanjiu ziliao xuanbian*, vol. 8: 189.

collectivization and the new relationships of production associated with it were taken as an evident sign of an accelerated transition toward communism, and as such was supposed to be appropriate. The inscription of an increasing number of workers under "ownership by the whole people" and under structures more closely approaching the SOE model was also desirable, not only for theoretical reasons, but because the newly collectivized laborers could potentially be entitled to expanded benefits and welfare. Yet, as that report by the bureau of industry cited above indicated, there remained a crucial tension at the core of the supposedly virtuous cycle of collectivization: The new conditions of ownership could not be advertised to the workers, because they would then be allowed to request the benefits linked with their newfound status too soon, and that could have consequences in terms of welfare costs and enterprise profits. This was one of the main contradictions that the experience of the urban communes had revealed.

Officers and cadres who argued that communes instead should remain firmly under "collective ownership" shifted the emphasis to those aspects of collectivization that were not yet fully realized. First, legally, commune workers were city residents (*jumin* 居民); they were not state employees.[59] While the state could provide help in founding enterprises, investment capital came from various sources: enterprises below the district level, funds of the handicraft co-ops, small entrepreneurs (*getihu* 个体户) who joined the commune, money raised among residents, donations by overseas Chinese (*huaqiao* 华侨), and profit and accumulation by commune companies.[60] Similarly, while there were enterprises belonging to "ownership by the whole people" under the commune administration – mostly city- or district-owned companies that pre-dated the Great Leap – only their management rights had been transferred to the commune, not their ownership. They did not "belong" to the commune, nor did they affect its overall benefit or remuneration structure.[61] So, while it was

---

[59] BMA 001-028-00031-12 Guanyu Erlonglu gongshe suoyouzhi wenti de baogao 关于二龙路公社所有制问题的报告 [Report on the issue of ownership system of the Erlonglu commune]. The term *"jumin"* deserves a closer analysis. While this is not its fixed or original meaning, in the sources the term seems to be applied specifically to urban residents outside the *danwei* system. So urban communes were supposed to mobilize *jumin* and transform them into workers and producers. I am thankful to Lara Kusnetzky for pointing this out.

[60] Wang Congchao 王丛超, "Cong guojia caizheng jiaodu laikan, chengshi renmin gongshe suoyouzhi jibenshang shi jitixingzhi de" 从国家财政角度来看, 城市人民公社所有制基本上是集体性质的 [From the point of view of state finance ownership in urban communes is essentially collective in nature], *Zhongguo jingji wenti* 中国经济问题 [Economic issues in China], no. 8 (1960): 9–11.

[61] Wang Yongxi 王永錫, Zhao Guoliang 赵国良, Wang Fangtian 王方田, Guo Shaoxiang 郭绍湘, Li Bicheng 李必成, Xiao Deyu 肖德愚, "Guanyu chengshi renmin gongshe

recognized that in the urban communes, "ownership by the whole people" had a dominant position, collective ownership still should and did determine the aspects more directly connected with social reproduction and workers' conditions, that is, distribution of wages and services. If the communes were still under "collective ownership," workers and members could not even think about asking for the same salaries and welfare of their SOE counterparts, at least not until a distant and always postponed future; forms of more equitable distribution could be (and eventually were) condemned as excessive "egalitarianism" (*pingjunzhuyi* 平均主义); and commune leadership could deploy management tactics and compensation systems that were usually not adopted in the SOEs, such as piece-rate wages.[62] Under collective ownership, the commune was solely responsible for welfare and salaries, and that responsibility could be (and very often was) pushed down to individual units. Consequently, there were calls to increase the portion of profit kept at the factory level (up to 80 percent). This starved the commune administration of resources and made any collective management of *fuli* impossible.[63]

This debate probed the limits of what inhabiting a temporality of transition allowed and what it did not: It allowed for experimentation in new forms of production, ownership, social relations, and distribution of resources. But it did not allow for any transformation that could place further burdens on the state, as it was programmatically supposed to be only generating benefits without consuming precious resources.

## 2.4    Bourgeois Right

Deciding the forms of ownership to which the "new socialist things" created under the Great Leap belonged had profound and very practical implications, but it nonetheless remained firmly within the relatively

suoyouzhi wenti de chubu tantao" 关于城市人民公社所有制问题的初步探讨 [A preliminary study on the ownership of urban people's communes], *Caijing kexue* 财经科学 [Finance and economics], no. 4 (1960): 21–33.

[62] BMA 112-001-00783-3 Erlonglu gongshe diaochazu 二龙路公社调查组 [Erlonglu commune survey group], Guanyu Erlonglu gongshe suoyouzhi wenti de baogao 关于二龙路公社所有制问题的报告 [Report on the issue of ownership system of the Erlonglu commune]. On the reintroduction of piece-rate wages, see BMA 001-006-01864-1 Chengshi renmin gongshe diaocha cailiao zhiyi – dui chengshi renmin gongshe xingzhi, renwu, he suoyou youzhi wenti de yijian 城市人民公社调查材料之一 – 对城市人民公社性质、任务和所有制问题的意见 [Survey materials on the urban people's communes no. 1 – Opinions on the nature, tasks, and ownership system of the urban people's communes], August 24, 1961.

[63] BMA 112-001-00783-3 Guanyu Erlonglu gongshe suoyouzhi wenti de baogao.

narrow theoretical confines of Stalin's argumentation. The Chinese debate emphatically exceeded those confines, starting with Mao himself. As Benjamin Kindler has pointed out,

Mao's interventions over the course of key meetings held from early 1958 onward reveal a process of theoretical development in which Mao sought to locate a vocabulary to think the ways in which formal transformations in the status of ownership do not exhaust the problems of social relations under socialism, and how, therefore, to attend to the constant production and reproduction of sites of inequality in the lived fabric of social relations.[64]

The discussion over the persistence of wages and other capitalist relational forms – as well as the stubborn social inequalities that they continuously reproduced – while related to and overlapping with the discussion over forms of ownership, marked a more decisive move away from the parameters set by the Stalinist orthodoxy. This took the form of the 1958 debate over "bourgeois right."

At the beginning of his Beidahe speech (August 1958), before he even mentioned ownership, Mao addressed bourgeois right as both a cultural form and a principle determining social relations: "[We] must eradicate the ideology of bourgeois right. For instance, competing for position, competing for rank demanding overtime pay, high salaries for mental workers and low salaries for physical laborers – these are all vestiges of bourgeois ideology. 'To each according to his worth' is stipulated by law; it's also bourgeois stuff."[65] The term "bourgeois right" had been first introduced in this context a year earlier, in the summer of 1957, by Lu Dingyi, in a speech at the 27th enlarged session of the Party Group of the Chinese Writers' Union. Lu was contemplating the presence of so many "rightist" intellectuals under socialism, as revealed during the Hundred Flowers and the anti-rightist campaigns.[66] Or, in Kindler's phrasing, he was discussing "the question of how to theorize the reproduction of the capitalist intellectual under socialist conditions."[67] The answer to that question, Lu argued, lay not only in the continuing influence of bourgeois ideology or the "lagging behind" of individual consciousness, but also, and perhaps primarily, in the fact that "bourgeois right" still existed under socialism, and it informed the distributions of

---

[64] Benjamin Kindler, *Writing to the Rhythm of Labor: Cultural Politics of the Chinese Revolution, 1942–1976* (New York: Columbia University Press, 2025): 126. For this entire chapter, and in particular for the discussion of bourgeois right, I owe a huge debt to Kindler's work, and much of my own research and investigation on this topic has been conducted in close dialogue with him.

[65] "Talks at the Beidahe Conference," 406.

[66] Schoenhals, "Saltationist Socialism": 114.

[67] Kindler, *Writing to the Rhythm of Labor.* 98.

the means of consumption. Even under socialism, "[d]istribution is still not according to need, but according to work. The means of livelihood are distributed according to the principles of commodity exchange of equal values."[68]

The expression "bourgeois right," which appears first in Marx's *Critique of the Gotha Program*, summarized a series of organizational forms, legal structures, and economic arrangements typical of capitalism, which, according to Marxist theory, had the appearance of producing social relations of formal equality while in practice they preserved the capitalist system and the radical inequalities on which it was predicated. The question, for Mao and for others, was how much of this "bourgeois stuff" still remained and what functions it served under socialism, especially after the massive development and industrialization spurred by the FFYP. In his Beidahe speech, Mao had singled out the persistence of remuneration according to labor (*anlao fenpei* 按劳分配), "to each according to their work," specifically in the form of wages, as one of the most stubborn elements of bourgeois right. On this front the USSR had very little to teach. As Andrew Sloin highlighted, "Soviet industrial production, as well as the entire system of consumption, depended on the increasingly universal actuality of waged labor throughout the system. Wage labor provided the primary means for exchange and the accumulation of personal property while simultaneously structuring social relations between citizens, employers, and the state as owner of productive property."[69] According to official discourse, the supremacy of wage labor in the USSR was supposed to have been transformed by the fact that, after the revolution, the workers themselves were the putative owners of the means of production, and therefore could not also be the subjects of exploitation. But in the practice of the working day, everything remained mediated through waged labor, and "production based upon the appropriation of commodified, alienated labor remained basic to the Soviet system."[70] This labor could be valued more or less, and compensations did indeed increase during the Stalin era, but the centrality of waged labor was never radically challenged.[71]

At Beidahe, Mao criticized the salary system in the USSR, where wage grades among Soviet cadres were "too numerous" and "the gap [between the cadres and] the workers and peasants" too wide.[72] And while the

---

[68] Schoenhals, "Saltationist Socialism": 119.
[69] Andrew Sloin, "Theorizing Soviet Antisemitism: Value, Crisis, and Stalinist 'Modernity,'" *Critical Historical Studies* 3:2 (Fall 2016): 265.
[70] Sloin, "Theorizing Soviet Antisemitism": 267.
[71] Sloin, "Theorizing Soviet Antisemitism": 268.
[72] "Talks at the Beidahe Conference": 425.

salary system could not "be abolished immediately, because there are professors," he argued, "[we should] prepare for it in one or two years."[73] To the system adopted in the Soviet Union and (currently) in his own country, Mao counterposed the experience of the anti-Japanese and revolutionary war, "a twenty-two-year history of war communism, with no salaries"[74] when the Red Army, "[t]hrough several decades of battle,... always practiced communism."[75] The Chinese revolutionaries adopted a "supply system," in which army and civilians, officers and men were equal. Mao continued,

Originally we divided up the leftovers from the mess and had small subsidies. After we came into the cities, it was said that the supply system was backward, guerrillaism, a rural work style, [and] that it couldn't boost initiative, nor stimulate progress. [They] wanted to establish a salary system. [They] endured for three years, [and] in 1952 the salary system was established. [They] said bourgeois ranks and rights and such were very fine and called our old supply system a backward method, a guerrilla practice that affected activism. In effect [they] turned the supply system into a system of bourgeois right, [thereby] promoting bourgeois ideology. Did initiating the 25,000 li Long March, the Land Revolution and the War of Liberation rely on salaries? Two to three million people during the anti-Japanese war, from four to five million during the War of Liberation lived a life of war communism, no Sundays [off] – didn't [they all] risk their lives?[76]

For Mao, the experience of wartime communism proved that you could elicit enthusiastic mass participation, even in what was literally a life-threatening enterprise, without relying on material incentives, and he argued that the reintroduction of salaries and wages was a retreat from what was already a more progressive (revolutionary) form of social relations. Accordingly, he refused the naturalized assumption that salaries were necessary to spur people's activism and initiative: "Piece-rate wages are not a good system. I don't believe the adoption of the supply system will make people lazy, inventions fewer, or activism lower. Because decades of experience prove otherwise."[77] The problem, Mao concluded, was not excessive egalitarianism, but the reliance on the Soviet model, with its structural inequalities, and the continuous reproduction of capitalist forms under the organizing influence of bourgeois right: "The sources [of our problems] are two-fold: one is socialism, which has been borrowed from Elder Brother [the Soviet Union], and the

[73] "Talks at the Beidahe Conference": 435.
[74] "Talks at the Beidahe Conference": 434.
[75] "Talks at the Beidahe Conference": 435.
[76] "Talks at the Beidahe Conference": 434–435.
[77] "Talks at the Beidahe Conference": 437.

second is capitalism, which is home born and bred."[78] In his later annotations to the Soviet textbook on political economy, Mao further criticized the centrality of wages, and concluded that "[i]t is when politics is weakened that there is no choice but to talk about material incentives."[79]

Mao's critique of "remuneration according to labor" was forcefully restated and pushed to its logical political conclusions in an article by Zhang Chunqiao,[80] which is usually considered to be the first official salvo in the 1958 debate on bourgeois right. It was first published in *Liberation* 解放and then reprinted in the *People's Daily*, apparently at Mao's behest and with a short, unsigned introduction allegedly written by Mao himself, who praised the article as "basically correct, but somewhat one-sided."[81] Mao's praise is not surprising as Zhang started by re-threading Mao's analysis of the experience of the revolutionary war. Then the Party had instituted a "wartime communist life" (*junshi gong-chanzhuyi shenghuo* 军事共产主义生活) whose main distinguishing and foundational feature was a "supply system" (*gongjizhi* 供给制), according to which soldiers, militiamen, and party members were all provided with the same amounts of (meager) rations, no matter their rank or position. It was a hard life but one predicated on a principle of radical equality, of which the supply system was both the premise and the realization. After Liberation, however, Zhang continued, that system had come under attack from the bourgeoisie and had been progressively abandoned under the influence of the ideology of bourgeois right. The supply system was labeled "village style," "a bad guerrilla habit," not suitable for the cities, and that criticism was eventually accepted and absorbed by CCP cadres. The supply system was replaced by wages – remuneration according to labor – the central feature of bourgeois right. The result was that, in place of the radical equality of the revolutionary war, China developed increasing social differences, all inscribed in the wage system, between skilled and nonskilled labor, rural and urban labor, mental and physical labor, producing what Zhang called a "system of ranks" (*dengji zhidu* 等级制度). Zhang recognized how Marx himself had indicated that, in the initial

---

[78] "Talks at the Beidahe Conference": 437.
[79] Mao, *A Critique of the Soviet Economics*: 85. The textbook argued that socialism was superior to capitalism because under socialism wages steadily rise.
[80] At the time, he was a member of the Shanghai CCP city committee and editor at *Liberation*.
[81] Zhang Chunqiao 张春桥, "Pochu zichanjieji de faquan sixiang" 破除资产阶级的法权思想 [Do away with the ideology of bourgeois right], *Renmin Ribao*, October 13, 1958. An English translation is available at http://marxistphilosophy.org/BourgeoisRightWeb.pdf.

stages of socialism, the new state cannot implement the communist principle of "to each according to their needs," but it must still stick to "to each according to their work." However – and here Zhang pushed Mao's critique to the next political step – that does not mean that one should let the principles of bourgeois right determine the structure of society. Quite the contrary: One should keep striving to destroy those principles and replace them with elements belonging to the communist future. That, Zhang argued, was the essential goal of the socialist period. Marx had provided an example with his description and praise of the (1871) Paris Commune's adoption of radical equality in terms of salaries, which was later reiterated by Engels and Lenin. Should then the socialist state not follow the example of the first proletarian commune?

To extend Zhang's point in a slightly different idiom, under socialism, even if the development of the forces of production had not been transformed at a level that could guarantee a transition to more egalitarian forms of social relations, it was necessary to introduce principles of ownership and distribution that anticipated that transition, in order to proactively push it forward (while preventing any capitalist regression), even if it created a *"non-correspondence between the forms of property and their content,"* between productive forces and social relations.[82] Without such a political intervention, under the conditions imposed by bourgeois right, *bourgeois* forms of social relations will continue to reproduce themselves, endlessly re-creating new inequalities and differences incompatible with the Maoist revolutionary project, and thus making any transition to communism and "to each according to their needs" impossible. Zhang, following Mao, challenged what was, for others in the CCP, a naturalized *economic* assumption – different forms of work are paid differently, more work or more complex work is paid more – because forms of remuneration, as part of bourgeois right, were constitutive of social relations and therefore did not belong to any conceptual realm that could be separated from politics, culture, and the everyday.

In opening up the debate, both Mao and Zhang were hinting at the existence of something – a power to shape social relations – which could not be reduced to ideology. Bourgeois right's power to determine social organization did not operate through ideological means, although it had obvious ideological effects, for example, the systemic devaluation of certain forms of labor vis-à-vis others. We see here, still in a very inchoate and undeveloped stage, a prefiguration of what Søren Mau calls "economic power," which "is rooted in *the ability to reconfigure the material*

---

[82] Bettelheim, *The Transition to Socialist Economy*: 54. Emphasis in the original.

*conditions of social reproduction.*"[83] In Mao and Zhang's argument, bourgeois right functions through a series of material operations that tend to reproduce relations of production of a certain kind. The lingering power of capitalism does not express itself solely in the ownership of the means of production or in the control of the state and its apparatuses. Rather, and more insidiously, the logic of capital is woven into the fabric of social life. Similarly, the law of value could not simply be understood as a technical way of explaining and organizing prices, as many "economists" argued in 1958; rather, "value" was meant "to capture a specific form of *socialization* of labor, that is, a historically specific way of coordinating production." The continuing functioning of the law of value under socialism therefore could not but establish relations of production that mirrored those of capitalism.[84]

Zhang Chunqiao also rebuffed the main criticism of the supply system, the assumption that it hampered productivity by offering the same remuneration no matter the amount and quality of work performed ("whether you work or not, you still eat!"). To this strictly *economic* determination, Zhang responded by recalling once again the *political* experience of the revolutionary war, when people fought and sacrificed themselves without even the faintest notion of material incentives (did anyone on the Long March receive wages?). This was the form of labor epitomized in Mao's 1944 formulation "serve the people," in which that "service" by selfless revolutionaries had the function of making immanent a new ethical social formation, "the people," constituted along the lines of socialist equality.[85] During the anti-Japanese and civil wars, labor, service, and sacrifice prefigured and made real, through the practice of the revolutionary army, the possibility to remake social relations. During the Great Leap, Mao and Zhang argued, labor in service of the people, without consideration of waged rewards, could similarly bring closer the temporality of communist equality.

Zhang pointed at the distortions that a formal system of "equal pay for equal work" produced in a society that was supposedly in the process of being restructured under a set of increasingly equalitarian relationships: Wage grades created a separation between cadres and workers, promoting bureaucratism and hierarchies, while the monetization of work time through salaries fomented real laziness, because labor became valuable

---

[83] Mau, *Mute Compulsion*: 17.        [84] Mau, *Mute Compulsion*: 150.
[85] Rebecca Karl, "Serve the People," in Christian Sorace, Ivan Franceschini, and Nicholas Loubere, eds., *Afterlives of Chinese Communism: Political Concepts from Mao to Xi* (Canberra: ANU Press, 2019): 250.

only insofar as it brought a monetary remuneration.[86] Zhang concluded that, even if some elements of bourgeois rights necessarily remained operative under socialism, the goal was not to cherish them but to progressively and resolutely restrict them, reduce their role, and ultimately eliminate them. Reintroducing a form of supply system that would replace salaries with a direct distribution of products and welfare in the communes would be a crucial step in this effort.

As Guan Feng had argued in his 1958 *People's Daily* piece, the partial rationing system introduced by most communes was precisely a way of moving out of "remuneration according to labor." By providing collectivized services, communes were socializing birth, rearing, education, and health, but they were also weakening the hold of bourgeois right. While this form of rationing, Guan argued, was different from wartime communism and was not yet "fully achieved communism," it introduced a form of distribution based on the principle of "to each according to their needs," and, as such, it belonged to the category of communism. In another essay, published in *Philosophical Research* in August 1958, Guan stressed how collectivization was supposed to have not only practical but also massive ideological effects, breaking the shackles of private (bourgeois) ideology. Guan admitted that, under socialism, the continued existence of "remuneration according to labor" would unavoidably continue to create differences, but the role of social welfare and direct distribution of products and services was precisely to prevent those differences from becoming too big – and eventually to reduce them. He configured collectivization as part of a progressive expansion of welfare, eventually leading to the transition from one system (socialism) to another (communism).[87]

What Zhang and Guan proposed was the progressive reduction and eventual elimination of a system (the commodity economy, wages) in which labor, to use once again Rubin's formulation, "becomes social only in the sense that it becomes equal with all other forms of labor, in the sense that it becomes socially equalized." This is replaced with a system, a socialist community, where a "social organ," a planning institution, equalizes the labor of various individuals, but only after that labor is already socialized and allocated. Thus, in such a socialist community,

---

[86] In Chapter 3 we will see how cadres were forced into a contradictory position in relation to wages and economic incentives: On the one hand, they praised added income and access to commodity as transformational; on the other, they rebuked workers for their focus on economic rewards.

[87] Guan Feng 关锋, "Lüeyu renmin gongshe de weida lishi yiyi" 略論人民公社的伟大历史意义 [Brief discussion of the huge historical meaning of people's communes], *Zhexue yanjiu* 哲学研究 [Philosophical research], 5 (1958): 1–8.

the property of labor as equal or equalized is "the result of the production process, of the production decision of a social organ which socialized and distributed labor."[88] At the end of the production process, when things (products, not commodities) are *distributed* to people, a process of evaluation and equalization of these things is necessary, but it does not require things to be valued according the precise amount of labor invested in their production, as their evaluation is in large part function of specific policy goals. Then, "the decision on the equalization of things will be separate from the decision on the equalization of labor," unlike in the commodity economy, where equalization of things is necessarily carried out only through the equalization of labor.[89] In such a system, political concerns about what is thought to be more necessary and useful to the masses dominate over pure economic ones, as the very decision on how to evaluate things is placed outside the realm of the economic, narrowly construed.

For both Guan Feng and Zhang Chunqiao, the transformation of productive and social relations under socialism was prefigured as a gradual transition (*zhujian guodu* 逐渐过渡), but that process, while still connected to the development of the "productive forces," was far from being an almost natural outcome of economic expansion and industrialization, as many Chinese economists (then and now) seemed to imply. Here the two Chinese theorists were in line with Marx's own abandonment of his early productive force determinism, which, in Søren Mau's summation, relied "on the unwarranted assumption of a transhistorically necessary tendency for the productive forces to develop, regardless of the specific relations of production under which they are put to use." Instead, Marx later moved to the understanding, which Mao and Zhang shared, that "what drives history is not the immanent and necessary development of the productive forces, but human beings acting within a set of determinate social structures from which certain tendencies arise."[90]

The Great Leap was supposed to generate a massive push in industrialization and economic growth, and therefore in the development of the productive forces; but, as I have outlined, it was also aimed at engendering a series of more radical changes, including the transformation of social relationships at a granular level, and the attack on bourgeois right

---

[88] Rubin, *Essays on Marx's Theory of Value*: 97.
[89] Rubin, *Essays on Marx's Theory of Value*: 98–99. "A society directed by the goals of social policy may, for example, consciously introduce a lower estimate of the things which satisfy the cultural needs of the broad popular masses, and a higher estimate for luxury goods."
[90] Mau, *Mute Compulsion*: 95–96.

was part and parcel of that transformation. In this perspective, a structure of remuneration and welfare that privileged the direct distribution of products and services in lieu of monetary compensation did not function simply as a facilitator of production (allowing for larger participation in labor and increased productivity) but was instead the motor for social revolution. This social revolution could only be pushed forward through direct *political* intervention, continuously expanding and elevating those elements and forms that prefigured communist social relationships while actively restricting the power and scope of those that tended to reproduce capitalist relationships, like the law of value, commodity exchange, money, and wages.[91] As Benjamin Kindler has highlighted, Zhang referred to his opponents as "the economists" – even if they included a variety of social scientists – squarely placing his own intervention on the terrain of politics, separated from the Soviet discourse of the political economy. "[A]t the juncture of the Great Leap," Kindler concludes, "the language of bourgeois right may be better understood from the perspective of a critique of political economy in the sense of remaining autonomous from a discourse whose disciplinary logic remained part of the Soviet model of socialism, and the posing of politics as a distinct field of relations sharply demarcated from the logic of the economic."[92] That also provides us with a different – and perhaps more profound – meaning for the ubiquitous invocation "politics in command" (*zhengzhi guashuai* 政治挂帅). That is, we could acknowledge that Zhang's argument was grounded on the political premise of radical equality as a starting point, rather than as the result of a long process centered on economic development: Equality was the precondition of a real socialist transition, not the end product of fully achieved communism. As Jacques Rancière argued many decades later, "equality, in general, is not an end to be attained. It is a point of departure, a presupposition to be verified by sequences of specific acts."[93] Thus, political measures that introduced a more equal system of distribution of products and resources under a "supply system" – as opposed to a system of wages and the law of value – at the same time verified and instantiated the equality promised by socialism.

Zhang's piece – perhaps because it came with Mao's imprimatur, perhaps because it touched a central nerve in the contested understanding of socialist society – elicited an intense debate. I will limit myself here

---

[91] Guan Feng, "Lüeyu renmin gongshe de weida lishi yiyi."
[92] Kindler, *Writing to the Rhythm of Labor*: 130.
[93] Charles Bingham and Gert J. J. Biesta, with Jacques Rancière, *Jacques Rancière: Education, Truth, Emancipation* (London: Continuum, 2010): 9.

to the responses and rejoinders published in the *People's Daily*, but even those are too many to exhaustively summarize. In general, the initial reactions, for about a month or so, were positive and aligned, if with nuances, with Zhang's argument. But a shift took place in mid-November, following the realignment of Great Leap policies, and through 1959 the *Renmin Ribao* published dozens of contributions that rebuffed, with varying degrees of coherence and intellectual heft, Zhang's critique.

Early commentators supported the overall thrust of Zhang Chunqiao's argument, but with varying degrees of intensity and placing emphasis on different aspects. Some authors made direct references to Zhang's piece, others did not, while clearly taking part in the same debate. The most radical interventions were clearly in agreement with Zhang and in some cases pressed his point even more forcefully. Yin Jianqing outlined a direct attack on the introduction of the wage system after Liberation, singling it out as a major roadblock in the socialist transformation,[94] while Chen Ming called for widespread adoption of the supply system, chiding those who used Marx as a fig leaf to defend bourgeois right.[95] Similarly, writing from his position as an academic, Xu Hongzhong attacked those who, following the letter of Marx's *Critique*, hid the true nature of bourgeois right as a product of class society, cloaking it as the natural outcome of "differences in intelligence and working ability."[96] In an otherwise moderately worded and unsigned piece, "Declaring War on Bourgeois Right," the authors concluded that the very idea that material incentives are always effective was a reflection of the desire to maintain bourgeois right and "the ideological root of right-leaning conservatism in practical work."[97]

Other authors staked more moderate positions. Zheng Jiqiao and Wu Chuanqi, in their contributions, stressed the "transitional" character of "remuneration according to labor" ("a transitional principle of allocation" *yizhong guodu de fenpei yuancze* 一种过渡的分配原则) as well as the need for a gradual and long-term process leading to its elimination. But they also agreed with Zhang Chunqiao that accepting how "bourgeois

---

[94] Yin Jianqing 尹剑青, "Gai gongzizhi shi yige lishi jiaoxun" 改工资制是一个历史教训 [Reforming the wage system is a history lesson], *RMRB*, October 27, 1958.

[95] Chen Ming 陈明, "Bu gai tuichu gongjizhi de zhendi" 不该退出供给制的阵地 [We should not retreat from the battlefield of the supply system], *RMRB*, October 30, 1958.

[96] Xu Hongzhong 徐红中, "Dakai zichanjieji faquan de fangkongdong" 打开资产阶级法权的防空洞 [Break open the bomb shelter of bourgeois right], *RMRB*, October 30, 1958.

[97] "Xiang zichanjieji faquan guannian xuanzhan" 向资产阶级法权观念宣战 [Declaring war on bourgeois right], *RMRB*, November 1, 1958.

legal power inevitably remains in socialist society is not the same as accepting the legitimacy of such legal power, nor is it the same as sitting back and waiting helplessly for it to disappear of its own accord."[98] Rather, the wage system should be considered an unavoidable "shortcoming" (*quedian* 缺点) of the new socialist society, whose role should be progressively weakened at each step of socialist construction.[99] Lin Wei, in a piece titled "Let's Remove the Vestiges of Bourgeois Hierarchy," while supporting Zhang's main criticism, transposed it squarely to the field of (narrowly conceived) ideology, reducing "bourgeois right" to a set of ingrained mental habits and hierarchical concepts, which, far from eliciting productivity and individual initiative, stifled the masses' sense of responsibility, activism, and creativity, fostering the passive attitude of "I will do whatever you tell me to do."[100] The *People's Daily* also reported on the debate over forms of remuneration among workers at the plastic factory in Taiyuan, who, while agreeing that equal pay for equal work was the principle of distribution under socialism, pointed out the very practical and evident inequalities it fostered: "We have a comrade in the factory, with a family of three and a monthly salary of more than ¥200, and he can put more than ¥100 a month in the bank. But take Zhang Mingshan, with a family of seven people and a monthly salary of ¥45; his family life is more difficult. Can this be said to be the most reasonable [system]?"[101]

In a piece published on November 12, economist Luo Gengmo embraced the progressive restriction of remuneration according to labor, criticizing the past overemphasis of its positive aspects over its negative ones, which had fostered, especially among cadres and senior intellectuals, the tendency to detach themselves from workers and peasants, "first in life and then in consciousness." He concluded by endorsing the abolition of piece-rate wages in factories and mines and the substitution of salaries with a partial supply system.[102] A day later, in a quite

[98] Zheng Jiqiao 郑季翘, "Zaitan xiaochu zichanjieji faquan" 谈谈削除资产阶级法权 [Talking about the eradication of bourgeois right], *RMRB*, October 18, 1958.

[99] Wu Chuanqi 吴传启, "Cong renmin gongshe kan gongchanzhuyi" 从人民公社看共产主义 [Looking at communism from the people's communes], *RMRB*, October 1, 1958.

[100] Lin Wei 林韦, "Saochu zichanjieji dengjizhi de canji" 扫除资产阶级等级制的残迹 [Let's remove the vestiges of bourgeois hierarchy], *RMRB*, November 3, 1958.

[101] Zhang Minzhi 张民植 and Cui Chengshan 崔成善, "Jianshe shehuizhuyi shehui yao you gongchanzhuyi sixiang – Ji Taiyuan suliaochang chengpin chejiangongren de yichang da bianlun" 建设社会主义社会要有共产主义思想 – 记太原塑料厂成品车间工人的一场大辩论 [To build a socialist society we need communist ideology – A record of the debate among workers at the finished product workshop in the Taiyuan plastic factory], *RMRB*, November 5, 1958.

[102] Luo Gengmo 骆耕漠, "Gongzizhi he gongjizhi dou you liangchongxing" 工资制和供给制都有两重性 [Both wage and supply systems have a dual nature], *RMRB*, November 12, 1958.

detailed essay, historian Hu Sheng articulated a precise criticism of remuneration according to labor, pointing to the inherent difficulty of comparing different forms of labor:

[W]hat is the difference between an hour of teaching in a classroom and an hour of work at a lathe? I think it would be difficult for any economist to make a precise calculation. It should be admitted that in the implementation of pay for work, certain principles of the capitalist system are in fact recognized: for example, skilled labor is paid more than unskilled labor, mental labor is paid more than manual labor, the labor of the more educated is paid more than that of the less educated, and so on.[103]

That was even more inequal, Hu argued, in a system in which training and education provided by the state and society were then turned into a personal, individual property, reflected in wage differences. Hu did not push the argument further, but what he was hinting at was that, unless one adopted a system of distribution in which different forms of labor were socialized and allocated by a planning organization, the only way of comparing and equalizing them was through commodity exchange, through things embodying a certain quantity of abstract labor. That was what the wage system ultimately reproduced.

Finally, some of the articles, echoing the voluntaristic effort of the revolutionary war and of the Great Leap, introduced a discussion about *the kind of labor* that was necessary for this transitional phase. In the piece quoted above, Hu Sheng celebrated, in passing, the voluntary deployment of excessive overtime: "Some workers' wages have even been reduced a little due to the elimination of piece-rate wages and of unreasonable incentive systems. Instead of working eight hours a day, people now voluntarily work ten hours and twelve hours, with surprise overnight stints when necessary."[104] In October, the *People's Daily* reported on a meeting of fourteen weavers in the Tianjin canvas factory with CCP and *Renmin Ribao* propaganda officers, in which they stated their opposition to remuneration according to labor and their desire to work for communism, not for money. They promised to increase production by 240,000 meters without adding one single worker.[105] Similarly, Xiong Fu, at the time secretary of the Foreign Liaison Department of the CCP

---

[103] Hu Sheng 胡绳, "Cong gongjizhi shuoqi" 从供给制说起 [Bringing up the supply system], *RMRB*, November 13, 1958.

[104] Hu Sheng, "Cong gongjizhi shuoqi."

[105] Sun Piqi 孙丕祺, "Yao gongchanzhuyi, buyao jijian gongzi. Wei gongchanzhuyi, bushi wei qian" 要共产主义,不要计件工资 为共产主义,不是为钱 [We want communism, not piece-rate wages. For communism, not for money], *RMRB*, October 23, 1958.

Central Committee, celebrated the voluntary outpour of work during the Great Leap:

[T]here are currently 50 million people working around the clock for steel, without pay, without an eight-hour workday, without Sundays, without proper sleeping arrangements, resorting to makeshift shelters. What is this? This is conscious, unlimited, unpaid communist labor. Just imagine, without such labor, without this communist spirit, could we have achieved such high-speed construction? Such an enormous scale of labor, if it all required state funding and adhered to the principle of material incentives, would be utterly impossible. This massive, earth-shaking national labor movement is an unprecedented and profound revolutionary movement for the transition to communism. It is a revolution to transform the objective world as well as a revolution to transform the subjective world – this is how the transition to communism begins.[106]

In this vein, an article (written in response to Zhang's piece) in the *PLA Daily* stated, in no uncertain terms, that "[c]ommunist labor is *unpaid labor*, and communists should be unpaid laborers. The revolutionary's first concern should not be the material interests of the individual, but the common prosperity of the whole society."[107] Liu Shaoqi had celebrated the deployment of "free" labor, with workers toiling for "ten hours, twelve hours, twenty-four hours, some ... without interruption for forty-eight hours, fifty-six hours"; they had abolished piece-rate wages and refused overtime pay. That was the kind of labor required to achieve the transition to communism: "From what I see today, if you just all work like this," Liu concluded, "if workers and peasants all work like this, if workshop directors and factory managers work like this, if everyone works like this, then we will be able to build communism in no time at all."[108]

Benjamin Kindler sees here the emergence of a specifically communist concept of labor. If capitalist labor, even under socialism, was still defined by its exchangeability at a supposedly "equal" value, that is, by remuneration based on time or output or productivity, communist labor

---

[106] Xiong Fu 熊复, "Tongxiang gongchanzhuyi de daolu dakaile" 通向共产主义的道路打开了 [The road to communism is open], *RMRB*, November 7, 1958.

[107] "Yong gongchanzhuyi guandian kan fenpei zhidu. Gedi taolun zichanjieji faquan wenti" 用共产主义观点看分配制度。各地讨论资产阶级法权问题 [Looking at the distribution system using the concept of communism. Discussions on bourgeois legal rights in various places], *RMRB*, November 3, 1958. The original piece in the *Jiefangjun bao* 解放军报 was titled "Gongjizhi geng jiejin gongchanzhuyi" 供给制更接近共产主义 [The supply system is closer to communism]. Emphasis mine.

[108] Schoenhals, *Saltational Socialism*: 43. Liu's speech is from October 27, 1958, "Zai Jiangnan zaochuanchang gongren zuotanhui shang de jianghua" 在江南造船厂工人座谈会上的讲话 [Speech at the workers' symposium in the Jiangnan shipyard], in *Liu Shaoqi fangeming xiuzhengzhuyi huibian* 刘少奇反革命修正主义言论汇编 [Compilation of Liu Shaoqi's counterrevolutionary revisionist remarks]: 95.

could only be labor "gratis," meaning labor without remuneration, whose duration and effort were determined solely by the voluntary decision of politically conscious members of society.[109] Kindler makes it clear that this is not the humanistic idea of labor captured in Marx's passage about fishing in the morning and painting in the afternoon, but labor as necessary collective toil, the potential foundation of a new set of social relations. Yet it is one thing to argue that communist labor should be *unpaid*, meaning that it should be *unwaged*, subtracted from a system of commodity exchange and exploitative remuneration, workers being provided with what they need in an egalitarian system of distribution. It is quite another to reduce human life to laboring bodies, toiling incessantly, without interruption, and seemingly without end. The step from the former to the latter proved to be very small indeed.

We can see here in preliminary form that there was always the very implicit risk that "communist labor," rather than being foundational of a new society, could be reduced to extreme exploitation and further disciplining in the service of construction and accumulation, with disastrous consequences especially for how gendered work and social reproduction came to be evaluated, rewarded, and practically organized.[110] Liu Shaoqi quite ominously forecasted that, under communism, discipline will be firmer than at the present, and there will be less, not more, individual freedom.[111] As one of the Taiyuan weavers quoted in the *People's Daily* bleakly stated: "The happy life of communism is good, but now we have extra shifts and work hard around the clock; it is so stressful, what happiness is there to talk about if you die?"[112]

## 2.5    A Debate, Interrupted

The tone and direction of the debate turned almost abruptly by mid-November, and positive, radical assessments, ostensibly in line with Zhang Chunqiao's, disappeared. This shift in the public debate reflected one at the higher levels of the CCP and coincided with the first negative reports about the conditions in the newly created rural communes. That spurred Mao to much more cautious assessments concerning both the transition to communism and the question of ownership. At Zhengzhou,

---

[109] Kindler, *Writing to the Rhythm of Labor.* 131.
[110] Fabio Lanza, "The Search for a Socialist Everyday: The Urban Communes," in Alan Baumler, ed., *The Routledge Handbook of Revolutionary China* (London: Routledge, 2019): 74–88.
[111] Schoenhals, *Saltational Socialism*: 87–88.
[112] Zhang Minzhi and Cui Chengshan, "Jianshe shehuizhuyi shehui yao you gongchanzhuyi sixiang."

he cited "the proposals of various localities for a transition to ownership by the whole people (a necessary preparatory stage) in two to six years, or ten years to communism, as too short a period." He regarded a transition to communism as potentially feasible in fifteen years but did not want that forecast to be published, "presumably to avoid excessive pressure for that goal," according to Teiwes and Sun.[113] In what was clearly at least a partial retreat from his previous position, Mao also put the focus again on the issue of ownership, criticizing those comrades who objected to the dividing line between the two systems of ownership and arguing that the main goal of socialist construction was the transition to a higher stage of ownership.[114] In his later published notes, written during and after the Great Leap, Mao stressed that the expansion of QMSYZ to the entire country would take "a good many years" and that the transitional stage from "comparatively underdeveloped socialism to comparatively developed socialism, namely, communism," would take even longer than the one from capitalism to socialism.[115] At the Zhengzhou meeting, he criticized Chen Boda for having proposed the abolition of currency and of the commodity economy,[116] and, notwithstanding his approval of Zhang Chunqiao's critique of bourgeois right just a month earlier, "the Chairman now spoke of the need for unequal wages to remain for the time being."[117]

In the following months, the *People's Daily* published a steady stream of articles that vehemently rejected Zhang's critique and started shaping a new orthodox version of socialist economics, heralding what Maurice Meisner called "the Thermidorian reaction" to the Great Leap.[118] These contributions are too many, too repetitive, and too verbose for me to examine with any level of detail, so I will just try to provide here a quick summary of how this ideological resettlement was achieved and articulated. The repetitiveness and verboseness of this effort, however, should not be chalked up to the abstruse character of Party-speak or, worse, of Maoist politics. Rather, the size and the uniformity of the reaction to Zhang's (and Mao's) early prodding was symptomatic of the perceived danger their positions posed and aimed at re-creating some form of ideological stability. The debate on bourgeois right in 1958 had identified a crucial and unresolved issue in socialist society, the continued reproduction – not the lingering persistence – of capitalist categories

[113] Teiwes and Sun, *China's Road to Disaster*: 248.
[114] MacFarquhar, *The Origins of the Cultural Revolution*: 130. See also Chan, *Mao's Crusade*: 95.
[115] Mao, *A Critique of the Soviet Economics*: 68 and 58.
[116] MacFarquhar, *The Origins of the Cultural Revolution*: 130.
[117] Teiwes and Sun, *China's Road to Disaster*: 248.    [118] Meisner, *Mao's China and After*.

and social relations, which placed the very existence and raison d'être of the socialist state on much less firm footing.[119] The specter of the attack on bourgeois right needed to be exorcised, as it constituted a radical political challenge on the current organization of the state and its socioeconomic order. The verbal avalanche of 1959 aimed at obliterating that challenge.

Some essayists proceeded to deny the very premise of Zhang's criticism – that bourgeois right was constitutive of social relations under socialism and needed to be reduced and eliminated – either by willfully misrepresenting it or by discarding it wholesale. For example, "remuneration according to labor" was depicted as just a tool in the hands of the proletariat to force the exploiting classes to work in order to support themselves, thus eliminating (rather than re-creating) social differences.[120] In a socialist society, there can be no real bourgeois right, as there is no bourgeoisie whose interests it would be preserving.[121] Similarly, because under socialism there is no exploiting class, then exploitation itself must have also disappeared, and the wage differences within the socialist system cannot be confused with the hierarchy of the class society of the past.[122] The latter constituted real inequality, while in the socialist system, there were only "so-called inequalities" (*suowei bu pingdeng*所谓不平等). In the same way, one had to distinguish "bourgeois right" from "bourgeois-style right" (*zichanjieji shi faquan*资产阶级式法

---

[119]  Toward the end of the Cultural Revolution (and of his own life), Mao was candid about how easy it would be for the PRC to revert to capitalism, precisely because of the continuous operation of bourgeois right: "Our country at present practices a commodity system, and the wage system is unequal too, there being the eight-grade wage system, etc. These can only be restricted under the dictatorship of the proletariat. Thus it would be quite easy for people like Lin Piao [Biao] to push the capitalist system if they come to power. Therefore, we should read some more Marxist-Leninist works." "Marx, Engels and Lenin on the Dictatorship of the Proletariat," *Peking Review*, no. 9 (February 28, 1975): 5–12, www.marxists.org/subject/china/peking-review/1975/ PR1975-09a.htm. Originally published in *RMRB*, February 22, 1975.

[120]  Wu Dingqiu 吴定求, "Yao quanmian gujia 'anlaoquchou'" 要全面估价 '按劳取酬' [We have to fully appraise "remuneration according to labor"], *Renmin Ribao* (November 19, 1958).

[121]  Ji Xichao 池曦朝, "'Anlao quchou' bushi zichanjieji faquan" '按劳取酬'不是资产阶级法权 ["Remuneration according to labor" is not bourgeois right], *RMRB*, November 22, 1958; Hou Mingfang 侯明方, "Zichanjieji faquan canyu bushi zichan jieji faquan" 资产阶级法权残余不是资产阶级法权 [The remnants of bourgeois right are not bourgeois right], *RMRB*, January 3, 1959; Xue Muqiao 薛暮桥, "Shehuizhuyi shehui de anlaofenpei zhidu" 社会主义社会的按劳分配制度 [The remuneration according to labor system of socialist society], *RMRB*, October 23, 1959.

[122]  He Tianzhong 贺天中, "Anlaofuchou shi woguo muqian fenpei zhidu de jichu" 按劳付酬是我国目前分配制度的基础 [Remuneration according to labor is the foundation of the current distribution system of our country], *RMRB*, November 28, 1958.

权).[123] Therefore, what Zhang had called a "system of ranks" could only belong to the feudal past.[124]

Other contributors defused the substance of Zhang's critique by reducing the persistence of bourgeois right to a question of ideology (in the most basic and vulgar understanding of the term), thus turning a systemic issue inherent in the very organization of society and the economy into one of lack of education and low consciousness. According to this interpretation, bourgeois right was something that only existed in the minds of the majority of working people, who could not yet understand how to work for society without certain "rights."[125] Workers needed the material incentives provided under the wage system because they were not yet completely free from the shackles of the old ideological influences in their attitude toward labor.[126] So, while "remuneration according to labor" continued practically unchallenged, the masses had to be educated to see it within a historical concept of development, that is, as something necessary but neither sacrosanct nor impermanent, forecasting its always postponed elimination.[127]

Writing in *Hongqi* [Red flag], Xu Liqun reverted to the primacy of the development of productive forces to deny the possibility of any substantial expansion of the supply system at the present moment, postponing any such transformation to an undefined future. He argued that, under the existing conditions of relative scarcity, there were only two ways to enlarge the scope of the supply system: Reduce the communes' capital accumulation or request state subsidies. Needless to say, neither of these methods could be considered appropriate. It was therefore imperative to continue with "remuneration according to labor" and only very gradually increase the role of the supply system.[128]

[123] Cheng Zhaosheng 程钊生, "Fenqing liangzhong bupingdeng" 分清两种不平等 [Distinguish between two kinds of inequality], *RMRB*, December 3, 1958; Ren Zhongping 任仲平, "'Anlao fen pei' bushi zichanjieji faquan canyu" '按劳分配' 不是资产阶级法权残余 [Remuneration according to labor is not a remnant of bourgeois right], *RMRB*, February 12, 1959.
[124] Jiang Chunze 江春泽, "Gaixing gongzizhi bing mei you cuo" 改行工资制并没有错 [There is nothing wrong with switching to a salary system], *RMRB*, November 19, 1958.
[125] Xue Muqiao, "Shehuizhuyi shehui de anlaofenpei zhidu."
[126] Wang Pu 王璞, "Bu neng fouding wuzhi liyi yuanze" 不能否定物质利益原则 [We cannot deny the principle of material benefits], *RMRB*, January 20, 1959.
[127] Zhang Chengxian 张承先, "Jiaqiang gongchanzhuyi jiaoyu, jiasu shehuizhuyi jianshe" 加强共产主义教育 加速社会主义建设 [Strengthen communist education, speed up socialist construction], *RMRB*, January 22, 1959.
[128] Xu, Liqun, "Have We Already Reached the Stage of Communism?," in Robert R. Bowie and John K. Fairbank, eds., *Communist China, 1955–1959: Policy Documents with Analysis* (Cambridge, MA: Harvard University Press, 1962): 481. Originally published in *Hongqi*, November 16, 1958.

Perhaps the most interesting and most revealing strategy to foreclose the critical potential of the debate on bourgeois right was to firmly reinsert that discussion under the problematic of ownership, and thus within the boundaries of Stalin's conception of political economy, following here Mao's own shift at Zhengzhou. Zheng Jiqiao, revising his own position of just a couple of months earlier, stated that the ultimate difference between socialist and bourgeois society lay in the form of ownership; with the abolition of private ownership, then, "remuneration according to labor" "ceases to be the way the exploiting class exploits the working people (capitalist exploitation), and becomes the main principle of distribution among the working people."[129] Others refined that argument, stressing how the different conditions of production under socialism could not but determine different forms of distribution: "When ownership is changed, the principle of distribution of consumer goods, which is a consequence of ownership, cannot but be changed."[130] There was really no discussion about the fact that "conditions of production," even in their simplest understanding, could not be fully reduced to the form of ownership. It was simply assumed that "[u]nder capitalist private ownership, the surplus labor of workers creates surplus value for the capitalist. Under socialist public ownership (the collective ownership of the people's commune is a form of socialist public ownership), the entire product of labor is distributed according to the interests of the laborers."[131] The theoretical logic deployed here does not differ from the Soviet discourse on the political economy, and reduces the understanding of the problem of wages "as simply one of distribution, which is in turn made a mere function of the mode of ownership, rather than being explicated in dialectical terms as itself constitutive of social relations."[132] This was a dramatic political and theoretical retreat.

Two moments marked the official foreclosing of the debate on bourgeois right, at least in its Great Leap Forward phase. The first was the "Resolution on Several Issues Concerning the People's Communes," adopted by the Sixth Plenary Session of the Eighth Central Committee

---

[129] Zheng Jiqiao 郑季翘, "Zaitan xiaochu zichanjieji faquan" 再谈削除除资产阶级法权 [Discussing again the elimination of bourgeois right], *RMRB*, January 27, 1959.

[130] Sa Renxing 撒仁兴, "'Anlao fenpei' shi shehuizhuyi de yuanze" '按劳分配' 是社会主义 的原则 ["Remuneration according to labor" is a socialist principle], *RMRB*, February 19, 1959. Sa Renxing was the collective pen name for Wu Chuanqi, Lin Yushi, and the aforementioned Guan Feng.

[131] Chen Zhengren 陈正人, "Lun renmin gongshe de suoyouzhi he fenpei zhidu" 论人民公 社的所有制和分配制度 [About people's communes' ownership and distribution system], *RMRB*, October 18, 1959.

[132] Kindler, *Writing to the Rhythm of Labor*. 203.

of the CCP on December 10, 1958, which marked a temporary retrench-ment and a cooling-off of the Great Leap enthusiasm. The resolution made clear that the transition between forms of ownership depended on the "objective situation" of the development of the productive forces, thus pushing that transition to a much more distant and undefined future. But, more importantly, it made ownership once again the deter-minant factor on which the functioning of all other aspects of the socialist economy and socialist social relationship depended. It therefore reaffirmed that the socialist stage should continue to be defined by "remuneration according to labor," and that stage, rather than limiting and reducing the sphere of the commodity economy, should instead produce a massive increase in commodity production and exchange. The justification for that unfettered expansion was that "[s]uch com-modity production and commodity exchange differ from capitalist com-modity production and commodity exchange in that they are carried out systematically on the basis of socialist communal ownership and not anarchically on the basis of capitalist private ownership."[133]

The official line on the socialist economy was further solidified in a symposium on commodity production and the law of value held in Shanghai between April 3 and 22, 1959. Some 245 economists and social scientists attended the meeting where seventy-seven papers and surveys were presented. All the materials were later compiled by the Institute of Economics of the Chinese Academy of Sciences and published by the Science Press as a single, mammoth volume (1.27 million Chinese characters, over 800 pages).[134] This was clearly supposed to represent the final word in the debate, the manifestation of a reached consensus; it was specifically the consensus among those that Zhang Chunqiao had labeled as "the "economists," and the papers in the symposium strove to bring the discussion back under the confines of "the economic." The volume makes for an extremely long and frankly quite dull read, as the various authors tend to agree with each other and endlessly reiterate the main elements of the new doxa, focusing only on very minor and nuanced differences. They agreed that the commodity economy, the law of value, exchange at equal value, and remuneration according to labor were not only "capitalist remnants" that continued to exist under socialism, but essential, indispensable, and fundamentally beneficial fea-tures of the socialist economy, whose role for economic development

---

[133] "Guanyu renmin gongshe ruogan wenti de jueyi."

[134] See Zhang, ed., *Historical Perspectives on Chinese Economics*: 18. The volume was Zhongguo kexueyuan jingji yanjiusuo bian, *Guanyu shehuizhuyi zhiduxia shangpin shengchan he jiazhi guilüwenti. 1959 nian 4 yue taolunhui lunwen*.

went far beyond that of facilitating accounting and distribution of resources. Yet all these "capitalist" elements were also supposed to function in ways that were completely different from, if not alternative to, capitalism.[135] As for wages, which had been one of the focuses of the debate in the previous months, participants in the symposium decided that socialist workers, unlike workers under capitalism, were not selling their labor and that therefore salaries did not embody a form of commodity exchange; they just "represented" the quantity of labor expended by each worker rather than being given in exchange for labor.[136] In the discourse of the economists and social scientists gathered in Shanghai, the wage system was viewed simply as part of the "distribution" (*fenpei* 分配), and any real analysis of its function as "constitutive of social relations" was eschewed, precisely because this function did not belong squarely to the sphere of the economic. The same goes for all the other elements that were subsumed under the term "bourgeois right," which were reduced to an aftereffect of the level of productive development and of the forms of ownership. This was antithetical to the original articulations by Zhang Chunqiao and Mao Zedong, for whom "bourgeois right" was expressed by and embodied in social and productive relationships under socialism.[137]

By April 1959, then, the radical phase of the theoretical debate on the socialist economy, which had coincided with Great Leap collectivization, was forcefully terminated. I am tempted to add "temporarily" because some crucial issues within that debate (and some crucial figures, including Zhang Chunqiao) resurfaced in the discussion surrounding various editions of a volume on the political economy of socialism, associated with the so-called Shanghai School, in the 1970s.[138] Although the

---

[135] Zhongguo kexueyuan jingji yanjiusuo zhengzhi jingji xuezu 中国科学院经济研究所政治经济学组, "Guanyu shehuizhuyi zhiduxia shangpin shengchan he jiazhi guilu wenti de taolun" 关于社会主义制度下商品生产和价值规律问题的讨论 [Discussion on the production of commodities and the law of value under the socialist system], in *Guanyu shehuizhuyi zhiduxia shangpin shengchan he jiazhi guilüwenti*: 9. See also Zhang, ed., *Historical Perspectives on Chinese Economics*: 21–22.

[136] "Guanyu shehuizhuyi zhiduxia shangpin shengchan he jiazhi guilu wenti de taolun": 7. In his notes on the Soviet textbook on political economy, probably written in 1960, Mao accepted that the law of value served as an instrument of planning, but he made clear it should not be "the main basis of planning." He specifically stressed how the Great Leap was not conducted according to the law of value and would be completely incomprehensible if viewed from that perspective. Mao, *A Critique of the Soviet Economics*: 88.

[137] Kindler, *Writing to the Rhythm of Labor*: 204.

[138] See Christensen and Delman, "A Theory of Transitional Society"; Kindler, *Writing to the Rhythm of Labor*.

theoretical discussion was halted, the praxis associated with it endured. While communes in the countryside were restructured during and after the famine, experiments in collectivization continued unabated in the cities through 1959, and in early 1960, establishment of new urban communes was allowed even in China's five major cities, including Beijing, leading to a second, massive wave of the urban commune campaign. This will be the subject of the following chapters. Here I just want to stress that, while issues of wages, ownership, forms of remuneration, and the social inequalities they fostered had supposedly been explained away at the level of CCP orthodoxy by 1959, they continuously and stubbornly reemerged in the contradictory praxis of urban collectivization. And while practical attempts to veer away from that doxa were almost universally shut down, these issues remained unresolved and therefore always threatening.

# 3    The Gender of Labor

## 3.1    Retrenchment and Relaunch

The process of collectivization in the cities was dramatically slowed by the end of 1958, just a few hectic and potentially promising weeks since its inception in the late summer. This coincided with an ideological reversal, itself related to the emergence of a series of problems in the countryside, where collectivization had often proceeded very rapidly – and, at times, chaotically. Mao, who had been one of the early inspirations behind collectivization and of the theoretical discussion around it, was also central in this later slowdown. His November 1958 text, "Letter and Amendments on the 'Resolution of the Zhengzhou Conference on Certain Issues of the People's Commune,'" was approved by the central political bureau and transmitted to Party committees and Party groups at all levels. In the letter, Mao once again framed the problems of the communes as related to the issue of "transition," its pace, and the conditions for its completion. The achievement of socialist construction was supposed to be signaled by the universalization of "ownership by the whole people," and, Mao noted, that was far from being the case at the time. Newly founded rural communes practiced what Mao called "big collective ownership" (*da jiti suoyouzhi* 大集体所有制) or "small owner-ship by the whole people" (*xiao quanmin suoyouzhi* 小全民所有制), which had to be progressively transformed into full QMSYZ, by increasing the amount of commune products and means of production that were manufactured and distributed as part of the national plan. This 1958 letter sounded a note of caution. For if, just a few months earlier, Mao had framed a similar evaluation as ground for a hopeful call to action for communization, with the alluring prospect of achieved communism beckoning in the near future, here he cast the assessment as a forewarning. He proceeded to list a series of problems that afflicted the communes, affecting their organization, allocation system, forms of ownership, food, heating, and the balance of rest and work. And contrary to his rosy estimates of just a few months prior, here Mao forecasted that the solution to these problems would have to wait until the completion of the second or maybe even the third Five-Year Plan (or "ten years from now"). By then, the state would have reached an abundance of both means of production and consumer goods such as to guarantee the material basis needed for the adoption of QMSYZ and allocation according to needs.[1] Mao expressed even more restraint when it came to urban communes. While he left it to each locality to decide the pace of collectivization, he stated that "big cities should slow down" (*da chengshi yingdang fangman* 大城市应当放慢) and that "at the moment it was better not to excessively influence the existing habits and ways of life of city people" (*muqian buyi guoduo de qiandong chengshi renmin xianyou de shenghuo xiguan he fangfa* 目前不宜过多地牵动成市人民现有的生活习惯和方法).[2]

Mao's "amendments" were supposedly integrated in the resolution "On Some issues Concerning the People's Communes," adopted by the Sixth Plenary Session of the Eighth Central Committee of the CCP a month later and published in the *People's Daily* on December 19, 1958.[3] The resolution, briefly discussed in Chapter 2, cautioned that the three transitions – from cooperatives to communes, from collective to universal ownership, and from socialism to communism – were processes that, while interrelated, remained "distinct from each other." The transformation of the form of ownership depended "on the objective situation of the level of production development and the level of people's consciousness"; therefore, it could only be realized in stages and could not be left to the "subjective desires of the people." Similarly, the transition from socialism to communism was described as "a rather long and complex process of development" between two different economic systems, which relied primarily on the massive expansion of socialist commodity production and commodity exchange. Accordingly, if the socialist principle of "distribution according to labor" were to be prematurely abandoned, and a uniform supply system too hastily adopted, that would unavoidably "hamper people's enthusiasm for labor, which will not be conducive to the development of production, the increase of social products, and the realization of communism." The resolution chided those who, "attempting to 'enter communism' prematurely, try to

[1] Mao Zedong, "Dui 'Zhengzhou huiyi guanyu renmin gongshe ruogan wenti de jueyi' de xiugai he xinjian" 对 '郑州会议关于人民公社若干问题的决议' 的修改和信件, in *Jianguo yilai Mao Zedong wengao* 7 (November 11–12, 1958): 513–521 (516). See also MacFarquhar, *The Origins of the Cultural Revolution*: 131.
[2] Mao Zedong, "Dui 'Zhengzhou huiyi guanyu renmin gongshe ruogan wenti de jueyi' de xiugai he xinjian": 517.
[3] "Guanyu renmin gongshe ruogan wenti de jueyi."

abolish commodity production and commodity exchange prematurely and prematurely deny the positive role of commodities, value, money, and prices."[4] The resolution also cautioned against the uniformity that could be produced by a rash expansion of the supply system, arguing that people will continue to have different needs even under communism, and therefore commune members should be given as much freedom of choice as possible.[5] As discussed in Chapter 2, the persistence of commodity production, commodity exchange, and the law of value had been the central issue in the 1958 debate on the socialist economy and bourgeois right. With the December resolution, then the Central Committee directly entered that debate, taking a stand against those proposals and arguments that aimed at accelerating the socialist transition through political interventions and mass experimentations. The resolution brought that discussion back within the confines established by the Stalinist doxa but also reasserted the "productive forces determinism" supported by many of the "economists" and the role of "the economic" as a separate sphere, which should continue to function free of any political intervention.

Earlier that year, Zhang Chunqiao and others (including Mao) had specifically identified the praxis of urban collectivization as the way to reduce the role of those elements of "bourgeois right" operating in the socialist city, and the resolution addressed that experience directly, but restricted its import and relevance to the issues of ownership and ideological consciousness. While the resolution stressed once again the role of urban communes as a crucial tool for transforming old cities into new socialist cities, it also bluntly remarked that cities were indeed different from rural areas (*chengshi he nongcun you suobutong* 城市和农村有所不同). First, the situation in the cities was "more complex" than that of the countryside. Second, QMSYZ was already the main form of ownership in urban areas, and urban factories, schools, and agencies had already reached a high level of socialist organization. "Third, many capitalists and intellectuals in the cities are still strongly bourgeois in their thinking, and they still have concerns about the establishment of communes." Therefore, cities should continue to promote a limited number of pilot experiments in collectivization, but large urban centers should take it slow, and only engage in preparatory work (*yunniang gongzuo* 酝酿工作). For the time being, the goal was to gain more experience and continue to raise the ideological consciousness of urban residents.[6]

---

[4] Chen Boda was supposedly an eminent representative of this way of thinking. See MacFarquhar, *The Origins of the Cultural Revolution*: 130.
[5] On this issue, see Chapter 4.  [6] "Guanyu renmin gongshe ruogan wenti de jueyi."

The resolution de facto halted the creation of new communes in major urban centers (including, of course, the capital), but that does not mean that efforts at collectivization ceased abruptly. Quite the contrary. As I illustrate below, in Beijing, the period from early 1959 to early 1960 witnessed a rapid development of collective production and collective welfare services. Historian Li Duanxiang labeled it a period of "consolidation" or "rectification" (*zhengdun* 整顿), involving first and foremost the central link of the urban communes, that is, the development of production in order to build "a strong material foundation." The rectification was also intended to address issues affecting the economic relationships between the state, the commune, and its members, specifically the allocation of salaries and resources, as well as to reform the ideological consciousness of city residents through extensive and in-depth political education.[7]

The political line against communization lasted for about a year. By the end of 1959, after the Lushan conference, which marked both a rethinking and a restarting of the Great Leap,[8] Mao and other leaders at various levels of the Party showed renewed enthusiasm for the process of urban collectivization. On December 17, 1959, the Hebei provincial committee sent to the Central Committee a report on the "problems of the urban people's communes," which described the apparent success the province had in establishing communes in the cities.[9] The report called, once again, for caution and for the primacy of production: It urged against rushing to implement an universal ownership system, asserted that wages had to be kept low, and that the capital accumulation by the commune should be used first to expand reproduction and improve production conditions, and only at a later time to organize collective welfare undertakings.[10] Upon such provisions urban communes were to be reinvigorated. According to Li Duanxiang, the central authorities were satisfied with the Hebei report, and Liu Shaoqi instructed Deng Xiaoping to distribute it to all the members of the Politburo.[11]

In early March, in part in response to the Hebei report and to a similar one from Heilongjiang, the Central Committee of the CCP released their

---

[7] Li, *Chengshi renmin gongshe yundong yanjiu*: 96–100.
[8] MacFarquhar, *The Origins of the Cultural Revolution*: 250. Alessandro Russo provides an original and very interesting analysis of the Lushan conference in chapter 2 of his *Cultural Revolution and Revolutionary Culture* (Durham, NC: Duke University Press, 2020).
[9] Li, *Chengshi renmin gongshe yundong yanjiu*: 107. In the case of Hebei, all urban communes seemed to involve some combination of industry and agriculture and encompassed some cultivated land.
[10] Li, *Chengshi renmin gongshe yundong yanjiu*: 111.
[11] Li, *Chengshi renmin gongshe yundong yanjiu*: 110.

"Instructions on the Problems of the Urban People's Communes," which was slated for immediate distribution to all levels of the administration and the Party, including the Xinhua News Agency and the *People's Daily*. The document called for an enthusiastic attitude (*jiji de taidu* 积极的态度) in organizing and expanding urban communes. Citing the experience of the previous year, they celebrated the fact that communes could adopt different structures, sizes, and organizational models, and that different forms of ownership would continue to coexist, sometimes within the same commune. That was described as both unavoidable and very good. Because the communes had shown the potential to transform the city, and especially to transform the lives of a large number of housewives, they had been generally welcome by the laboring masses. However, the report warned, more affluent, upper-class families still harbored concerns about urban communes, so participation in collective enterprises and services should remain on a strictly voluntary basis. Possibly to allay those fears, local newspapers were encouraged to advertise the establishment of neighborhood factories and collective welfare services but were not allowed to print news concerning the founding of actual communes, nor should there be any mass public parade or celebration of such an event. Finally, in the five major cities of Beijing, Shanghai, Tianjin, Wuhan, and Guangzhou, it was advisable to proceed with some restraint and avoid putting up commune signs on every street. However, these cities were now allowed to slowly again start establishing communes, relying on the masses to carry on all the practical work, under the coordination provided by the All-China Federation of Trade Unions and its local branches.[12] The document was sent out with two attachments: "The Development of the Xiangfang Commune in Harbin" (*Ha'erbinshi Xiangfang renmin gongshe de fazhan qingkuang* 哈尔滨市香坊人民公社的发展情况, February 23, 1960) and "Report of the Henan Provincial Committee on the Consolidation and Development of the Urban Communes" (*Henan shengwei guanyu chengshi renmin gongshe gonggu he fazhan qingkuang de baogao* 河南省委关于城市人民公社巩固和发展情况的报告, February 28, 1960), both of which detailed successful models of urban collectivization. The Central Committee accordingly concluded by encouraging localities to send representatives to visit communes in Harbin (Heilongjiang province), Zhengzhou (Henan province), and Tianjin.

---

[12] HDA, 1-112-127 Zhongyang guanyu chengshi renmin gongshe wenti de pishi 中央关于城市人民公社問題的批示 [Central Committee's instructions on the problems of urban people's communes], March 16, 1960. This was a *pishi* 批示, a commentary by a superior (or a higher lever in the government structure) on a report by a subordinate.

Henan and Heilongjiang had indeed emerged as pioneers in the commune campaign, and according to a March 25, 1960, survey published in the *Neibucankao*, these were the two provinces with the highest rate of urban collectivization, with 90 percent and 80 percent of the population, respectively, already under the commune umbrella. But even in places like Shanghai and Zhejiang, where urban communes had not yet been officially formed, neighborhood collectivization had advanced during the previous year, and those locations had already achieved the "embryonic form" (*chuxing* 雏形) of the commune. Shanghai, the survey reported, had 947 *lilong* committees (*lilong* 里弄 being the typical Shanghai lane neighborhood); 4,600 neighborhood enterprises employing 12,000 workers; 1,600 canteens, with 11,000 employees and 400,000 customers; 2,100 child care centers with 13,000 caregivers and 130,000 children served; 3,200 service centers with 20,000 employees; and 880 locally run (*minban* 民办) middle and elementary schools, with about 200,000 students.[13] The survey gave a similarly impressive picture for the entire country: Industrial production of commune and neighborhood enterprises (not including SOEs under the commune jurisdiction) had reached 20 billion yuan nationally in 1959, which was equivalent to 65.8 percent of the entire production of SOEs and joint state-private companies in 1949. As for collective welfare, 50,000 childcare centers and 53,000 canteens had been created. About three quarters of the communes were organized around neighborhood enterprises, the remaining being centered around a factory or a government agency. The survey once again pointed out that even places where the label of "commune" had not yet been officially adopted had reached an "embryonic form." Setting aside the issue of the accuracy of such estimates, it seems evident that this surfeit of data was deployed to highlight the progress and overall success of urban collectivization in the previous months, despite the partial slowdown of 1959, and to set the stage for relaunch. Accordingly, the rest of the survey was devoted to listing and examining (again, with abundance of nationwide data) proofs of the "powerful vitality and unparalleled superiority" (*qiangda de shengmingli he wubi de youyue* 强大的生命力和无比的优越) of the communes. These included developing production through mobilization of latent labor force, improving residents' lives through collective welfare and increased revenue, transforming forms of ownership, as well as profoundly

---

[13] "Quanguo chengshi renmin gongshe qingkuang diaocha" 全国城市人民公社情况调查 [Survey of the situation of urban people's communes nationwide], March 25, 1960, *Neibucankao*: 2.

changing both the people's ideological outlook and their daily practices.[14]

In Beijing, the shift in policy was echoed in a March 26, 1960, speech by Peng Siming, vice president of the Beijing Federation of Trade Unions, the organization tasked with coordinating communization, in which, while admitting the complexity of the urban situation, he celebrated the successes of pilot communes, mentioning Beixinqiao and Shijingshan by name. Given the success of these pilot programs and "at the Party's request," Peng stated, the urban people's commune movement should be carried out everywhere. It was a big endeavor, but one that should be pursued quickly; some places around the country were making rapid progress, therefore Beijing should move even faster.[15]

The official relaunch of full-fledged urban collectivization took place at the meeting of the second session of the Second National People's Congress (NPC) (March 30 to April 10, 1960). An article in the March 31 issue of the *People's Daily* entitled "We Definitely Must Continue to Leap Forward, We Definitely Can Continue to Leap Forward" recounted the opening of the Congress, with speeches celebrating the achievements of the previous year, which included reaching the goals of the second Five-Year Plan with three years to spare.[16] The draft economic plan for 1960 reasserted "the policy of developing industry and agriculture simultaneously under the condition of giving priority to the development of heavy industry," and the forecast was equally auspicious, with a prospected 23 percent yearly increase in the industrial and agricultural output. Significantly, the article concluded with an extremely positive evaluation of the experience of the urban communes since 1958: They were praised for the development of production and social services, but also for having freed from tedious household chores "tens of millions of urban housewives," who were now "participating in neighborhood industries, cultural and sanitary undertakings, and various collective welfare undertakings." "The new and tremendous development of the urban people's commune movement," the *People's Daily* reported, "is an event of great historical significance, as the communes

---

[14] "Quanguo chengshi renmin gongshe qingkuang diaocha": 4–6.

[15] BMA 101-001-00768 Guanyu chengshi renmin gongshe wenti Peng Siming fuzhuxi xiang youguan gonghui ganbu de baogao jilu ji benhui de diaochabiao 关于城市人民公社问题彭思明副主席向有关工会干部的报告记录及本会的调查表 [Records of the report of Vice President Peng Siming to relevant trade union officials on the issue of urban people's communes and survey by the union], March 26, 1960.

[16] "Yiding yao jixu yuejin, yiding neng jixu yuejin" 一定要继续跃进，一定能继续跃进 [We definitely must continue to leap forward, we definitely can continue to leap forward], *RMRB*, March 31, 1960.

will not only free urban housewives from domestic work and create more favorable conditions for the development of urban production and construction, but they also represent a very good organizational form for further restructuring people's economic and cultural life in the cities and completely transforming the old cities." On the basis of that evaluation, speakers at the meeting concluded that the growth of urban people's communes would be "a new and significant positive factor in achieving our continued leap forward in 1960 and beyond."[17]

A few days later, on April 9, the secretaries of the municipal committees of the five major cities (Beijing, Shanghai, Tianjin, Wuhan, and Guangzhou) delivered a joint statement at the NPC in which they summarized the discussions of the previous months and repeated (often verbatim) many of the main points. Wan Li, Cao Diqiu, Wan Xiaotang, Song Yiping, and Zhu Guang praised the results achieved since 1958, when urban collectivization started "on a trial basis": More than one year of practice had "proven that people's communes are also perfectly suitable to big cities, and they are warmly welcomed by the general public." Therefore, the secretaries argued that major cities should be allowed to proceed with further collectivization, step by step.[18] Cities should first establish communes centered around neighborhoods, and only later those around factories and government agencies. Yet "because of the differences in ideological consciousness, income, living standards and habits" of city residents, and the consequent lingering suspicions about communes, especially among merchants and intellectuals, participation in communes and collective services should remain strictly voluntary, and no one who harbors concerns should be forced to take part.[19]

As a result of this shift in policy, "China's cities were basically transformed into people's communes." A survey by the ACFTU reported that, by the end of July 1960, 1,604 people's communes had been established in 190 large- and medium-sized cities in China, with more than 55 million members, 77 percent of the total population of those cities.[20] Urban communes had set up 76,000 public canteens, to which one should add

[17] "Yiding yao jixu yuejin, yiding neng jixu yuejin."
[18] "Zhonggong Beijing, Shanghai, Tianjin, Wuhan, Guangzhou wushi shiwei shuji zai rendahui shang lianhe fayan dachengshi bixu zhubu fenpi shixian gongshehua" 中共北京、上海、天津、武汉、广州五市市委书记　在人大会上联合发言　大城市必须逐步分批实现公社化 [The municipal party committee secretaries of Beijing, Shanghai, Tianjin, Wuhan, and Guangzhou spoke jointly at the National People's Congress], *RMRB*, April 10, 1960.
[19] "Zhonggong Beijing, Shanghai, Tianjin, Wuhan, Guangzhou wushi shiwei shuji zai rendahui shang lianhe fayan dachengshi bixu zhubu fenpi shixian gongshehua."
[20] Li Duanxiang 李端祥, "Chengshi renmin gongshehua yundong de xingwang yu lishi jiaoxun" 城市人民公社化运动的兴亡与历史教训 [The rise and fall of the urban people's

the 170,000 public canteens run by SOEs, government institutions, and schools, for a total of 60 million customers. Over 9 million children were enrolled in childcare centers, and over 8.5 million "idle" residents had been mobilized, including more than 5.8 million women.[21]

In the rest of this chapter, I focus on the evolution of the urban commune campaign in Beijing during the "rectification" stage in 1959 and the full-blown relaunch in 1960. While no new communes were formed in the capital after the initial wave of 1958, the existing ones remained in operation, and further experiments in collectivization were put in motion in several other areas. When the campaign was restarted in earnest in 1960, a high tide of collectivization ensued, during which there was a massive explosion in the number of communes. For the sake of organization, I will split the analysis according to the three main goals of urban collectivization: production, welfare, and women's liberation/new daily life. For all three aspects, the sources recorded very positive outcomes, not only by laying out a plethora of statistical data (rising production outputs, number of residents fed and children cared for, improvements in hygiene and literacy), but also and more significantly by reporting women's voices. Female workers celebrated their liberation from household chores and their productive life in commune enterprises, and, more vividly, they cherished the newly found freedom and ability to satisfy long-repressed yet everyday desires – for leisure, entertainment, and often, very simply, free time.

Yet the promises of collectivized life were eventually undermined by a series of problems, and in 1959 and especially in 1960 the contradictions already inherent in the initial phase of this project became fully evident. It is not surprising that each of the three arenas experienced deficiencies, given the monumental tasks collectivization was supposed to tackle, the speed with which it proceeded, the limited resources allotted to it, and, more critically, the very brief span of time in which such a complex experiment was allowed to be conducted. Yet what emerged more clearly in this phase was that the major tensions lay in the presupposed reciprocal relationship among these three areas – production, welfare, liberation. This relationship tied a radical social revolution to forms of labor and

---

commune movement and its lessons for history], *Qiusuo* 求索 [Explore], no. 7 (2004): 233.

[21] Liu Zhenqing, "Chengshi renmin gongshe shulun": 98. See also Li Duanxiang 李端祥 and Xiao Chuchu 肖楚楚, "Chengshi renmin gongshe gonggong shitang chengyin tanxi" 城市人民公社公共食堂成因探析 [An analysis of the causes for the formation of public canteens in urban people's communes], *Hunan keji daxue xuebao (shehui kexue ban)* 湖南科技大学学报（社会科学版）[Journal of the Hunan University of Science and Technology (Social Science Edition)] 17:6 (November 2014): 102–106.

structures of remuneration that remained antithetical to it and was grounded on the attempt to replace the complex process of social reproduction with collectivized services, still poorly managed. "Liberation" was conceived simply as moving people into productive labor, housewives included, whereas any genuine form of liberation cannot be that, as I explore in the last section of the chapter, engaging the debates on social reproduction theory among Marxist feminists. The experiment of urban communes brought to the fore women's desires, but these desires were often deemed antithetical to the kind of selfless labor and participation required by collectivization. In narrating their newly achieved freedom, commune housewives-turned-workers implicitly highlighted some of the blind spots of that project of liberation, specifically that it disregarded and overlooked much of the hidden labor of social reproduction and ended up reducing it to a set of dull, repetitive, and mundane tasks that could be easily transferred to canteens and kindergartens. In that context, newly collectivized female workers kept toiling to achieve the promises of liberation, while vocally pointing out the inherent limitations in how that project had been conceived.

## 3.2    Communal Production and What Made It Possible

Two reports compiled a few months apart in 1960 provide a detailed picture of the situation in Beijing. The first, "Survey of Urban People's Communes," was released on April 30, just a few weeks after the period of "rectification" had ended, and the commune movement had been restarted. The impression it conveys is that of a massive, city-wide push, which clearly relied on previous preparatory work. Beijing now featured thirty-eight communes (a huge jump from the original six founded in 1958), with almost 1.4 million members, or 63.8 percent of the city's population. (See Map 3.1.) Three of the communes were centered on a SOE factory, with the other thirty-five based on neighborhood enterprises; thirty-four of those had between 10,000 and 50,000 members and only one exceeded 200,000 members. The data concerning industrial production is quite staggering: The overall output of collective enterprises was reported to be three times that of December 1959, and yet in the same period the average salary of commune workers had dropped from ¥25.11 to ¥21.64. A large part of that output took the form of contract work for SOE factories, but there were also a fair number of products for daily use (*wei shenghuo fuwu* 为生活服务). Beijing commune factories were not involved in steel production.[22] By the end of the year,

---

[22] BMA 133-010-00462, Chengshi renmin gongshe yici xing diaocha 城市人民公社一次性调查 [One-time survey of urban people's communes], April 30, 1960.

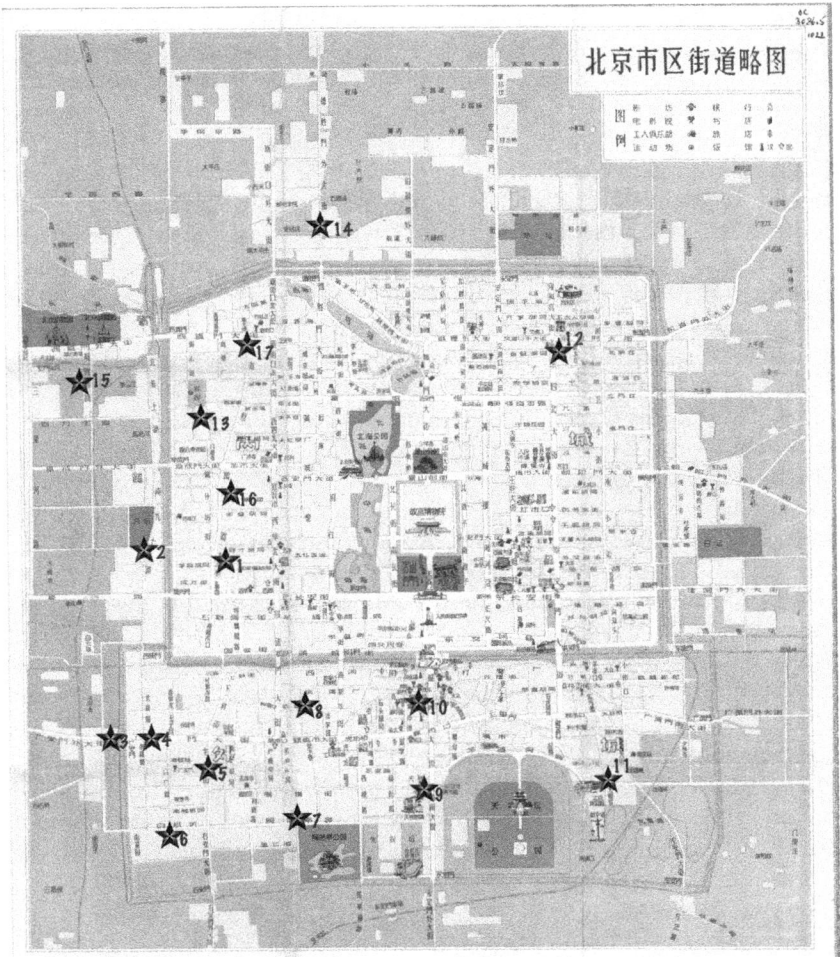

Map 3.1 Approximate locations of some of the communes in central Beijing (based on a 1959 Beijing travel map). 1. Erlonglu; 2. Yuetan; 3. Guang(an'men)wai; 4. Guang(an'men)nei; 5. Niujie; 6. Baizhifang; 7. Taoranting; 8. Chunshu; 9. Tianqiao; 10. Dashilar; 11. Tiyuguanlu; 12. Beixinqiao; 13. Fusuijing; 14. De(shengmen)wai; 15. Zhanlanlu; 16. Fengsheng; 17. Xinjiekou.

according to a shorter, less exhaustive survey, Beijing had forty-eight communes, albeit at different stages in their organizational development, which comprised 67.8 percent of the city population and 23.78 percent of its labor force.[23]

According to documents produced at the district level, arrangements for further collectivization had been made in advance of the second session of the NPC and collective industrial enterprises had continued to steadily develop throughout 1959. The picture was, once again, one of unmitigated success, at least at the level of sheer productive output. In Xuanwu, the district had created an Office for the People's Commune Movement (*Renmin gongshehua yundong bangongshi* 人民公社化运动办公室), and by early April they transmitted to the CCP municipal committee requests from seven of the eight subdistrict offices to officially establish communes. The committee granted all the requests, and the official inauguration was set for April 15.[24] The Guang'anmennei subdistrict office boasted that it had already mobilized 77.7 percent of the "unused labor" in the area; these workers were now staffing eighteen factories and five small production groups, manufacturing 118 different kinds of products (including sulfuric acid reagent, sewing machines, and radios) for a total value of 3 million yuan just for the month of March.[25] Guang'anmennei was representative of the other aspiring communes in Xuanwu, all of which recorded high levels of mobilization among the available labor force (between 68 and 86 percent of all the people who could participate in labor), despite different social compositions among the various areas, as well as similarly impressive production outputs, in terms of both value and variety. The industrial sector in the Niujie subdistrict had recorded an output value of about 6 million yuan in 1959, but they had already reached that quota by the

[23] BMA 133-010-00463, Chengshi renmin gongshe jiben qingkuang diaocha 城市人民公社基本情况调查 [Survey on the basic situation of urban people's communes], December 1960.

[24] The district already had one commune, Chunshu, founded in 1958. The other seven were Guangnei 广内、Guangwai 广外、Dashilar 大栅栏、Baizhifang 白纸坊、Tianqiao 天桥、Taoranting 陶然亭、and Niujie 牛街. XDS 1-23-202-1, [Xuanwuqu gongshehua bangongshi] chengli renmin gongshe xiang shiwei de qingshi, shiwei de pifu ji gongshehua yunding zongjie [宜武区公社化办公室]成立人民公社向市委的请示、市委的批复及公社化运动总结 [Xuanwu District Communization Office's request to the Municipal Committee for the establishment of a people's commune, the Municipal Committee's approval and a summary of the communization campaign], April 1960.

[25] XDS 1-23-202-1 Zhonggong Xuanwu quwei guanyu jianli Guangnei danshichu renmin gongshe de qingkuang 中共宜武区委关于建立广内办事处人民公社的请示 [Request for instructions from the Xuanwu District Party Committee on the establishment of a people's commune in the Guangnei subdistrict], April 3, 1960.

first quarter of 1960.[26] Even more impressive was the improvement at Dashilar, whose 1959 output was valued at almost 10 million yuan, an achievement they had already surpassed in the first three months of 1960, reaching over 13 million yuan. Dashilar also touted the excellence of their products, which included high-quality tools, such as current sensors (*dianliu ganyinqi* 电流感应器), for which they had supposedly attained the level of SOE factories.[27] Similarly, factories in the Tianqiao subdistrict had produced ferric oxide at a 99.12 percent level of purity, the national standard for "advanced level."[28]

Overall, the collectivized industries in the district were reported to be manufacturing a wide array of products, ranging in level of sophistication from objects for everyday use, like electrical equipment and hardware, to materials for larger factories – chemicals, insulation, mica condensers, machine tools, and tungsten from discarded light bulbs – and even hypodermic needles. This remarkable industrial effort was supported, in all of these communes, by a set of new collective services, canteens, childcare centers, and service centers, and some localities provided educational opportunities in after-hours classes. Yet in these overall glowing assessments, we can see a hint of one major problem that will affect urban communes in the months ahead: the relatively low percentage of workers and members making use of the collective welfare offerings, primarily childcare and communal eating, with canteens registering attendances as low as 25 percent and rarely above 50 percent, even in this initial, feverish phase.[29]

In Xicheng district, neighborhood factories had realized an overall revenue of 30 million yuan and a profit of 6 million by the end of 1959. Their output of over 500 products was in large part (about 67 percent) absorbed by SOEs, who subcontracted work to these enterprises and often provided materials. For example, the talcum factory at Yuetan

---

[26] XDS 1-23-202-1 Zhonggong Xuanwu quwei guanyu Niujie jiedao banshichu jianli renmin gongshe wenti qingshi 中共宣武区委关于牛街街道办事处建立人民公社问题请示 [Request for instructions from the Xuanwu District Party Committee on the establishment of a people's commune in the Niujie subdistrict], April 8, 1960.

[27] XDS 1-23-202-1 Zhonggong Xuanwu quwei guanyu Dashilar jiedao banshichu jianli renmin gongshe wenti qingshi 中共宣武区委关于大栅栏街道办事处建立人民公社问题请示 [Request for instructions from the Xuanwu District Party Committee on the establishment of a people's commune in the Dashilar subdistrict], April 8, 1960.

[28] XDS 1-23-202-1 Zhonggong Xuanwu quwei guanyu Tianqiao jiedao banshichu jianli renmin gongshe wenti qingshi 中共宣武区委关于天桥街道办事处建立人民公社问题请示 [Request for instructions from the Xuanwu District Party Committee on the establishment of a people's commune in the Tianqiao subdistrict], April 8, 1960.

[29] Dashilar had the lowest recorded attendance, 24 percent of the people involved in production and social services. XDS 1-23-202-1 Zhonggong xuanwuquwei guanyu Dashilar jiedao banshichu jianli renmin gongshe wenti qingshi.

produced fifty tons of quartz powder (*shiyingfen* 石英粉) and the paint factory at Erlonglu over ten tons of paint solvent, all for SOE production. The Fengsheng model factory made electric resistors for use in high-tech industries, and one factory at Fusuijing fulfilled one third of the production quota for the (state-owned) Tiantan hat factory. Some of these factories, in pure Great Leap style, used discarded materials, such as a chemical factory at Xinjiekou, which recycled caustic soda mud to produce over 500 tons of calcium carbonate. Neighborhood industries also took over production lines that had been discontinued or abandoned by SOEs, including goods for the commercial sector, thus "freeing" larger factories, which were less flexible in responding to "the needs of the [consumer] market." By December 1959, twenty-eight factories in the district were devoted to manufacturing consumer goods: They produced 250,000 pairs of shoes, but also handicraft objects for export (cloisonné, embroidery, and jade). In 1959, the hardware factory at Xinjiekou had produced 64,400 coal shovels, 44,900 metal dustpans, and 900 ovens.[30] In April 1960, on the anniversary of two years of "street-level collectivization," the high tide of establishing communes took over Xicheng as well, with eight new communes created. By then, the district had 143 factories, 102 of them with more than 100 employees, manufacturing over 600 products, including millivoltmeters, carbon rods (*tanjingban* 炭精棒), electric controllers, and electric switches, all as part of contracts with larger SOE factories. Their overall output value had gone from ¥8,230,000 in January to over ¥30 million in May, an almost four-fold increase.[31] Most of the communes in the district comprised schools, government agencies, and residential areas, and, aside from Yuetan,

---

[30] XDN 7-1-211-3 Xicheng quwei guanyu jiedao shengchan fuwu gongzuo qingkuang de baogao 西城区委关于街道生产服务工作情况的报告 [Report of the Xicheng District Committee on the situation of neighborhood production and services], December 28, 1959. The report was addressed to the city party committee. The archive file also has an alternative number, 7-1-211-45.

[31] XDN 7-1-807 Zhonggong Beijingshi Xicheng quwei guanyu chengshi jiedao renmin gongshe gongzuo wenti de baogao (cao'an) 中共北京市西城区委关于城市街道人民公社工作问题的报告 (草案) [Report of the Beijing Xicheng District Committee of the CCP on the work of urban people's communes in neighborhoods (draft)], June 16, 1960. The eight new communes were East Chang'an 西长安, Guangqiao 广桥, Fusuijing 福绥境, Fengsheng 丰盛, Xinjiekou 新街口, De(shengmen)wai 德外, Zhanlanlu 展览路, plus Erlonglu 二龙路, which had been established in 1958. Yuetan 月坛 also petitioned to become a commune but that was delayed. Chongwen district witnessed a similar development: The district also had one commune founded in 1958 but the other six subdistrict offices all petitioned to establish communes in April 1960. BMA 001-006-01703-13 Chongwenqu guanyu jiedao banshichu zuzhi qilai de qingkuang he chengli renmin gongshe riqi de qingshi baogao 崇文区关于街道办事处组织起来的情况和成立人民公社日期的请示报告 [Report of Chongwen District on the organization of subdistrict offices and on the request for a date to establish people's communes], April 8, 1960.

did not have any significant industrial production before the Great Leap. Here too rates of mobilization of the "idle" (*xianzhi* 闲置) population ranged between 78 percent and 87 percent, except for Zhanlanlu, which only managed 62 percent.[32]

Given the central role it was supposed to have in the functioning of communal enterprises, a brief aside is needed here on the status of what these sources call "the market." A series of new studies have revised the widely held assumption that the Mao era was "void of market activity"; rather, rural and urban residents continued to engage in underground, illegal, or semi-legal private trade exchanges, which were often essential for their survival and at times grew to constitute a sizable portion of the economy.[33] However, this is not what these government documents mean when they call for responding to "the needs of the market." Here that term refers first and foremost to those forms of trade and services that satisfied the social needs of urban residents and that were not inscribed under the plan. That was, for example, the case for a section of the haircutting trade, which I will describe in the next chapter, with small or itinerant barbers providing services outside any form of planned economy or cooperative organization. By the mid 1950s, while the state had become dominant in wholesale trade, retail trade presented a much more complex picture, with private enterprises and co-ops taking a larger share. And while the share of private retail kept diminishing (down to 2.7 percent in 1957), the state was not supposed to be dominant in retail trade.[34] In 1956 a new policy was introduced, stipulating that "for 'commodities supplied in fragmentary quantities and of varied and complicated patterns,'… factories in future were to manufacture these goods for their own account. State commerce was to have priority for their purchase which would be on a selective basis." The rest could be marketed directly by the factories or consigned to state commerce and sold on commission. Similarly, except for materials in short supply, factories were to purchase them on the "free market." "It was hoped that the new system would lead factories to pay closer attention to consumer demand."[35] Urban commune production was specifically

---

[32] XDN 7-6-88-9 Zhonggong Xichengqu zhanlanlu dangwei guanyu shenqing chengli renmin gongshe de baogao 中共西城区展览路党委关于申请成立人民公社的报告 [Report of the Xicheng District Zhanlanlu Party Committee on the application to establish a people's commune], April 10, 1960. The folder 7-6-88 includes a series of similar reports on the founding of all the other communes in the district.

[33] Adam K. Frost and Zeren Li, "Markets under Mao: Measuring Underground Activity in the Early PRC," *China Quarterly* 258 (June 2024): 309–328; Chunying Wang and Y. Yvon Wang, "Gray Markets in the Great Leap: Prosecuting 'Profiteering' in Liangshan County, Shandong, 1958–1960," *Modern China* 48:5 (2022): 948–981.

[34] Audrey Donnithorne, *China's Economic System* (New York: Praeger, 1967): 279.

[35] Donnithorne, *China's Economic System*: 281–282.

geared, as mentioned earlier, to remedy shortages by either locally manufacturing products that were needed by urban residents (and that were not
included by the state plan) or helping to supply semi-manufactured goods
to SOEs or larger factories. Commune products for everyday social needs
were commercialized and distributed by the municipal commercial departments (branches of the state commercial organs). These commercial
departments were considered to be in the best position to determine the
gaps in supply and unfulfilled demands to which commune production
was supposed to respond, and they were also charged with distributing the
finished products.[36] Finally, "the market" for commune products, especially handicrafts, also included foreign trade, which remained very
important as a source of foreign currency throughout the Mao era.[37]

Documents about the "pilot" communes of Erlonglu (Xicheng) and
Chunshu (Xuanwu) restated, with a sometimes-excruciating level of
detail, the successes of rapid industrialization at the street level in
1959 and early 1960, while also hinting at the specific conditions in
which this process took place and to which it was supposed to respond.
The commune industrial sectors at Erlonglu had developed steadily and
at dazzling speed, with total output in the fourth quarter of 1959 reaching
141.4 percent of that in the third quarter. About 1,500 residents had
entered the commune's fifteen factories as of December 1959, but that
number had grown to over 3,200 by July 1960.[38] Commune production
was explicitly supposed to make up for the collapse in the availability of
daily necessities during the Great Leap, in large part due to the transformation of handicraft co-ops into subsidiaries of SOE production.
Erlonglu's factories stepped in and reportedly produced 32 percent of
everyday necessities in the area. The relatively small size of these enterprises and their labor-intensive, low-technology character made them
flexible and therefore able to adapt to the shifting needs – and unpredictable scarcities – of the period. An Erlonglu stovepipe factory resolved the

[36] Donnithorne, *China's Economic System*: 289.
[37] Jason M. Kelly, *Market Maoists: The Communist Origins of China's Capitalist Ascent* (Cambridge, MA: Harvard University Press, 2021).
[38] XDN 7-1-211-1 Erlonglu renmin gongshe shidian qingkuang de baogao (Erlonglu jiedao dangwei); XDN 7-1-211-2 Xicheng quwei guanyu Erlonglu renmin gongshe shidian qingkuang de baogao 西城区委关于二龙路人民公社试点情况的报告 [Report by the Xicheng district party committee on the situation at the pilot test of Erlonglu people's commune]; XDN 38-1-34-2 Zhonggong Erlonglu gongshe weiyuanhui 中共二龙路公社委员会 [Party committee of the Erlonglu commune], Beijingshi Erlonglu gongshe gongye jiben qingkuang 北京市二龙路人民公社工业基本情况 [Basic conditions of the industrial sector of the Erlonglu people's commune in Beijing], July 30, 1960.

issue of a shortage of metal, by converting its entire production to clay chimneys.[39] Commune factories at Chunshu were also asked to intervene in similar situations and reported similar levels of output improvement. In June 1959, when there was a city-wide scarcity of vials for eyedrops, the commune glass factory manufactured 370,000 vials between June and October. At its founding, the factory could only produce a small number of simple glass objects and had only a couple of skilled workers; about a year later, it turned out eleven kinds of ampoules and several common glass instruments. Among the 113 workers who had been there for eight to nine months, 34 had already reached the equivalent skills of first- or second-level workers in a larger factory.[40] In February 1959, when schools reopened, there was a sudden need for chalk, and by April the Chunshu Fine Arts Factory (*meigongchang* 美工厂) had fulfilled the task of producing 39,000 boxes of chalk. By the end of 1959, this factory was responsible for 50 percent of the plasterwork objects produced in the entire city.[41] Also singled out for praise was the Chunshu chemical factory, which had started in July 1958 with only seven workers in one room, with one big pot and one bellow, where they could only produce ferrous sulfate ($FeSO_4$). By November 1959 they had 300 workers, 90 rooms, and seven ball mills, and they had added six chemical compounds to their output, for a monthly total value of ¥555,800, 11.2 times what they had achieved in January of the same year.[42] The factory recycled discarded sulfuric acid and by December 1959 had become the sole provider of ferrous sulfate for the city's chemical industry.[43] The eight factories in the Chunshu commune were responsible for a total of 71 products, forty of which they marketed directly, not only providing for the "needs of the [consumer]

---

[39]  XDN 38-1-34-2 Beijingshi Erlonglu gongshe gongye jiben qingkuang.
[40]  XDS 15-1-13-2 Dali fazhan jiedao shengchan wei dagongye wei renmin shenghuo xuyao fuwu (Xuanwuqu Chunshu jiedao dangwei shuji Liu Yong) 大力发展街道生产为大工业为人民生活需要服务(宣武区椿树街道党委书记刘涌)        [Vigorously develop neighborhood industry to serve big industries and to serve the people's needs (Liu Yong, secretary of the party committee of the Chunshu neighborhood, Xuanwu District)], 1959; XDS 15-1-13-5 Chunshu renmin gongshe yinianlai fazhan qingkuang de diaocha 椿树人民公社一年来发展情况的调查 [Survey on the development of the Chunshu People's Commune in the past year], December 28, 1959.
[41]  XDS 15-1-13-2 Dali fazhan jiedao shengchan wei dagongye wei renmin shenghuo xuyao fuwu.
[42]  XDS 15-1-13-5 Chunshu renmin gongshe yinianlai fazhan qingkuang de diaocha.
[43]  XDS 15-1-13-10 Zhonggong Chunshu dangwei guanyu renmin gongshe shidian gongzuo de baogao (chugao) 中共椿树党委关于人民公社试点工作的报告(初稿) [Report of the Chunshu Party Committee on the pilot work of the people's commune (preliminary draft)], December 31, 1959.

market" in Beijing, but also sending their wares all the way to Baotou, Datong, and Zhangjiakou.[44]

If we take these reports to be more or less accurate – and I don't see why we should not, at least for the overall picture, if not for the granular data – then it seems clear that the industrial sector of the Beijing communes was considered to provide a positive contribution to the development of the socialist economy. As already noted, and as I analyze further below, urban communes were supposed to collectively organize productive labor, and their overall goals programmatically exceeded the confines of the factory and of industrial work. Yet even if one focuses only on the side and sites of production, communes' successes and failures were not to be measured as if they were normatively economic (i.e., capitalist) forms, that is, according to their sheer profitability. Even those economists and social scientists who had maintained that the law of value and other elements of bourgeois right should continue to operate under socialism argued that their main function was to guarantee the maximum efficiency of the planned economy, or to "achieve the maximum economic effect with the minimum labor consumption."[45] In this perspective, the law of value was what assured "economy of time and the planned distribution of labor time among the different sectors of production." Under socialism, "price, profit, price of production, etc. reflected the conscious and organized relations of production of the workers who possess the means of production."[46]

Urban collectivization was described as a central feature in the nationwide push to "increase production and reduce expenses" (zengchan jieyue 增产节约),[47] and, as I illustrated in Chapter 1, communes were organizations born out of conditions of scarcity and were programmatically based on principles of extreme frugality. Yet while, as Lu Duanfang has argued, the production of urban space under Maoism was overwhelmingly defined by those conditions of scarcity and by the need to keep urban consumption down to the minimum,[48] urban collectivization was

---

[44] XDS 15-1-13-5 Chunshu renmin gongshe yinianlai fazhan qingkuang de diaocha.

[45] Sun Yefang 孙冶方, "Qian guilü, wan guilü, jiazhi guilü diyitiao" 千规律，万规律，价值规律第一条 [There are a thousand laws, but the first is the law of value], *Guangming Ribao* 光明日报, October 28, 1978.

[46] Sun Yefang 孙冶方, "Yao quanmian tihui Mao Zhuxi guanyu jiazhi guilü wenti de lunshu" 要全面体会毛主席关于价值规律问题的论述 [We must fully appreciate Chairman Mao's exposition on the question of the law of value], *Jingji Yanjiu* 经济研究 [Economic research] 11 (1978). Sun Yefang wrote this piece during the Socialist Education Movement but did not publish it until 1978.

[47] XDN 7-1-211-3 Xicheng quwei guanyu jiedao shengchan fuwu gongzuo qingkuang de baogao.

[48] Lu, *Remaking Chinese Urban Form*: 11 and 58. The restrictions on urban consumption were meant to promote (heavy) industrial development.

configured and thought of as *the way* to overcome those conditions, with frugality, efficiency, and meticulous use of resources eventually leading to a shared abundance. Therefore, the effectiveness of collectivized production, as the examples above indicate, could be measured on the basis, first, of its overall output, its ability to effectively manufacture a variety of goods; and, second, of its ability to reduce waste, that is, to achieve maximum efficiency, in terms of both resources (hence the emphasis on recycling) and labor time. Most of the surplus revenue generated by the industrial sector – after salaries and taxes – was supposed to go to the commune administration to be reinvested in production, with only a portion allocated for welfare and educational activities.[49] In August 1959, the Erlonglu commune reinvested 96.7 percent of its profits,[50] while at Chunshu, in 1959, 53.3 percent of the commune's gross revenue was allocated to capital accumulation and expanded reproduction (*kuoda zaishengchan* 扩大再生产), with the rest going mostly to salaries, welfare, hygiene, and education, with salaries being ten times more than welfare. Stated expectations were that the proportion of capital accumulation would steadily increase, and that of expenses decrease.[51] In so doing, commune enterprises would be creating an ever-efficient loop of continuously boosted production and continuously reduced waste and expenses. As historian Joshua Goldstein has argued, recycling under socialism "was framed as a momentary inversion of capitalism," turning consumption into a productive contribution, returning consumed materials into the productive cycle.[52] That commune production often centered the recycling of discarded materials was due to practical conditions of scarcity but also was evidence of its superior socialist character. Collective socialist production was supposed to be not only more profitable but better in every aspect, including in its use of labor and resources.[53]

Yet there were inherent and profound strains affecting communes' collective organization of productive labor. First and foremost, that labor

[49] XDN 38-1-13-2 Beijingshi Xichengqu renmin gongshe shixing zhangcheng (cao'an) 北京市西城区人民公社试行章程（草案）[Experimental charter of the people's communes in Beijing's Xicheng district (draft)], April 5, 1960.

[50] XDN 7-1-211-2 Xicheng quwei guanyu Erlonglu renmin gongshe shidian qingkuang de baogao.

[51] XDS 15-1-13-10 Zhonggong Chunshu dangwei guanyu renmin gongshe shidian gongzuo de baogao (chugao).

[52] Joshua Goldstein, *Remains of the Everyday: A Century of Recycling in Beijing* (Berkeley: University of California Press, 2020): 137.

[53] Hanchao Lu notes that even human hair and nails were traded in, and "barbershops routinely collected customers' hair to sell to the depots. A saying went that 'there is no useless garbage, only misplaced resources.'" Lu, *Shanghai Tai Chi*: 147.

remained, at least in part, waged, and as discussed in Chapter 2, the salary form and remuneration according to labor remained a thorny issue at the core of the socialist economy. In this phase, communes purposely moved to more "progressive" forms and structures of remuneration. Reports from Beijing communes were all adamantly supportive of the widespread adoption of time-based wages (hourly or monthly), plus possible bonuses, and of the gradual elimination of piece-rate wages. Piece-rate was considered a more "primitive" form and one that directly promoted "economism" (*jingjizhuyi* 经济主义), that is, workers' tendency to focus exclusively on immediate monetary rewards.[54] Workers on piece-rate wages also tended to receive higher salaries. In Dongcheng district, piece-rate wages were ¥4.8 higher than hourly ones, and at Erlonglu the average difference was ¥30 versus ¥21.[55] Commune salaries were meager by design, and both service and factory jobs were defined as "low pay." This was part and parcel of a system that was supposed to reduce the role of direct monetary rewards and material incentives, while increasing both production and the direct allocation of goods and services. Low salaries meant increased capital accumulation at the commune level, to be devoted to expanded reproduction and welfare. Commune documents explicitly connected the elimination of piece-rate wages with depression of average wages and concurrent increase of commune's capital accumulation.[56] Low remuneration for collective labor was supposed to be made tolerable by and was essential to the expansion of both production and welfare services.

At Xicheng, the average salary in 1959 was ¥19, with five ranks ranging between ¥15 and ¥30,[57] while at Dongcheng it was ¥24.56, which was considered very high according to the city regulations.[58]

[54] XDN 7-1-211-3 Xicheng quwei guanyu jiedao shengchan fuwu gongzuo qingkuang de baogao.

[55] XDN 28-1-94-2 Dui Erlonglu renmin gongshe xiezuopian zonghechang zuzhi qingkuang de diaocha cailiao 对二龙路人民公社协作片综合厂组织情况的调查材料 [Investigation materials on the organization of the collaborative sectors in the general factory of the Erlonglu People's Commune], May 17, 1960; BMA 110-001-01098 Beijingshi laodongju dangzu 北京市劳动局党组 [Party Leadership Group of the Beijing Municipal Labor Bureau], Guanyu chengshi renmin gongshe laodong gongzi he laobao fuli gongzuo de wenti he jiejue yijian 关于城市人民公社劳动工资和劳保福利工作的问题和解决意见 [Problems and suggestions concerning labor wages, labor insurance and welafare in urban people's communes], July 1960.

[56] XDS 15-1-13-10 Zhonggong Chunshu dangwei guanyu renmin gongshe shidian gongzuo de baogao (chugao).

[57] XDN 7-1-211-3 Xicheng quwei guanyu jiedao shengchan fuwu gongzuo qingkuang de baogao.

[58] BMA 110-001-01098 Guanyu chengshi renmin gongshe laodong gongzi he laobao fuli gongzuo de wenti he jiejue yijian.

At Baizhifang (白纸坊, in Xuanwu district) the average pay for a neighborhood factory worker was ¥24 (in February 1960), while the Erlonglu General Factory paid only ¥15 per month (as of May 1960).[59] And while a few of the communes had announced plans for a slight rise in the average pay,[60] most of the attention seemed to be geared toward keeping the salaries as low as possible, limiting increases, and actively reducing the income of those few workers who were considered to be overpaid. At Dongcheng, 5.6 percent of the newly mobilized "housewives" earned more than ¥40 per month, which was more than the starting salary of a teacher or an apprentice. Salaries of specialized workers in commune factories were also uncommonly high, in part because these workers were more likely to have been transferred from other factories (meaning they were not "housewives"; they were male workers), and the same was the case for "model skilled workers."[61] As a rule, wages in commune enterprises had to be kept below those of SOE employees.[62]

And here another crucial tension emerges, one intimately tied to the different characterization of commune and SOE labor: The former was gendered female, the latter male. Low salaries for (female) commune workers were directly connected with and partially justified by the perceived lack of technical skills among the newly recruited labor force. Officers at various levels complained repeatedly of the cultural and technical levels of both industry and service workers, which made it difficult, if not impossible, for them to adapt to the developing needs of production and to achieve the goal of full mechanization and technological revolution.[63] But while reports celebrated the occasional instance of workers acquiring high technical abilities,[64] mechanization was, in fact, usually postponed to a distant future, precisely because commune

---

[59] XDS 14-2-6-10 Dui Beizhifang guanjie ge danwei dangwei shuji huiyi yanjiu zuzhi renmin jingji shenghuo de jianghua gao 对白纸坊管节各单位党委书记会议研究组织人民经济生活的讲话稿 [Transcript of the speech delivered at the meeting of the party committee secretaries of the work units under the Baizhifang area to discuss organizing people's economic life], February 1960; XDN 28-1-94-2 Dui Erlonglu renmin gongshe xiezuopian zonghechang zuzhi qingkuang de diaocha cailiao.

[60] XDN 7-1-211-2 Xicheng quwei guanyu Erlonglu renmin gongshe shidian qingkuang de baogao; XDN 7-1-211-3 Xicheng quwei guanyu jiedao shengchan fuwu gongzuo qingkuang de baogao.

[61] BMA 110-001-01098 Guanyu chengshi renmin gongshe laodong gongzi he laobao fuli gongzuo de wenti he jiejue yijian. The report cited one male employee of the auto repair factory, who had been an officer for the KMT and then sent to a reeducation camp, where he learned the skills that now gained him a monthly salary of ninety yuan.

[62] XDN 38-1-13-2 Beijingshi Xichengqu renmin gongshe shixing zhangcheng (cao'an).

[63] XDN 7-1-807 Zhonggong Beijingshi Xicheng quwei guanyu chengshi jiedao renmin gongshe gongzuo wenti de baogao (cao'an).

[64] XDS 15-1-13-5 Chunshu renmin gongshe yinianlai fazhan qingkuang de diaocha.

production was supposed not to require capital investment and was therefore by definition based on low-skill, labor-intensive processes. Low skill and low pay were therefore as much a feature as they were a bug; commune work was labor-intensive, repetitive, and underpaid because it was supposed to be labor-intensive, repetitive, and underpaid. As such, it fit "housewives" with no training; thus, while being performed by women, that labor was gendered as "simple," in an unvirtuous cycle of reproductive logic.

Reports from a jade factory at Dashilar provide an example of both the conditions in which commune production often took place and the kind of effort that was ideally required from female workers to achieve that production. This was a factory founded in late 1958, originally staffed by eight "housewives" and equipped with eight old pedal-propelled machines to grind jade; they were subcontracted for finishing work by the Beijing municipal jade factory. The workers hated the grinding sound of the machines; in the winter, they had to spend the day with their hands in freezing water, and it was very easy to cut oneself. Initially, productivity was incredibly low and so was quality: it took them half a month to produce one fish-shaped piece, which also did not look lifelike at all. Yet by December 1959, the factory employed ninety-six workers, they had acquired three electric machines, and they had made significant improvements in both productivity and quality – no mention whether working conditions had also improved. This transformation was achieved through intense ideological pressure from local leaders, who convinced workers not to leave the factory and pushed them through a series of "socialist competitions" aimed at increasing productivity through labor self-discipline. The effects were recorded at the individual level. One of the workers, Su Jinhai, had three children, and she had no peace of mind while at work, so she would sneak home to check on her kids; but when the competition started, she was afraid of lagging behind, so she stopped. Another worker, Lu Aju, used to tease her coworkers and make them giggle, but she became focused solely on her productivity and stopped laughing during the competitions. Two workers, Liu Yuhua and Jin Suyin, engaged in a fierce battle over individual productivity, challenging each other on who could make more jade fishes in a month. Liu was described as working fanatically, not stopping even for a drink of water or to use the bathroom, while Jin managed to maintain her promised quota despite missing two days of work to care for a sick child. Perhaps the best model of what kind of labor was implicitly (and explicitly) prescribed for these workers was exemplified by Zhang Xingzhen, who was so impressed by the life-like quality of the fishes an old master had produced that she became "obsessed," thinking non-stop about how to draw the tail or the cheeks, tossing and turning in bed, sleeplessly drawing fish shapes on her own belly. Spurred by this frantic effort, productivity did indeed double, with faster workers teaching the others how to work more quickly.[65] Other reports single out an individual case of abnegation and dedication: At Erlonglu, Sun Guilan, who, despite the biting cold that made her hands bleed, kept repairing trucks through the winter and who, in less than a year, had mastered the technique to work on lathes.[66] Meanwhile, at the electric tools factory at Dashilar, Zhao Chunli was named district model worker for never taking time off and often working past midnight.[67]

The pressure of this labor-intensive production could become an issue, as factory leaders demanded – and workers sometimes self-imposed – longer workdays. This was the case in Xuanwu district, where neighborhood factory workers worked for twelve to thirteen hours a day, with worrisome rates of safety accidents. The district had to intervene and mandate rest days, breaks for nursing, and the eight-hour day.[68] Given that, in most cases, the work was also boring and repetitive and often involved using recycled scraps,[69] it is not too surprising that in some areas the mobilization of "housewives" became difficult, with potential workers, especially those who were young and with some elementary schooling, refusing to be employed by the commune and asking instead for jobs in SOE factories, where the conditions were better and there were possibilities for career improvement.[70]

---

[65] XDS 13-2-17-3 Dashilar yuqi jiagongchang pinglun cailiao 大栅兰玉器加工厂评比材料 [Evaluation materials about the Dashilar jade processing factory], December 24, 1959. I assume that jade objects were produced for export, which was a crucial source of foreign currency for the state.

[66] XDN 7-6-88-2 Erlonglu renmin gongshe choubei weiyuanhui gongzuo baogao 二龙路人民公社筹备委员会工作报告 [Report on the work of the preparatory committee of the Erlonglu people's commune], 1960.

[67] XDS 13-2-17-3 Dashilar yuqi jiagongchang pinglun cailiao.

[68] XDS 15-1-13-4 Zai Dang de lingdaoxia dagao qunzhong yundong, zhe shi yinianlai jiedao gongzuo qude de lingyitiao zhongyao de jingyan 在党的领导下大搞群众运动，这是一年来街道工作取得的另一条重要的经验 [The mass movement under the leadership of the Party is another important experience achieved in the neighborhood work over the past year], January 29, 1959.

[69] BMA 101-001-00782-1 Chongwenqu zixingche lingjian chang qionggan kugan, zili gengsheng shixian jixiehua banjixiehua shengchan 崇文区自行车零件厂穷干苦干、自力更生实现机械化半机械化生产 [The Chongwen District bicycle components factory works hard and self-reliantly to achieve mechanized and semi-mechanized production], February 15, 1960; XDN 28-1-94-2 Dui Erlonglu renmin gongshe xiezuopian zonghechang zuzhi qingkuang de diaocha cailiao.

[70] BMA 110-001-01098 Guanyu chengshi renmin gongshe laodong gongzi he laobao fuli gongzuo de wenti he jiejue yijian. At the Caoguang 草厂 residential committee in Dongcheng district, 30 percent of the available labor force (all healthy, relatively educated people, with no major family obligations) refused to work in a commune factory.

The frantic, bare-bones, bottom-up character of commune industrial work also led to other issues, which reports recorded next to the sky-rocketing outputs. Many of the collective factories, created as part of a mass movement, had not been integrated into the overall state plan for industrial production, meaning that there was no designated system for either the provision of raw materials (another reason for the emphasis on recycling scraps) or the distribution of finished products. Even if factories were solely responsible for procuring their own supplies, some materials were only available as part of the state plan, in which the communes were not participant. At Xicheng, out of 143 commune factories, 38 had major issues either in receiving a steady supply of materials or in selling their finished products, or both.[71] This uncertainty affected every aspect of management and production, including technical improvement and labor organization. Factories were forced to send out supply and marketing personnel, wasting time and resources, and making unified management of the market impossible.[72] Factory managers were left to decide what to produce, blindly following what was available and possible, often falling prey to "capitalist mentality" and "selfish departmentalism."[73] These tendencies sometimes manifested in practices such as using state-distributed materials for one enterprise's own use, exchanging products among enterprises, engaging in barter trade, or purchasing illegally from the market, often with precious commune capital. Such scavenging was widespread. The Erlonglu Art Accessories Factory illegally purchased 500 leather balls for kids, and cut them open to make drumming sticks. The Yuetan electric factory apparently sold motors they were supposed to repair to buy chemicals they needed for production. Four factories of the Zhanlanglu commune were all found to be pilfering large quantities of materials (including wires, steel, etc.), even stealing within the commune, with a factory taking bricks from a child-care center. Prices were often set arbitrarily, leading to speculation and

---

[71] XDN 7-1-807 Zhonggong Beijingshi Xicheng quwei guanyu chengshi jiedao renmin gongshe gongzuo wenti de baogao (cao'an).

[72] BMA 119-001-00400-8 Fang Shi 方石, *Guan Baozhang* 关保章, *Ouyang Dou* 欧阳斗, "Guanyu Beixinqiao diqu gongshehua hou caimao gongzuo bianhua qingkuang de dianxing diaocha he dui chengshi renmin gongshe caimao tizhi de yijian" 关于北新桥地区公社化后财贸工作变化情况的典型调查和对城市人民公社财贸体制的意见 [Survey on changes in finance and trade work in the Beixinqiao area after communization and opinions on the finance and trade system of the urban people's communes], April 16, 1960.

[73] BMA 001-006-01703-4 Xicheng quwei guanyu zhengdun jiedao renmin gongshe de yijian de baogao 西城区委关于整顿接到人民公社的意见的报告 [Report of Xicheng District Committee on correcting the opinions received from the people's commune], July 20, 1960.

profiteering.[74] Under those conditions, personnel were also a problem, with managers hiring people independently, sometimes from other factories, or workers taking up second jobs and hopping from one factory to the next (*tiaochang* 跳厂).[75]

In some cases, this devolved into overtly corrupt practices, like one factory at Yuetan that borrowed ¥90,000 from a bank but only needed ¥20,000, and ended up wasting the extra money on food and booze (*dachi dahe* 大吃大喝); at the Erlonglu General Factory, they spent ¥603 between January and April 1960 on lodging and entertainment (*zhaodaifei* 招待费), of which ¥431 was for food and ¥172 for alcohol, tea, and sweets. A worker at Xi Chang'an named Wang went on a purchasing mission for two months, spent ¥375 inviting people to dinner, and used company funds to buy 1,000 *jin* of stuff to give a friend of his, while getting reimbursed for all his expenses (which included barbers, a camera, shoes, and other items).[76]

Officers often tended to blame the corruption and the problems on the ideological deficiencies of workers and managers, among whom they identified an alarming presence of "bad elements," and they called for heightened educational work and thought reform, together with a cleansing of the cadre ranks. Yet while there might have been plenty of untrustworthy elements within the commune leaderships, the problems, as the reports document, were structural and systemic, and went far beyond the individual characters of managers or leaders. I will examine

---

[74] XDN 7-1-807 Zhonggong Beijingshi Xicheng quwei guanyu chengshi jiedao renmin gongshe gongzuo wenti de baogao (cao'an).

[75] BMA 110-001-01098 Guanyu chengshi renmin gongshe laodong gongzi he laobao fuli gongzuo de wenti he jiejue yijian. In Dongcheng district, there were 468 people in areas under commune jurisdiction who had temporary jobs outside the district, and there were 201 people from outside with temp jobs in the communes. In Chongwen district, communes were reported to have "illegally" hired people who should be working in some other *danwei*, people without *hukou* (rural residents), people who had voluntarily quit or retired from another job, people who had been laid off by other units, and people who did not reside in that district. BMA 001-006-01703-14 Chongwen quwei guanyu ge renmin gongshe lanshou renyuan de jiancha baogao 崇文区委关于各人民公社滥收人员的检查报告 [Chongwen district committee's inspection report on the indiscriminate hiring of personnel by the people's communes] (May 17, 1960). Rural residents flowing into the city in search of better jobs (and escaping the famine) were of particular concern, see BMA 001-006-01703-2 Dongchengqu weiyuanhui 东城区委员会 [Dongcheng district party committee], Guanyu chunjie gongshe shengchan, fuwu zuzhi lingdao chengfen jinxing chuli gongzuo de yijian 关于纯洁公社生产、服务组织领导成分进行处理工作的意见 [Suggestion on how to conduct the cleansing of the class status of leaders in communal production and service organization], May 14, 1960.

[76] XDN 7-1-807 Zhonggong Beijingshi Xicheng quwei guanyu chengshi jiedao renmin gongshe gongzuo wenti de baogao (cao'an).

in Chapter 5 how these problems reached a crisis level in the final, declining phase of urban collectivization.

## 3.3    Socializing Housework

Collective welfare services were, as described in Chapter 1, a necessary counterpart to the mobilization of "housewives" for neighborhood production, a counterpart that, while indispensable, often remained logically, ideologically, and practically secondary to it. As concisely summarized in a late 1959 report, "neighborhood services are a part of the social welfare sector, and they are organizations created by the masses of urban residents to provide services to the residents themselves, *on the basis of the development of neighborhood production.*" They were supposed to take over the trivial "household chores."[77] Paralleling the expansion of collective production, social welfare services were also reported to have witnessed a massive increase in 1959 and early 1960. The archival documents are, once again, effusive, at least in terms of numbers. A report by the Beijing ACWF praised the increase in childcare centers, which in June 1959 had gone from 418 to 1,300 citywide, with over 5,000 caregivers serving 70,000 children. They also cited two anecdotes to exemplify the benefits provided, both to children and to production: They singled out the case of a child suffering from generalized edema who was cured thanks to the tender care of the staff at a nursery in Chongwen; and they recognized a female worker who had achieved stellar productivity in her factory once the neighborhood kindergarten had solved the problem of her children's care.[78] A few months later, in April 1960, Beijing had 3,151 communal canteens, 2,423 childcare centers (among which 903 kindergartens and 181 nurseries), 12 old people's homes, and 1,952 service centers, which provided housework, washing and mending clothes, and also bathhouses and barbers.

---

[77] Original text: "街道服务事业是社会福利事业的一部分，是在街道生产发展的基础上，居民群众组织起来进行自我服务的组织." Emphasis mine. See also XDN 7-1-211-3 Xicheng quwei guanyu jiedao shengchan fuwu gongzuo qingkuang de baogao.

[78] BMA 084-001-00149-4 Beijingshi funü lianhehui dangzu 北京市妇女联合会党组 [Party committee of the Beijing ACWF], Guanyu fazhan he gonggu jiedao tuo'er zuzhi de qingkuang baogao 关于发展和巩固街道托儿组织的情况报告 [Report on the development and consolidation of neighborhood childcare organizations], June 19, 1959. The report does not specify what was the cause of the child's swelling, but it mentions that he was cured with a "special diet" (*tebie yingyang* 特别营养). Given that this episode took place during the famine, one wonders whether the child wasn't simply malnourished.

Communes and neighborhoods had established 157 schools, 155 of which offered after-hours instruction.[79]

By the end of 1959, Chunshu, one of the earlier communes, comprised thirty childcare centers and nine canteens, all adhering to the principle of "serving production." If the factory worked overtime, so did the kindergarten; in the canteens, hot food was available all hours of the day and could also be delivered to the factory.[80] The centers had 187 employees and served a total of 1,555 children. This was the result of a long, concerted effort, starting from a shoestring operation run by "housewives," who were initially reluctant to engage in service work, which they considered as "having no future." Improvement and expansion required both ideological and professional education through a series of internal campaigns. Throughout 1959, the commune sent 132 childcare workers to training classes promoted by the district education and healthcare offices while also organizing research groups and classes in every single center. In May they launched the movement "in loving children, the *ayi* rivals the mom" (*re'ai haizi, ayi sai mama* 热爱孩子,阿姨赛妈妈), followed by a "study, compare, and catch up" campaign (*xue, bi, gan* 学, 比, 赶), which invited units to learn from model enterprises until they achieved comparable outcomes.[81] When the Chunshu commune first evaluated the quality of the centers and ranked them, only five of them (16.7 percent) were deemed "first level," but by December twenty-three of them had achieved that status. Caregivers also took responsibility for washing the kids, mending their clothes, cutting their hair, and making bibs. One kindergarten, at Sichuan ying, was singled out for praise, in part for implementing strict hygiene rules, with health checks in the morning and at noon, and a full-body examination once per season, thus making sure diseases were detected early. That summer, no child was sick with dysentery.

The Chunshu commune canteens employed twenty-nine people and served 682 customers; in the previous year they had been allocated thirty-seven rooms, big stoves had replaced briquet ovens, and they also now had vegetable choppers, roasting ovens, and dough presses, leading to improved hygiene, better service, and extended hours. The canteen in

---

[79] BMA 133-010-00462 Chengshi renmin gongshe yici diaocha.
[80] XDS 15-1-13-2 Dali fazhan jiedao shengchan wei dagongye wei renmin shenghuo xuyao fuwu.
[81] XDS 15-1-13-6 Chunshu renmin gongshe yinianlai fazhan qingkuang de diaocha (er) 椿树人民公社一年来发展情况的调查(二) [Investigation report on the development of the Chunshu people's commune over the past year (two)]. Here the term *ayi* ("auntie," "nanny") is used to indicate the caregiver. It's an affectionate term, commonly used for both nannies at home and professional caregivers in kindergarten.

the fourth lane of Xianglu ying grew from forty to over a hundred customers, with only three people doing food prep plus the manager, fifty-six-year-old Zheng Wenxiu, who went to the market every morning at 5 am to buy vegetables. The canteen was praised for cleanliness and good accounting, which allowed for equitable prices: ¥7 per month for children, ¥12 for adults. They did not have fixed times for meals, but they saved the food for regular customers and delivered it to the pregnant, the elderly, and the sick.[82]

Despite inherent limitations, communes attempted to make up for as much as possible of the practical and emotional labor of social reproduction, which, however, they did not (and perhaps could not) understand as an integrated process, so they reduced it to a list of "trivial and burdensome" (*fansuo* 繁琐) matters, the endlessly repetitive and minute tasks of housework. For example, the Chunshu service centers provided washing and repairing of clothes, but also helped with things like starting the fire, boiling water, taking people to the doctor, caring for the old and the pregnant, and accompanying kids to and from school.[83] One service center in the commune provided over 100 different services, and they were accordingly praised for "a full list of services, delivered in a flexible way, and very popular with the masses."[84] Xuanwu district, of which Chunshu was part, celebrated a similar expansion of service centers, which official reports explicitly connected with a massive improvement in the overall quality of life. Specifically, the "washing and dyeing" subsector (*xiranye* 洗染业) had grown by 280 percent in 1959 and by a further 14 percent in early 1960. This corresponded to an increase in the quality of the clothing that was washed and dyed (wool and cotton), which in turn meant an increase in the consumption of high-end clothing (84.5 percent more from 1959 to 1960). At the same time, they embarked on a campaign to economize cotton, taking apart old clothes and making new ones (*chaizuomianyi lingxiusuibu* 拆作棉衣 另修碎补), and between September and November 1959, they made 4,845 items of clothing. By January 1960, the district service centers had 1,515 employees, used 342 sewing machines, and, in the busy season of September to November, they had washed and mended over 400,000

[82] XDS 15-1-13-6 Chunshu renmin gongshe yinianlai fazhan qingkuang de diaocha (er).
[83] XDS 15-1-13-2 Dali fazhan jiedao shengchan wei dagongye wei renmin shenghuo xuyao fuwu.
[84] BMA 001-006-01703-12 Chunshu gongshe diyi dadui fuwuzhan de qingkuang 椿树公社第一大队服务站的情况 [The situation of the first brigade service center at the Chunshu commune], April 23, 1960.

pieces of clothing.[85] Besides taking care of washing and mending clothes, the Xuanwu centers also provided other major services, including distributing goods in local stores, conducting sanitation and hygiene work, going door to door to help with household chores and family care, and cutting hair.[86]

In Xicheng district, progress had been slower and more modest. At the end of 1959, district service centers did not have the capacity to take over much of the housework, and the CCP committee suggested developing service teams that were smaller in size, dispersed, and easy to be run by the masses (the method of *xiao, tu, qun* 小, 土, 群). Similarly, collective canteens were asked to develop a self-sufficient production base for foodstuff by linking up directly with rural communes. They were also supposed to start raising chickens, ducks, and rabbits, and to make their own pickles and condiments, without harming the sanitation of the city. Food was supposed to be of high quality but also fit the desires of the masses, cheaper and better than what could be made at home.[87] By March, the situation seemed to have substantially improved, according to a survey of the Fusuijing subdistrict that included fifty-eight collective canteens, with widely varied conditions: Most had been created just a month before and were therefore in different stages of development, but the three canteens that had been founded in 1958 were singled out as positive examples. They were cheap, the food offering was varied, and they were well attended, with factory and service workers accounting for 76.3 percent of the total attendees, the rest being local employees and students. They had also become a central place for the masses to engage in political and cultural activities (*qunzhong jinxing zhengzhi, wenhua yundong de zhongyao zhendi* 群众进行政治、文化活动的重要阵地).[88] By July 1960, the district had 701 canteens, with 2,802

[85]  XDS 22-2-133-1 Xuanwuqu fuwugongsi guanyu jinyibu jiaqiang xiranye de qingshi 宣武区服务公司关于进一步加强洗染业的请示 [Request for instruction from the Xuanwu District Service Company on further strengthening the washing and dyeing industry], January 12, 1960.
[86]  BMA 001-006-01703-11 Xuanwu quwei jiegongwei guanyu Chunshu gongshe fuwuzhan gongzuo wenti ji jinhou yijian de baogao 宣武区委街工委关于椿树公社服务站工作问题及今后意见的报告 [Report by the neighborhood work committee of the Xuanwu district committee on the Chunshu commune service centers and suggestions for the future], June 6, 1960.
[87]  XDN 7-1-211-3 Xicheng quwei guanyu jiedao shengchan fuwu gongzuo qingkuang de baogao.
[88]  XDN 7-1-211-5 Xicheng quwei guanyu jiedao shitang de qingkuang diaocha he xiayibu kaizhan gongzuo de jidian yijian de baogao 西城区委关于街道食堂的情况调查和下一步开展工作的几点意见的报告 [Report of the Xicheng district committee on the survey of the situation of neighborhood canteens and a few ideas for the next step], March 22, 1960.

employees serving 57,607 customers, but only 85 of those pre-dated the relaunch of collectivization in 1960. The new canteens were mostly small in scale (80 percent of them served fewer than 100 customers each) and only one quarter of them were judged to be "well run." In 1960, the district communes had established eight large-size canteens – with over 500 customers and staple food–processing capabilities (*zhushi jiagong* 主食加工) – and they planned to open five more. Those thirteen canteens would then be able to feed 6,500 people and provide staples for 33,000 more.[89]

Here too, progress was even more evident in the district's flagship commune Erlonglu, where the number of "advanced" childcare units, which was only nineteen at the time of the evaluation in August 1959, rose to forty-one at the end of the year. The Xitiejian hutong kindergarten had been named a city Red Flag Unit – a very high honor – in August and did not register any case of either minor or major infection among its children for the rest of the year. The commune canteens expanded from the initial four makeshift sheds to twenty-five rooms, feeding over a thousand people, and now deployed electric and hand-cranked dough-making, dough-cutting, and vegetable-cutting machines, as well as a steam boiler that could cook buns for 240 people every ten minutes.[90] By April 1960, the commune had 566 canteens with 1,076 employees, 146 childcare centers, and 105 service centers, which offered almost any service imaginable, including helping with marriages and funerals, minor repairs, cutting hair, and taking pictures.[91] Commune residents conveyed their appreciation in a rhymed couplet on a *dazibao*: "Neighborhood work has blossomed, and great joy has come to my home / a simple canteen was set up, and since then we never worry about food / We cross the door and food appears in our hands, and after eating we have time to go to work / First of all thanks to the Communist Party, and then thanks to my elder sisters and aunties."[92]

[89] XDN 7-1-812-1 Xichengqu 1960 nian xiaban jiedao renmin gongshe shitang gongzuo yijian 西城区1960年下半街道人民公社食堂工作意见 [Suggestions on the work of people's commune canteens in Xicheng district in the second half of 1960], July 1, 1960.

[90] BMA 101-001-00782-7 Yong zuikuai de bufa jianshe shehuizhuyi xin xhengshi: Beijing shi Erlonglu renmin gongshe diaocha.

[91] XDN 38-1-13-3 Erlonglu renmin gongshe jiben qingkuang jieshao 二龙路人民公社基本情况介绍 [Basic information on Erlonglu people's commune], April 12, 1960. The report singles out the case of the Haosheng canteen 好省食堂, which was expanded twice to include thirty-six rooms, and served over 900 people. They had a new heavy-duty boiler that could cook *mantou* (steamed bread) for over 200 people in twenty minutes and *zhou* (congee) for over 300 people in fifteen minutes, and they provided staples for other smaller canteens. This was also a place where people met, students did their homework, and the Peking opera groups practiced.

[92] XDN 28-1-94-4 Guanyu Erlonglu Jingjidao jumin weiyuanhui dui Xiaotuqun shitang shixing tongyi guanli de qingkuang de baogao 关于二龙路京畿道居民委员会对小土群食

Documents from the Beixinqiao commune, in Dongcheng district, detail another story of advancement through education and ideological work, leading to the situation in April 1960: 161 canteens, with 605 employees and 20,101 customers, serving 80.4 percent of the commune members; 144 childcare centers, with 445 employees and caring for 4,800 children, 42 percent of the total; 35 service centers, with 638 employees, offering over 170 service items; plus a series of communal banks and stores, employing 1,572 people. The commune had also managed to switch a fair amount of its commodity exchange to direct supply, in line with the projected transformation of the wage economy. For example, in the month of April, one of their sales offices had distributed 55 percent of its products within the commune, 28 percent to canteens, 7 percent to childcare centers, 20 percent to residents.[93] These quite impressive results – except for the not-so-minor issue of low childcare attendance – were not achieved overnight, however. The commune held a total of more than 500 propaganda meetings (*xuanchuanhui* 宣传会) of various sizes, educating more than 100,000 people on the benefits of social welfare and the responsibilities of service work. People were initially suspicious of collective services. Cadres and activists worried about where these services would be housed, who would staff then, and whether they would be run well and cheaply. Residents suffered from the "four fears": fear that the food would not be good, that it would not be cheap, that it would not be provided at appropriate times, and that it would be cold.

As noted earlier, many commune members despised the work of the "three service staff" (cook, caregiver, service personnel), believing it did not offer any chance of career advancement. In order to dissipate these prejudices, the commune organized activities such as a meeting for over 200 youths, during which some city-wide model caregivers extolled the "glorious practice" of service work. At the end of the meeting, thirty-one young women put their names down for childcare duty. Models of extreme dedication and personalized care were deployed, such as Wang Shuzhen, a cook who had joined the canteen despite having nine children, or a volunteer who had patiently spent two days helping one infant,

堂实行统一管理的情况的报告 [Report by the Jingjidao neighborhood committee at Erlonglu on the implementation of centralized management for the Xiaotuqun canteen], May 16, 1960. Original text: "街道工作开红花,天大喜专到我家。/ 简易食堂 庆成立,从此吃饭不抓瞎。/ 进门饭菜全到手,吃完上班有余暇。/ 首先感谢共产党,再谢 大嫂与大妈。"

93 BMA 119-001-00400-8 Guanyu Beixinqiao diqu gongshehua hou caimao gongzuo bianhua qingkuang de dianxing diaocha he dui chengshi renmin gongshe caimao tizhi de yijian.

the child of a canteen employee, acclimate to the nursery. The commune conducted training classes for service workers. At the end of one such class, with 150 women enrolled, Sun Xiuling recounted her change of heart: "In the past, I thought it was just cooking food and eating food, so I did not intend to be a cook for a long time, but after listening to the reports, I realized that the work of a cook is very important, and I am determined to do a good job in the canteen." Welfare services were also supposed to produce practical benefits, for the individual and the collective: At Beixinqiao, unlike in other cases, eating in the canteen was reportedly cheaper than eating at home (for a family of four).[94]

In reports, officers and surveyors often found it necessary to stress how the apparatus of social welfare organizations was primarily in the service of production, its principal role to free labor time for factory work. At Beixinqiao, the cosmetics factory initially could not fulfill its production quota, but once all the workers joined the canteens and sent their children to childcare facilities, they went 60 percent over the plan in the month of February. In the case of the communal carpet factory, reports once again took an almost Taylorist approach to time management, calculating that the twenty-six workers wasted fifty-two hours in food preparation at home, and eating at the canteen thus corresponded to fifty-two extra feet of carpet. One of the employees, Li Shuzhen, had to go home after work and cook for her family of seven people, so she could not go to sleep before midnight, and, waking up at six, she was always tired and could cut only fourteen feet of carpet per day. After the whole family started eating at the canteen, she was full of energy and could cut eighteen feet per day, a 30 percent increase in productivity.[95] Communal services were therefore described as functionally essential to achieve the virtuous cycle of increased production and reduced waste; while they were meant to introduce the embryonic form of a "supply system" that would replace material incentives and monetary remuneration, they also allowed for a maximum concentration of labor and labor time. As cogently synthesized in another report, the establishment of collective welfare had allowed for the "four concerns" (*sitiaoxin* 四条心) – production, food, childcare,

[94] BMA 002-012-00132-1 Shirenwei gongying bangongshi 市人委供应办公室 [Supply office of the Municipal People's Council], Beijingshi Dongchengqu Beixinqiao diqu zuzhi renmin jingji shenghuo yundong de qingkuang 北京市东城区北新桥地区组织人民经济生活运动的情况 [Current situation of the campaign for organizing people's economic life in the Beixinqiao subdistrict, Dongcheng district, Beijing], April 1, 1960. The report cites the example of the family of Fan Weijuan, two parents and two children, for whom eating in the canteens was ¥10 cheaper than eating at home, ¥52 vs. ¥62.
[95] BMA 002-012-00132-1 Beijingshi Dongchengqu Beixinqiao diqu zuzhi renmin jingji shenghuo yundong de qingkuang.

cleaning and sewing – to become *one* concern, namely, production.[96] In the words of one worker at the Fusuijing commune, "[T]he factory is my home, the party is my parents, the machine is my husband, the product is my baby."[97] I discuss later how a "liberation" framed as a reduction of life concerns (and of the connected physical and emotional labor) to the single issue of production revealed itself to be not only practically impossible but also politically problematic.

One final, and usually less heralded, benefit of collectivization was in the field of education and culture, as the collectivized life in the commune created new demands among the new workers.[98] These demands included raising the level of basic literacy, with communes opening after-work courses. At Dewai, over 700 women attended those courses, while over 2,000 people had thrown off the "ignorance hat" (*mangmu maozi* 盲目帽子), and the overall literacy rate in the commune reached 87 percent in April 1960.[99] At Chunshu, they both created an after-work school in January 1959 and later added schools in various commune factories, the latter achieving a much better attendance rate than the former (77.1 percent vs. 24.3 percent).[100] But there were also other, more creative endeavors, such as at Fusuijing, where 90 percent of the new workers took part in cultural and physical activities, using whatever time was available to sing, dance, perform theater pieces, create art, or read. Since April, the commune laborers had created over 600 works of art (poetry, songs, theater pieces, dances, etc.) At the Zhaobei service center they used a record player and the broadcasting system to teach workers the lines of a play titled "Women's Service Center" (*Funü fuwuzhan* 妇女服务站). Fusuijing also established a Commune Center Club, a

---

[96] BMA 119-001-00400-8 Guanyu Beixinqiao diqu gongshehua hou caimao gongzuo bianhua qingkuang de dianxing diaocha he dui chengshi renmin gongshe caimao tizhi de yijian.

[97] BMA 001-024-00110-1 Fusuijing renmin gongshe dangwei guanyu kaizhan wenhua gongzuo de qingkuang baogao 福绥境人民公社党委关于开展文化工作的情况报告 [Report by the party committee of Fusuijing people's commune on the development of cultural work], June 1960.

[98] BMA 001-024-00110-2 Fusuijing renmin gongshe dangwei guanyu tushu zulinye gaizao de qingkuang baogao 福绥境人民公社党委关于图书租赁业改造的情况报告 [Report by the party committee of Fusuijing people's commune on the reform of the book rental sector], June 1960.

[99] XDN 46-1-1-9 Dewai renmin gongshe choubei weiyuanhui de gongzuo baogao 德外人民公社筹备委员会的工作报告 [Work report of the Dewai people's commune preparatory committee], April 1960.

[100] XDS 15-2-18-1 Xuanwuqu Chunshu renmin gongshe yijiuliuling nian saomang he yeyu jiaoyu gongzuo guihua 宣武区椿树人民公社一九六零年扫盲和业余教育工作规划 [Literacy and after-work education plan for 1960 of the Chunshu people's commune, Xuanwu district], December 17, 1959.

children's library, and an amateur cultural team.[101] This represented the fulfillment of the promise of a new, richer life to come with collectivization, a life that included access to and enjoyment of a certain communal luxury, in terms of not just material goods and improved services, but also culture, leisure, and participation in intellectual and artistic activities. A world where everyone "would have his or her share of the best."[102]

Despite the massive expansion and the general impression of improved conditions in welfare services, many of the problems that had already emerged in the first few months of collectivization continued to bedevil the Beijing communes. First and foremost, some of the collective facilities remained significantly unattended, with obvious consequences for their long-term economic sustainability. At Dashilar, only 24.5 percent of the newly mobilized labor force ate at the canteens,[103] and at Qinghe commune, in Haidian district, over half of the members did not take advantage of any of the services.[104] The situation was slightly better at Erlonglu, where 55 percent of the commune members had joined a canteen; another 25 percent of them had someone who could cook at home, but there was clearly 20 percent of members who needed the canteens but did not use them.[105] The commune childcare centers served only 1,973 children out of the 13,000 total in the area, as of March 1960, and while the commune leadership expected an increase, given the recent expansion of production, their rosier projection was to reach 5,200, which was still only 40 percent of the total number of

[101] XDN 44-1-24-2 Zai Fusuijing renmin gongshe wenhua gongzuo. Xianchanghui shang de jianghua tigang 在福绥境人民公社文化工作。现场会上的讲话提纲" [Cultural work at the Fusuijing People's Commune. Outline of the speech at on-site meeting], June 4, 1960. The commune also incorporated the existing four (privately owned) book lending centers, which had over 6,000 books. See BMA 001-024-00110-2 Fusuijing renmin gongshe dangwei guanyu tushu zulinye gaizao de qingkuang baogao.

[102] Kristin Ross, *Communal Luxury: The Political Imaginary of the Paris Commune* (London: Verso, 2015): 65.

[103] BMA 001-006-01703-6 Zhonggong Xuanwu quwei guanyu Dashilar jiedao banshichu jianli renmin gongshe wenti de qingshi 中共宣武区委关于大栅栏街道办事处建立人民公社问题的请示 [Request for instructions from the Xuanwu District Party Committee on the establishment of a people's commune by the Dashilar subdistrict committee], April 8, 1960.

[104] BMA 001-006-01493-8 Zhonggong Beijing shiwei bangongting 中共北京市委办公厅 [General office of the CCP Beijing municipal committee], Qinghe renmin gongshe jumin shengchan fuwuzhan zuzhi jumin canjia shengchan laodong de qingkuang he wenti 清河人民公社居民生产服务站组织居民参加生产劳动的情况和问题 [Report on the Qinghe people's commune residents' production service centers: Participation of residents in productive labor and related issues], June 9, 1959.

[105] XDN 7-1-807 Zhonggong Beijingshi Xicheng quwei guanyu chengshi jiedao renmin gongshe gongzuo wenti de baogao (cao'an).

preschool children.[106] Reports from Chunshu detailed an improvement of services but also a surprising decrease in attendance during 1959. When the commune was funded, there was an obvious and massive need for social services, but because of a lack of capital and resources, the facilities created were of low quality, and people quickly stopped eating at the canteens and sending their children to kindergartens. Through 1959, following the steady development of industrial production, the commune consolidated and improved the service enterprises, which nevertheless registered only 1,555 children enrolled in childcare (vs. 6,590 in 1958) and 682 canteen customers (vs. 5,510). Welfare services, the report admitted, lagged behind production. In just in one alley, Qiujia jie, where eighty "housewives" were involved in industrial work, there were 120 children under six years of age in need of care.[107] An earlier report from the same alley tellingly noted that 490 dependents who had been targeted for mobilization could not join centralized production (only 109 of them were in "scattered production"), because they shouldered the entire responsibility of running the household, raising and educating more than 1,400 children. In a rare and clear admission of the indispensable and ultimately productive character of domestic work, the report remarked how these women were "inextricably linked to the general workforce" and their labor was "directly related to every item of work and production."[108]

In Xicheng district, a survey revealed that at least 12,000 workers who should have joined the collective canteens had not yet done so, and they provided five major reasons: (1) It was economically unprofitable, especially for people who were on a tight budget; (2) it was not convenient, especially if each family member had to eat in a different canteen; (3) workers who were employed in "scattered production," meaning they did contract work at or around the home, did not want to join; (4) people were afraid they wouldn't be served enough food; and (5) they believed the canteens were poorly managed.[109] All these concerns were, to different degrees, justified, yet one has to remember these services had been

---

[106] XDN 7-1-211-2 Xicheng quwei guanyu Erlonglu renmin gongshe shidian qingkuang de baogao.

[107] XDS 15-1-13-10 Zhonggong Chunshu dangwei guanyu renmin gongshe shidian gongzuo de baogao (chugao).

[108] XDS 15-1-13-9 Xuanwuqu Chunshu renmin gongshe jiedao qunzhong zuzhi qingkuang diaocha he gaixuan shidian gongzuo baogao (cao'an) 宣武区椿树人民公社街道群众组织情况调查和改选试点工作报告(草案) [Report on the survey on the situation of neighborhood mass organizations of the Chunshu people's commune in Xuanwu district and the pilot work of reelection (draft)], June 10, 1959.

[109] XDN 7-1-812-1 Xichengqu 1960 nian xiaban jiedao renmin gongshe shitang gongzuo yijian.

created through a bottom-up effort of mass mobilization, in conditions of scarcity, and had been in operation for, at most, a year, and in some cases for only a few months, a time too brief to iron out the kinks and fix the issues of what were novel and complex endeavors.

Financially, many of the welfare services were not yet self-sustainable and could function only with subsidies from the commune administration or fees from members, or both. This deterred participation. The service centers at Chunshu were "working inefficiently and losing money," in large part because they seemed to be overstaffed: One laundry had washing machines, but they were not any better or any faster than what could be achieved by hand washing, while another center had a productivity level ideal for thirty-four employees, but it employed ninety-four workers. The commune had to supplement ¥2,940.71, or 64.4 percent of the total expenses, which was clearly untenable.[110] As full employment logic came up against logics of efficiency, the commune social services proved inefficient. In June 1959, when the ACWF surveyed the situations of neighborhood childcare in the city, they realized that, while all the centers were supposed to be self-funding, nurseries were much more costly to operate than kindergartens and could not survive only on fees – they needed subsidies. Faced with financial shortages, some subdistrict committees siphoned money away from kindergartens to finance nurseries, while others used capital from neighborhood factories. But only half of production workers had children in nurseries, so some nurseries started rejecting children whose parents were not employed in a factory. There was always the possibility of hiking fees, but when a subdistrict committee in Chongwen district raised the nursery fees by ¥2 for non-factory children, 300 children stopped using the service.[111] At the Qinghe commune, in Haidian, all workers contributed between 10 and 40 percent of their salaries to the commune's provident and welfare funds, which in turn were used to pay salaries of service workers in childcare and canteens. However, out of 698 workers, only 100 ate at the canteens and only 175 had children in collective childcare. Eliminating subsidies and raising fees made welfare services completely unaffordable for the vast majority of people.[112] Yet even when communes decided to provide substantial help, such as at Erlonglu – where they subsidized 50 percent of daycare and 40 percent

[110] BMA 001-006-01703-12 Chunshu gongshe diyi dadui fuwuzhan de qingkuang.
[111] BMA 084-001-00149-4 Guanyu fazhan he gonggu jiedao tuo'er zuzhi de qingkuang baogao.
[112] BMA 001-006-01493-8 Qinghe renmin gongshe jumin shengchan fuwuzhan zuzhi jumin canjia shengchan laodong de qingkuang he wenti.

of full-board childcare and eliminated canteen fees for commune workers – that was still not enough for poor families with several children, the ones who most needed those services. A March 1960 report mentioned the case of a woman with eight children and a family income of ¥57, who, even counting her factory salary and a ¥15 subsidy, could not afford communal childcare.[113] This remained a crucial obstacle to the socialization of housework.

However they were financed, those services often varied widely in terms of quality: As the next chapter will illustrate, uniformity of service was neither an operating principle nor a political goal of the Great Leap transformation. Of the fifty-five canteens operating in Xicheng district in 1960, twenty-nine were ranked "first class," meaning they were cogently organized, appreciated by the masses, and sufficiently equipped. Below that, there was a steep drop, as the second tier included canteens that rented a room from a commune member and used the kitchen to cook meals or that were distributing meals under a porch (weather permitting). Some could only do some "finishing labor" (*jiagong* 加工) on whatever raw ingredients, mostly staples, the customers brought, something akin to a "you buy, we fry" system: They could only "cook as much food as the people brought."[114] However, as the reports noted, the masses were not satisfied with being served enough to eat; they also wanted to eat well and in comfortable surroundings.[115]

In 1959, the All-China Women's Federation produced a similar classification for the childcare centers in Beijing suburban districts, which they arranged according to three levels. In those that achieved the top status, children were "relatively clean," each of them had their own towel and teacup, and the canteen could make good dishes out of coarse grains (*culiang xizuo*粗粮细做). In other, lower-ranked organizations, however, washbasins and towels were all in common, and rooms never got swept, not even once a year; caregivers let infants pee wherever they wanted, and never washed the children's faces and hands – or their own hands. Caregivers were said to completely ignore the children, or they resorted to yelling and even tying them up. One child ended up falling asleep in a

---

[113] XDN 38-1-13-1 Erlonglu jiedao dangwei 二龙路街道党委 (Erlonglu neighborhood party committee), Erlonglu renmin gongshe shiban qingkuang 二龙路人民公社试办情况 [Situation at the Erlonglu pilot people's commune], March 13, 1960.

[114] XDN 7-1-211-5 Xicheng quwei guanyu jiedao shitang de qingkuang diaocha he xiayibu kaizhan gongzuo de jidian yijian de baogao.

[115] XDN 7-1-807 Zhonggong Beijingshi Xicheng quwei guanyu chengshi jiedao renmin gongshe gongzuo wenti de baogao (cao'an). Some canteens could serve a variety of high-quality dishes, but even those were not considered to have achieved the Great Leap standard of "saving grains, saving money, and providing a comfortable and appetizing meal" (节约粮食、省钱又能吃的舒服适口等标准).

haystack, and another one had a millstone fall on his foot, crushing it. Because of this disregard for hygiene, in the winter, these lower-ranked centers registered several cases of measles, scarlet fever, whooping cough, and other diseases; 89,842 children got sick (20 percent of the entirety of kids under seven) and 1,040 died.[116] This situation was replicated at the city level, where 30 percent of the childcare centers were reported as lacking any fixed location and any respect for basic sanitary rules.[117]

Reports almost uniformly laid the blame for these failures squarely on the people who ran those services: the managers and workers. For managers, the issue was invariably their ideology and class background: At one service center in Chunshu, one out of three leaders had an "impure" class background and the center head was a former brothel manager,[118] while in Xicheng, placing "bad elements" in charge had led to a lack of attendance – people did not trust them with their food rations – and even sabotage.[119] This issue could be solved with a cleansing of the leadership ranks. Deeper and more intractable problems were attributed to the caregivers themselves, usually described once again as "housewives" (sometimes "old housewives") with low professional abilities and little knowledge of childrearing and pedagogy.[120] A large number were either illiterate (24.4 percent) or semi-literate (60.6 percent), thus had received a minimal education. Caregivers were reported complaining that childcare was tiring, the workload was heavy, the pay low, and it was a job with no future and no sense of whom they were serving.[121] In the suburban districts, many of the kindergarten

[116] BMA 084-001-00149-3 Guanyu xiaoqu tuo'er zuzhi de fazhan qingkuang he gonggu yijian xiang shiwei de baogao 关于郊区托儿组织的发展情况和巩固意见向市委的报告 [Report to the municipal committee on the development and consolidation of childcare organizations in the suburban districts], February 7, 1959.

[117] BMA 084-001-00149-5 Guanyu Beijing xiaoqu tuo'er zuzhi fazhan he gonggu de baogao 关于北京郊区托儿组织发展和巩固的报告 [Report on the development and consolidation of child care organizations in Beijing suburban districts], June 29, 1959.

[118] BMA 001-006-01703-12 Chunshu gongshe diyi dadui fuwuzhan de qingkuang.

[119] XDN 7-1-211-5 Xicheng quwei guanyu jiedao shitang de qingkuang diaocha he xiayibu kaizhan gongzuo de jidian yijian de baogao.

[120] XDN 7-1-807 Zhonggong Beijingshi Xicheng quwei guanyu chengshi jiedao renmin gongshe gongzuo wenti de baogao (cao'an).

[121] BMA 084-001-00149-4 Guanyu fazhan he gonggu jiedao tuo'er zuzhi de qingkuang baogao. A survey of the commercial sector of the Beixinqiao commune noted the relatively old age of the personnel: 17 percent were over sixty (the oldest eighty-four), 22 percent between fifty and fifty-nine, 43 percent between forty and forty-nine. The remaining 18 percent included many weak and sick people. BMA 119-001-00400-8 Guanyu Beixinqiao diqu gongshehua hou caimao gongzuo bianhua qingkuang de dianxing diaocha he dui chengshi renmin gongshe caimao tizhi de yijian.

employees were old, weak, or sick. In Haidian they recorded seventeen cases of syphilis and four of tuberculosis among the caregivers.[122]

Improving the educational level of caregivers (teaching them pedagogical methods, childrearing, and basic rules of hygiene) and raising their ideological awareness were identified as the obvious solutions to the problems of collective childcare. I could not find any pedagogical material for urban commune caregivers in the archives, but pamphlets drafted for their rural counterparts might prove useful, especially as they address the same kinds of problems. These pamphlets, geared at training the illiterate or barely literate employees in communal kindergartens and nurseries, combined a relatively limited amount of text with illustrative pictures, and conveyed instructions that ranged from the rudimentary to the commonsensical. Rooms should be well-ventilated and well-lit, and they should be swept every day. One pamphlet explained the basic process of weaning. But caregivers were also reminded not to let children urinate and defecate wherever they liked, eat dirty food, or play with knives, scissors, or fire. They should neither overdress nor underdress the children, nor should they feed them with their hands or chew food for them. Children should not be left alone, even when they were napping.[123] Most of the caregivers, according to reports, were indeed "housewives" and often mothers themselves who, illiterate or not, had raised their own children. With that in mind, the level of details of these instructions and the blame imputed to caregivers seem excessive, and even a sign of condescension. As noted earlier, there was an evident tendency to identify the cause for communes' problems in the gendered character of the labor force. And then, paradoxically, even the kind of labor that was supposed to replicate motherly duties and housework could be tainted when it was associated with the category of "housewife," which stood here for a general gendered characterization of inferiority, devaluation, ignorance, and incompetence. I will return to this issue, but here I want to highlight how blaming the low educational level of caregivers was perhaps also a way to gloss over more systemic issues, such as lack of resources, poor organization, low pay, bad labor conditions, mismanagement, and the absolute frenzy with which these services were established.

As the blame for the issues afflicting communal services was cast in gendered and personalized terms, so were the examples illustrating what

---

[122] BMA 084-001-00149-3 Guanyu xiaoqu tuo'er zuzhi de fazhan qingkuang he gonggu yijian xiang shiwei de baogao.
[123] *Baomu shouce* 保姆手册 [Manual for children's caregivers] (山西省卫生厅编印, 1958); *Nongcun baoyuyuan shouce* 农村保育员手册 [Manual for children's caregivers in the countryside] (上海市卫生局, 1958).

kind of work was required by each and every employee to make this collective endeavor possible in the current conditions. The system's functioning relied heavily on a select group of "activists" (*jijifenzi* 积极分子) who were usually already over-tasked and overworked. At Xuanwu, most of the cadres responsible for the service center were also leaders in neighborhood committees, and they found it very difficult to juggle both sets of tasks.[124] At Chunshu, the director of a commune nursery was also a member of the Law Enforcement and Mediation committee and a household registrar, and she was so overwhelmed with work that she ended up losing the key of the *hukou* (household registration) box, which they could not open again for two months.[125] Childcare work was hard, tiring, and underpaid: The workday in a kindergarten was between 9.5 and 10.5 hours, in a nursery 11 hours on average. Most childcare organizations (62 out of 102) did not provide any welfare or paid leave, and caregivers often found themselves facing the double burden of work and housework, rushing home to cook lunch and dinner, and managing only to quickly ingest a few mouthfuls of cold rice and cold vegetables, before hurrying back to work.[126]

The anecdotal evidence about those individual workers presented as models is perhaps the most vivid and the most revealing. At the Dewai commune, a nursery employee, Zhang Huimin 张惠敏, was singled out for her positive attitude. She carried the children in her arms when the *hutong* was flooded in mud after a summer storm, but, even more impressively, she routinely took home those children whose mothers worked late. In the case of a female worker who did not get off until midnight, Zhang took two children to her own home, fed them, and put them to sleep every night for an entire month. The mother is reported having commented: "If it weren't for comrade Zhang who took such good care of our kids, there is no way I could have left the house to go to work."[127] At Chunshu, the Xianghuying sitiao canteen achieved advanced status on the back of the work of the manager, the aforementioned Zhang Wenxiu, who almost singlehandedly succeeded in keeping it clean and running efficiently, offering a larger variety of dishes.[128]

[124] BMA 001-006-01703-11 Xuanwu quwei jiegongwei guanyu Chunshu gongshe fuwuzhan gongzuo wenti ji jinhou yijian de baogao.

[125] XDS 15-1-13-8 Xuanwuqu Chunshu renmin gongshe qunzhong zuzhi gongzuozu qingkuang de diaocha baogao 宣武区椿树人民公社群众组织工作组情况的调查报告 [Investigation report on the mass organization working group at the Chunshu people's commune in Xuanwu district], April 22, 1959.

[126] BMA 084-001-00149-4 Guanyu fazhan he gonggu jiedao tuo'er zuzhi de qingkuang baogao.

[127] XDN 46-1-1-9 Dewai renmin gongshe choubei weiyuanhui de gongzuo baogao.

[128] XDS 15-1-13-10 Zhonggong Chunshu dangwei guanyu renmin gongshe shidian gongzuo de baogao (chugao).

Documents from Xuanwu district record a similar, more elaborated story of another exceptional canteen employee, Niu Zhuqin, thirty, mother of two children, and illiterate, who had joined neighborhood enterprises in October 1958 and, after being moved from one position to another, had landed at the Xiezimiao canteen. She immediately showed great initiative, fetching firewood when needed, even bringing coal from home, with no fear of getting dirty or tired. Through ideological education, she learned how to put collective interest over personal advantage and decided that she needed to improve her cooking skills. Taking advantage of her "personal time" – that is, sacrificing rest and leisure – she went regularly to the famed Xingsheng restaurant and established a good relationship with the chef there. Quickly she mastered how to cook 103 dishes. She also conducted a series of experiments aimed at saving valuable ingredients without sacrificing flavor. She used cabbage to make "caramelized yams" (*basi shanyao* 拔丝山药), mixed celery leaves with steamed bean curd as a fried dish, and deployed several methods to economize on cooking oil, so that she saved ten *jin* of oil in the month of June. She became so proficient that she was also asked to cook for banquets. With the improvement of Niu Zhuqin's cooking skills, the canteen managed to serve at least seven or eight dishes, a marked improvement over the two or three they could produce in the past.[129]

As commune production was ultimately based on the deployment of low-skill, high-intensity labor, welfare services were similarly predicated on each worker's single-minded devotion and seemingly unending exertion. And here we see a crack in the project of "complete female liberation." Not only did liberation depend on a series of collective services still in their early stage of development, chronically underfinanced and underresourced, and which could not ultimately replace the complex labor of social reproduction, but the very functioning of both industrial and service collective enterprises seemed possible only under a continuously reaffirmed – and always gendered – strict labor discipline.

## 3.4    What Is Liberation?

The promise of "liberation" – in the sense both of women's emancipation and of the overall transformation in the organization and understanding

---

[129] XDS 13-2-17-5 Niu Zhuqin geren pingbi cailiao 牛柱琴个人评比材料 [Niu Zhuqin's Personal Assessment Documents], January 8, 1960. Xingsheng was a 100-year-old restaurant just outside Qianmen in central Beijing, which was also singled out as a model after 1957, and became a red flag unit. See *Xingsheng fanguan* 兴昇饭馆 (Renmin meishu chubanshe, 1959).

of the everyday for urban residents – featured quite prominently in the reports that hailed the successes of collectivization and urban communes. What was singled out for celebration is revelatory of both the goals and the limitations of that promise. The lives of "housewives" were declared to have changed, as they now worked in factories and childcare was provided; that had led in turn to a high tide of cultural activities and studying. At Xicheng in 1959, over 5,000 women had been lifted out of illiteracy, thanks to classes before and after work.[130] At the Tiantan subdistrict office, 98 percent of illiterate and semi-literate people under the age of forty were enrolled in classes, while many were also involved in recreational and sports activities.[131] These women, "liberated from household chores and free from illiteracy," now expressed a desire for culture, and, as mentioned earlier, in 1960 one commune collected over 600 songs, poems, and *kuaiban* (rhymed stories with rhythmic accompanying) written by the newly literate workers.[132]

Literacy and the desire for "culture" were just outward manifestations of what reports claimed to be a much deeper transformation of both the structure of social relations and individual consciousness, and this, as much as production quotas, was the true measure of the radical character of the Great Leap. Since Liberation, a report from the Erlonglu commune summarized, while the appearance of city street had improved greatly, some things had remained stubbornly unchanged. As the report narrates,

Factories, institutions, schools and other grassroots units have achieved a high level of organization according to socialist principles. Yet the residents of these streets remain largely unorganized. A large number of women remain confined to their narrow domestic spheres, burdened by trivial household chores, which results in a massive waste of labor and hinders their political awakening. This situation is incompatible with the socialist economy and politics of the cities, creating a significant contradiction.

Collectivization and participation in production had "gradually transformed the backward, one-family, scattered street of consumption into the socialist, organized street of production, fundamentally solving that contradiction."[133] Participation in communal enterprises had "liberated

[130] XDN 7-1-211-3 Xicheng quwei guanyu jiedao shengchan fuwu gongzuo qingkuang de baogao.
[131] BMA 001-006-01703-13 Chongwenqu guanyu jiedao banshichu zuzhi qilai de qingkuang he chengli renmin gongshe riqi de qingshi baogao.
[132] BMA 001-024-00110-1 Fusuijing renmin gongshe dangwei guanyu kaizhan wenhua gongzuo de qingkuang baogao.
[133] XDN 7-1-211-2 Xicheng quwei guanyu Erlonglu renmin gongshe shidian qingkuang de baogao.

the masses of residents from the narrow world in which they spent their day thinking only about the interests of their individual family life and had linked their lives directly with the cause of socialist construction," fostering their collective spirit and a new perspective on labor. As one worker at Dewai summarized, "In the past, we revolved around our husbands, our pots and pans, and our children. Now we revolve around machines and factories, and we work for socialist construction."[134] It was, another report averred, "a fundamental change in the spiritual outlook of street residents."[135] At Chunshu, this change was once again manifested in a steep decline in the number of civil disputes: There had been 178 cases between January and September 1958, about 19 per month, but since the founding of the commune, there had been only 90 in 14 months.[136]

That ideological revolution was embodied in transformed practices, ranging from the seemingly mundane – listening to news on the radio instead of dramas – to the foundational – shifting allegiance from the family to the factory. At Erlonglu, when, during a major rainstorm, workers' houses were flooded, they nonetheless first rushed to the factory to mop up the water, then they went to help neighbors, and only at the end did they move on to clean up their own homes.[137] The effects of women's participation in collective labor were perhaps most clearly visible in those changes that affected the intimate realm of family relationships. Descriptions of those changes, however, were heavily tinged by the dismissal of any possible productive value of domestic labor and of any meaning for domestic life. Before the Great Leap, one document from the All-China Federation of Trade Unions remarked, many women did not take part in production, so they had very little of a collective life; "their political and cultural levels were low, therefore between husband and wife there was nothing to talk about except for house chores." Now, with women abandoning those house chores for factory work, spouses could talk about production, their studies, and current affairs, creating a new foundation for their feelings.[138] As another report synthesized, highlighting the newly achieved equality not only between spouses but

---

[134] XDN 46-1-19 Dewai renmin gongshe choubei weiyuanhui de gongzuo baogao 德外人民公社筹备委员会的工作报告 [Report on the work of the preparatory committee of the Dewai People's Commune], April 1960.
[135] XDN 7-1-211-1 Erlonglu renmin gongshe shidian qingkuang de baogao (Erlonglu jiedao dangwei).
[136] XDS 15-1-13-10 Zhonggong Chunshu dangwei guanyu renmin gongshe shidian gongzuo de baogao (chugao).
[137] XDN 38-1-13-3 Erlonglu renmin gongshe jiben qingkuang jieshao.
[138] BMA 101-001-00782-5 Zhigong jiashu chengle shehui caifu de chuangzaozhe: Shijingshan Zhongsu youhao renmin gongshe jieshao.

also between daughters-in-law and mothers-in-law, "real quality and harmonious coexistence have taken the place of the backward feudal patriarchal system and of a family system centered on the vestige of husband's authority."[139] This also apparently led to women finally overcoming what was described as their "inferiority complex," accepting that they were indeed equal to male workers.[140] However, as the history of urban collectivization proves, the problem of gender equality, even among workers, could not be reduced to one of self-awareness; rather, it was grounded on the systemic devaluation of any work performed by women, in the home as well as in the factory.

One 1960 report singled out the case of a woman named Zhang, who lived in the third alley at Erlonglu and who in the past was often the target of her husband's anger: They had a fight every time she asked him for some cash. The situation changed completely once she joined production and started making her own money, with which she could buy whatever she wanted. Her relationship with her mother-in-law had been fraught as well, but once they both worked outside the home, the mother-in-law on the day shift and the daughter-in-law on the night shift, they took turns doing work around the house and stopped quarreling.[141] At the other pilot commune in Chunshu, they celebrated the transformation in daily life and ideological attitude of the residents of an entire building compound, the no. 3 *dayuan* at Mianhua toutiao (棉花头条). Fifteen families lived in the compound for a total of seventy-two residents, including thirty children. Before collectivization, the place was described as "very backward," with bad hygienic conditions, and with disputes between mothers and daughters-in-law exploding out in the open all the time. After the founding of the commune, fourteen housewives joined productive labor, as industrial workers, shop clerks, and caregivers, bringing radical changes to interpersonal relationships and the spiritual outlook of the *dayuan* residents. For example, Zhang Shumin 张淑敏, mother of six, became the manager of the food store, and was so good at her job that she was named a city advanced worker. Forty-year-old Guo Chunhua 郭春华, who had spent half of her life busy only with family chores, rose to become a leading cadre in a nursery. "She now understands that being a caregiver is noble work, and one cannot behave like the old ladies taking care of kids at home in the past.

[139] XDN 7-1-211-3 Xicheng quwei guanyu jiedao shengchan fuwu gongzuo qingkuang de baogao.
[140] BMA 101-001-00782-5 Zhigong jiashu chengle shehui caifu de chuangzaozhe: Shijingshan Zhongsu youhao renmin gongshe jieshao.
[141] XDN 38-1-13-1 Erlonglu renmin gongshe shiban qingkuang.

It is a job that requires studying and culture. So, while she has never held an [ink] brush since she was a kid, now every night she sits at a table studying indefatigably in the lamplight." In the past, Liu Wenying was famous among the residents for being one who just liked to eat and do nothing (*haochi lanzuo* 好吃懒做), dirty and messy, going around with unkempt hair and unwashed face; the money she received from her husband every month was never enough; they often quarreled and wanted to get divorced; and she used to pick fights with the neighbors for silly reasons. The previous year activists had pushed her to join production; she had gone through some training; and she had even started studying in the factory. All her neighbors reported how she had changed: She now understood the principles of frugally and diligently running a house; all the family expenses were well arranged; the husband and kids were always cleanly dressed; her husband had even started helping with domestic chores; and they had stopped fighting with each other. While a year previously she had not even understood what the word "socialism" means, now she actively called for building socialism.[142] Finally, Li Fulan, now an apprentice at the No. 1 machine factory, used to have a really awful relationship with her mother-in-law. When she decided to join production, both the husband and the mother-in-law disapproved, but she went ahead anyway, studying hard and improving quickly, to the point that she was chosen as a red banner pacesetter (*hongqi shou* 红旗手). With each month's salary Li bought something for the mother-in-law, while the latter prepared meals for her to eat after work. With everyone away all day, busy with production and commune operations, only four elderly people were left in the compound, so they became the de facto managers, in charge of cleaning the courtyard, taking care of the mail, bringing in the coal, and other chores.[143]

These personal stories and testimonials were collected in surveys and reports produced at the commune, district, and city level, and while there was probably plenty of embellishment and selective description, there is no reason to discount them as outright fabrications by zealous cadres aiming to please superiors. As Aminda Smith has pointed out, the CCP routinely criticized lower-level cadres for committing the grave methodological error of discarding local stories as "chicken feathers and garlic skins" (*jimao suanpi* 鸡毛蒜皮), and inventive reporting could get people

---

[142] XDS 15-1-13-10 Zhonggong Chunshu dangwei guanyu renmin gongshe shidian gongzuo de baogao (chugao). It is worth noting here that no matter how extensive the social transformations produced by collectivization were (or were portrayed to be), they did not fundamentally change the gendered division of labor and did not take away the wife's responsibility for the frugality and diligence of the household.

[143] XDS 15-1-13-6 Chunshu renmin gongshe yinianlai fazhan qingkuang de diaocha (er).

in serious political trouble.[144] And even if we cautiously ignore the excessive positivity of these narratives, what they certainly provide is a depiction of the kind of radical transformations that urban collectivization should and could achieve, in the expectations of both cadres and those who took part in the campaign. And, more significantly, they reveal how the expectations of participants, cadres, and leaders were never univocal and were instead often in contradiction with each other.

For example, beyond the narrated radical changes in ideology and interpersonal relations, the aspect to which reports devoted the most attention and praise was the financial improvement provided via women's entrance into the wage economy. In 1958, Mao had remarked that the simple fact of receiving a salary as individuals would constitute a crucial step in the liberation of women and the destruction of the patriarchal family. This was not his most radical position, or a radical position at all, as it basically replicates the stance of bourgeois feminism, but Beijing cadres followed suit in stressing the transformative power of added income. For example, at Jiuxianqiao 酒仙桥, in Chaoyang district, they recorded an increase of about 40 percent in family income, with families previously in dire straits now saving money.[145] At the tailoring factory at Erlonglu, surveyed in the summer of 1960, out of sixty-nine workers, twenty-eight had a salary that counted for 10–20 percent of the overall family income, another twenty-eight 20–40 percent, five 40–70 percent, and eight 100 percent.[146] In Erlonglu's West Alley (Xixiang), the thirty-two female workers, all model laborers, earned 56 percent of their family income.[147] As a worker at Erlonglu described, "once upon a time I had my palms facing up [asking people for money], now I have my palms facing down [putting money away at home]; this is something no one can underestimate."[148]

The effect of that increased revenue, however, mainly took the form of commodities, purchased with the salaries of the new female workers and which the reports were very keen to minutely describe. In the Jiuxianqiao case cited above, seventy families in the area were able to buy radios, leather shoes, bicycles, watches, and other products for a total of

---

[144] Aminda Smith, "Foreword: The Maoism of PRC History," *positions: asia critique* 29:4 (2021): 666.

[145] BMA 001-006-01703-18 Chaoyang quwei guanyu zai Jiuxianqiao diqu chengli yi dagongchang wei zhongxin de chengshi renmin gongshe 朝阳区委关于在酒仙桥地区成立以大工厂为中心的城市人民公社 [The Chaoyang District Committee on the establishment of an urban people's commune centered on a large factory in the Jiuxianqiao area], April 8, 1960.

[146] XDN 38-1-34-2 Beijingshi Erlonglu gongshe gongye jiben qingkuang.

[147] XDN 38-1-13-1 Erlonglu renmin gongshe shiban qingkuang.

[148] XDN 38-1-13-3 Erlonglu renmin gongshe jiben qingkuang jieshao.

¥9,535.[149] At the Beixinqiao commune, the average salary for female workers was around ¥20, and for most of these women this constituted "pure income," of which they spent 46 percent on foodstuff, 25 percent for nonfood items, 17 percent on noncommercial expenses, and they saved the remaining 12 percent.[150] In one workshop of the electric tool factory at Erlonglu, the salaries of the seventy workers represented on average 38.9 percent of their families' income: twenty-four of them purchased twenty-four items of nylon clothing, twenty-three items of cotton clothing and sheets, ten pairs of leather and rubber shoes, plus a table, an iron coal-burning stove, an alarm clock, and a bicycle, while nine workers put away some savings.[151] Another report from Erlonglu recorded how all women were now able "to buy new clothes, new appliances, and many permed their hair."[152] Perhaps the most extreme cases of this consumption-centered reporting was in a survey of the Chunshu commune from December 1959, where the aggregate sum of the salaries disbursed to the "housewives" in the previous eleven months (¥500,380) is described solely – and quite strangely – in terms of purchasing power: With that money, one could buy 3,210 Flying Pigeon bikes, or 55,980 bags of flour, or 12,549 bolts of cloth, or 50,382 sets of warm undergarments. In the case of Mianhua toutiao no. 3 cited above, the fourteen "housewives" who had joined production earned an average salary of ¥22.2 per month, and their families were able to purchase 185 commercial items, including clothes, bedding, and watches, for a total value of more than ¥2,140. While in 1958 only two of those families had some savings, by the end of 1959 ten did. Four of them used to be in dire straits, but none of them was anymore. The report cited the exemplary case of Zhao Xigeng, a sales clerk with five children. His wife and two kids went to work for a commune factory, and when the elder son graduated from technical school, he too got a job. Their income went from ¥30 to ¥139, and that more than covered their fixed expenses (¥119). Therefore in the previous year they managed to buy five sets of cotton-padded clothes, four sets of long undergarments, five sets of unlined garments, five bedding sets, and also watches, leather shoes,

---

[149] BMA 001-006-01703-18 Chaoyang quwei guanyu zai Jiuxianqiao diqu chengli yi dagongchang wei zhongxin de chengshi renmin gongshe.

[150] BMA 119-001-00400-8 Guanyu Beixinqiao diqu gongshehua hou caimao gongzuo bianhua qingkuang de dianxing diaocha he dui chengshi renmin gongshe caimao tizhi de yijian.

[151] XDN 7-1-211-3 Xicheng quwei guanyu jiedao shengchan fuwu gongzuo qingkuang de baogao. See also XDN 7-1-211-2 Xicheng quwei guanyu Erlonglu renmin gongshe shidian qingkuang de baogao.

[152] XDN 38-1-13-3 Erlonglu renmin gongshe jiben qingkuang jieshao.

and other items. Zhang was quoted saying: "I certainly have to work hard to repay the Party and repay chairman Mao."[153]

There is no doubt that social change could be practically embodied in the availability of necessary and useful products, nor do I want to dismiss how the newfound (relative) abundance could be interpreted and experienced as the prefiguration of the "communal luxury," the "red plenty" to come. Yet what distinguishes this from the promises of capitalism? There is an obvious unresolved tension in a movement promising radical socialist transformation whose revolutionary potential ends up being expressed predominantly in the form of salaries and commodities, two categories strictly connected with capitalist social relations, and which had been at the critical center of the debate on the socialist economy in 1958–1959 (described in Chapter 2). This is one of the incongruities that was never quite overcome.

This tension comes to the fore directly and explicitly in other archival documents, reports in which CCP officers blame the newly recruited "housewives" specifically for indulging in those opportunities – added income leading to purchase of commodities – that they had otherwise singled out as the main achievements of urban collectivization. This became visible most clearly during a training class for commune Communist Youth League cadres, which took place in Beijing in the summer of 1960.

The officers identified three kinds of problems among the young commune cadres. First, and perhaps most importantly, they were criticized for having the wrong life goals and for lacking any long-term ideals. Out of the seventy (all female) cadres from the suburban districts, only eleven declared that "building socialism and communism' was their ultimate goal in life. Most of the others professed much more basic aspirations, like "earning a living for myself" (*ziji yanghuo ziji* 自己养活自己) or "working and eating" (*ganhuo chifan* 干活吃饭). Others stressed that their ideals had already been largely realized once they gained the ability to work and take care of themselves, free from family oppression. Eight women said they just wanted to have fun: "My highest ideal is to go see a movie after work, take a stroll on the street, adults and children all together."[154] Another report about the same training course, this one about cadres from Xuanwu district, described similar attitudes even more vividly. Forty-four cadres from the district communes took part in the course, thirty-seven of them women, some of whom conveyed their

---

[153] XDS 15-1-13-5 Chunshu renmin gongshe yinianlai fazhan qingkuang de diaocha.
[154] BMA 100-001-00659-6 Qingkuang jianbao disanhao 情况简报第3号 [Briefing no. 3], July 19, 1960. The document was listed as *neibu ziliao*, only for cadre education.

desires very directly. "Eating at the canteen, not slaving around the stove, not being subject to my mother-in-law's temper, that was my greatest ideal," said Zhang Jin'ai, a worker at the Tianqiao landscape painting factory. After she joined commune production, that ideal had been achieved. Fang Guiying, a metalworker in a Guangwai factory, chimed in: "In the past, women were objects of anger and oppression, they were controlled by their mothers-in-law, were closeted in the house and cut off from the outside world, but now that I have a job, I believe that learning skills well and earning more money is the greatest happiness." Zhang Jing of the Niujie commune radio factory stressed how the highest ideal was to earn money without having to work overtime; once one has money, one can enjoy oneself. She stated her belief that the greatest joys in one's life are to eat well, dress well, go to movies, and skate in the park. Zhang Yuying of the Dashilar commune electrical factory also expressed similar simple ambitions: She had grown up without a father, and she had always hoped she could make a bit of money, improve her life: "Buy a radio, a sofa, tidy up my small apartment, how good that would be. On Sunday, go to the movie, listen to a play, do what I feel like doing." Qi Fusheng of the Baizhifang commune hardware factory had migrated to Beijing to escape the hard and dirty work in the countryside; she just wanted to be able to go back to the village dressed in her finest and stroll up and down, looking impressive. In the end, many of the workers agreed that "people's lives do not have any other goal: just let me eat a bit more, because dying without having eaten well is a strange injustice."[155]

What these reports give us is a vivid depiction of these women's desires, displayed here as objects of criticism by CYL officers, and of the difficult relationship between these desires and the project of socialist construction. These are simple and understandable aspirations: for leisure, for fun, for relative abundance, for affection, for independence, and for time to oneself. They speak of a pre-commune everyday often stripped down to its bare functions of production and reproduction, when even a small amount of disposable income or disposable time appeared as a newly gained privilege. And in these women's claims to their own time, we can perhaps see a still inchoate gesture toward what Henri Lefebvre called "appropriated time," a time subtracted and defended from being organized by others (the state and capital, first

---

[155] BMA 100-001-00659-11 Gongqingtuan Xuanwuqu weiyuanhui 共青团宣武区委员会 [Communist Youth League Xuanwu district committee], Woqu gongshe tuanganbu zai Beijingshi tuanxiao xuexi zhong baoluchu de jige wenti 我区公社团干部在北京市团校学习中暴露出的几个问题 [Several issues identified among our district communes' CYL cadres during their training at the Beijing Youth League school], September 16, 1960.

and foremost); a time reconquered from alienation, from the discipline of labor, from social fragmentation.[156] So, while these gendered everyday desires might seem distant from the lofty goals of communism, they were not necessarily in contrast to them, the small improvements in the daily lives of neighborhood residents offering perhaps a taste of the new society to come. Yet these desires were disparaged, and the female cadres' attitudes decried as "economistic" by officers who otherwise had no qualms in celebrating the successes of collectivization in terms of disposable income and purchase ability, but who found it reprehensible when these achievements were expressed through women's daily practices and in women's own voices.

The CYL young cadres also shared their disparaging assessments of working conditions in commune factory and services. The sources report critically on their attitude: They did not generally want to work under the commune, because the pay was too low, there was barely any welfare, no work protection, and no prospects for a future career, unlike in SOEs.[157] Zhang Jing from the Niujie commune complained of the low salaries: "In the past I used to work as a temp worker and made more than ¥1 a day, but since I got to the commune I only make ¥12 a month, and that's not even enough to send the kids to childcare. And nobody reimburses your medical expenses if you are sick." Some of the new cadres were students who believed that neighborhood work had no future, and in that there was no real difference between laboring in a commune factory or doing housework: They were both a waste of talent. Things were different if you were a man and had a bit of education, but work in the neighborhood factory required no skill and the low pay was not worth the while. It was, as one (female) student remarked, echoing the prejudice toward those who performed domestic labor, something fit only for "housewives" who spend all day chattering. As Wang Xiuwen of the Baizhifang glass factory trenchantly remarked, "I came to the neighborhood to work while looking for another job; I am not spending my life here."[158]

Given those premises, it is quite obvious that these cadres were not really that keen about doing voluntary work for the Youth League, as it cut into the time they could devote to studying and learning skills, thus potentially damaging their status as advanced workers. In general, the surveyors were quite dismayed at the ideological awareness of the CYL

---

[156] Kristin Ross, *The Commune Form: The Transformation of Everyday Life* (London: Verso Books, 2024): 61. Ross is making reference to Henri Lefebvre and Catheirne Régulier, "Le projet rhythmanalytique," *Communications* 41 (1985): 194.

[157] BMA 100-001-00659-6 Qingkuang jianbao disanhao.

[158] BMA 100-001-00659-11 Woqu gongshe tuanganbu zai Beijingshi tuanxiao xuexi zhong baoluchu de jige wenti.

cadres: Many were content to "stay in the middle," avoiding exposing themselves for doing either too much or too little; they did not know what class struggle, revisionism, imperialism, and so on were. Most of them were not really willing to die for the cause.[159] Thirteen of them were identified as having major right-leaning tendencies: They believed that people in the countryside were starving, that rural cadres had made false reports, and they were vocally unhappy with the products available in the market.[160] In the end, these commune cadres were found to be ideologically lacking precisely because they valued specific practical benefits of collectivization (increased purchasing power, access to products and services, more leisure time), while criticizing the continuing subordinated and purposefully discriminated conditions of the female labor that made these benefits possible. Other reports, as we have seen, mirrored that assessment by celebrating those very same practical benefits as the manifested realization of women's liberation within the commune movement while at the same time restating the necessity of continuously devaluing female labor. The CYL commune cadres were criticized because they made that tension explicit, because they voiced their own mundane and everyday desires and framed the benefits of collectivization as the realization of those personal longings – and not of a much larger "liberation" or a path to communism – while refusing to overlook the harsh labor conditions and the gender discrimination that made that realization possible. The devaluation of women's labor here was compounded with the devaluation of their desires, as recognizing the latter would have meant recognizing the very contradiction at the core of liberation through communal labor.

## 3.5    From Housewife to Worker?

One of the main arguments I am making in this book is that most of the problems and tensions afflicting urban collectivization were not simply the result of practical constraints or bureaucratic mismanagement but were instead instantiations of deeper political and theoretical fissures.

---

[159] BMA 100-001-00659-11 Woqu gongshe tuanganbu zai Beijingshi tuanxiao xuexi zhong baoluchu de jige wenti.

[160] BMA 100-001-00659-8 Qingkuang jianbao diwuhao. Chengshi renmin gongshe tuanganbu xunlianban guanyu sandafabao wufang chulai de wenti 情况简报第5号. 城市公社团干部训练班关于三大法宝鸣放出来的问题 [Briefing no. 5. Issues raised during the "three great magic weapons" discussion at the urban commune CYL cadre training class], July 20, 1960. This is one of the very few sources I consulted that mentions the famine in the countryside. The "three great magic weapons" were the Party's leadership, the united front, and armed struggle.

Now I want to set the empirical analysis displayed above in the context of the theoretical debates over social reproduction theory (SRT) and Marxist feminism that have taken place outside China. "Social reproduction" was not an issue addressed *directly* during urban collectivization. The term itself never appears in the documents of the period (including during the debate over the law of value and the socialist economy), and the word "reproduction" (*zai shengchan* 再生产), when used, refers primarily to simple or expanded (economic) reproduction. However, the praxis and theory of urban collectivization were connected and logically justified by references to the few texts in the Marxist canon dealing with domestic labor and the condition of women – Engels's *The Origin of the Family* first and foremost. On the other hand, Marxist feminists, especially Italian Marxist feminists in the 1970s and 1980s, took the experience of the Chinese communes as a largely negative but crucial reference for their analysis.

The recent debate over social reproduction has organized itself into two camps, the "autonomists" versus the "Marxists," or the "old" Marxist feminism versus the "new" social reproduction theory. To put it simply, while both sides agree on reaffirming the crucial (and always hidden) role that social reproduction plays in the formation, expansion, and preservation of capitalism, they differ on one crucial point: whether social reproduction work produces value or does not.[161] Or rather, whether it produces value within the circuit of capital. This is an important debate, but it exceeds the scope of my analysis here. Given the specific set of historically situated relationships I am exploring, I feel confident I can sidestep the split between the two camps of SRT and deploy the full array of their contributions. In the case of Great Leap China, while the configuration of the "socialist economy" remains unclear, it was not a capitalist economy (there was, for example, no labor market), but rather a system in which the "mute compulsion" of forms and structures associated with capitalism (wages, the law of value, etc.) continued to affect and shape social relations and social reproduction. In this case, then, the question of whether social reproduction generates value within the circuit of capital is not the crucial one. Here the main issue is how, under the guise of "female liberation," urban collectivization constituted an attempt to tackle one set of issues raised by social

---

[161] Useful summations of this debate have been produced on the two opposite sides: see Alessandra Mezzadri, "On the Value of Social Reproduction: Informal Labour, the Majority World and the Need for Inclusive Theories and Politics," *Radical Philosophy* 2:4 (Spring 2019): 33–41; Paula Varela, "Social Reproduction in Dispute: A Debate between Autonomists and Marxists," *Spectre*, December 10, 2021, https://spectrejournal.com/social-reproduction-in-dispute/.

reproduction theory via the submission of women to waged labor outside the home.

I start here by summarizing the Marxist feminist analysis of social reproduction within capitalism and later evaluate how such an analysis might help us in the case of Maoist China. As Silvia Federici outlined in her book *Caliban and the Witch*, with the advent of the new monetary regime of capitalism, "only production-for-market was defined as a value-creating activity, whereas the reproduction of the worker began to be considered as valueless from an economic viewpoint and even ceased to be considered as work." While reproductive work was paid, if very little, when performed outside the home (nannies, cleaners, servants, wet nurses, etc.), reproductive work within the home became invisible as labor, and so did its crucial role for capital accumulation.[162] What happens with primitive accumulation is the separation of reproduction and production, so that "the general process of commodity production appears as being separate from, and even in direct opposition to, the process of reproduction. While the first appears as the *creation of value*, the second, reproduction, appears as the *creation of non-value*." Capital must pose domestic labor, housework, as the opposite of the real labor that takes place in the factory, "the *mirror* image, the photographic negative of production," thus displacing the former outside capitalism itself, in the realm of the "natural."[163] "For bourgeois ideology, the woman does not work in the proper sense, but carries out a mission, that of wife and mother (more or less emancipated)."[164] With capitalism, women became nonworkers, and "all female work, if done in the home, was defined as 'housekeeping.'"[165] In Margaret Benston's trenchant summation, women are defined by housework; they are the group of people

who are responsible for the production of simple use-values in those activities associated with the home and family ... The material basis for the inferior status of women is to be found in just this definition of women. In a society in which money determines value, women are a group who work outside the money economy. Their work is not worth money, is therefore valueless, is therefore not even real work. And women themselves, who do this valueless work, can hardly be expected to be worth as much as men, who work for money.[166]

---

[162] Silvia Federici, *Caliban and the Witch: Women, the Body, and Primitive Accumulation* (New York: Autonomedia, 2004): 74–75.
[163] Leopoldina Fortunati, *The Arcana of Reproduction: Housewives, Prostitutes, Workers and Capital*, translated by Arlen Austin and Sara Colantuono (London: Verso, 2025): 15.
[164] Fortunati, *The Arcana of Reproduction*: 37.      [165] Federici, *Caliban and the Witch*: 94.
[166] Margaret Benston, "The Political Economy of Women's Liberation," *Monthly Review* 41:7 (December 1989).

In turn, all the forms of labor that take place in the household, all deemed to be creative and unproductive, became feminized, gendered, part of what Maria Mies called *housewifization*, "a complex process entailing both the subordination of women's unpaid labour to male paid labour and the cheapening of women's paid contributions beyond the household."[167]

Indeed, the absolute devaluation of any work performed by "housewives" within the home, and the concurrent association of women with valueless, uncreative, unproductive labor, also radically affected women's waged work. As Antonella Picchio has argued, women are supposed to be dependent on someone else's wages; they are also presumed to be unskilled, domestic labor being "natural" and untrained.[168] This, of course, means that women, even when they find salaried work outside the home, are systematically paid lower wages. This is not a transitory situation that can be amended through a struggle for equal rights, but part and parcel of the basic structure of capitalism itself, and it is grounded in the separation between production and reproduction: "the discrimination that women have suffered in the waged work-force has been directly rooted in their function as unpaid laborers in the home."[169] In the words of Leopoldina Fortunati:

the exchange between women and capital is mediated by the worker. Women's labor power, under the guise of domestic labor, is sold by the housewife to the waged worker as a commodity. However, domestic labor is not formally a commodity. When the free woman worker meets the owner of money (in the form of the wage) on the market, they enter into relations with each other, but not on a footing of equality as owners of commodities, and not as equals in the eyes of the law. It follows that the inequality in the relation between man and woman is neither a dysfunction in the capitalist mode of production nor a legacy of some pre-capitalist barbarity. It is, instead, inherent and ingrained in the functioning of the capitalist mode of production. Equality of exploitation between man and woman cannot exist in a capitalist society precisely because such exploitation is based on power differences that are present within the class itself.[170]

Therefore, in this schema, no liberation can be achieved through women's entry into the labor market; "while it can undoubtedly solve

---

[167] Alessandra Mezzadri, "A Value Theory of Inclusion: Informal Labour, the Homeworker, and the Social Reproduction of Value," *Antipode* 53:4 (2021): 1189. See also Kalindi Vora, "After the Housewife: Surrogacy, Labour and Human Reproduction," *Radical Philosophy* 2:4 (Spring 2019): 44; Mies, *Patriarchy and Accumulation on a World Scale.*

[168] Antonella Picchio, *Social Reproduction: The Political Economy of the Labour Market* (Cambridge: Cambridge University Press, 1992): 80.

[169] Federici, *Caliban and the Witch*: 94–95.

[170] Fortunati, *The Arcana of Reproduction*: 60–61.

many problems in their lives, [it] cannot really 'liberate' them. In reality it does not even bring liberation from patriarchy, because the waged labour market, as we have seen, is based on a particular sexual division of labour in reproduction."[171] Also, if the problem is that "the wage labor relation suffuses the spaces of non-waged everyday life," putting more people directly under that relation could not offer any respite or solution.[172] That was one of the more obvious and clearer ways in which Marxist feminists departed from the Leninist or the bourgeois theory of women's liberation, whose central tenet was indeed "the resort to a second job outside the home" complemented by a (gentle) demand for social services. This is what Fortunati describes as "a sort of migration: from the home to the factory, the only place where an effective fight against the extraction of surplus value is possible"; and this, she concludes, can only lead to the "the atrocious mockery of performing twice the work for a single discriminatory salary."[173] It was one of the tenets of the Italian Marxist feminists (and one that is shared by more recent SRT) that liberation could not be achieved through labor, because the only freedom guaranteed to the wage earner was that of selling their labor power to capital. "Slavery to an assembly line," as Mariarosa Dalla Costa pithily posited, "is not a liberation from slavery to a kitchen sink."[174]

The economic system of 1958 China was neither aspirationally nor actually capitalist, yet several of the gendered and exploitative aspects targeted by the SRT critique were still very much present. Maoist economists and politicians saw the liberation of women very much along the lines traced by Engels and Lenin, that is, through women's participation in waged labor and the concomitant socialization of housework. And while there had been, at the time of the Great Leap, a serious debate on the inherently capitalist and unequal character of waged labor (as shown in Chapter 2), wages remained the measure of the difference between productive and unproductive work, and there was no serious reconsideration of the value of domestic labor. Unproductive/reproductive work was postulated, as in capitalism, as the opposite of productive/factory work, a series of "trivial tasks" requiring no skill and creating no value.[175]

---

[171] Picchio, *Social Reproduction*: 111–112.
[172] Tithi Bhattacharya, "How Not to Skip Class: Social Reproduction of Labor and the Global Working Class," *Viewpoint Magazine* (October 31, 2015), https://viewpointmag .com/2015/10/31/how-not-to-skip-class-social-reproduction-of-labor-and-the-global-working-class/.
[173] Fortunati, *The Arcana of Reproduction*: 2.
[174] Dalla Costa, "Women and the Subversion of the Community."
[175] The characterization of domestic labor as a set of repetitive, cumbersome, onerous, but essentially *trivial* tasks is widespread in the sources. One of the Chinese terms used for

In this sense, it is not surprising that, even under collectivization, female workers in commune factories and service organizations were identified with repetitive, low-skilled, and underpaid forms of labor. This is because, even outside the home, they remained associated with reproductive work, that is, "work that can be reduced to simple work where the woman's simple labor-power – that contained within her body – is used as it is, without any need of specific development," "unskilled labor par excellence." In the commune factory as in the home, women's work then continued to be considered as "undifferentiated labor, uniform, always qualitatively homogenized,"[176] and women continued to be identified as "housewives." So even when, as described earlier, women workers celebrated their newly achieved freedom from the house and the realization of everyday desires in the form of income and leisure, they also highlighted that the factory and service labor which allowed for that income continuously reproduced the very status they were supposed to have left behind and was necessarily grounded on gendered inequality. It was work fit only for "housewives."

Urban collectivization during the Great Leap also presents a very practical case for why housework, that is, the work of social reproduction, cannot be easily transferred to social services or sublimated through technological advances (mechanization of the household). And that was not simply because of the obvious and quite important practical constraints of the time. Rather, this is because, following Antonella Picchio,

[h]ousework is not merely a combination of tasks necessary for the daily reproduction of households and for the physical and psychological life of their members. Housework's job is to restore a relation between production and reproduction that makes sense from the point of view of the people involved. It is expected that within the family, through women and their housework, the alienated relation that structures the system of production and the social system will be reversed, and its conflicts absorbed.

In the family, through the care work of women, the process of accumulation that turns people into commodities is supposed to be reversed,

---

"household chores" is *jiawu suoshi* 家务琐事, and while the compound does not convey an overtly negative tone, the last two characters (琐事) mean "trivia," and that connotation is intimately associated with housework. In some of the documents, domestic labor is often directly described as *fansuo* 繁琐 (tedious, overly detailed, cumbersome) or *fanzhong, suoshide jiawu laodong* 繁重、琐事的家务劳动 (burdensome and trivial housework). Liu Song 刘松, "Guanyu jiawu laodong de jitihua, shehuihu" 关于家务劳动的集体化,社会化 [Concerning the collectivization and socialization of household labor], *Qingnian gongchanzhuyizhe congkan* 青年共产主义者丛刊 [Youth Communist] (November 1958): 91.

[176] Fortunati, *The Arcana of Reproduction*: 149.

restoring them into people.[177] And this is true in the case of Great Leap China, where forms of alienation and inequalities remained inscribed into production and the social fabric. In that, the promise of liberation through social services is largely illusory. First, because social services "not only presuppose domestic work but constantly demand it," thus reproducing incessantly the need for women to take on a double burden. Second, and more importantly, because a large share of domestic work, specifically "the immaterial aspects of domestic work (including affection, love, consolation and, above all, sexuality)," cannot be socialized.[178] This does not mean that we should give up any attempt or even hope to make social reproduction into a communal and collective process, but that this is an incredibly complex and difficult endeavor, which requires a wholesale and radical remaking of the social.

Once analyzed in the light of the critical analysis of Marxist feminism, the urban commune sources detail a process that was riddled by contradictions which not only were due to practical limitations and management issues but were also entangled in some fundamental misunderstanding on the sides of both production and reproduction. The debate on the law of value in 1958 and 1959 had highlighted some of the fundamental problems that continue to affect the functioning of the socialist economy and continuously reproduced "capitalist" forms at its core. That debate, however, had been foreclosed by early 1959, and that reflection also never seemed to apply to the issue of women's liberation, which remained solely entrusted to production, and specifically anchored to one of those "capitalist leftovers": wages. There was no similar debate on the side of social reproduction, so domestic work continued to be framed in an extremely reductive way, either as nonwork if performed inside the home (a set of meaningless chores) or as a constraint to the full release of labor force once it was (incompletely) socialized. In the Maoist framing, then, social reproduction remained ultimately separated from production, and ancillary to it, its role recognized only when its fulfillment interfered with industrial development. Without a total rethinking of the relationship between production and reproduction, not only could the issue of women's liberation not be tackled, but the transition out of a specific mode of production could not even be thought, as the gendered division of labor, with all its nefarious corollaries, is ultimately constitutive of that mode.

We will see how those unresolved contradictions doomed the project of urban collectivization in Chapter 5. But first, a slight detour.

---

[177] Picchio, *Social Reproduction*: 98.    [178] Fortunati, *The Arcana of Reproduction*: 4.

# 4    The Barbers of Beijing

While gathering archival materials about the urban commune movement in Beijing, I kept bumping into documents concerning barbers. Initially, I skipped them, considering them largely irrelevant, one of those strange shards of archival oddity that are at best amusing and in the worst case a waste of precious research time. But these sources kept surfacing, in different archives, authored by different sectors of the state. I was puzzled, so I started collecting and reading them. In retrospect, had my memory served me better, I should not have been surprised. Revolutionary concern for the people's hair was not a new thing. Mao Zedong himself had devoted a few pages of his famed 1930 *Report from Xunwu* to local barbers, meticulously listing their business structure, prices, revenue, profit margins, and even detailing the evolution of (male) hairstyles in the area since the 1911 Revolution, when men had had their Manchu queues cut off.[1] Mao decried the social status and economic conditions of barbers:

Very few barbers and tailors, whether workers or bosses, save up enough money to become rich. The reason is that these two types of people, though generally bright and capable, indulge in whoring and gambling and are fond of fine food and nice clothing. Why are they like this? It is probably because their social position is low. During the Qing Dynasty barbers were regarded by society as one of the "nine low classes."[2]

The documents in the Beijing archives display a similar meticulousness in tracing the fairly complex evolution of the haircutting sector around the time of the Great Leap Forward. And that level of documentary precision was in part justified by the fact that, unlike under the Qing,

---

[1] Mao Zedong, *Report from Xunwu*, translated, and with an introduction and notes by Roger R. Thompson (Stanford: Stanford University Press, 1990): 103–105. Thanks to Rebecca Karl for reminding me of this reference. For a later controversy involving women's hairstyles, see Lung-kee Sun, "The Politics of Hair and the Issue of the Bob in Modern China," *Fashion Theory* 1:4 (1997): 353–366.

[2] Mao Zedong, *Report from Xunwu* 104.

under socialism, barbershops – together with bathhouses and sometimes photographers – were considered to provide an essential service to the people, so much so that frequent haircuts were often included in the benefits that *danwei* provided to employees.[3] The haircutting industry was described as "serving urban residents' cleanliness and beauty, thus being closely integrated in people's livelihood."[4] In 1962, the movie *Female Hairdresser* (*Nü lifashi* 女理发师), starring the famous actress Wang Danfeng 王丹凤, celebrated, in comedic form, the importance of that vocation and skewered the prejudices against barbers, showing at the same times how those prejudices lingered in the socialist era and how much attention the CCP devoted to that sector of the service industry.[5] Making socialist barbers was therefore a not unimportant element in the totalizing transformation of the urban everyday that Great Leap collectivization aimed at achieving. With a revolutionized haircutting sector, urban residents would finally have access to barbering services delivered more efficiently and with higher aesthetic standards, thus fulfilling one of the stated goal of the Leap, "to make people's lives more beautiful" (*meihua renmin shenghuo* 美化人民生活).[6] That transformation was also supposed to radically improve the lives of the barbers themselves, many of whom still toiled in small family shops or as itinerant peddlers, and therefore "lagged behind" in the path to the promised achievements of socialism, let alone the future of communism. Finally, barbers, who worked in close contact with other people's bodies and were tasked not only with their customers' looks but also with their cleanliness, were

---

[3] A December 1956 survey estimated the average individual to need eighteen haircuts per year. BMA 068-001-00025-0094 Beijingshi chengqu lifaye, yuchiye qingkuang huibao cailiao (caogao) 北京市城区理发业、浴池业情况汇报材料（草稿）[Draft report on the situation of bathhouses and barbers in Beijing inner city districts], February 19, 1957.

[4] *Lifaye gongzuo yewu shouce: zhuangong ge lifadian gong zuo renyuan xuexi yewu zhi yong* 理发业工作人员业务手册: 专供各理发店工作人员学习业务之用 [Manual for employees of the haircutting industry: To be used for study by personnel in every barbershop] (上海市福利事业公司编印, January 1958): 33.

[5] *Nü lifashi* 女理发师 (Female hairdresser), dir. Ding Ran, 1962. Available at https://youtu.be/KE6fszfli4c?si=4ZzGodepsHwHhy0W (accessed June 2025). The movie depicts a hypocritical husband who vehemently opposes his wife's desire to become a hairdresser – a profession not suited for the spouse of a "director" – while instructing everybody else on how all jobs are equally dignified under socialism. I am thankful to Benjamin Kindler, who told me about this movie.

[6] HDA 030-101-0109 Beijingshi, Haidianqu fuwuju guanyu yinshi, lifaye jishu biaoyan qingkuang tongbao he Haishunju fanguan zhongzhi mogu de qingkuang jieshao北京市、海淀区服务局关于饮食、理发业技术表演情况通报和海顺居饭馆种植蘑菇的情况介绍 [Beijing Municipal and Haidian District Service Bureaus' circular on technical demonstrations by the hairdressing and catering industries and report on mushroom cultivation at the Haishunji restaurant].

considered to be involved in the larger Great Leap push to make the cities – and the people who lived in them – more "hygienic."

The sources on Beijing barbers[7] from the late 1950s and early 1960s describe a process of collectivization and decollectivization, which was paralleled by radical changes in *fenpei* (allocation of resources and funds), welfare, salary, and ownership, and which produced quite profound social effects, for workers and customers. Collectivization of barbers started before the Leap (in 1956) but it significantly accelerated in 1958–1960, only for that process to be largely reversed after 1960. In that, the history of Great Leap barbers mirrored the development and dénouement of the urban communes and offers some specific insights into that process. Barbers' collectivization, while socially and economically eventful, did not bring about disastrous consequences, but this relatively minor case sheds light on questions of productivity, developmentalism, welfare, and labor under socialism, hotly debated issues that defined the larger urban commune movement and the Great Leap in general. The sources also document another, perhaps more trivial detail, but one that significantly alters the stereotypical image of collectivized life in the socialist city: During the Great Leap not only did hairstyling fashions and a corresponding hierarchy of hairdressers persist, but they were recognized and actively fostered by local and state authorities. The case of hairdressers and barbers in Great Leap Beijing, then, shows the attentiveness some cadres paid to the most minute aspects of the quotidian but also testifies to the resilience of subtle (and not so subtle) social differences in the midst of what was supposed to be one of the more aspirationally "egalitarian" movements in the Maoist era. It was not just that the end of the movement brought back "petit bourgeois" strategies and methods and restored inequalities in salaries, treatments, and so on. Rather, what the barbers of Beijing show is that the very process of collectivization was not necessarily meant to eliminate social and economic differences, as those differences were integral to the process, and they were often at the center of cadres' perspectives. Similar to what Tina Mai Chen has highlighted for the rhetoric surrounding fashion and clothing, this case also reveals "the contradictions inherent in Maoist ideals that simultaneously produced alternative visions while locating alternatives within hierarchical structures."[8]

---

[7] I here use the term "barber," which usually refers to men who cut the hair of male customers, to translate the Chinese "*lifayuan* 理发员" or "*lifashi* 理发师," which can identify both (male) barbers and (female) hairdressers, who were cutting and styling hair for both male and female residents.

[8] Tina Mai Chen, "Proletarian White and Working Bodies in Mao's China," *positions: east asia cultures critique* 11:2 (Fall 2003): 364.

The case of barbershops' collectivization and decollectivization then underlines how our view of the Great Leap is often myopic and distorted by converging stereotypes, in that we overestimate the extent of the social leveling the campaign was supposed to produce – maybe because there was a definite and tragic overestimation of its economic effects. Productivity and unending need for capital profit accumulation almost invariably trumped any consideration of social change and reduction of inequality; actually, the preservation of inequalities was often inscribed in the process, as it was functional to profit, increased accumulation, and reduced expenses. Yet collectivization came with political promises, stated *and* implicit, and central among them was that of a more egalitarian society. Nor do I believe that those promises were empty, that their fulfilment was supposed to be endlessly postponed, or, worse, that they were ruses to force people into deploying more and more self-sacrificing labor. As we have seen, the Great Leap was predicated on the possibility of an accelerated transition into a more equal society (communism), and that ideal manifested itself in practical ways. First and foremost, in the attempt to provide services and benefits to people who currently did not enjoy them, people who had been kept out of the SOE *danwei* system. And that often meant including their labor under the umbrella of "ownership by the whole people," with very concrete consequences for livelihood and security. Those consequences were much more significant for those urban workers in very precarious positions, in terms of income and status, such as many of the barbers. If the socialist economy, achieved in 1956, had created a unified socialist market where production and commodity exchange could happen "without fear of speculation and manipulation by private capital,"[9] then, at least to some, the Great Leap looked like the next logical step toward a market in which not commodities, but necessary products and services were provided (and not exchanged) to the entire population. If you expect communism to arrive relatively soon, it is not surprising that you would push now for a society with reduced inequalities, increased availability of cheap or better free services, and an increasingly diminished role for "capitalist" forms of relationship and organization. And there were indeed plenty of efforts to steer the Leap in the direction of more egalitarian social relations, usually coming from the bottom up, from street-level cadres and organizations. However, as the examples in this chapter illustrate, when these efforts, even at the neighborhood or commune level, came close to impeding overall capital accumulation or requiring disbursements from the state, they were

---

[9] Hsue Mu-chiao, Su Hsing, and Lin Tse-li, *The Socialist Transformation of the National Economy in China* (Peking: Foreign Language Press, 1960): 239.

invariably tamped down and social differences were reaffirmed. Here we see once again the crucial tension between the promise of a revolution-ized and egalitarian everyday and the impossibility – or at least the strong reluctance – to instantiate that promise in the present, because of the belief that doing so could potentially put that very future at risk. This was the tension embodied in the contradictory temporality of socialism as *transition*, one defined by the lag between different components of the social formation, between those elements that prefigured a new revolu-tionized set of relations and those that continued to re-create the old (capitalist) ones.[10] That tension affected the evolution and the destinies of every single aspect of collectivization, including hairstyling.

## 4.1    Collectivizing Barbers

In 1956 the Chinese state, on its path to declaring the elimination of private ownership of the means of production and thus the achievement of socialism, faced the task of transforming the structure of those busi-nesses that provided daily services, including barbering, to city residents. This led to a proliferation of surveys, tracing the history and the current situation of that enterprise. Being a barber in Beijing had supposedly been relatively lucrative in the early Republican period, but the situation had radically worsened during the Japanese occupation, and then again with the inflationary crisis culminating in the 1947 collapse of the econ-omy. By the time of liberation in late 1949, 138 barbershops (probably around a third of the total) had closed, and yet a good barber could feed a family, and an average one could provide for themselves.[11] The situation improved after 1952, following the state's coordinated efforts in "city construction," with a steadily increasing number of barbershops (from 600 to 822 between 1949 and 1955)[12] and average income – in 1954, ¥120 per month constituted a high salary, ¥70–80 a medium one.[13] With the exception of those shops operated by larger work units, most individ-ual barbers' income was determined as a percentage of the shop's overall

---

[10] Alberto Toscano, "Transition Deprogrammed," *South Atlantic Quarterly* 113:4 (Fall 2014): 761–775.
[11] BMA 068-001-00025-0094 Beijingshi chengqu lifaye, yuchiye qingkuang huibao cailiao (caogao).
[12] BMA 068-001-00025-0002 Beijingshi lifaye jiben qingkuang he youguan gaozao wenti de yijian 北京市理发业基本情况和有关改造问题的意见 [Suggestions on the situation of the hairdressing industry in Beijing and problems related to its reform], March 6, 1956.
[13] BMA 068-001-00025-0094 Beijingshi chengqu lifaye, yuchiye qingkuang huibao cailiao (caogao).

revenue, a system that had been adopted at the time of the Japanese occupation.[14]

At the end of 1956 there were 1,225 barbershops in the city, most of them privately owned, and organized according to six different levels of quality and service. Some 325 of those "shops" were small family businesses, often no more than itinerant peddlers, operating in the inner city. The Beijing Social Welfare Bureau (*Jingshi shehui fuli shiye ju* 京市社会福利事业局) produced elaborate statistics, recording the average number of haircuts per barber (between 8.4 and 12.3 per day) and the composition of the clientele, which varied significantly according to the quality of the establishment. Beijing barbers were often from poor families, and 29 percent of them were illiterate.[15] Tuberculosis (*feibing* 肺病) was common, and of the 485 barbers in the Xidan area (in Xicheng district), thirty-three were reported to be sick. Barbers were also particularly affected by Beijing's chronic housing scarcity, and employees often slept on the shop floor. The prejudice toward the profession that Mao had noted had not yet dissipated, and barbers were considered to be of low social and political status: "barbers were not fit to be seen" (*lifayuan jianbuderen* 理发员见不得人), it was a degrading trade (*disan xiasi* 低三下四), not to be mentioned (*buzudao* 不足道).[16] A young barber in a Sanlihe shop in 1958 apparently refused to tell anybody what his job was, while some of his colleagues wrote down as their actual employer the government agency in whose building the shop was located.[17] Of the "necessary" services, working as a photographer in a hotel was a much more coveted position than being a barber or a bathhouse employee, and, in Beijing, that led to an enduring shortage in personnel. Even after an initial phase of collectivization in early 1956, the existing establishments could satisfy only 35.5 percent of the total demand for haircuts in the capital. As a result, barbers were overworked, and customers had often to endure long queues. The unequal distribution of barbershops in the city, the concentration of customers during specific times (after work or on days off), and the increased demand for perms among female customers all made the

---

[14] BMA 068-001-00025-0094 Beijingshi chengqu lifaye, yuchiye qingkuang huibao cailiao (caogao). Female hairdressers were originally paid more, but the difference had been reduced after 1949.

[15] BMA 068-001-00025-0002 Beijingshi lifaye jiben qingkuang he youguan gaozao wenti de yijian.

[16] *Lifaye gongzuo renyuan yewu shouce*: 2. Preconceptions about the trade were considered one of the causes behind the seemingly chronic lack of barbers in Beijing and Shanghai.

[17] BMA 001-021-00095-0035 Dayuejin zhong de Sanlihe lifaguan 大跃进中的三里河理发馆 [The Sanlihe barbershop during the Great Leap Forward], 1958.

situation worse.[18] Sources celebrated the massive improvement in the overall quality of life for urban residents, due to industrialization and the increase in production, but that had also led to a more sophisticated clientele with higher aesthetic standards, which the extant supply of services struggled to satisfy.[19]

Collectivization aimed at transforming the larger and higher-quality stores into public/private joint ventures while medium- and small-sized shops would be reorganized in cooperatives, on a profit-sharing system. The overall goal of the city administration was to shut down a fair number of small establishments, while opening new, larger ones (or expanding the size of the existing ones), upgrading hygienic conditions and the overall quality of the offerings. Cooperatives were supposed to improve all aspects of business, including management, internal democracy, political study, and transmission of skills, while centralizing expenses, purchasing, and taxes. Shops were also to be redistributed in areas of the city that chronically lacked services, merging smaller shops in crowded neighborhoods. The major obstacle was the large number of very small family operations and itinerant street barbers, who provided an indispensable service in a very nimble fashion but who were difficult to organize into cooperatives, as in many cases there was no real separation between work and family, shop and housing. Those who could not be collectivized, one report sanctioned, were not to remain a "permanent feature of the socialist economy."[20]

Collectivization, however, was not supposed to produce uniformity or even to reduce differences in either prices or salaries. The Social Welfare Bureau noted with a certain dismay that current prices, if adjusted for inflation, were lower than during the war with Japan and the early 1950s. Prices did not accurately reflect the hierarchy of barbers and shops in the city,[21] leading to overcrowding of the better shops while the cheaper or less skilled ones remained empty and unprofitable. The proposed solution was to increase both prices overall and price differences among

---

[18] BMA 068-001-00025-0094 Beijingshi chengqu lifaye, yuchiye qingkuang huibao cailiao (caogao). The increase in the demand for perms was connected to the "reform of women's clothing."

[19] *Lifaye gongzuo renyuan yewu shouce*: 2. See also "Jinyibu zhankai jingsai, tigao fuwu zhiliang (Beijingshi fuwu shiye guanliju fujuzhang Ding Tiefeng)" 进一步展开竞赛,提高服务质量 (北京市服务事业管理局副局长 丁铁峰) [Further develop the competition to improve the quality of services (Ding Tiefeng, Deputy Director of Beijing Municipal Service Administration)], *Beijing Ribao* 北京日报, August 2, 1959: 2.

[20] BMA 068-001-00025-0002 Beijingshi lifaye jiben qingkuang he youguan gaozao wenti de yijian.

[21] ¥1 between special and first grade, and ¥0.5 between all other levels. BMA 068-001-00025-0094 Beijingshi chengqu lifaye, yuchiye qingkuang huibao cailiao (caogao).

shops. Similarly, the Bureau expressed dissatisfaction with the current salary system, based on an even distribution of a percentage of the daily revenue, which they blamed for "egalitarianism," and proposed to replace it with a hybrid system of fixed salaries plus piece-rate wages and bonuses.[22] If changing the entire salary system proved to be impossible, the Bureau stressed that individual salaries should at least reflect much more closely differences in term of hours, kinds of work, and skill levels.[23] Socialist labor competitions and ideological work were deployed to increase productivity and promote training, as, for example, in April 1959, when service enterprises in the city, including barbers, were first involved in the "'five goods' red banner competition movement," and then in the "three rivals" (rivalling in skill, efficiency, and quality).[24]

Finally, it is worth noting that while all reports remarked how most barbers did not receive any welfare provisions and that medical coverage was especially needed, no comprehensive solution emerged to tackle the issue. Only some of the newly and better organized cooperatives were deemed able to provide medical coverage for employees and even to reimburse their bathhouse fees, but these were model shops, cited as exemplary cases. Barbers in state-owned shops, on the other hand, enjoyed both fixed monthly salaries (there was no piece-rate wage) and welfare provisions.[25]

Collectivization of services did not necessarily represent an economic benefit for some of the city residents either. In January 1957, the *People's Daily* printed a letter in which a reader from Tianjin remonstrated against the price hike at his local barbershop, which he blamed on the expansion of nonproductive personnel that took place with the creation of private/public joint enterprise. He noted that they had added a management office for barbers, six district main stores, and thirty-three management areas, and had transferred 123 cadres, for a total expense of ¥200,000, equal to 15.6 percent of the total revenues of all city barbers, who were therefore forced to increase prices. As this letter-writer put it, hypocrites who filled their mouths with sentences like "running enterprises like businesses" (*qiyehua* 企业化) and "specialization" (*zhuanyehua* 专业化)

[22] BMA 068-001-00025-0002 Beijingshi lifaye jiben qingkuang he youguan gaozao wenti de yijian.
[23] BMA 068-001-00025-0094 Beijingshi chengqu lifaye, yuchiye qingkuang huibao cailiao (caogao).
[24] "Jinyibu zhankai jingsai, tigao fuwu zhiliang (Beijingshi fuwu shiye guanliju fujuzhang Ding Tiefeng)." The text does not specify what the "five goods" are in this case, but the term usually includes good leadership, good party members, good working structure, good work performance, and high appreciation from the public.
[25] BMA 068-001-00025-0094 Beijingshi chengqu lifaye, yuchiye qingkuang huibao cailiao (caogao).

had no issue inflating the size of management, and the cost fell on the people, who still needed haircuts.[26]

That same year, 1957, the Beijing municipal government abolished rations for haircuts and showers, leaving the *danwei* to pick up the slack, leading to a certain amount of confusion and, eventually, to an overall reduction of subsidies. The Local Industry Bureau had to issue guidelines to local factories stating unequivocally that the value of coupons provided under the new system should not exceed what used to be paid by the municipality; if prices went up, workers should pay the difference. Given that prices, as we have seen, were meant to go up, we can surmise that this move had deleterious effects for the pocketbooks of individual workers.[27] The same office conducted a survey of seventy-six local factories, which, in the first half on 1957, had subsidized showers and haircuts for a total of ¥224,546, an average of ¥0.76 per employee per month, equal to 1.34 percent of the average employee monthly salary. Some factories had barbershops on-site, but the majority relied on outside shops, and there were a variety of arrangements – agreements with barbers, coupons, and so on – and of subsidies, with women receiving a larger allowance per haircut. The bureau's suggestion was to terminate all these arrangements and unload the burden of payment onto the employees – and the barbers. For those factories that hosted a shop, they should simply stop paying a salary to the barbers and let them survive on the fees they could extract from employees, now without subsidies. As for the other factories, the document states that rations should simply be discontinued.[28]

From these relatively random sources from the earlier (pre–Great Leap) phase of collectivization of service enterprises, it appears that this process was primarily supposed to establish collective (if not state) control over individual businesses with the goal of improving the supply, quality, and distribution of hairstyling and haircutting services. That this came with an overall price hike, increased differences among shops, and diminished subsidies seemed to have largely been accepted and even

[26] Bao Chang鲍昌, "Lifa yougan" 理发有感 [Reflections on a haircut], *RMRB*, January 13, 1957.
[27] BMA 019-002-00169-071 Guanyu zhigong lifa, xizaofei baoxiao banfa de lianhe tongzhi 关于职工理发、洗澡费报销办法的联合通知 [Joint notice concerning the method for reimbursing expenses for haircuts and showers], December 2, 1957. The notice was by the Beijing No. 1, No. 2, and No. 3 Local Industrial Bureaus (北京市第1、2、3 地方工业局) and the Beijing Municipal Building Materials Industry Bureau (北京市建筑材料工业局).
[28] BMA 061-001-00156-0089 Guanyu zhigong lifa xizao de jiben qingkuang diaocha 关于职工理发洗澡的基本情况调查 [Survey of the general conditions of employees' haircutting and showering], 1957.

welcomed by Beijing planners, as, at this stage, reducing socioeconomic differences, expanding welfare provisions, or shifting economic burdens away from the individual were not among the main objectives of barbers' reorganization. Efficiency, capital accumulation, and improvement of service were paramount. That would change the following year, however, because the Great Leap embraced, both implicitly and explicitly, the goal of prefiguring more egalitarian social relationships and instantiating a more egalitarian distribution of resources.

## 4.2 How to Be a Good Barber

Just a few months before the start of the Great Leap Forward, the Shanghai Municipal Welfare Company compiled and published an incredibly detailed manual for the newly collectivized barbers, describing (or rather prescribing) with stubborn precision haircutting techniques, customer service procedures, safety and hygiene rules, tool maintenance, and successful management processes. The booklet provides a snapshot of what was expected from barbers and how the hairstyling industry was conceived under collectivization.

The preface offers a brief history of hairdressing, from the Tang dynasty to the present. It insists that great improvements had taken place in the Republican period, especially following the revolutionary tide initiated with the May Fourth movement and the ideological change it produced: Women started wearing their hair shorter and in bobs; people's demand for more beautiful hairstyles increased; and different styles and new techniques were developed, all of which led to the thriving situation at the present time, when the barbers' skills had become an art geared toward the production of beauty (*zaomei de yishu* 造美的艺术).[29] The authors highlight the improvements achieved in recent years, especially under collectivization, in terms of the popular opinion about barbers, their skills, methods, enthusiasm, and creativity. Following the rapid industrialization and increase in production that had taken place under socialism, urban residents' tastes had also developed, leading to a demand for more sophisticated styles and higher aesthetic standards. This assessment echoes the coeval debates on what socialist fashion should look like, how the new woman and the new man that socialism was creating should be dressed, and what principles should determine that fashion, debates that had taken place through the 1950s and had culminated just a couple of years earlier, in 1956, with the Beijing

---

[29] *Lifaye gongzuo renyuan yewu shouce*: 1.

clothing exhibition. How to create fashion styles that were at the same time uniquely Chinese and uniquely socialist remained a seemingly unsolvable problem, but by the mid 1950s a shared agreement had emerged on the fact that, if the establishment of the new state had led to improvements in industrial technology, living standards, and social organization, then outward standards of beauty should reflect that improvement, thus making evolving ideas of fashion a desired feature – rather than an unwanted epiphenomenon – of socialist development. "The aim of socialism … was 'the improvement of the material life and culture of the people,'" and that, as Antonia Finnane has pointed out, included the beautification of dress "in accordance with the principles of attractiveness, economy and usefulness."[30] People had become more beautiful, their lives had become more beautiful, so their clothes – and their hair – should also be beautiful.[31] In the 1950s, "a diverse wardrobe" and diverse hairstyles "could reflect success according to socialist norms set by the CCP rather than a bourgeois proclivity for self-indulgence," as fashion options demonstrated how goods and services that used to be the "luxuries of an earlier age" were now available to the socialist masses.[32] The Great Leap famine and the desperate needs for resources it engendered overwhelmed any concern for fashion – albeit not completely, as the case of Beijing barbers show – and frugality became the primary criterion. But in the early stage of the Great Leap, it is not at all surprising that a movement that was presented as a massive push for a radical progress in all aspects of everyday life should also include fashion and personal beauty as a central preoccupation.

The barbers' manual devotes several pages to promoting good service practices: Customers should be welcomed at the door, their coats stored in a safe place, reading materials should be made available, and they should be offered a clean towel – warmed at a temperature fitting the weather – when they arrive and before they leave. Barbers should also avoid chatting with colleagues and customers, focusing their attention solely on the task at hand. Instructions about actual haircutting and shaving are even more impressively meticulous. Men's cuts are divided between short and long hair: Styles for short hair include the bowl cut (*yuanding* 圆顶), the flat top (*pingding* 平顶), and complete shave (like monks), but it is with long hair that things get complicated.[33] When a

---

[30] Antonia Finnane, *Changing Clothes in China: Fashion, History, Nation* (New York: Columbia University Press, 2008): 220.

[31] Finnane, *Changing Clothes in China*: 210.

[32] Tina Mai Chen, "Dressing for the Party: Clothing, Citizenship, and Gender-Formation in Mao's China," *Fashion Theory* 5:2 (2001): 152–153.

[33] *Lifaye gongzuo renyuan yewu shouce*: 10.

customer sits down, the barber should pay careful attention to his age, stature, and existing haircut in order to figure out what style is most appropriate. Cutting is described as a fairly complex procedure, involving combing with a wooden comb, using both electric and manual razors, trimming, washing, shaving the beard, and massaging the face. Blow-drying, the final step, also required a specific skill in order to create the "youthful style" (*qingnianshi de chuifa* 青年式的吹法) – one of the two styles listed for long-haired men.[34]

The hairstyling procedures for women were more intricate and the explanations even more painstakingly detailed. Besides cutting and blowing, perms featured prominently, with four different techniques: hot, electric, water-based, and chemical, the latter being a new safer, method. According to the manual, the electric perm just made the hair wavy, while the water one consisted in applying coils onto permed hair so to create all kind of ripples and waves, allowing to shape the hair in "new and original styles." The electric perm, on the other hand, allowed for limited choices and could only reproduce "old styles."[25]

The manual then included a section devoted to hygiene, with detailed instructions (down to the percentage of Lysol or alcohol in the cleaning solution) on how to disinfect both tools and the shop area, requirements for the personal cleanliness of the barbers, and advice on how to take care of one's own hair. After chapters on razor sharpening and equipment repair, democratic management and internal organization, the last section of the manual provides a series of suggestions on "how to follow the policy of running the enterprise diligently and thriftily, and actively participate in the movement to increase production and reduce expenses."[36] Here the authors bring attention back to a crucial element in how the collectivized service industry was supposed to function: It was a question not just of providing needed services to the largest number of people in the best possible way, but also of delivering them at no cost to – and possibly with profit for – the state, whose main objective remained industrial development. They remark how the hairstyling enterprise had long-standing issues, and how, despite the improvements of recent years, employees still lived on very low wages, and many barbershops relied on state support and were incapable of serving the people well. Even more serious, however, were the economic losses being sustained throughout the industry, which presented an obstacle to further development at the state level – meaning that the state subsidized barbers with capital it

---

[34] *Lifaye gongzuo renyuan yewu shouce*: 9–10.
[35] *Lifaye gongzuo renyuan yewu shouce*: 10–16.
[36] *Lifaye gongzuo renyuan yewu shouce*: 33.

should instead invest in production. What follows is a long list of meticulous recommendations aimed at helping "establish the glorious feeling of
turning over more capital to the state."[37] Barbers were asked to improve
skills and workplace organization so to reduce service time and to adjust
working hours to fit the needs of the residents and increase income.
To reduce overall electricity consumption by 5 percent, the manual gives
specific instructions on using lights and fans, but also regulates blow-
drying time, which should be five to eight minutes for men, ten minutes
for the "youth" style, and five to ten minutes for women. Similar scru-
pulously comprehensive rules are offered to economize on the use of fuel,
lotions, Vaseline, soap, perm solution, and water. The manual displays
and summarizes both the kind of attitude required from collectivized
service workers and the systemic constraints in which that effort was to be
deployed. The combination of voluntary overwork, overwhelming attention to detail, and obsessive cutbacks on expenses was functional to
providing stratified and differentiated services at no cost to the state –
the cost being absorbed by deployment of selfless labor and resourceful
avoidance of waste. This combination of strategies characterizes the
development of the hairstyling industry during the Great Leap.

## 4.3    A Great Leap in Haircutting

In the movie *Today Is My Day Off*, set in Great Leap Shanghai, a haircut
functions as the fulcrum for the comedic plot. Ma Tianming, an altruis-
tic, committed, yet hapless police officer, stops at the local barbershop to
get his hair cut before his movie date. The barber welcomes him with a
smile, and despite Ma's protestations, volunteers to skip lunch and cut
the officer's hair, so that he can go on his date looking his best. The
barber has just started trimming Ma's hair (with electric clippers) when
his customer is called out for an emergency. This is followed by another
emergency, and another, and then yet another event that requires poor
Ma's attention. The barber reappears at the very end of the movie:
Ma finds him waiting in Ma's own room, late at night, clippers in hand,
ready to finally provide his services. If Ma is the embodiment of Party-
inspired selfless dedication, the barber exemplifies an extraordinary yet
supposedly commonplace "serve the people" attitude. That portrayal,
idealized as it may be, appears to be a relatively accurate representation of
the efforts of Beijing barbers during the Great Leap.[38]

---

[37] *Lifaye gongzuo renyuan yewu shouce*: 34.
[38] *Jintian wo xiuxi* 今天我休息 (Today is my day off), dir. Lu Ren (1959). Available at www
.virtualshanghai.net/Films/Collection?ID=109 (accessed March 2025).

With the launch of the Great Leap in 1958, the pace, scope, and form of collectivization increased. Building on earlier efforts, the Leap also had the stated goal to socialize domestic labor and care-providing services, extending *fuli* to people who had so far been excluded. Haircutting was one of those services to be "socialized," shifted from an individual burden to a collective responsibility, and even before the full (re)launch of the urban commune movement in 1960, barbers in Beijing were absorbed by a massive push for productivity and labor activism. Municipal documents record this transformative effort at the level of daily business practice.

In downtown Beijing, two models of Great Leap success were the Tianqiao Department Store and the Mishi street grocery store. Employees of the Sanlihe barbershop (a state-owned business established in September 1956) visited the Tianqiao location and decided to remold their business practices in that image. The first decision was to abandon the eight-hour workday: Barbers started working from dawn till dusk, indefatigably. This produced a profit of over ¥7,800 but also led to a drastic reduction of personnel, from thirty-two to twenty. Barbers also worked to improve customer service: They now welcomed every customer with a smile, handed them a magazine, and politely asked them to wait for the next available barber. Yet it appears that most employees at Sanlihe were not particularly apt at displaying cordiality and ended up looking fake and pretentious. One exception was a barber named Li Wenfu, who was so effortlessly good at expressing enthusiasm that he had received up to twelve notes of commendations from customers in one day.[39] The shop then started a "learn from Li Wenfu" campaign, which focused on ideological transformation of services in the name of serving the people. More substantially, they radically changed the practical working of the shop: Surrounded by offices, it used to keep normal office hours and was therefore inaccessible for most of the workers in the area, who themselves were at work during the shop's opening hours. So, not only did the barbershop extend their hours of operation, but they also reserved appointments and sent barbers to make rounds, cutting hair door to door, very much like the fictional Ma Tianming's barber.[40]

The following year, the Sanlihe barbershop (now a Red Star work unit) reported further progress. As the *People's Daily* recounted, all barbers at Sanlihe had mastered both male and female hairstyles, thus reducing

---

[39] The text does not explain how these letters or notes were collected; possibly there was something like a suggestion box.
[40] BMA 001-021-00095-0035 Dayuejin zhong de Sanlihe lifaguan.

waiting times for customers.[41] They added scalp massages and back rubs to their services and increased yearly profits by 21.35 percent compared with 1958. This was achieved through a quite impressive increase in productivity, with male and female barbers styling the hair of 19.4 customers per day on average (up from 16), while significantly reducing expenses.[42] Another Red Flag work unit, the No. 1 barbershop in Fengtai District (in the southwest of Beijing), detailed a similar successful expansion of services: They offered massages, but also lent out their tools, with roaming barbers (*liudong lifa* 流动理发) visiting communes, offices, and individual residences.[43]

The barbershops at Sanlihe and Fengtai provide us with another example of what kind of labor Great Leap collectivization required. First of all, it required *more* labor: In Fengtai, workers started providing their own perm solution and repairing their own tools.[44] In the same vein, the manager of the No. 1 Barbershop at Xidan celebrated the large amount of extra work his employees had contributed during the National Day festivities, coming to the shop extra early, leaving extra late, and

---

[41] "Jinyibu zhankai jingsai, tigao fuwu zhiliang (Beijingshi fuwu shiye guanliju fujuzhang Ding Tiefeng)."

[42] BMA 001-021-0148-0109 1959 nian caimao xitong hongqi danwei cailiao – Xichengqu Sanlihe lifaguan 1959 年财贸系统红旗单位材料 – 西城区三里河理发馆 [Materials on the 1959 Red Flag work units in the financial and trade system: The Sanlihe barbershop in Xicheng District], 1959.

[43] BMA 001-021-00148-0114 1959 nian caimao xitong hongqi danwei cailiao – Fengtaiqu di yi lifaguan zhuyao xianjin shiji 1959 年财贸系统红旗单位材料 – 丰台区第一理发馆主要先进事迹 [Materials on the 1959 Red Flag work units in the financial and trade system: The advanced achievements of the No. 1 barbershop in Fengtai District]. Repairing barber tools was economic but was not necessarily a good idea. In the same year, a barber in Guanqumen Zhongcheng barbershop in Chongwen district was electrocuted and died while using faulty hair clippers. BMA 001-021-00131-0139 Caimao diandi (47) – Shangbannian benshi jieyue meitan chengji xianzhu, zuijin you xie waidi guanqie liuru qiyou 11 dun duo, Chongwenqu yi lifayuan wushi Anquan chongdian shensi 财贸点滴 (47) – 上半年本市节约煤炭成绩显著、最近有些外地惯窃流入汽油11顿多、崇文区一理发员无视安全触电身死 [Finance and trade briefs (47) – Notable achievements in our city's coal conservation effort during the first half of the year; over 11 tons of gasoline stolen by non-local thieves; A barber in Chongwen district electrocuted due to safety negligence], September 10, 1959. In 1959, Fengtai District was also extolled as a model in training new barbers: Neighborhoods sent young apprentices to various district barbershops to learn from practice, while shops sent experienced barbers into neighborhoods to share skills and techniques. By August, the seven apprentices at the No. 1 Barbershop had already achieved a basic skill level and could work independently. "Fengtaiqu ge lifadian bangzhu jiedao peiyang lifa renyuan" 丰台区各理发店帮助街道培养理发人员 [All barbershops in Fengtai district help neighborhoods train hairdressing staff], *RMRB*, August 12, 1959.

[44] BMA 001-021-00148-0114 1959 nian caimao xitong hongqi danwei cailiao – Fengtaiqu di yi lifaguan zhuyao xianjin shiji.

working extra hard through the holidays.[45] But longer hours and extended efforts were not the only or even the main requirement. Collectivized shops were also supposed to be more productive, serving a larger number of customers through a more efficient deployment of labor, increasing profit and cutting expenses at the same time. Sanlihe, as noted, had achieved those goals while also reducing its personnel, thus becoming a smaller but more productive and efficient shop, and the assumption was that excess personnel could be deployed elsewhere in the ever-expanding effort of the Great Leap. There was, however, as we have seen in previous chapters, a precarious balance to be struck between improvements in work methods and resource utilization, on the one hand, and increased extraction of labor, on the other, either through intensification of work effort or through simple extension of the workday. The Great Leap promise was that increased accumulation and cheaper, better services could be achieved by emphasizing the former element, especially with the prospect of further mechanization, including for barbers. Yet falling back on ever-increasing extraction was always a tempting possibility for managers and bureaucrats.

Newspapers reported anecdotes about the outstanding service attitude of some barbershops in the capital, highlighting the ethics of sacrifice they embodied. The *Beijing Ribao* recounted how a female customer had come to a barbershop in Xidan around 7 pm, asking for a perm. Perms usually required at least two hours, but she was leaving town the next day and needed to get something to eat before 8 pm. Then all the barbers rallied and, working as a team, they sped up the process, completing the perm in about one hour. They even went to the nearby restaurant and got a bowl of noodles delivered so that the customer could have dinner while having her hair styled.[46] A few years later, the model barbershop at Sanlihe was similarly extolled in the news. A Beijing resident was looking to get a haircut during the weekend, but all shops were busy; by the time he got to Sanlihe, it was already 9:40 pm and there was a line. He stood there, undecided about what to do, until one of the barbers called him in, saying they were all going to work overtime, no problem. Once all the customers were taken care of, the barbers vied with one another over who was going to stay and clean up – they all wanted to – only for the

[45] BMA 001-021-00146-0026 Xidan diyi lifaguan jingli Jin Guangshou Tongzhi de fayan gao 西单第一理发馆经理金广寿同志的发言稿 [Speech by comrade Jin Guangshou, manager of the No. 1 barbershop at Xidan], August 19, 1959.
[46] "Guke you jishi, tangfa zhi yong yi xiaoshi" 顾客有急事 烫发只用一小时 [The customer is in a rush so the perm takes only one hour], *Beijing ribao* 北京日报, December 27, 1959: 2.

customers to take up brooms and sweep up the place as a thank you to the selfless employees.[47]

This wave of politicized and enthusiastic overwork in the service of the people did not produce a uniformly egalitarian provision of affordable services, nor did it erase distinctions in taste, or overcome inequalities in purchase power.[48] It doesn't seem that CCP leaders and officers intended for it to do any of those things. For example, in 1958, in Xuanwu district, barbers and hairdressers, spurred by revolutionary fervor, left their stores, and went to offer their services in factories, offices, and dormitories. However, the district service department noted that prices did not often match the quality of services and the expertise of the personnel, and the department intervened, establishing and enforcing a strict hierarchy of hairdressers with related price tags.[49] Similarly, in June 1959, the Beijing Municipal Service Management Bureau found out that four hairdressers in the Dongcheng and Xicheng districts were charging too little for washing and dyeing hair, and they promptly stepped in by increasing the prices of each service item.[50]

The barbers at the Sanlihe and Fengtai shops not only were making efforts to be nice to customers and provide services to the people in the most convenient and widespread fashion possible, but also were working to improve their skills so to offer differently priced services to individuals of different socioeconomic status. That must have been some kind of municipal priority as well, given that in 1959, with the Great Leap famine looming, the manager of the Sanlihe barbershop was sent for three

---

[47] Yu Yingshi 于英士, "Zhoumo lifa ji" 周末理发记 [A weekend haircut], *RMRB*, June 26, 1963.

[48] Hanchao Lu notes a similar attention to different tastes, including high-end tastes, in the case of the management of the city restaurants by the Shanghai Municipal committee. Under the Shanghai Municipal Public Food and Drink Company, founded in January 1956, the city government hired, retained, and ranked top chefs. "Numerous training programs and cooking competitions eventually led to the establishment of the Shanghai Culinary School in 1963." Lu, *Shanghai Tai Chi*: 36.

[49] XDS 0022-002-81 Xuanwuqu fuwu gongsi youguan tiaozheng zhaoxiang, lifa, fangdian, yuchi jiage de yijian he fuwuye xiafang gongshe guanli jihua cao'an ji mingdan 宣武区服务公司有关调整照相、理发、旅店、浴池业价格的意见和服务业下放公社管理计划草案及名单 [Proposal by the Xuanwu district service company on price adjustments for photographers, hotels, barbers, and bathhouses, and draft plan with name list for transferring the management of the service sector to the communes], 1958.

[50] BMA 090-001-00139-009 Beijingshi fuwuju guanyu tiaozheng si liandeng 4 hu lifaguan xi, ranfa jiage de tongzhi 北京市服务局关于调整四联等4户理发馆洗、染发价格的通知 [Notice by the Beijing Municipal Service Bureau about regulating the prices for washing and dying hair at Silian and three other barbershops], June 17, 1959. The minute level of intervention is quite astonishing, as we are talking of a handful of shops. The bureau provided pricing for men and women, short and long hair, washing and dyeing.

months to Shanghai to improve his technique, and specifically to learn how to style women's hair. He recounted his experience in a speech, stressing his debt to the CCP but also the very mundane experience of struggling to learn new skills, practicing daily with curlers, combs, and hairpins.[51] The 1962 movie *Female Hairdresser* offers a vivid depiction of the variety of services a barbershop was supposed to deliver and the variety of customers' needs it was supposed to satisfy. We see the all-female staff tend to men and women, with clippers, scissors, combs, dryers, curlers, and even a contraption with wires attached to the ceilings (I suspect that's the "electric perm" described in the manual). The success of this fictional shop, aptly named "March 8 barbershop,"[52] is proved by its clientele, which includes cadres, teachers, and even a dapper sailor – who looks very pleased with his haircut – all people coded as supposedly having more refined taste than an average factory worker.[53] That this aspect was highlighted in what was definitely an idealized, propaganda version of a socialist barbershop created by the Great Leap mobilization suggests that the people's aspiration to fashionable hairstyles neither disappeared nor was discouraged following the famine – something confirmed by the Sanlihe manager's trip to Shanghai. That shared aspiration was recognized in official discourse and in state cultural production but, in lived practice, it was still largely allocated in a postponed future. While collectivization aimed to – and seemingly did – improve barbers' skills so that they could offer superior services to a larger number of people, for the moment, the persistent differences in quality among hairdressers corresponded to a stark difference in prices, making the better shops largely unaffordable for lower-income residents.

---

[51] BMA 001-006-01764-00128 Beijingshi gongye, jiaotong, jijian, caimao fangmian xianjin jiti he xianjin gongzuozhe daibiao dahui zhongxing huiyi fayan gao 北京市工业、交通、基建、财贸方面先进集体和先进工作者代表大会中型会议发言稿 [Drafts of speeches for the Beijing mid-level conference of advanced collectives and advanced workers of the industrial, transportation, infrastructure, finance, and trade sectors], 1960.

[52] The *People's Daily* reported on another, nonfictional March 8 barbershop located in Harbin, part of the Xiangfang commune (founded in 1958). It employed seventeen young female hairdressers, with an average age of twenty-one. The barbers had apparently made use of the small space (only 85 square meters) to the utmost: There was a little reading room with newspapers and magazines and even a small store. They also provided baby-sitting for customers while they were getting haircuts. To solve the problem of storing clothes and personal items, they had created a closet in a wall, and even placed a safe box behind a mirror. The barbers had also invented a portable perm machine; with that, they could provide services (including perms) in factories, in the fields, and at home. Liu Jing 刘竞, "Ruguo ni xiang lifa ... 如果你想理发 ... [If you want a haircut ...], *RMRB*, May 4, 1960.

[53] *Nü lifashi.*

The Sanlihe barbers had been criticized in the past for being capable of giving only shapeless, uniform haircuts, which, customers complained, looked like a "toilet cover," so they established after-work sessions to learn new techniques, for example, how to use electric clippers.[54] Electric clippers were also viewed as a technological solution to the chronic lack of personnel, as they shortened the time of each haircut, thus reducing the need to hire new barbers. One young barber in Xidan was celebrated as a model worker, and one of his achievements was precisely doubling his productivity by mastering the use of electric clippers, after a long trial-and-error process.[55] The Fengtai district barbers focused on electric trimmers too, but they also learned how to perm women's hair and even went as far as developing their own tools, including a sanitizing lamp and a lightweight chair for hair-washing.[56] Great Leap barbers were supposed to learn how to continuously create new artistic hairstyles, which would make old people look younger, female comrades look even more beautiful, and children look as pretty as flowers. Improving technical skills was a way to increase the artistic value of a haircut (*tigao lifa yishu* 提高理发艺术), creating attractive and tasteful styles, which fitted the customer's age but also their individual characteristics.[57] At the same time, this process was also supposed to remake the city barbers, formerly despised for peddling a lowly trade, into skilled workers, whose effort was crucial in shaping a more beautiful socialist everyday.

As of June 1958, the 6,398 barbers and barbershop employees in Beijing belonged to four different administrations: the city Service Bureau, the suburban districts Supply and Marketing Cooperative (*Xiaoqu gongxiaoshe* 郊区供销社), the Handicraft Cooperatives (these would mostly be merged into communes in 1960), or a specific *danwei*. In most cases, barbers were paid either a monthly salary or a basic monthly salary supplemented either by a food/welfare allowance or by a percentage of the shop profits. The latter was the case in Haidian district, the only place where the earlier pre-liberation system was maintained. The district implemented four levels of basic salaries (from ¥40 to ¥55 per month), but if the monthly percentage exceeded the basic salary,

[54] BMA 001-021-00095-0035 Dayuejin zhong de Sanlihe lifaguan.
[55] BMA 100-003-00695-0036 Xidan lifa yuchi shi ruhe jinxing tuanzhibu gongzuo de 西单理发浴池是如何进行团支部工作的 [How barbershops and bathhouses in Xidan should conduct CYL branch work], 1959.
[56] BMA 001-021-00148-0114 1959 nian caimao xitong hongqi danwei cailiao – Fengtaiqu di yi lifaguan zhuyao xianjin shiji.
[57] BMA 001-021-00146-0026 Xidan diyi lifaguan jingli Jin Guangshou Tongzhi de fayan gao.

that's what the barbers were paid. The barbers' cut used to be 20–30 percent but was raised during the five-anti campaign to 35–40 percent. The system created massive seasonal imbalances. For example, the barbers near the eight universities in the district made an average of ¥36 per month between January and April but would make twice that amount in the summer. It was not unusual for them to almost starve during the winter months and then go on a spending spree (even patronizing restaurants) in the summer.[58]

Salaries, in general, were far from uniform and varied significantly not only according to location but especially according to skill levels and price of services. In the city at large, there were eight price levels just for male haircuts. The shops with higher prices also tended to pay higher salaries: A shop charging ¥0.8 per haircut would pay an average of ¥97 per month, while in a ¥0.3 or ¥0.4 shop salaries hovered around ¥45–55. The Xiangong barbershop at Xidan had thirteen pay grades, corresponding to a hierarchy of prices, ranging from ¥0.25 to ¥1.2. Six barbershops in the city had an eight-level salary scale (from ¥96 to ¥33), while suburban districts adopted a six-level scale (from ¥80.5 to ¥41.5), and barbers in bathhouses were on a four-level scale (from ¥62 to ¥56).

This elaborate system was not a pre-socialist legacy that the Party-state had failed to amend; rather, it was the product of the collectivization of the previous years, which, in some cases, had exacerbated preexisting salary gaps. In one shop, the difference between the monthly compensation of two barbers had originally only been ¥1.2, but it rose to ¥6.5 when they were classified in two different skill levels in 1956. Reportedly, that created "bad feelings" among coworkers. Conversely, those shops where the introduction of fixed salaries had leveled down the differences between workers of different ability were criticized in government sources, and the few establishments that did not differentiate for skill level and paid all barbers the same were condemned for adopting an "irrational" system.[59] As viewed from the perspective of the Beijing barbers, Great Leap collectivization did not – and did not aim to – erase differences, neither among residents, nor among workers. The formers' varied tastes and varying purchasing abilities had to be catered to, while barbers' diverse skills had to be encouraged and adequately rewarded. This project clearly did not mean to produce the uniform, gray-and-blue, ant-like urban population that we often associate with high Maoism. And while access to fashionable hairstyles remained at the time restricted by

---

[58] BMA 001-021-00118-0029 Beijingshi lifaye renyuan gongzi qingkuang diaocha ziliao 北京市理发业人员工资情况调查资料 [Survey of the salaries of Beijing barbers], June 1958.
[59] BMA 001-021-00118-0029 Beijingshi lifaye renyuan gongzi qingkuang diaocha ziliao.

purchasing power or access to *fuli*, the promise was that this access would be eventually extended to the entire urban population. The "red plenty" that the transition to communism would deliver was supposed to be one of diversely expressed aesthetic beauty. The problem, both theoretical and practical, was how to achieve that transition if social relationships had to continue to be determined by "capitalist elements" such as the wage form.

## 4.4    Not the Property of the Whole People

The year 1960 brought forth an expansion of the urban commune movement to the major cities, including the capital. That rapid push for collectivization was almost immediately followed by (or it often over-lapped with) a rectification campaign that aimed at increasing productivity by any means possible, while amending the "egalitarian" distortions that the Great Leap had produced (see the next chapter). These adjustments significantly affected all those welfare provisions that collectivization had at least partially instituted. In the haircutting business, the repercussions were not necessarily life-changing, but they were nonetheless quite visible. Price differences became starker and the efforts to nail them down citywide more aggressive. In November 1960, the Beijing Supply and Marketing Cooperative substantially raised the prices of almost every service offered by barbers in two service centers, in Guang'anmenwai and Deshengmenwai.[60] They had done the same with a barbershop in the suburban district of Daxing (in the south of the city), which had recently improved in terms of quality and services offered, and whose prices there-fore had to be set according to a higher level in the city hierarchy.[61]

Classifications of barbers according to level and price were produced in the Dashilar commune in 1961[62] and in Haidian district in 1961 and 1962. The Haidian cases include perhaps the most detailed analyses of

[60]  BMA 119-001-00465-0005 Guanyu tiaozheng lifa jiage de baogao ji pifu + tiaozheng lifa feibiao 关于调整理发价格的报告及批复+调整理发收费标 [Report and official response on the issue of regulating barbers' price + amended table of barbers' fees], November 3, 1960. The official reply was addressed to the Beijing Municipal Supply and Commercial Bureau 北京市供食品商业局. The highest priced service was an electric perm, ¥1.5.

[61]  BMA 119-001-00465-0010 Guanyu xinding lifa jiage qingshi ji pifu + xinding lifa jiage biao 关于新订理发价格请示及批复+新订理发价格表 [Request and approval regarding newly established haircut pricing + newly established haircut price list].

[62]  XDS 0013-002-50 Dashilar gongshe guanyu dashitang shidian huibao zongjie, zhidu, jihua, pingbi jingsai he lifa guanli zhidu, yijian, lifayuan jishu biaozhun, gongzi wenti qingshi 大栅栏公社关于大食堂试点汇报总结、制度、计划、安排、评比竞赛和理发管理制度、意见、理发员技术标准、工资问题请示 [Dashilar commune's request for instruction concerning the report summary, regulations, plans, arrangements, and evaluation competitions for the pilot canteen program as well as the management system of barbershops and the wages and technical standards of barbers], 1961.

what the authorities labeled the "haircutting problem" in the district. In 1961, the Service Bureau (*fuwuju* 服务局) estimated that the district was facing a shortage of hairdressers. After a series of relatively complex calculations – How many seats were available? How many heads could the current barbers serve per day? And per month? – they concluded that over 500,000 residents of the district had to go with their monthly hair needs unmet. The report described long waiting times (up to two hours) at the better-rated facilities, with people queuing up before the shops opened. In contrast, other facilities were less frequented because they were poorly advertised or located in run-down buildings. The problem, however, was not just the number of providers. The report stressed how, since the establishment of the communes, the quality of life had improved and common people had now greater demands in term of services.[63] And that was specially the case in Haidian, which hosted a large number of universities, military facilities, and central government agencies. The district residents comprised a large number of high-level intellectuals and people with high income, who "because of their large purchasing power, put a lot of pressure on the hairdressing services to increase its quality." Intellectuals, central government cadres, and military officials (and their families) required better, more fashionable hairstyles than commoners, and the collectivized service sector under the communes was tasked with catering to this class-based demand.[64] The district coordinated with the subdistrict offices and the communes to train more and better hairdressers but also instituted a hierarchy of facilities, at different prices, tasked with providing haircuts to residents of different status and economic means.[65] In November, the district organized a public demonstration of apprentice hairdressers' skills:

---

[63] This was a common refrain. For example, in 1959, the *People's Daily* reported on the effort to expand services in Guangzhou, writing: "because life has improved, Guangzhou residents demand increasingly more and higher-quality services." "Tiaohui fuwuyuan huifu fuwudian Guangzhou dali jiaqiang lifa, ziran, yinshi, saiying deng fuwu xingye jishu zhiliang he fuwu taidu shoudao qunzhong huanying" 调回服务员 恢复服务点 广州大力加强理发、洗染、饮食、摄影等服务行业 技术质量和服务态度受到群众欢迎 [Reassigning service staff and reopening service outlets: Guangzhou intensifies efforts to strengthen the hairdressing, washing-dyeing, catering, and photography sectors; technical quality and service attitudes are welcomed by the masses], *RMRB*, June 18, 1959.

[64] In Xidan, the same model worker who had been praised for his mastery of electric clippers was also recognized for his ability to fathom whether a customer was a worker, a student, or a cadre, and to style their hair accordingly. BMA 100-003-00695-0036 Xidan lifa yuchi shi ruhe jinxing tuanzhibu gongzuo de.

[65] HDA 002-113-0044 Haidianqu fuwuju, weishengju, qinghe jiedao banshichu guanyu zhengdun ifaye Qinghe gongzuozhan fangzu, chengli chanyuan, tuo'ersuo de qingshi, pifu, tongzhi 海淀区服务局、卫生局、清河街道办事处关于整顿理发业清河工作站房租、成立产院、托儿所的请示、批复、通知 [Haidian District service bureau, health bureau, and Qinghe subdistrict office: request, approval, and notice on rectifying rent issues

Thirty-one of them showcased various techniques, from washing to blow-drying to styling. At the end they were treated to a blow-drying performance by the winner of the city-wide hairdressing competition, Guo Shouchen.[66]

The following year (1962), the hierarchy of skills and facilities was codified in a district-wide system of five levels and ten sublevels – from master to apprentice. The required skills for each level were painstakingly detailed: A master hairdresser had basic knowledge of chemical processes, could repair and service tools, but was also an expert in three different kinds of perm (electric, hot, and cold) and kept up-to-date with the changing fashion in men's and women's hairstyles and makeup.[67] By then, this hierarchy of skills was being connected not just to a system of diverging price tags but also to the salary reform in the commune system. It was decided that a portion of the salaries of the hairdressers should be based on their abilities – which corresponded to a specific percentage of work points – and productivity. This was done "in order to muster the enthusiasm of the employee in the haircutting service, in conformity with the interest of the individual, the collective, and the nation, to appropriately manage the relationships among workers and to effect the best possible distribution of income, thus spurring hairdressers to give free rein to their initiative."[68] By 1962, in terms of prices, services, and salaries, the collectivized hairdressing industry seemed to have not only preserved but actively increased social and economic differentiation.

The aspect in which the readjustment to correct what were perceived to be the dysfunctions of collectivization – in terms of egalitarianism,

---

for barbers at the Qinghe workstation, and establishing a maternity hospital and a nursery], 1961.

[66] HDA 030-101-0109 Beijingshi, Haidianqu fuwuju guanyu yinshi, lifaye jishu biaoyan qingkuang tongbao he Haishunju fanguan zhongzhi mogu de qingkuang jieshao. Tables detailing each participant's strength and weaknesses are included in the report.

[67] HDA 030-101-0117 Lifaye jishu dengji biaozhun 理发业技术等级标准 [Technical standards for the hairdressing industry].

[68] HDA 030-101-0117-3 Beijingshi Haidianqu fangwuju guanyu lifa xingye shidian jiben gongzi jia lirun ticheng gongzi zhidu de banfa 北京市海淀区房屋局关于理发行业试点基本工资加利润提成工资制度的办法 [Beijing Haidian District housing bureau's measures for the trial implementation of a basic wage plus profit-sharing system in the hairdressing industry], August 11, 1962. Even in Huairou, a rural district north of Beijing, in 1961, the commerce bureau, citing economic improvement leading to new demand, proposed the establishment of a high-end restaurant and high-end barbershop, with significantly higher prices for a wealthier clientele. BMA 119-001-00564-0097 Guanyu zengshe gaoji fanguan he gaoji lifabu de qingshi ju pifu yijian 关于增设高级饭馆和高级理发部的请示及批复意见 [Request and official reply about adding a high-end restaurant and a high-end barbershop].

daily life, and socialism – was more forceful and therefore more evident was that of ownership. As we have seen, an essential element of the Great Leap and the urban commune movement was a rapid acceleration in the process of transforming forms of ownership within the country, a process that had already reached a publicly acknowledged milestone in 1956, with the elimination of private ownership of the means of production – and the consequent achievement of "socialism." The accelerated transition to the stage of communism that the Great Leap Forward promised was predicated on a further, radical, and quick expansion of the collectivization of ownership. If earlier it had been a question of turning private into collective ownership (or joint public/private ventures), with the Great Leap, the task became moving those enterprises recently placed under some form of collective ownership into "ownership by the whole people." Several barbershops had undergone that transformation with varying and often contradictory results. In Changping township, the two barbershops with their thirty-three employees had been transferred from the county handicraft association to the Ministry of Commerce, and from collective ownership to ownership by the whole people in 1958. Consequent to that, the compensation system had been changed from a percentage of profits to a fixed monthly salary. While the reports cited substantial improvements in political consciousness, service, and, significantly, overall profit (in 1960, 14.2 percent more than the previous year, and the profit went to the state), they also recounted a series of problems. It appears that barbers had quickly developed a "dependent mentality" (*yilai sixiang* 依赖思想), coming to believe that they could rely on the collective and the state instead of their own individual efforts. For example, as customer satisfaction did not affect their income, quality of service had declined; similarly, management had become careless and expenses had risen, as now this did not affect the workers' share but only the state's profit margin. Finally, the new pay structure had led to reductions in the average salary and the abandonment of material incentives, which in turn dampened the workers' enthusiasm and productivity. As one of the barbers, Hao Baoshan, remarked, "my work is truly meaningless, no matter how much energy I put into it, I still get the same forty yuan. So now I put my family first, and my work second."[69]

---

[69] BMA 001-021-00265-0020 Guanyu Changping zhen guoying lifabu tuihui dao yuanlai suoyouzhi de lifashe de qingkuang gei Ke Han, Hong Yi, Su Yifu tongzhi, Changping xian de han 关于昌平镇国营理发部退回到原来所有制的理发社的情况给克寒、宏毅、苏一夫同志、昌平县的函 [Letter to Ke Han, Hong Yi, Su Yifu, and the Changping county about reverting the Changping township state-owned barbershop back to its original collective ownership structure], June 18, 1961.

This sentiment was allegedly echoed by skilled barbers in Xicheng district (which hosted 93 barbershops with 974 employees), who complained that the pay system (a monthly salary plus bonuses) did not properly reward their work and did not incentivize productivity: "if you work more you don't make more, if you work less you don't make less, so working hard is just wasted effort." The district authorities remarked that the system allowed for different pay for equal work, was biased toward excessive egalitarianism (*pingjunzhuyi* 平均主义), and was ultimately incompatible with the socialist principle of remuneration according to labor. Workers tended to slack off, often called in sick, or asked for days off. For example, in March 1961 in the Wan'guo barbershop, the twenty-six employees worked an average of 20.5 days per month (instead of the expected twenty-six), and barbers complained about their coworkers who claimed to be sick and got paid anyway.[70]

The solution adopted in Beijing in the early 1960s, while the urban commune campaign officially continued, was to implement rapid decollectivization, returning these enterprises to previous forms of ownership. Political education was deployed to convince workers that it was politically correct and economically advantageous to abandon "ownership by the whole people" and return to collective ownership. In Changping, the proposal/decision to return the barbershops to the county handicraft association generated political instability and worried reactions: Party and Youth League members considered it a retreat, ordinary employees were wary of another massive reform, and apprentices fretted over their future outside state ownership. All mentioned the risk of lower salaries and of decline in management and welfare. The authorities then organized separate meetings on each of the issues, explaining how this shift paralleled what was happening with the communes and the collective canteens, and arguing that this was all for the sake of "sparking enthusiasm, freeing the productive forces, better serving people's lives, and accelerating socialist construction." As for welfare, it would now be the responsibility of the handicraft association, leaving those provisions on a much less stable footing.[71]

[70] BMA 001-021-00288-0032 Zhonggong Xichengqu fuwu gongsi dangweihui 中共西城区服务公司党委会 [Party committee of the Xicheng district service company], "Guanyu zai lifa xingye shixing jishi jijian jia lirunjiang de gongzi zhidu de baogao + lifaye gongzi dengji biaozhun biao" 关于在理发行业试行计时计件加利润奖的工资制度的 报告+理发业工资等级标准表 [Report on experimenting with a time-rate/piece-rate/rewards on profit salary system in the barber business + table of standard wage scale for barbers], June 20, 1961.
[71] BMA 001-021-00265-0020 Guanyu Changping zhen guoying lifabu tuihui dao yuanlai suoyouzhi de lifashe de qingkuang gei Ke Han, Hong Yi, Su Yifu tongzhi, Changping xian de han.

Barbers in Xicheng were generally more supportive of the change in ownership, and the few recalcitrant ones were convinced after some propaganda work and reassurances from the top. While some of them were pushing to a return to the pre-liberation system, when employees received a cut of the profits, this suggestion was rejected as that method was considered to favor young, skilled, highly productive workers over older, very skilled, but not as productive ones. Moreover, it did not incentivize workers' love for the enterprise, and it did not connect the individual's interest with the nation's interest. Eventually, the district opted for a compensation system that preserved a portion of the extant basic monthly salary (about 48 percent) but supplemented it with piece-rate wages and rewards for increased profits. This reform was accompanied by a reorganization of barbers into a more precise salary scale (with five levels), making sure that differences in skill corresponded to marked differences in pay. They estimated that, under the new arrangement, the shop's overall revenue was going to increase by 40 percent, the net profit by 68 percent, and salaries by 33 percent.[72] Reports from Changping celebrated the successes of the new/old ownership system: Barbers were happy and worked extremely hard, even those who had been notorious slackers under the previous system. They were also zealously looking for expedients to increase productivity and profits, including selling hair to purchase new tools or keeping manual razors at hand in case of blackouts. The initial worries about welfare, however, proved not to have been unfounded, as under collective ownership, barbers quickly found out that funds to cover medical expenses were either scarce or not available and that the state was not backing those expenses anymore.[73]

In June 1961, at Erlonglu, one of the earliest and most celebrated communes in Beijing, barbers who had been previously reorganized under the umbrella of joint private/public enterprises and moved into QMSYZ were returned to collective ownership, each shop managed as a cooperative, with independent accounting, solely responsible for profits and losses. Under the new statute, remuneration was strictly "according to labor" (*anlao fuchou, duolao duode* 按劳付酬, 多劳多得); work points were supplemented by bonuses, which, however, could not be distributed equally to all employees, but were specifically aimed at rewarding highly productive individuals. The cooperative statute guaranteed a

[72] BMA 001-021-00288-0032 Guanyu zai lifa xingye shixing jishi jijian jia lirunjiang de gongzi zhidu de baogao + lifaye gongzi dengji biaozhun biao.
[73] BMA 001-021-00265-0020 Guanyu Changping zhen guoying lifabu tuihui dao yuanlai suoyouzhi de lifashe de qingkuang gei Ke Han, Hong Yi, Su Yifu tongzhi, Changping xian de han.

modicum of *fuli*, including sick leave, partial coverage of medical expenses, bereavement and maternity leaves, and even allowances for hardships, but this was all based on the shop's public welfare fund, which was in turn dependent solely on the continuing profitability of the enterprise.[74]

As discussed in Chapter 2, the retreat from QMSYZ was not simply an effect of the foreclosure of the debate on the socialist economy, which, by 1960, had been forcefully, if unstably, reinscribed into the confines established by the Stalinist doxa. Rather, abandoning the prospect of moving enterprises to ownership by the whole people or even forcing them to revert to collective ownership was largely a consequence of what was perceived to be possible under the current conditions of capital accumulation, and it implied a significant redistribution of responsibilities for welfare and social services. Under collective ownership, these services (healthcare, childcare, food, etc.) were now once again reliant on the individual enterprise's capital accumulation, which in turn could only depend on each employee's longer work hours or increased productivity. This turned into a renewed effort to extract as much surplus labor from workers as possible, in order to spare any financial burden to the state. Another case, from Xuanwu district, exemplifies this process. In June 1961, the Commercial Sector Survey Working Group of the CCP Xuanwu District Committee decided to reorganize the (mostly itinerant) barbers who were operating along the perimeter of the old city wall. Just the previous year, they had been turned into a public/private partnership barbershop (*gongsi heying lifadian* 公私合营理发店), thus passing from collective ownership to ownership by the whole people. Now that process was being reversed. Salaries were switched to a system of remuneration according to labor, with work points disbursed according to political consciousness, quality and attitude of service, skill level and productivity, attention to the company finances, study, and collaborative work. In the new system, the state stepped away from all responsibilities, which were devolved to the co-op or to the individual workers – who now owned and were responsible for their own tools, for example. This led to an increase in overall revenues and salaries but made every form of welfare and security dependent on the labor of individual barbers. The report remarks that while the state received less in taxes, that loss was offset by the fact that there was no disbursement of *fuli*, leading to a net gain – for the state. The report concluded by arguing

---

[74] BMA 001-028-00031-15 Erlonglu diqu lifa hezuo shangdian shixing zhangcheng (cao'an) 二龙路地区理发合作商店试行章程 (草案) [Experimental statute for the cooperative barbershops in the Erlonglu area (draft)], June 9, 1961.

that only workers who were young, strong, and already ideologically committed were fit for a job under QMSYZ. In the case of barbers, especially itinerant barbers, who had low ideological awareness, collective ownership was the better system: for them, for the people, and for the state.[75] We see here, in the case of barbers, a tension similar to the one described in the previous chapter for the labor of housewives-turned-workers, whose gendered – and therefore ideologically and technically inferior – character justified the continuous postponement of most promises of advancement and improvement. For barbers, both male and female, the prejudice connected with their low social status could be used as a reason to make them remain always unfit for the promises of socialist welfare.

Decollectivization did not just affect barbers; rather, the shift of emphasis to profitability, productivity, and diversification led to a general increase in prices, especially in certain areas. In 1961 the Beijing Labor Bureau conducted a survey of haircutting prices. While only fifty-five barbershops (out of 503) had raised prices, and the average increase for the city was a bit over 2 percent, certain downtown areas had experienced much more substantial price hikes. In Xuanwu district, the shops around the Dashilar area had initially increased their price by 86.8 percent, but they were later forced to reduce that to a mere 63 percent. In Guanganmennei, the report registered the vociferous complaints of workers in the area, who lamented that while the barbers had hiked their prices, their own salaries and welfare provisions had remained the same. Shops had raised prices on the fake pretense of providing "high-end" services: "the barbers are still the same, but they give a coat of a paint to the door, and they immediately hike the prices." One of the stated reasons for this increase was to more closely parallel the skill levels of local shops, which had hired highly skilled barbers to attract high-end customers. The price hike, however, did not produce the desired outcomes, and most stores reported a loss compared with the previous year.[76]

---

[75] BMA 001-006-01859-00120 Zhonggong Xuanwu quwei shangye diaocha gongzuozu guanyu huifu lifaye hezuo shangdian, hezuo xiaozu de shidian qiangkuang baogao 中共宜武区委商业调查工作组关于恢复理发业合作商店、合作小组的试点情况报告 [Report by the commercial survey work group of the CCP Xuanwu district committee about a pilot project resuming the cooperative store and cooperative small group system for barbers], July 27, 1961.

[76] BMA 001-006-01855-00071 Zhonggong Beijing shiwei bangongting zhigong shenghuo diaocha ziliao zhi liu – Beijingshi laodongju guanyu lifaye tijia qingkuang de diaocha baogao 中共北京市委办公厅职工生活调查资料之六 – 北京市劳动局关于理发业提价情况的调查报告 [Document no. 6 of the survey series on the living condition of employees by the Beijing Municipal Party Committee Office – Beijing Municipal Labor Bureau's investigative report on rising prices in the barbering industry], September 12, 1961.

The emphasis on each shop's profitability led to other, unwanted consequences that the government had to restrict and regulate. In 1963, the practice of sending barbers door-to-door during idle hours, which during the Great Leap had been heralded as a service to the people, now produced chaotic competition, with barbers encroaching upon each other's districts and other shops' territory, offering services at an incoherent range of prices, and potentially damaging the normal functioning of their own shops. The Service Administration Bureau had to intervene, setting fees and imposing rules.[77] In late 1963 and early 1964, the same Bureau reported the case of ten barbershops that had erroneously been involved in the massive decollectivization of 1961, when thousands of peddlers and small tradespeople were moved out of SOEs and joint ventures. This had damaged "the frontline of the private/public joint venture" and over forty expert barbers had been transferred to cooperatives, with massive personal losses in terms of *fuli* and salary. In June 1964, the Finance and Trade Office of the Beijing Municipal People's Committee approved the return of these shops to QMSYZ.[78]

The partial decollectivization of the early 1960s was impactful at a very practical level, because it took away the security of welfare and *fuli* from people who had just received those provisions, but also at a political level, as it signaled the demise of any expectation of a quickly coming era of shared and more equal prosperity. The tensions between economic status and distribution of services, productivity, and welfare that Great Leap barbers illustrated also reflected, at a macro-economic level, the demise of the last and most radical attempt to overcome commodity exchange and subvert the law of value. The next and final chapter is devoted to analyzing that demise.

---

[77] BMA 090-001-00584-028 Beijingshi fuwu shiye guanliju guanyu lifa yewai chu lifa shoufei biaozhun de tongzhi + tongyi jiage biao 北京市服务事业管理局关于理发业外出理发收费标准的通知+统一价格表 [Notice by the Beijing Municipal Service Management Bureau about standard fees for barber providing services outside the shop + unified price list].

[78] BMA 002-021-00425-026 Guanyu shouhui 10 hu lifa hezuo shangdian wei gongsi heying qiye de qingshi ji gongwen piban tongzhi dan 关于收回10户理发合作商店为公私合营企业的请示及公文批办通知单 [Request for instruction about reverting ten cooperative barbershops back to private/public joint venture and corresponding official notice of approval].

# 5    Foreclosing on Liberation

## 5.1    How to End a Movement

According to historian Li Duanxiang, August 1960 marked the beginning of the last phase of the urban commune movement, one that he labels alternatively as "decline" (*shuailuo* 衰落) or "withering away" (*xiaowang* 消亡).[1] Li identifies a series of causes, both exogenous and pertaining to the movement itself, for this gradual demise: There had been a rapid and large influx of population into urban centers, connected first to the expansion of urban industries and then to the famine, which had put pressure on the distribution of consumer goods;[2] urban residents of means, afraid of the potential excesses in collectivization, had gone on a buying spree, leading to an increase in prices for several commodities; and, perhaps more significantly, the urban communes, in large part because of the speed with which they had been established, were plagued by disorganization and poor administration, as well as by jurisdictional conflicts emerging between commune management and municipal administration. These issues were already evident in May 1960, when the central party group of the ACFTU convened a meeting of all the trade union presidents at all levels, after which they issued the "Report on the Current Situation and Several Problems in the Development of

---

[1]    Li Duanxiang, "Duiyu Beijing chengshi renmin gongshe lishi de kaocha" 对于北京城市人民公社历史的考察 [An examination of the history of urban people's communes in Beijing], in Li, ed., *Chengshi renmin gongshe yanjiu ziliao xuanbian*, vol. 1: 16–26. Originally published in 北京党史, no. 1 (2005). And Li, *Chengshi renmin gongshe yundong yanjiu*.

[2]    According to MacFarquhar, the Great Leap encouraged a massive flow of laborers from the countryside to the cities, leading to an increase in the urban labor force "from just over 9 million in 1957 to well over 25 million in 1958 and over 28.5 million in 1959." MacFarquhar, *The Origins of the Cultural Revolution*: 299. Or, in Kam Wing Chan's assessment: "Rural-urban migration peaked in 1959 with an estimated annual net inflow of about 15 million. The influx of rural peasants pushed China's urban percentage from 16.2 per cent in 1958 to 19.7 per cent in 1960, the all-time high in the pre-1980 era." Kam Wing Chan, *Cities with Invisible Walls: Reinterpreting Urbanization in Post-1949 China* (Oxford: Oxford University Press, 1994): 38.

Urban People's Communes" (*Guanyu dangqian chengshi renmin gongshe fazhan qingkuang he jige wenti de baogao* 关于当前城市人民公社发展情况和几个问题的报告). At the time, these problems were attributed to the ideological makeup of the cadres and the nefarious work of class enemies; accordingly, the solution was a two-month campaign of "purification," with the goal of cleansing the cadres' ranks and reestablishing the Party's leadership.[3] When these measures failed to produce any significant result, the ACFTU Party Group sent to the Central Committee the "Report on the Problems in Consolidating and Rectifying the Urban People's Communes" (*Guanyu zhengdun he gonggu chengshi renmin gongshe wenti de baogao* 关于整顿和巩固城市人民公社问题的报告), which acknowledged some fundamental issues (waste of resources, poor management, etc.) and called for halting any further development of urban collectivization. As a result, on January 14–18, 1961, the ninth meeting of the eighth plenum of the CC adopted the eight-character policy of "adjust, consolidate, replenish, improve" (*tiaozheng* 调整, *gonggu* 巩固, *chongshi* 充实, *tigao* 提高).[4] Despite the seemingly positive spin of the motto, this new strategy was construed to amend the "leftist" tendencies of the past, and what it produced, at the national level, was a complete reversal of the policies adopted just a few months earlier, a retreat from the stated goals of urban collectivization, and the ultimate demise of the entire campaign. Separation of commune administration from city and neighborhood government was rigidly enforced, thus putting the end to any pretense of *zhengshe heyi* 政社合一, the idea that the commune should integrate economic, political, social, and administrative work in one organization. More significantly, most of the structures that embodied the promises of a revolutionized everyday were either significantly curtailed or simply eliminated. Communes ceased to be organized under the principle of achieving "ownership by the whole people" in the near or distant future; reform of canteens, childcare centers, and welfare institutions resulted in a drastic reduction in such services; and commune industrial production declined rapidly in terms of overall output, number of enterprises, and number of workers. On September 15, 1961, the Central Committee of the CCP ordered SOE industries to withdraw from urban communes, firmly separating the ownership by the whole people (SOEs) from collective ownership (the communes).[5] The most

---

[3] Li, *Chengshi renmin gongshe yundong yanjiu*: 129. On the cleansing of rank, see also XDN 7-1-807 Zhonggong Beijingshi Xicheng quwei guanyu chengshi jiedao renmin gongshe gongzuo wenti de baogao (cao'an).
[4] Li, "Duiyu Beijing chengshi renmin gongshe lishi de kaocha": 23.
[5] Li Duanxiang, "Chengshi renmin gongshehua yundong de xingwang yu lishi jiaoxun": 233.

profitable factories were eventually placed under the jurisdiction of the handicraft cooperatives (*shougongye hezuoshe* 手工业合作社), thus leaving the communes as easily-disposable empty shells.[6] This process also included a net urban outflow of people from the cities back to the countryside, and "18 million urban workers and another 6 million dwellers, most of whom had migrated to the cities during the Great Leap Forward, were returned to their home villages during the period 1961–3." This was meant to reduce the cities' need for food and ease unemployment, but, of course, dumped the task of providing for these people to the already overburdened and famine-plagued rural areas.[7]

After 1961, neither Mao nor anybody else in the central government had anything to say about the urban communes, which were then allowed to slide quietly into obscurity and dissolution. In most cases, communes all over the country were simply shut down, transferring the remaining responsibilities to subdistrict offices. A few exemplary communes were allowed to continue "experimenting," and these were the ones often toured by friendly foreign visitors. Finally, in two cases, Heilongjiang province and the capital city of Beijing, communes persisted for much longer. Urban communes in Beijing had certain characteristics that made them less problematic and more resilient – for example, they overlapped geographically with subdistrict offices, thus avoiding any confusion or disruption in administrative boundaries. More important, it seems that Beijing commune enterprises were more profitable and better functioning compared with the national average and were therefore allowed to remain in operation. In 1964, when the Socialist Education movement started, forty-four communes still nominally operated in the capital, and the Four Cleanups were first tested in one of them. There were probably communes in Beijing up until the eve of the Cultural Revolution, although their roles had been significantly curtailed.[8] The decline of urban collectivization in Beijing happened at a much slower pace than in the rest of the country and materialized as a gradual emptying-out of economic resources, practical functions, and political significance from those collective units. As such, the Beijing case allows for a closer analysis of the reasons behind the end of the campaign, of what happened when collectivization started to wane and the promises of a revolution in the everyday dissipated, and of how urban residents

---

[6] Li, *Chengshi renmin gongshe yundong yanjiu*: 139. This happened much later in Beijing, where, as of May 1964, commune industries were still under commune leadership and had not been transferred to the handicraft cooperatives. Li, "Chengshi renmin gongshehua yundong de xingwang yu lishi jiaoxun": 233.
[7] Chan, *Cities with Invisible Walls*: 39. See also Brown, *City versus Countryside*.
[8] Li, *Chengshi renmin gongshe yundong yanjiu*: 146–147.

(and especially women) were affected by and reacted to that demise. As I have argued before and as I analyze in detail in this chapter, while I do not discount the very concrete reasons for the end of the urban collectivization campaign that Li Duanxiang and others offer, I see the collapse of this experiment not only as the result of practical constraints but also and more importantly as the outcome of a series of unresolved tensions and contradictions within the very animating principles and conditions of collectivization, socialist development, and women's liberation. Those had been productive tensions at the beginning of the Great Leap, in that they generated both theoretical discussion and practical experimentation on crucial issues of Marxist political economy, but most of those possibilities were foreclosed by the Thermidorean reaction after 1959. In this final chapter, I take up again the fundamental issues that I began to discuss in Chapters 1 and 3, and I trace how they came fully to the fore and led to the unraveling of any hope of a new collectivized life. Section 5.2 examines the reorientation of commune industrial production and of collective industrial labor in terms of both products and organization, leading to the progressive decentralization and precarization of commune labor. Section 5.3 details how, during this reversal of Great Leap policies, commune enterprises, commune services, and even individual workers were subjected to increased disciplinary control, through imposition of strict accounting of time and resources as well as deployment of material incentives. Finally, Section 5.4 looks at how this led to the overall collapse of collective services and at how commune residents, and especially female workers, reacted to the dismantling of the enterprises and organizations they had created.

Documents from Beijing dating from 1960 and 1961 provide a preliminary but clear picture of how the devolution of communal enterprises was supposed to work and what principles informed it. Commune enterprises should continue to rely on cheap (female) labor[9] and remain focused on simple production processes, avoiding involvement with any project too ambitious or too technical. Instead of large factories with hundreds of employee, small neighborhood workshops were to be favored, following the principle of "suiting measures to local conditions, drawing on local resources" (*yindi zhiyi, jiudi qucai* 因地制宜, 就地取材).[10]

---

[9] XDN 7-1-807 Zhonggong Beijingshi Xicheng quwei guanyu chengshi jiedao renmin gongshe gongzuo wenti de baogao (cao'an).

[10] XDN 7-1-807 Zhonggong Beijingshi Xicheng quwei guanyu chengshi jiedao renmin gongshe gongzuo wenti de baogao (cao'an); BMA 112-001-00782-2 Guanyu chengshi renmin gongye jige wenti de yijian (gao) 关于城市人民公社工业几个问题的意见 (稿) [Opinions on several issues concerning the industry of urban people's communes (draft)], August 10, 1961.

What was perceived to be the prevailing tendency toward egalitarianism in salaries and treatment had to be reversed. A report by the Beijing General Society of Handicraft Cooperatives singled out the lack of marked differences in the salary scale operating in Beijing's 651 commune factories. The average salary was ¥23 and variations were limited to only ¥2–3, so they noted that there was no real way either to reward those who worked themselves to death or to incentivize the slackers. The report did not record any qualms against but rather quietly supported the introduction of hourly or even piece-rate wages.[11] By then, as I described in Chapter 2, the debate over "economism," the role of material incentives, and the centrality of the wage form (as well as of wage differences) had been resolved and foreclosed, and the relatively unstable consensus reached in 1959 was mirrored in the muted acceptance and sometime full-throated endorsement of practices of inequal distribution.

Another report from Xicheng district (August 1960) extolled the success of the collective industrial enterprises, whose output had tripled and whose overall profit had doubled in the previous year, yet it lamented the persistent lack of sound financial management, leading to waste, excesses, and unlawful appropriation of resources by cadres and personnel. The solution was the introduction of detailed rules for bookkeeping, leading to the development of a system of what was torturously called "economic accounting with a mass character" (*qunzhongxing de jingji hesuan* 群众性的 经济核算). It was geared at making every single individual worker care personally and deeply about expenses and revenues, and at making accounting an integral part of every activity, every (productive) moment of the day, so that "where there is production, there must be accounting" (*nali you shengchan, nali you hesuan* 哪里有生产, 哪里有核算).[12] Given that this applied to factories that were admittedly already quite profitable, what we see prefigured here, in its aspirational and inchoate form, is a system aimed at achieving maximum profitability through the self-disciplining of labor (something already visible in the case of barbers, as described in the previous chapter) and the contemporary reduction in the deployment and use of all kinds of resources and capital, except for labor itself. This is once again a reflection and a manifestation of the Thermidorean reaction, which restated the absolute primacy of pure economism after the brief

---

[11] BMA 112-001-00782-2 Guanyu chengshi renmin gongshe gongye jige wenti de yijian (gao).
[12] XDN 28-1-86-3 Zhonggong Beijingshi Xichengqu caizheng dangzu 中共北京市西城区 财政党组 [Beijing Xicheng district finance leading party group], Guanyu jiaqiang chengshi renmin gongshe caiwu guanli de yijian 关于加强城市人民公社财务管理的意 见 [Suggestions on strengthening the financial management of urban people's communes], August 11, 1960.

radical political intervention by Mao, Zhang Chunqiao, and others in the early phase of the Great Leap, culminating in the debate on the socialist economy and bourgeois right. Once collective enterprises and collective services had been thus largely divested of any role in producing political and social change, the value of communes could then be reduced to a simple numerical estimate of profits and losses, to be entrusted to the exclusive supervision of bean-counters. This had obvious repercussions not only for the promised technological revolution of commune production – which was endlessly postponed – but also for the viability of any kind of "nonproductive" social service. Reports stressed repeatedly how participation in canteens and kindergartens had to remain eminently voluntary, which ultimately made them unsustainable.[13]

This shift configured an overall reduction in the objectives, scopes, and missions of urban communes, which went from the essential vehicles for the radical transformation of urban everyday life to largely marginal organizers of production, with purely economic purposes. A set of draft provisions in 1961 described the urban commune as "a socialist collective economic organization combining the resources of working people in the area, with working women as the foundation" (*yi bendiqu laodong funü wei zhude laodong renmin ziyuan jiehe de shehuizhuyi jiti jingji zuzhi* 以本地区劳动妇女为主的劳动人民资源结合的社会主义集体经济组织).[14] Nothing was left in this definition about the collectivization's potential to transform everyday life in all its aspects, revolutionize the family form, achieve gender equality, provide needed social services, or even accelerate the transition to communism. Basically, all the *political* promises associated with the urban communes in 1958 had been removed, and what was left was the technical function of organizing locally available labor for increased production. That was a massive political retreat, and one that was not and could not be completely justified by practical constraints and harsh conditions; it was a political decision that followed a clear positional shift within the CCP. However, as it became rapidly clear, once deprived of those political horizons and political functions, there was no way the communes could pursue even that minimum economic objective.

[13] At the Lushan conference, Mao stressed the voluntary character of rural communes' mess halls, and he was apparently unperturbed by the notion that two thirds of them would have had to be dissolved. McFarquhar, *The Origins of the Cultural Revolution*: 220.

[14] BMA 112-001-00782-4 Guanyu xian jieduan chengshi renmin gongshe ruogan wenti de guiding (cao'an) 关于现阶段城市人民公社若干问题的规定 (草案) [Provisions on some issues concerning the urban people's communes at this stage (draft)]. In the original typed document, a draft, someone crossed out the characters "*laodong funü weizhu de* 劳动妇女为主的" (centered on laboring women), thus changing the meaning of the sentence to "a socialist collective economic organization combining the resources of working people in the area." I have no evidence on whether this change was accepted in the final version.

Another report, surveying the situation after the restructuring of the Qianmen commune, pointed out that service and industrial workers in that commune comprised only 6.2 percent of the population of the district. Urban communes were therefore completely different from rural ones, as they were only relevant to a miniscule proportion of the urban population and could not yet constitute the "grassroots units" (*jiceng danwei* 基层单位) of the new socialist society. For the same reasons, they could not claim any administrative or political authority. At the time, the commune was, at best, "a socialist collective economic organization formed by the voluntary association of urban housewives and a few socially idle laborers." And that, in the end, the report concluded, was not much different from handicraft cooperatives.[15] Originally singled out as the urban embodiment of that vaunted bridge to the heaven of communism, communes were then reduced to structures whose only task was to mobilize, on a strict voluntary basis, people considered to be previously idle. They thus became just another form through which labor could be extracted from the urban population. Accordingly, in these later sources, while some of the revolutionary language about transforming the city, promoting educational improvement, and producing ideological change still vaguely lingered on, any hint to the transition to more advanced forms of ownership had disappeared and the goals of the commune had been redefined as strictly geared to productivity and capital accumulation. Ultimately, "the urban people's communes should make sure that production and service workers implement the principles of from each to the best of their ability, distribution according to labor, and more pay for more work; they should organize the necessary collective welfare according to what is needed and what is possible, so as to encourage the increase of labor efficiency and the improvement of living conditions."[16]

As we have seen, production through the deployment of poorly paid female labor had always been the element on which the very possibility of urban collectivization as a transformative enterprise hinged. Similarly, possibilities for radical social change through welfare, mechanization, or technological improvements had already been stalled or postponed. Yet the redefinition that took place in 1960–1961 emptied collective production of any residual revolutionary value or possibility, and separated it, at a practical and theoretical level, from all the other features of communal

---

[15] BMA 001-006-01864-1 Chengshi renmin gongshe diaocha cailiao zhiyi – dui chengshi renmin gongshe xingzhi, renwu he suoyouzhi wenti de yijian.
[16] BMA 001-006-01864-1 Chengshi renmin gongshe diaocha cailiao zhiyi – dui chengshi renmin gongshe xingzhi, renwu, he suoyou youzhi wenti de yijian.

life, making them redundant and rendering radical promises completely moot. What remained was poorly remunerated, highly disciplined, low-skilled, and *gendered* labor.

Commune (female) workers and commune residents did not remain silent when faced with the dissolution of their collective enterprises, and the last section of this chapter describes those vociferous reactions. The complaints and vocal protests over the dissolution of the urban communes present us with a vivid reminder both of the promises of that campaign and of its intrinsic limitations and contradictions. These voices, even when filtered through official government documents, convey the passion and devotion of many of those – most of them women – who participated in urban collectivization; who built workshops, nurseries, and canteens out of meager resources and often crushing amounts of labor; and who managed them through shifting policies from the top, regularly shouldering the weight of a huge social burden. And this was all done not only for the prospect of personal advancement and individual improvement, but for the belief that "liberation" was possible: liberation from the social relations that the label "housewife" embodied, coming closer to the aspirational sociality of the socialist "worker." As historian Kimberley Manning has summarized, while discussing the gendered memory of the Great Leap Forward,

Liberation cannot be achieved by waiting for the state to grant rights and protections, these women seemed to be saying, but rather women must go out and struggle for it – and sometimes even physically suffer in the process. At the heart of many of these recollections, therefore, lies a basic conflict over the means to achieve sexual equality. Is protection from or engagement with suffering the road to freedom? During the Great Leap Forward, many chose "suffering." And today, many women leaders still see that particular period of suffering, at least parts of it, as a legitimate means to achieve a desired end: women's liberation.[17]

The real, lived value of that political promise is often erased in analyses of the Great Leap, buried under the overall tragedy of the movement, and one of the goals of this book is to bring it front and center again. On the one hand, the historical experience of the millions who toiled and strove should not be erased. But more importantly, that experience continuously brings us back to the radical political horizon of the Great Leap and perhaps of the entire Maoist project, and here I would push Manning's point even a bit further. The Great Leap promised to achieve, through the liberation of (suffering and toiling) women, a "complete liberation" from structural social inequality, from want, from the hidden

---

[17] Kimberley Ens Manning, "Making a Great Leap Forward? The Politics of Women's Liberation in Maoist China," *Gender & History* 18:3 (November 2006): 586–587.

exploitations of capitalism – a liberation inscribed and experienced in the workplace, the family, the street, in the minute details of the quotidian, and achieved through a collective and shared process of transformation – rather than being imposed or mandated.

This liberation was not achieved, and as this chapter illustrates, the search for it was truncated. But while it lasted, the search also revealed unsolved fundamental issues within the project of the Maoist revolution, issues that often were summarized under the figure of the "housewife" and embodied in the lived praxes of women defined as such, but that were inherent in the process of social reproduction under bourgeois right. I will return to that at the end of the chapter.

## 5.2 Re-localizing Production

At the end of 1962, Beijing still had forty-nine communes, comprising a total of 1,242 production units. Thirty-eight communes had been created by local residents, ten were centered around a larger factory, and there were also fifteen more locations where the neighborhood offices provided welfare services and organized production.[18] While the industrial sector had allegedly grown steadily between 1959 and 1961, the number of employees, compared with June 1960, had plummeted by 51 percent by June 1962 and by 57.8 percent by November, with the largest drop in the suburban districts of Haidian and Fengtai. The number of units under commune management had decreased by 77.2 percent.[19] The majority of the factories were either doing contract work for larger SOE enterprises or manufacturing products of everyday use for the market, with 20 percent of unplanned, piecemeal tasks filling up production gaps (*renwu suosui, shiyi buque de* 任务琐碎,拾遗补缺的).[20]

---

[18] BMA 002-020-01135-1 Youguan chengshi renmin gongshe yixie qingkuang de huizhai 有关城市人民公社一些情况的汇摘 [Excerpts of selected materials on the urban people's communes], November 21, 1962; BMA 001-028-00036-12 Zhonggong Beijing shiwei chengshi gongshe gongzuo xiaozu 中共北京市委城市公社工作小组 [Urban People's Commune Working Group of the Beijing Municipal Party Committee] "Guanyu chengshi renmin gongshe de jiben qingkuang" 关于城市人民公社的基本情况 [Basic conditions of the urban people's communes], June 4, 1962. The latter document reports forty-eight, not forty-nine communes.

[19] BMA 001-028-00036-12 Guanyu chengshi renmin gongshe de jiben qingkuang; BMA 001-028-00036-18 Zhonggong Beijing shiwei chengshi gongshe gongzuo xiaozu 中共北京市委城市公社工作小组 [Urban People's Commune Working Group of the Beijing Municipal Party Committee], Guanyu chengshi renmin gongshe gongye de qingkuang he jinhou yijian de baogao 关于城市人民公社工业的情况和今后意见的报告 [Report on the situation of the urban people's commune industry and recommendations for the future], November 28, 1962.

[20] BMA 002-020-01135-1 Youguan chengshi renmin gongshe yixie qingkuang de huizhai.

Despite the drastic reduction in personnel (or maybe because of it), Beijing communes' industrial sector was deemed to be quite profitable and useful: Local factories manufactured over 490 kinds of finished products for a total output value of over ¥900 million and a net profit of ¥105 million between 1958 to 1961. In 1961, two communes, Chunshu and Guang'anmennei, registered profits over ¥2million.[21] The quality of products was reported to have steadily increased, production costs to have steadily decreased, and improved factory management had set a stable relation between supply and demand. Much of what was produced in the capital was produced in commune factories. Given those results, the municipal CCP working group concluded in November 1962 that the commune industrial sector needed to be preserved and fostered; industries were at the very core of the commune, and without them, there was no commune to speak of.[22] Even at the time when urban collectivization was being abandoned, Beijing commune enterprises seemed to have remained productive and profitable. But under what conditions?

Survey materials from the Beixinqiao commune praising the success of some local factories provide insight into *what kind of production* was supposed to take place at this stage of urban collectivization. The cotton thread processing factory employed 104 workers (81 of them women), mostly older (forty-four was the average age), who took discarded or recycled cotton scraps and repurposed them for cotton thread, felt, gloves, and other products in high demand. This was one of the factories created by "popular initiative" in April 1958, when a group of local residents from indigent families implemented "production self-help" (*shengchan zijiu* 生产自救) and built a workshop with scrap bricks and wood. Over the years, the factory had become extremely profitable, and the report lists how much it produced in taxation, in salaries, and how much it contributed in terms of national wealth per average employee (¥3,419). Participation in production had also reduced the poverty rate among the workers, whose wages had eased their families' financial difficulties. Yet, with no provision of social services, here we have a case in which the harsh reality of a meager salary in exchange for low-skilled labor supplanted any promise of collective welfare.[23] That is, if this was

---

[21] BMA 001-028-00036-12 Guanyu chengshi renmin gongshe de jiben qingkuang. As mentioned, there are minor discrepancies between these two 1962 reports.

[22] BMA 001-028-00036-18 Guanyu chengshi renmin gongshe gongye de qingkuang he jinhou yijian de baogao.

[23] BMA 001-028-00036-5 Bian wuyong wei youyong, hua xiaoji yinsu wei jiji yinsu de miansi jiagong chang (Beixinqiao gongshe gongye diaocha cailiao zhiyi) 变无用为有用、仁消极因素为积极因素的 棉丝加工厂 (北新桥公社工业调查材料之一) [A cotton thread processing plant that turns uselessness into usefulness and negativity into positivity

"liberating," it was liberation through labor alone, which resulted only in poorly remunerated labor. The Beixinqiao electroplating factory was celebrated as another success story. Founded in 1958 by amalgamating preexisting small private workshops and with capital contributed by the workers themselves, who had asked for technical guidance from spouses, friends, and neighbors, the factory had expanded in 1961, and by 1962 it had 165 employees (152 of which were women). Only two workers had a minimum of technical expertise, and because the factory lacked a chemical laboratory, all quantities of inputs were ballparked, so quality was erratic and unreliable. Yet the factory was still profitable and successful precisely because the production process was of low technical level; skilled laborers would find it boring and a waste of their talents. It was deemed work for "housewives."[24]

A February 21, 1961, piece in the *Beijing Ribao*, "Urban Commune Industries Should Be Content with Small, Proficient at Small," offered a succinct statement of *what kind of output* was to be the target of commune production – and indirectly of *what kind of labor* was best suited to that objective. Aside from a small portion of productive effort going to serve the needs of the agricultural sector and of large industrial SOEs, the article contended that commune factories should devote themselves to manufacturing handicrafts and light industrial products "for the lives of the productive masses."[25] The refrain of "serving the people's lives as the main objective" by producing a steady stream of "small commodities" (*xiaoshangpin* 小商品) was repeated in several sources from Beijing, which also stressed how that kind of production, which was varied and did not require much in terms of equipment, fitted the *flexible and nimble nature* of the commune industry, capable of filling gaps and making up for sudden deficiencies.[26] The shift to almost exclusively producing everyday objects in response to continuously shifting social needs, while

(Survey documents of the industrial sector of the Beixinqiao commune No. 1)], September 1962.

[24] BMA 001-028-00036-6 Jidong linghuo, fangbian yonghu de dianduchang (Beixinqiao gongshe gongye diaocha cailaio zhier) 机动灵活、方便用户的电镀厂 (北新桥公社工业调查材料之二) [Flexible and customer-oriented electroplating plant (Survey documents on the industrial sector of the Beixinqiao commune No. 2)], October 4, 1962.

[25] "Chengshi gongshe gongye yao an yu xiao, jing yu xiao (shelun)" 城市公社工业要安于小、精于小 (社论) [Urban commune industries should be content with small, proficient at small (editorial)], *Beijing Ribao* 北京日报 (February 21, 1961), reprinted in Li, ed., *Chengshi renmin gongshe yanjiu ziliao xuanbian*, vol. 7: 117–118.

[26] BMA 001-006-01864-3 Chengshi renmin gongshe diaocha cailiao zhi san – guanyu gongshe de gongye shengchan 城市人民公社调查材料之三 – 关于公社的工业生产 [Survey documents on the urban People's Communes No. 3 – About commune industrial production], August 31, 1961; XDS 13-1-37-2 Guanyu xian jieduan chengshi renmin gongshe ruogan zhengce wenti de yijian (cao'an) 关于现阶段城市人

not a complete about-face from previous priorities, nonetheless represented a shift for commune industries, which had been praised for their contract work in service of large SOEs and for taking over entire sectors of the city supply (see Chapter 3).

This reorientation was justified in part as a response to a series of lingering issues that continued to affect communal production. In many instances, commune factories were not deemed capable of maintaining a stable output of quality products. One 1962 survey of Xuanwu district showed that more than half of the products were of bad or mediocre quality, and twenty-four enterprises were operating at a loss.[27] While these problems were sometimes written off as the result of shoddy management, they were more often and more correctly identified as symptomatic of a more structural flaw in collective enterprises. As we have seen in Chapter 3, commune production was not part of the planned economy, or, at least in the initial phase of the Great Leap, it was "not yet" inserted into the plan. The promise of a transition to "ownership by the whole people" also implied that communes would be eventually placed into the planning schema, and therefore they would be assigned a steady supply of raw materials while their products would be directly absorbed by the state distribution system through purchase or allocation. By 1961, the possibility of that transition had been erased, or at least endlessly postponed, largely because that transition, as I have described in previous chapters, required a more expansive role of the state in the form of the services provided by the SOE *danwei*. With that possibility gone, it had become evident that commune factories, if they operated at all, had to do so outside the *planned* system of supply and purchase, often leaving them exposed to shortages of provisions and a surfeit of unsold (or unsellable) products. For example, five of the seven tailoring factories surveyed in Xuanwu district could not maintain any stability in terms of either materials or purchasing orders.[28] With the exception of those services and products for which commune factories could set up contracts with SOEs, it was then assumed that they should

民公社若干政策问题的意见 (草稿) [Suggestions on certain policy issues concerning the urban people's communes at the present stage (draft)], October 30, 1961.

[27] XDS 5-2-8-6 Xuanwuqu gongyeju Cao Jinxue fujuzhang zai qugongshe guanyu zengchan jieyueyundong jingyan jiaoliu hui shang de baogao di 宜武区工业局曹进学付局长在区公社关于增产节约运动经验交流会上的报告摘 [Excerpts from the report by Cao Jinxue, deputy director of the Xuanwu District Industrial Bureau, at the meeting of the district communes to exchange experiences on the campaign to increase production and minimize costs], November 2, 1962.

[28] XDS 5-2-8-6 Xuanwuqu gongyeju Cao Jinxue fujuzhang zai qugongshe guanyu zengchan jieyueyundong jingyan jiaoliu hui shang de baogao di.

produce based on their understanding of "social needs," which could only be expressed via "the market," meaning the exchange that continued to exist outside the planned sector of the economy.[29] Given how that understanding was at best partial and flawed, and that "social needs" were often quickly shifting, the "flexibility" of commune production, their ability to swing from one (simple) production line to another, was singled out as their distinctive characteristic.[30] And while "flexibility" had been identified as *one* of the inherent features of (some) communal production (see Chapter 3), after 1961, it became *the* central and defining character, with serious consequences, especially for the organization of communal labor.

A survey of the industrial sector at Beixinqiao in late 1962 depicts a situation characterized by systemic unpredictability, where production was solely dependent either on complex arrangements by individual factories or on workers' initiatives. The commune manufactured 256 products, all outside state planning, and organized under four different provisions. Some 14 percent (thirty-seven products) were manufactured under long-term arrangements with SOE enterprises, which issued a monthly plan that the commune guaranteed to fulfill on time. Another 10.5 percent (twenty-seven items) were objects that the commune factories produced of their own initiative, usually with locally recycled waste. These two types of production were relatively stable, but they accounted for only one quarter of the overall output of commune industry, the rest of which was subject to much more aleatory constraints. Some 172 products (67.1 percent) were manufactured on request, when SOEs, agencies, or schools needed something done quickly, usually in small batches, a form of production almost prefiguring the type of just-in-time manufacturing that has come to define neoliberal capitalism. The remaining twenty products (7.8 percent) were produced under temporary arrangements with the Commercial Department and the district Supply and Marketing manager and were contingent on both "the needs of the market" and the availability of materials in the commune. As for the latter, the supply of materials was subject to similarly unreliable conditions, as more than 67 percent of those materials depended on the ability of the commune itself to procure them

---

[29] See Chapter 3 for what "the market" means here.
[30] BMA 002-020-01135-1 Youguan chengshi renmin gongshe yixie qingkuang de huizhai; BMA 001-028-00036-5 Bian wuyong wei youyong, hua xiaoji yinsu wei jiji yinsu de miansi jiagong chang (Beixinqiao gongshe gongye diaocha cailiao zhiyi); XDS 5-2-8-6 Xuanwuqu gongyeju Cao Jinxue fujuzhang zai qugongshe guanyu zengchan jieyueyundong jingyan jiaoliu hui shang de baogao di.

independently. In such a situation, planning, even for the medium term, was simply impossible.[31]

Flexibility, however, did not simply apply to production lines and factory outputs. Rather, it also came to define where and how production took place, and the kind of labor it required. In order to become nimbler, commune enterprises had to be shrunk in size, and large factories (over 100 employees), considered too cumbersome and unwieldy, had to be divided into smaller units. Since their inception, urban communes had integrated "concentrated" (*jizhong* 集中) and "scattered" (*fensan* 分散) production, but if in the initial phase of the Great Leap the emphasis was on the former, in this later stage scattered production was clearly being privileged, following the principle of "if it can be scattered, then do not concentrate it, if it can be small, then do not make it big" (*neng fensande jiu buyao jizhong, neng gaoxiao buyao gaoda* 能分散的就不要集中, 能搞小不要搞大).[32] Scattered production took place in proximity to the workers' homes and was often accomplished within the home; it was programmatically centered on simple processes, with even lower mechanization – or, rather, with no mechanization at all – and requiring very basic technical skills.[33] It was a kind of labor perfectly suited to piece-rate wages, and "flexibility" here meant that workers could potentially be paid only when there was a task to be completed or a request to be satisfied, rendering them a largely disposable or at best contingent workforce. As Hanchao Lu notes, "a woman could register in the workshop and have work assigned to her, but the whole family, typically children and

---

[31] BMA 001-028-00036-7 Beixinqiao gongshe gongye de shengchan anpai, yuan cailiao gongying he chanpin xiaoshou qiangkuang (Beixinqiao gongshe gongye diaocha cailiao zhi san) 北新桥公社工业的生产安排、原材料供应和产品销售情况 (北新桥公社工业调查材料之三) [Production arrangements, supply of raw materials, and sales of products in the Beixinqiao Commune industry (Survey documents of the Beixinqiao Commune industry No. 3)], November 6, 1962. The large majority of finished products, 78.9 percent, were sold directly to the commissioning party (a SOE, for example). Historian Lin Chaochao describes a similarly dire situation in Shanghai, where workers in a neighborhood factory fought for raw materials with workers from a SOE factory, and where issues in the provision of raw materials had led to reliance on back-door markets and illegal purchase and reselling. Lin Chaochao 林超超, "'Dayuejin' shiqi Shanghai jiedao gongye de dingwei yu zhuanxing" '大跃进' 时期上海街道工业的定位与转型 [The orientation and transformation of Shanghai street industry at the time of the Great Leap Forward], *Zhonggong dangshi yanjiu* 中共党史研究 [CCP history research] 8 (2018): 51–52.

[32] XDS 13-1-37-2 Guanyu xian jieduan chengshi renmin gongshe ruogan zhengce wenti de yijian (cao'an).

[33] Of course, embroidery, needlework, tailoring, and weaving all require high technical skills. But because those forms of production were gendered female and associated with "housewives," they were systemically undervalued, and completely "un-valued" when performed within the home.

the elderly in particular, could help with the work she took home."[34] The localized nature of this work and the fact that it was done near or in the home also meant that the communes did not consider it necessary to provide collectivized welfare for these laborers and therefore did not provide any such services.[35]

Sources from one of the earliest Beijing communes, Erlonglu, document in impressive detail the devolution of the commune's productive sector and the progressive precarization of its labor force; this was a sector that had been singled out for praise just months earlier and was now instead identified as a case study for critique and restructuring. In the summer of 1962, the commune comprised 76,497 residents (17,570 families), 7,000 of which were labeled "scattered labor." But the history of the commune productive sector had not been linear or unproblematic, or at least that was not how it was described in these later sources. While the size of the commune had remained relatively stable in 1958 and 1959, at least in terms of employment (4,330 workers in 1958, and 4,654 in 1960), there had been a significant drop after the restructuring in 1960, so that in June 1960 the commune had 3,177 employees (a 25 percent reduction). A similar shift affected the kind of products manufactured by the commune. While originally Erlonglu's commune enterprises were focused on repair and finishing work, they quickly started tackling more ambitious projects, with higher production value and higher revenue, which by June 1960 represented 65 percent of the total output and occupied 70 percent of the personnel.[36] Some factories purchased expensive pieces of equipment, but ultimately did not use them. In some cases, they simply did not need such equipment; in other cases, they could not even get the machinery through the doors of the workshop, or they did not have enough electric power to make it work.[37]

These circumstances coincided with an expansion in the size of individual factories: Many of the "scattered production groups" established in 1959 were absorbed into regular enterprises and small factories were combined into large ones, so that they went from only two factories with

---

[34] Lu, *Shanghai Tai Chi*: 159.
[35] BMA 001-006-01864-3 Chengshi renmin gongshe diaocha cailiao zhi san – guanyu gongshe de gongye shengchan.
[36] XDN 38-1-34-1 Erlonglu gongshe dangwei 二龙路公社党委 [Party Committee of the Erlonglu commune], Beijing Erlonglu renmin gongshe jiben qingkuang (cao'an) 北京市二龙路人民公社基本情况 (草稿) [Basic information on the Erlonglu people's commune in Beijing], July 28, 1962.
[37] XDN 11-4-57-3 Guanyu Erlonglu renmin gongshe jilei yu fenpei qingkuang de diaocha baogao 关于二龙路人民公社积累与分配情况的调查报告 [Investigation report on capital accumulation and income distribution at the Erlonglu people's commune], May 14, 1961.

over 100 workers in 1958 to twelve in 1961. During such expansion, commune cadres were accused of falling prey to their own ambitions of grandeur (*zhuida qiuyang* 追大求洋), ignoring the directives of the Beijing CCP committee, which had advised against excessive concentration and favored smaller factories with specific and diverse production lines. This led to a reduction in the kinds of products manufactured at the commune but also a drop in workers' participation, especially among those women who had found it possible to join a "scattered" production center close to home but could not really abdicate family responsibilities and move to a larger factory farther away for hours a day. In one case, out of seventy workers, thirty-two left when their small production center was merged into a bigger factory. Conversely, larger concentrated production centers with hundreds of employees were expected to provide welfare services for their employees, which increased the financial burden for commune enterprises and worsened the housing crisis in downtown Beijing, as canteens and kindergartens took over residential buildings. In the process of expanding the size of the commune factories, managers sometimes ended up combining disparate production lines, with no coherence, with a single factory merging processes related to five or six different industries, making the provision of materials extraordinarily complicated. Documents and surveys often reverted to placing the blame on the inherent gendered failures of those in charge, "housewives" turned factory or line managers, whose skills and organizational capacities were not considered to be good enough to supervise more complex production processes.[38]

The solution to these problems was found in restructuring the Erlonglu commune production sector through a process that unfolded over several months. In November 1960, the district reorganized the commune factories and placed them under the central administration (*guikou* 归口). The existing thirteen factories were reassigned to four bureaus: electrical, light industry, textile, and chemical, a move that provoked a certain amount of resistance from the commune side – the sources do not specify how this resistance materialized. The goal from the central administration was to streamline production, eliminating redundancies – several factories manufactured the same merchandise – as well as products that were considered unnecessary or, more tellingly,

---

[38] BMA 112-001-00783-2 Erlonglu gongshe diaochazu 二龙路公社调查组 [Erlonglu commune survey group], Guanyu Erlonglu gongshe shengchan zuzhi de guimo he xingshi wenti de baogao 关于二龙路公社生产组织的规模和形式问题的报告 [Report on the scale and structure of production organizations at the Erlonglu commune], August 17, 1961.

"unfit for female workers," which in this case I assume to mean requiring high technical skills or complex production procedures.[39]

In early 1961, it was decided by central administrators to rearrange the Erlonglu commune factories from the existing twelve (or thirteen; there is some discrepancy in the sources) to seventeen, assigning them to five industrial bureaus (the four mentioned above plus metallurgy), and reducing the workforce from 3,225 to 2,524. Two factories remained under the commune's jurisdiction.[40] In August, the plan was altered to further fragment commune production into twenty-one factories.[41] Some of the existing factories were deemed too big and unwieldy to be properly managed. This was the case of the Erlonglu General Factory and its 587 employees, which was split into three separate enterprises, with 150 workers each. This was the very same factory that had been singled out for praise in 1959, when the value of its daily output had grown ten times (see Chapter 1).

In other cases, productions lines that were considered to be unconnected were separated. For example, the plumbing plant included a leather belt workshop, which was then turned into an independent factory and placed under commune administration.[42] The restructuring also meant a return to "scattered production," which was a recommended option for the old, the weak, and those who were too busy with housework, who were better suited for smaller workshops fulfilling simple tasks. By July 1961, the number of employees in Erlonglu factories was down to 2,190.[43] While reports argued that both concentrated and scattered production were to be pursued at the same time, each form fitting different manufacturing processes, the emphasis was clearly on the latter, with sources celebrating factory work done in the home. Such was

[39] XDN 11-4-63-2 Erlonglu renmin gongshe gongye zu 二龙路人民公社工业组 [Industry group of the Erlonglu people's commune], Erlonglu renmin gongshe gongye guihua de chubu yijian (diyi gao) 二龙路人民公社工业规划的初步意见（第一稿）[Preliminary views of the industrial planning of the Erlonglu people's commune (first draft)], April 3, 1961.

[40] XDN 11-4-63-3 Erlonglu renmin gongshe gongye zu 二龙路人民公社工业组 [Industry group of the Erlonglu people's commune], Gongye guihua shuoming 工业规划说明 [Explanation of industrial planning], April 10, 1961. Another coeval source provides slightly different numbers: from twelve to eighteen factories, and from 3,225 to 2,614 employees. XDN 11-4-63-6 Erlonglu renmin gongshe gongye zu 二龙路人民公社工业组 [Industry group of the Erlonglu people's commune], Erlonglu renmin gongye 'wunian' guihua 二龙路人民公社工业'五年'规划 ["Five year" plan of the Erlonglu people's commune industry] (April 14, 1961).

[41] BMA 112-001-00783-2 Guanyu Erlonglu gongshe shengchan zuzhi de guimo he xingshi wenti de baogao.

[42] XDN 11-4-63-3 Gongye guihua shuoming.

[43] BMA 112-001-00783-2 Guanyu Erlonglu gongshe shengchan zuzhi de guimo he xingshi wenti de baogao.

the case of Wang Caixia, thirty-four, a mother of five who did work for the No. 1 Sewing Factory at Erlonglu in her own home and made ¥10 monthly. While workers in the main factory were probably more efficient and produced more per capita, they received higher salaries and required at least a minimum of welfare, so, in purely economic terms, it was in the end more profitable to keep workers employed at home. Perhaps the most extreme case reported in the Erlonglu sources was that of commune workers spinning asbestos yarns at home, something that even commune authorities found too dangerous and eventually decided to move to a separate workshop.[44] The same source details the case of two commune workers, both manufacturing cotton thread at home:

The most productive spinner is Yang Zuoxiu and the family depends primarily on her income. There are three children and the oldest one (about 14 and a half years old) also helps her with spinning, getting the cotton, and delivering the thread. She works 15–16 hours per day, laboring day and night, spinning up to 185 pounds. Her husband is a counter-revolutionary undergoing reform through labor, so the three children rely on her to survive. The least productive worker, spinning only 10 pounds for a monthly income of ¥2.5, is Guo Yurong. She has five children, the oldest one just started elementary school, the youngest is less than 3 years old, and she is now pregnant again. Her husband's salary is low, so life is quite difficult, but childcare and domestic chores are too much of a burden, and she has little time to spin, therefore the [economic] impact of her work is limited.[45]

Overall, what documents about the 1961–1962 restructuring illus-trate is the return to forms of labor that had existed in urban and especially rural China long before the modern era, when women's work in the home was both an essential element for the family economy and a crucial contributor to certain productive sectors – textile first and foremost – with the loom and the needle indispensable parts in a woman's everyday life.[46]

This restructuring of the processes and locations of production had a parallel in the kinds of products manufactured. At Erlonglu, products of

---

[44] BMA 001-028-00031-7 Erlonglu renmin gongshe guanyu jizhong shengchan he fensan shengchan qingkuang diaocha 二龙路人民公社关于集中生产和分散生产情况调查 [Survey of centralized and decentralized production at the Erlonglu people's commune], May 15, 1961.

[45] BMA 001-028-00031-7 Erlonglu renmin gongshe guanyu jizhong shengchan he fensan shengchan qingkuang diaocha.

[46] Gail Hershatter notes how during the Great Leap, "Women themselves, sometimes used the language of compulsory, regular, disciplined labor to talk about their needlework; they spoke, for instance, of 'adding a night shift working for the children.'" Hershatter, *The Gender of Memory*: 195. On women's labor in late imperial China, see Francesca Bray, *Technology and Gender: Fabrics of Power in Late Imperial China* (Berkeley: University of California Press, 1997).

everyday use went from 31 percent of the total in 1960 to 54.6 percent in 1961 to 62 percent in 1962. Products for SOE factories decreased to 32 percent. Overall, variety of products drastically declined, so that in 1962 Erlonglu's output comprised 71 kinds of products, 6 of them part of the state plan, 32 on a contract basis with other units, 18 processing materials provided by clients (*lailiao jiagong* 来料加工), 4 for processing at retail store (*menshi jiagong* 门市加工), and 11 produced and sold directly by the commune (*zichan baoxiao* 自产报销). Everyday objects (62 percent of the total, 61 percent of the personnel) included small spoons, thermoses, pipes (for smoking), medical ointment, washstands, clay chimneys, clasps, and other products.[47] This kind of production was overtly described as "labor intensive" and akin to handicraft, and, if done in a SOE, where salaries were higher, it would not have been cost effective.[48] Some 6 percent of the commune output was for export, including leather hats, leather collars, and needlework: These were good-quality items that also garnered foreign currency for the state. Overall, reports estimated that 65 percent of commune factory workers were in production lines that manufactured either daily necessities or export goods, for which there was a strong need in the market. Raw materials for these lines were usually not an issue, and they would come from planned distribution, recycled scraps, or the commercial sector. One Erlonglu factory made cloisonne mugs using recycled materials from a washbasin factory, while their own scraps were used by another commune factory to produce shoe eyelets. The belt factory cited above collected leather scraps from all over town to manufacture wallets and satchels.[49] These factories were celebrated for their undercapitalized, simple production processes, which could be easily relocated close to or in the home, and which remained highly profitable under conditions of low wages and no benefits. They

[47] A similar shift in production took place at the Fusuijing commune: The commune's eleven factories (3,280 workers) used to do contract work on components and parts for SOEs. However, because of supply issues, in 1960, all factories except for three switched to produce objects for everyday use – kettles, buckets, spoons, vegetable knives – and renovating old clothes. BMA 084-003-00072-5 Fusuijing renmin gongshe gongye shengchan de jige wenti 福绥境人民公社工业生产的几个问题 [Several problems of industrial production in the Fusuijing people's commune], June 30, 1961.

[48] A 1962 report from Jiuxianqiao listed the forms of labor appropriate for the commune (which included rough processing of raw materials and sorting of industrial waste). Besides increasing the family's income, (female) commune labor also had the added benefit of reducing the burden of SOEs and saving state expenditures, as it was programmatically underpaid and with very few welfare provisions. BMA 001-028-00036-9 Guanyu Jiuxianqiao renmin gongshe de diaocha baogao (caogao) 关于酒仙桥人民公社的调查报告 (草稿) [Investigation report on the Jiuxianqiao people's commune (draft)], January 18, 1962.

[49] XDN 38-1-34-1 Beijing Erlonglu renmin gongshe jiben qingkuang (cao'an).

participated in the push for a no-waste economy inaugurated in early 1953 with the "Double-Anti Movement" (*shuangfan yundong* 双反运动)[50] – opposing waste and conservative thinking – which was supposed to combine boldness in economic experimentation with maximum utilization of available resources, including recycled ones.[51] Conversely, other *danwei* in the same commune were criticized and eventually disbanded for tackling tasks considered to be too complex, too technical, and too sophisticated, especially for "housewives."

As described in previous chapters, commune production was programmatically based on a bottom-up effort and on the deployment of low-skilled, underpaid, gendered labor, but that had been at least in part counterbalanced by the assurance of future technological progress, career advancement through education and training, and "women's liberation" through a radical transformation of the everyday. And despite the fact that efforts in that direction had been regularly frustrated, the continued insistence of the possibility of such a future had a political and theoretical significance, especially as women had often and vocally expressed their support for such a project and devoted their labor to achieve that future. In that light, the declared acceptance and the sometimes unabashed celebration of forms of labor suited to "scattered production" could not but represent an abrupt course reversal, compared even with just a few months later, when Beijing officials lavished praise on the improved technical abilities and the high level of quality achieved by commune production. By 1961 and 1962, even when they mentioned the rarer and rarer educational achievements of commune workers, reports continued to emphasize the "simple" production process as the standard to be maintained.[52] Gone was any prospect of improvement, either through education or mechanization. Yet, as we have seen, many women workers embraced decentralization, preferring the home to a distant factory. This shift, I argue, was a reflection of changing practical conditions in the communes' last phase but, more importantly, of the unsolved tension between domestic and "productive" labor, between home and factory, a tension embodied in the figure of the housewife-turned-worker.

Even under socialism, the condition of the "housewife" was constituted by and constitutive of a set of social relations that were still determined, as many Maoist theoreticians explicitly recognized, by elements and structures similar to those of capitalism and bourgeois society. Under those constraints, "housewives" and the domestic labor they performed were made invisible by the very ideology surrounding

---

[50] Kelly, *Market Maoists*: 132.    [51] See Chapter 3.
[52] XDN 38-1-34-1 Beijing Erlonglu renmin gongshe jiben qingkuang (cao'an).

"productive" work, which in turn made their own work programmatically nonproductive. In that perspective, the factory remained the sole place where production took place, where productive labor was performed, and where the identity of worker was located and shaped. Even under socialism, without factory work, there was no worker. And even if the work in commune factories had to be reduced to the simplest processes and tasks, because of the prejudices and assumptions associated with female labor (Mies's housewifization), the potential for socialization, technical improvement, education, and women's liberation remained strictly associated with the factory.

With disappearing social services and the increasingly simplified and mind-numbing nature of commune labor, several women embraced scattered production. As in the case of Yang Zuoxiu cited above, whose husband was in a labor camp, they could gain much needed income while keeping an eye on the home and the family, even if it came with a punishing double burden and a never-ending workday. Under the particular conception of labor adopted by the CCP – which was in turn still defined by elements of bourgeois right – it remained impossible to square the circle of social reproduction and to grant "scattered work" or any work conducted in the home any recognition beyond some minimum of monetary compensation. There was no "liberation" to be found in a form of production brought back to the home and deprived of any prospects of welfare benefits.[53] Liberation, if it came, had to come through the factory.

At the end of this process of restructuring, in the summer of 1962, Erlonglu had seventeen factories and six production groups, for a total of 2,611 employees (1,799 of them in the factories). There were six metal factories, five for everyday products, two for clothing, one for leather and fur, one for transportation, one for wood, and one for chemicals. Most of them (71 percent) were functioning well, with a steady supply of materials; they were on average small, with very low levels of mechanization. The largest factories had between 150 and 200 employees, and they were all based on manual labor. They were therefore all very flexible, and it was easy to shift from one production line to another when needed.[54]

Yet despite its declared success, the movement "to increase production and diminish expenses" had not fully eliminated a series of lingering problems. Blame fell first and foremost on cadres and management.

---

[53] These forms of "scattered" production lingered on after the dismantling of the communes, but, as Delia Davin noted, offered little monetary compensation and no benefits. They were also very vulnerable to any shift in the economic climate. Davin, *Woman Work*: 164.

[54] XDN 38-1-34-2 Beijingshi Erlonglu gongshe gongye jiben qingkuang.

In Xuanwu district, for example, cadres of 22 out of 132 factories were reported as not having yet fully mobilized the workers in joining the movement.[55] At Erlonglu, managers of most factories were reproached for their lack of planning: Only two commune factories had a plan for the following month laid out by the 25th.[56] At Fusuijing, one worker complained about the lack of any rhyme or reason in their schedule: "Today you tell us to get the shears, tomorrow to get the hammer, today you move us to this group, tomorrow you transfer us to another group; can you finally tell us what you want us to do?"[57] Another survey of Xuanwu pointed at more structural issues concerning the coordination between various levels of administration (commune, district, city, and party) and the distribution of responsibilities among them in the new system.[58] Factories also struggled at maintaining a stable overall quality of products, with some units still failing to grasp the contradiction between quantity and quality, emphasizing the former while neglecting the latter. In the third quarter the output of Xuanwu district factories comprised four products of outstanding quality, six of good quality, four middling, and eight bad.[59] At Erlonglu, only a few products were considered to be of high quality: For example, 30 percent of rivets produced by commune enterprises were not good, and 25 percent of chimneys had issues.[60] Surveys identified the main reason for this in the lack of expert master workers: There were only seventy-nine skilled workers in Erlonglu factories, and just three of them were above "third class," with experience in automotive, mechanical, or electrical engineering.[61] More worryingly for city authorities, there were still commune *danwei* that were hemorrhaging money: Twenty-four enterprises in Xuanwu accrued a total loss of ¥66,000 in the third quarter of 1962, mostly because of low productivity, bad quality, and high consumption of materials.[62] At Erlonglu, they identified seventy-one kinds of products losing money, a total of ¥8,500 in the second quarter of 1962, which was attributed to bad accounting and irrational use of expensive resources.[63]

---

[55] XDS 5-2-8-6 Xuanwuqu gongyeju Cao Jinxue fujuzhang zai qugongshe guanyu zengchan jieyueyundong jingyan jiaoliu hui shang de baogao di.
[56] XDN 38-1-34-1 Beijing Erlonglu renmin gongshe jiben qingkuang (cao'an).
[57] BMA 084-003-00072-5 Fusuijing renmin gongshe gongye shengchan de jige wenti.
[58] BMA 002-020-01135-1 Youguan chengshi renmin gongshe yixie qingkuang de huizhai.
[59] XDS 5-2-8-6 Xuanwuqu gongyeju Cao Jinxue fujuzhang zai qugongshe guanyu zengchan jieyueyundong jingyan jiaoliu hui shang de baogao di.
[60] XDN 38-1-34-1 Beijing Erlonglu renmin gongshe jiben qingkuang (cao'an).
[61] XDN 38-1-34-2 Beijingshi Erlonglu gongshe gongye jiben qingkuang.
[62] XDS 5-2-8-6 Xuanwuqu gongyeju Cao Jinxue fujuzhang zai qugongshe guanyu zengchan jieyueyundong jingyan jiaoliu hui shang de baogao di.
[63] XDN 38-1-34-1 Beijing Erlonglu renmin gongshe jiben qingkuang (cao'an).

Finally, in line with the new policies, reports identified another problem, one that came to be considered at the very foundation of almost all others: excessive "egalitarianism" in remuneration. Up until 1959, most commune industrial workers were on piece-rate wages, but they were moved to per-time remuneration in the second half of that year, with salaries ranging between ¥18 and ¥23.[64] At Erlonglu, only 12.3 percent of the workers were paid on a piece-rate basis, and the differences in salaries among the various levels of skill and proficiency were negligible, with allegedly adverse effects on the enthusiasm and activism of commune laborers.[65] A similar egalitarianism was practiced not only among workers but among enterprises, with commune administration appropriating 80–90 percent of the profits with no real consideration of the individual factory's performance, so enterprises that operated well and those that did not ended up being very similar to each other in terms of material incentives.[66] This critique of egalitarianism was another example of the newly reestablished orthodoxy in political economy achieved after the foreclosure on the debate on bourgeois right, in which the wage form had featured prominently as a target. With wages and wage differences once again naturalized, workers and labor processes were available to be newly subjected to a much stricter disciplining through more widespread and detailed accounting practices.

## 5.3    The Discipline of Accounting

The solutions proposed to these lingering problems followed the general directions that the process of rectification had adopted after 1960, which, as mentioned earlier, prefigured an arrangement designed to achieve the maximum extraction of profit from each unit and the concomitant reduction – or complete elimination – of any disbursement of resources and capital from the upper administration. As 95 percent of the factories

---

[64] BMA 002-020-01135-1 Youguan chengshi renmin gongshe yixie qingkuang de huizhai.
[65] XDN 38-1-34-2 Beijingshi Erlonglu gongshe gongye jiben qingkuang.
[66] BMA 001-028-00036-17 Chengshi renmin gongshe gongye bu neng yifeng chui – guanyu Beixinqiaorenmin gongshe gongye de qingluang diaocha 城市人民公社工业不能一风吹 – 关于北新桥人民公社工业的情况调查 [Industries in urban people's communes cannot be suddenly eliminated – Survey of the situation of the industry in the Beixinqiao people's commune]; BMA 002-020-01135-1 Youguan chengshi renmin gongshe yixie qingkuang de huizhai. Similarly worded critiques of "egalitarianism" were leveled at urban communes in other locales. For the case of Zhengzhou, see Yao Ertao 姚二涛, "Chengshi renmin gongshe 'gongchanfeng' tanwei" 城市人民公社 '共产风'探微 [Exploring the 'communist winds' in urban people's communes], *Guangdong dangshi yu wenxian yanjiu* 广东党史与文献研究 [Guangdong Party history and literature research], no. 1 (2022): 87.

were still the collective property of the commune, reports critically noted, the commune was the basic accounting unit and could step in to make up for losses at the unit level, leading industry cadres to ignore financial accounting and develop an "eat from the big pot" (*chi daguofan* 吃大锅饭) attitude.[67] It was therefore deemed necessary to shift responsibility for profits and losses from the commune to each individual productive or service unit – and, ultimately, to each individual worker – so to quash any mentality of "dependence." In bureaucratic terms, that meant the transformation of all commune *danwei* into independent units of accounting. This applied to commune factories and production groups that, as part of the aforementioned push toward efficiency and productivity, were encouraged to provide rewards for quality improvements and punishments for lack thereof, as well as to reduce the proportion of nonproductive personnel to a maximum of 5 percent.[68] More pointedly, this devolution of responsibilities and accounting also applied to service units, with the goal of making canteens, childcare centers, and service centers into efficient and self-sufficient (*ziji zizu* 自给自足) organizations. This had momentous consequences, which I explore below.

In November 1961, when the Xuanwu district drafted guidelines for the commune canteens, the main principle was that canteens had to account for themselves and were solely responsible for profits and losses. The district authorities alerted canteen managers that the commune could step in and help only when there were extenuating circumstances, but if a unit lost revenues because of endogenous issues (bad service, bad attitude, bad food), no subsidy could be expected. The guidelines included the proviso that, in order to remain solvent, canteens had to maintain an employee/customer ratio of 1:25; failing that, personnel had to be cut.[69] An August 1961 report from Erlonglu retells the story of the supposed decline in efficiency of commune canteens and childcare centers. Created as part of a mass mobilization effort, these organizations belonged to the commune but continued to be administered as independent units until 1960, when they all were subsumed under the commune accounting, with salaries and expenses being provided for at the commune level. This allegedly led to carelessness and waste in the use of material and human resources: Some nurseries and

---

[67]  BMA 112-001-00782-4 Guanyu xian jieduan chengshi renmin gongshe ruogan wenti de guiding (cao'an).

[68]  XDS 13-1-37-2 Guanyu xian jieduan chengshi renmin gongshe ruogan zhengce wenti de yijian (cao'an).

[69]  XDS 13-2-50-3 Zjiji zizu shouru, zhichu ji guanli zhidu (cao'an)" 自给自足收入、支出及管理制度 (草案) [Self-sufficient income, expenditure, and management system (draft)], November 7, 1961.

kindergartens were overstaffed, with several employees who performed no actual labor; they wasted supplies and did not take good care of toys and equipment; and the attitude of workers had also worsened. The solution adopted in 1961 was "to abolish the system of commune guarantee, making canteens and childcare centers solely responsible for their own funding."[70] The same principle was applied to the commune repair centers, which were "granted" administrative and economic autonomy in July 1961; this resulted in an increase in both the employees' motivation and their salaries.[71] The Fusuijing commune service sector also reported the same tale of excessive reliance on the commune and lack of any notion of economic accounting (*jingji hesuan gainian* 经济核算概念), leading to large losses. Only one of the ten service centers had registered a profit in 1961, while forty-one service centers did not even keep any form of centralized accounting, letting the commune make up for any loss; the commune subsidized 65.5 percent of the salaries on average. Devolution of accounting to the *danwei* level was once again the proposed solution. The commune remained responsible only for the maintenance and repair of major pieces of equipment for canteens and factories, but almost every other expense was transferred down to the individual unit.[72]

Localized accounting did not simply mean that commune enterprises were now supposed to be self-sufficient and were left to "sink or swim" based on their own profitability; rather, it was also an attempt at configuring a detailed system of control of both labor and resources to enhance profitability to the utmost. The goal of full employment and potentially universal provision of services gave way to profit as the sole standard. Xuanwu district, for instance, not only introduced a reform of the management system, but commune factories and their employees were also supposed to become subject a regime of continuous evaluation and self-evaluation (*pingbi* 评比), pushed forth by a combination of mass

---

[70] BMA 112-001-00783-6 Erlonglu gongshe diaocha zu 二龙路公社调查组 [Erlonglu commune survey group], Guanyu Erlonglu gongshe shitang, tuo'er zuzhi shixing ziji zizu wenti de baogao 关于二龙路公社食堂、托儿组织实行自给自足问题的报告 [Report on the implementation of self-sufficiency in the Erlonglu commune canteen and child care organizations], August 17, 1961.

[71] BMA 002-020-01135-1 Youguan chengshi renmin gongshe yixie qingkuang de huizhai; XDS 13-1-37-2 Guanyu xian jieduan chengshi renmin gongshe ruogan zhengce wenti de yijian (cao'an).

[72] XDN 11-4-57-9 Xichengqu caizhengju 西城区财政局 [Xicheng district finance bureau], Fusuijing gongshe de fuwusuo, zhan caiqu 'tongyi hesuan, gongfu yingkui' de houguo 福绥境公社的服务所、站采取'统一核算、共负盈亏' 的 后果 [Consequences of adopting "unified accounting and shared profit and loss" by the service centers and stations at the Fusuijing Commune], May 29, 1961.

movements and material incentives, and conducted among and within workshops every yearly quarter, every month, and even every week.[73]

In canteens, this disciplining first and foremost manifested itself in the management of foodstuff (primarily grains, oil, and vegetables), something perhaps to be expected in what were the bitter months of the famine. In 1961, the Taoranting commune issued a series of instructions on that subject: Each canteen should have a locked storage for foodstuff, with officers specifically responsible for its management, whose access was regulated through a double layer of security. Those canteens that did not yet have locked storage were supposed to build it within a month. Each canteen should also keep daily accounts, balancing every night what they had sold with the ration tickets they had received. Those accounts should be made public every month.[74] At Dashilar, the district mandated a similar system and instructed that monthly surplus and losses in stored food could not exceed 0.5 percent of the total (1.2 percent yearly). Canteen workers were furthermore solicited to increase their service ratio to one worker per forty customers in the span of two months.[75]

Increase in workers' productivity (together with reduction of expenses) was a leitmotif of early 1960s reports, and it was usually achieved through the disciplining produced by closely tying salaries and material incentives to rigidly measured performance. At the Mishi hutong canteen (Taoranting commune), although personnel were cut, the number of customers increased; productivity rose to one employee for 26.5 customers; the average salary grew accordingly; and expenses went down by 40 percent.[76] The Jiajia hutong service center at Taoranting – a small workshop, with seven employees plus one popsicle seller – had incurred major losses. The commune identified the reasons as "absenteeism, low efficiency, an ideology of dependency, and low motivation." In July 1961, they introduced independent accounting and a system of fixed and

---

[73] XDS 5-2-8-6 Xuanwuqu gongyeju Cao Jinxue fujuzhang zai qugongshe guanyu zengchan jieyueyundong jingyan jiaoliu hui shang de baogao di.

[74] XDS 41-2-14-2 Taoranting gongshe shitang he fuwu gongzuo jihua 陶然亭公社食堂和服务工作计划 [Canteen and service work plan for the Taoranting commune], January 5, 1961.

[75] XDS 13-2-50-4 Shitang pingbi jingsai neirong 食堂评比竞赛内容 [Criteria for the canteen assessment contest], March 6, 1961. The criteria were described as the "four good, three low, two high, and one convenient" (sihao, sanshao, ergao, yi pianli 四好、三少、二高、一便利), meaning: good management of foodstuff, good quality of dishes, good service, good hygiene; low operating costs, few people exempted from productive labor, low use of coal; high attendance, high productivity; convenient for the masses.

[76] XDS 41-2-14-4 Taoranting gongshe fuwubu 陶然亭公社服务部 [Taoranting commune service department], Mishi hutong shitang guanyu zifuyingkui wenti shidian qingkuang 米士胡同食堂关于自负盈亏问题试点情况 [Pilot implementation of financial self-sufficiency at the Mishi hutong canteen], July 21, 1961.

variable assignment of work points (*sifen huozhi* 死分活值), meaning that the work points assigned to each individual worker, instead of being set, were subject to increase or decrease according to a periodical evaluation of the work produced, the worker's labor, and the enterprise's revenues. In half a month, the station not only stopped losing revenue, but they increased capital accumulation; five workers got a pay raise, and two a pay cut, all as a function of their individual productivity. In the past, when work was poorly done, the responsibility was collectively shared; under the new system, it fell onto the individual worker, with the result that there was no shoddy work that needed redoing.[77] Another workshop for repairing iron objects at Taoranting also introduced a new remuneration system in July 1961, with a significant portion of the profit going to bonuses. That led to an increase in average compensation (38 percent over the previous month), which was achieved through interiorized self-discipline by the small cohort of workers, who adopted the attitude that "if you are a little sick you keep going, if there is a small issue you don't take time off" (*xiaobing jianchi gan, xiaoshi bu qingjia* 小病坚持干，小事不請假). This was exemplified by Zhang Runying, who on July 7 had a fever and a headache but kept working nonetheless; while in the past she could repair only two to three basins per day, now she was now up to four to five. The productivity rush spurred by material incentives also generated some (predictable) adverse effects, as workers started adopting a "purely economic perspective" (*danchun jingji guandian* 单纯经济观点), choosing only what was best for them individually (*tiaofei jianshou* 挑肥拣瘦), privileging quantity over quality. Sources also registered a breakdown in the relationship between master and apprentice, each now caring only for their own selfish interests.[78] In July, the Tongfa temple kindergarten (also at Taoranting) adopted independent accounting and the fixed/variable assignment of work points, with workers distributed on a scale of twenty-five to thirty points, each point valued at ¥0.9. The workers, who had been criticized in the past for caring only for their salaries (working eight hours and wanting to be paid), were now praised for their newfound activism and enthusiasm – which was, ironically, also

---

[77] XDS 41-2-14-3 Taoranting gongshe fuwubu 陶然亭公社服务部 [Taoranting commune service department], Jiajia hutong fuwuzhan guanyu fenpei fangfa de shidian qingkuang 贾家胡同服务站关于分配方法的试点情况 [Pilot implementation of distribution methods at the Jiajia hutong service center], July 21, 1961.

[78] XDS 41-2-14-5 Taoranting gongshe fuwubu 陶然亭公社服务部 [Taoranting commune service department], Heibaitie dier menshibu guanyu caiqu chao'e jiangli de fenpei xingshi de shidian qingkuang he jinhou de yijian 黑白铁第二门市部关于采取超额奖励的分配形式的试点情况和今后的意见 [Pilot implementation of an overfulfillment bonus distribution system at the No. 2 hardware retail store and recommendations for the future], July 21, 1961.

motivated by monetary rewards. A report mentions two young, strong women, very good workers, whose salaries had increased from ¥20 to ¥26. As in other units, here too a rise in productivity was accompanied by a reduction in personnel, and while in the past they had 18 workers for 110 children, in 1961 they needed only 12 to care for 118.[79]

The disciplining of workers for the sake of increased productivity was also achieved through a system of repeated evaluations, often taking the form of labor competitions between and within communes, as, for example, in 1962, when the Beijing Handicraft Management Office invited each commune to select one or two factories to take part in a city-wide contest. They assessed products in terms of quality, productivity, cost, and how well they fulfilled the national plan. To be chosen as a "red flag" enterprise, a factory had to satisfy a series of requirements, including outstanding quality (80 percent at least on the national scale), a continuous effort to reduce costs and increase productivity, and the use of recycled materials.[80] This was just one instance in a series of campaigns pitching factories, small groups, individuals, and managers against one another, as part of a system that, through the assignment of mostly nonmaterial rewards, potentially placed every single worker and cadre under unremitting competitive evaluation.[81]

However, the effort to increase productivity and enthusiasm among commune workers relied primarily on *material* incentives, that is, monetary compensation. While in the first months of the Great Leap, wages had been singled out as one of the vestiges of capitalism, a crucial component of bourgeois right, and the main generator of inequalities under socialism, a short four years later, in this later stage, wages were instead celebrated as the necessary remedy for pernicious "egalitarianism," as the sole guarantor of individual productivity and originator of workers' enthusiasm. And that meant a return to forms of remuneration "according to labor" that actively emphasized differences, focused on value extraction, and were functional to disciplining workers' activities.[82]

---

[79] XDS 41-2-14-6 Taoranting renmin gongshe youjiaobu 陶然亭人民公社幼教部 [Taoranting people's commune early childhood education department], Youjiao shiye guanyu gaibian suoyouzhi de shidian qingkuang 幼教事业关于改变所有制的试点情况 [Experimental implementation of ownership reform in early childhood education], July 21, 1961.

[80] XDS 5-2-8-3 Beijingshi shougongye guanliju guanyu erjidu changji jingsai pingbi gongzuo de tongzhi 北京市手工业管理局关于二季度厂际竞赛评比工作的通知 [Notice by the Beijing Municipal Handicraft Industry Administration on the second quarter inter-factory competition evaluation], June 14, 1962.

[81] XDS 5-2-8-6 Xuanwuqu gongyeju Cao Jinxue fujuzhang zai qugongshe guanyu zengchan jieyueyundong jingyan jiaoliu hui shang de baogao di.

[82] There was a gendered aspect in this process, as authorities remarked how "housewives" were supposedly incapable of adhering to these rigid disciplinary measures.

As a 1962 city-wide report on commune services summarized, the main purpose of wages in the service sector was

to overcome past practices such as not valuing economic accounting, or the commune underwriting [the unit's] losses, or the tendency toward egalitarianism in the wage system; to further implement the principle of distribution according to work, paying more [to those] who work more; and to better mobilize the enthusiasm of the production staff, so that we can correctly deal with the relationship between the state, the collective, and the individual with regard both to accumulation and distribution, making sure that the interests of the three parties are closely integrated.[83]

While piece-rates had originally been the norm in urban communes, since mid 1959, "due to a one-sided understanding of piecework wages," they had been switched to monthly salaries. This was in line with Mao's own assessment, who, even when taking a more moderate position on collectivization in 1959, criticized piece-rates for fostering among workers "a psychology of 'going for the big ones,'" prioritizing individual income over the collective cause, and even impeding technological innovation and mechanization. Instead, he supported the time-rate system plus rewards.[84] However, later reports noted how, under that system, it quickly became impossible to follow the principle of "remuneration according to labor," and that had negatively influenced the workers' zeal. The switch to factory financial autonomy was supposed to also include the reintroduction of piece-rate wages[85] or fixed and variable assignment of work points,[86] as well as more differentiated pay scales,[87] often through a careful disbursement of bonuses. At Qianmen, the existing system of pay-per-time, which had been criticized for not allowing for the differentiation of productive workers from slackers, was replaced by piece-rates for the majority of workers. Similarly, the old bonus scheme, which allegedly rewarded 80 percent of the employees – one just needed to show some diligence – was replaced by bonuses more precisely targeted according to productivity, technical achievements, and

---

[83] BMA 001-028-00036-13 Guanyu chengshi renmin gongshe xiuli fuwu hangye jilei, fenpei cunzai de wenti ji jiejue yijian 关于城市人民公社修理服务行业积累，分配存在的问题及解决意见 [Existing problems of accumulation and distribution in the urban people's commune repair service industry and proposed solutions], January 1962.

[84] Mao, *A Critique of Soviet Economics*: 89.

[85] BMA 112-001-00782-4 Guanyu xian jieduan chengshi renmin gongshe ruogan wenti de guiding (cao'an).

[86] XDN 11-4-57-3 Guanyu Erlonglu renmin gongshe jilei yu fenpei qingkuang de diaocha baogao.

[87] BMA 001-028-00036-18 Guanyu chengshi renmin gongshe gongye de qingkuang he jinhou yijian de baogao.

quality.[88] The Dashilar commune held a series of meetings in November 1962 to assess the reform of their bonus scheme. In the past, 60–70 percent of workers received bonuses, and their disbursal was characterized by shoddy management. While quantity and quality of production were the basic criteria, nobody really know how to assess labor that was not directly productive (such as repairing machinery), so there were employees who exaggerated how much of that they had performed and others who simply refused to perform it. The reformed system was instead centered on a set of statistical data assembled by group leaders on whose basis one could evaluate the productive output of every single worker, in terms of time, consumption of materials, quantity, and quality. This "elicited the enthusiasm of the masses," with sharp increases in productivity at the level of both production groups and individual workers – one worker increased her daily productivity by 60 percent, another one tripled it.[89]

At the end of 1962, the Niujie commune conducted a survey of its service center, where three out of four production groups had shifted from monthly salaries to work points in 1961, a move that was once again described as better implementing the socialist principle of "who works more makes more" and which had led to an impressive rise in productivity (41 percent for the washing and dyeing group, 23.18 percent for the whole station). And while the station went from thirty-five to twenty-four workers, capital accumulation increased by almost 20 percent. As a result, work points were extended to the entire station. However, it is worth highlighting that in this case this was not a question of remedying a situation of crisis or financial losses: Most of the groups had been profitable enough to provide all workers with a basic monthly salary, it was just that the current system did not offer them enough *material* incentives to continuously raise their productivity.[90]

[88] BMA 001-006-01864-2 Chenghsi renmin gongshe diaocha cailiao zhier – guanyu chengshi renmin gongshe de jilei he xiaofei 城市人民公社调查材料之二 – 关于城市人民公社的积累和消费 [Survey documents concerning the urban people's communes No. 2 – On accumulation and consumption in urban people's communes] (August 24, 1961). In other cases, such as the Dashilar commune canteens, they did not introduce piece-rate but enforced strict pay scales with substantial differences in wages, which ranged between ¥20 and ¥36. XDS 13-2-91-5 "Dashilar gongshe shitang guanyu gaibian gongzi xingshi zanxing banfa" 大栅栏公社食堂关于改变工资形式暂行办法 [Interim measures for reforming the wage system in the Dashilar commune canteens], May 25, 1962.

[89] XDS 13-2-89-7 Guanyu Dashilar gongshe qiche peijian chang zhigong pingjiang gongzuo de diaocha 关于大栅栏公社汽车配件厂职工评奖工作的调查 [Investigation report on employee award evaluation at the Dashilar Commune Auto Parts Factory], December 6, 1962.

[90] XDS 31-3-92-9 Niujie gongshe fuwu xiuli shidian gongzuo zu 牛街公社服务修理试点工作组 [Niujie commune service and repair pilot work group], "Niujie fuwuzhan shidian

Fusuijing commune, in Xicheng district, had been experimenting with piece-rates in some of its workshops, with the usual profitable results. In the refilling ink bottle workshop at its stationery factory, the return to piece-rates elicited a series of improvements synthesized as "three less, two early, one increase" (*sanshao, liangzao, yitigao* 三少, 两早, 一提高): less absenteeism and tardiness, less slacking, less stealthily running home; getting to work early, and preparing for production early; and there was a whopping 78 percent increase in productivity in the first month. This report went so far as to tout piece-rate as a *more equitable method*: It recorded the case of two employees, one who showed up for work only six days out of ten and yet refilled far more bottles than her colleague, who had perfect attendance, and yet the former earned three yuan less. The new system was not necessarily uniformly welcomed by the workers, nor did it necessarily have positive effects in terms of attitude and collective spirit. Diligent but slower laborers were afraid of this change; some workers who had enjoyed relatively high wages but were not very active mocked the new "productivity winds" and ended up influencing others so that they didn't deploy their full potential for fear of being labeled "traitors"; and some became single-mindedly obsessed with improving their productivity, overlooking everything else.[91] The reduction of the entire enterprise to the simplest logic of economic profit could not but affect the social relationships in the workplace.

Overall, reports from commune welfare organizations almost uniformly blamed their dire financial situation on the excessive egalitarianism of their remuneration scheme, which once again was singled out as having failed to elicit the workers' enthusiasm and to foster their productivity.[92] The sixteen centers at Xinjekou registered a loss of 35 percent in the second half of 1960 and a loss of 55.5 percent in the first quarter of 1961, and this was imputed to an irrational remuneration system and an excess of salaried employees. In one service center, for example, while salaries remained on average very low (¥17), they still constituted 150 percent of the total revenue, and this had been the case since February 1960, when they had moved away from piece-rate and work

gongzuo xiaojie" 牛街服务站试点工作小结 [Summary report on the pilot work of Niujie service centers], January 1963.

91 BMA 084-003-00072-6 Xichengqu Fusuijing renmin gongshe suoshu shengchan danwei shixing jijian gongzi de qingkuang 西城区福绥境人民公社所属生产单位试行计件工资的情况 [Experimental adoption of piece-rate wages in production units under the Fusuijing people's commune in Xicheng District].

92 XDN 37-1-62-2 Xichang'an jie renmin gongshe guanyu diaozheng fuli zhidu youguan jige guiding de tongzhi 西长安街人民公社关于调整福利制度有关几个规定的通知 [Notice of the people's commune of Xi Chang'an jie on the adjustment of several provisions related to the welfare system], June 11, 1962.

points and adopted a fixed salary system. Then productivity had immediately dropped, from an average of ¥89.78 yuan per person per month
to ¥36.33 in the case of bike repair; from ¥43 to ¥23.9 for tailors; and
from ¥58 to ¥25 for barbers. While there had been other changes in the
area that had affected the business, the report noted that, even where
there were pressing demands for services, they could not really satisfy it,
and they were still losing money. The district then reconstituted the
commune's service centers as independent accounting units, following
the principle of "using profit to motivate service personnel."[93] The same
reasoning was applied to the childcare centers in Xuanwu district, where
once again commune-level accounting and wages were identified as the
main causes for financial difficulties. They had fostered dependency,
carelessness, and even the feeling among workers that "the fewer children we take in the better; it saves us worries." Under those conditions,
salaries had not been "rationally" distributed "according to labor," so
that half of the employees had been on the same salary, resigned to the
fact that "no matter if one is good or bad, it's still the same eighteen
yuan." So, in 1961, financial assistance from the commune was revoked,
and, as centers were prohibited from raising fees, they were forced to
increase productivity and reduce expenses.[94]

Marx had deemed piece-rates to be "the form of wage most appropriate to the capitalist mode of production."[95] With piece-rates, the quality
and intensity of labor are controlled by the very form of the wage, and it
becomes "in the personal interest of the worker that he should strain his
labor-power as intensely as possible," leading to an increase of the pace
of work and a voluntary lengthening of the workday.[96] By fostering
competition among workers, Marx argued, piece-wages tend to raise
the wages of individuals above the average, but to lower the average
itself.[97] Piece-wages, he concluded, "become, from this point of view,
the most fruitful source of reductions in wages, and of frauds committed

---

[93]  XDN 11-4-57-8 Xichengqu caizhengju 西城区财政局 [Xicheng district finance bureau],
Xinjiekou gongshe suoshu fuwusuo weishenme changqi kuijuan 新街口公社所属服务所
为什么长期亏损 [Why the service offices under the Xinjiekou Commune have been
operating at a loss for a long time], May 29, 1961.
[94]  XDS 1-11-5-9 Zhonggong Beijingshi Xuanwu quwei jiegongwei, Xuanwuqu fulian 中共
北京市宣武区委街工委、宣武区妇联 [Street work committee of the CPC Xuanwu District
Committee and Xuanwu district ACWF], Guanyu gongshe xitong tuo'ersuo, you'eryuan
shixing dandu hesuan zifuyingkui de gongzuo qingkuang baogao 关于公社系统托儿所、幼
儿园实行单独核算自符盈亏的工作情况报告    [Report    on    the    implementation    of
independent accounting and financial self-sufficiency for the commune's nurseries and
kindergartens], August 29, 1961.
[95]  Marx, *Capital, Volume 1*: 698.    [96]  Marx, *Capital, Volume 1*: 695.
[97]  Marx, *Capital, Volume 1*: 697.

by the capitalists."[98] It was no surprise that this form of wages had been restricted or eliminated in the first, more radically equalitarian phase of the Great Leap. The full-scale reintroduction of piece-rates and other overtly "capitalist" forms of compensation in Beijing urban communes after 1961 was therefore quite a shocking reversal, in Marxist terms, and very difficult to square with any prospect of a transition toward communism. This regressive move was justified with a reasoning that followed the line of Marx's critique, but with opposite outcomes. Piece-rate wages were described not only as a way to incentivize and discipline commune labor but also as a more fitting way to organize its (desired) "flexible" nature. Piece-rates were considered particularly appropriate for "simple" production lines, with basic and low-tech manufacturing processes, which had been identified as the direction that commune production should take.[99] "Flexibility" under a piece-rate system, however, went beyond that: It configured precarious arrangements in which commune labor often became temporary, discontinuous, unpredictable, and eminently disposable. As commune industries were now mostly devoted to everyday objects, which were outside the national plan and usually produced in an ad hoc fashion, commune laborers were supposed to be able to move from one line to another, from one factory to the next, or from production to service units.[100] To avoid idle periods, employees were required to work in shifts, take forced rest periods (without pay), or do part-time labor.[101] Ultimately, the "flexible" production that the early 1960s restructuring designed was one based on a set of elementary manufacturing processes that could be potentially completed inside or near the home, whose output could be easily quantified and remunerated, and whose nature was ultimately easily discontinued and restarted. The stated principle, often repeated through various reports, was that "if there is work they can do it, if not they can go home and take care of household chores" (*youhuo jiu gan, meihuo jiu huiqu liaoli jiawu* 有活就干,没活就回去料理家务).[102] While cadres argued that such a principle "met the requirements of a wide range of

---

[98] Marx, *Capital, Volume 1*: 694.

[99] XDS 13-1-37-2 Guanyu xian jieduan chengshi renmin gongshe ruogan zhengce wenti de yijian (cao'an). Marx argued that piece-wages "form the basis for the modern 'domestic labor.'" Marx, *Capital, Volume 1*: 695.

[100] BMA 001-028-00036-17 Chengshi renmin gongshe gongye bu neng yifeng chui – guanyu Beixinqiaorenmin gongshe gongye de qingluang diaocha.

[101] XDS 13-1-37-2 Guanyu xian jieduan chengshi renmin gongshe ruogan zhengce wenti de yijian (cao'an).

[102] BMA 001-006-01864-3 Chengshi renmin gongshe diaocha cailiao zhi san – guanyu gongshe de gongye shengchan. See also XDN 38-1-34-2 Beijingshi Erlonglu gongshe gongye jiben qingkuang.

production and service personnel,"[103] it is evident that what this system relied on was an extreme form of precarious and disposable labor, whose "flexibility" was largely a function of its gendered character – women could always be sent home to cook and clean and take care of children or elders. The emancipatory promises originally associated with collectivization melted away.

It is not surprising that this restructuring of accounting and the disciplining of labor was also accompanied by the demise of any discussion about a potential transition to forms of ownerships that heralded the progress toward communism and the principle of "to each according to their needs." Not only did the urban communes categorically *not* belong to "ownership by the whole people"; they were and could only be under "collective ownership," and units within the communes could be placed under even more regressive arrangements. For example, smaller factories and service centers could be moved to collective ownership at the factory level, and dispersed production units could become "family side business with individual ownership under socialist economic leadership" (*shehuizhuyi jingji lingdaoxia de geti suoyouzhi de jiating fuye* 社会主义经济领导下的个体所有制的家庭副业).[104] This retrenchment – part of the Thermidorean reaction of post–Great Leap adjustments – was connected with the extreme "flexibility" now required from commune labor. If one placed commune units under QMSYZ, then it would have been impossible to dispose of (female) workers according to the shifting needs of the market, sending them home during idle periods; and that would have "increased the burden for the state, with no benefit."[105]

At Erlonglu, which was in many ways exemplary, ownership was avowedly a central issue in the restructuring of the commune. Reports described the process of capital accumulation in the collective industry: Initial funds for the establishment of factories had been provided directly by the state or by SOEs (in one case, to the tune of 79.5 percent). Then, because the state did not levy taxes on commune profits, those were deployed for further expansion; furthermore, the state provided materials at low prices and bought the commune factory's products at increasingly higher prices, in order to avoid losses and to keep them profitable. Because of this support from the state and SOEs, the commune factories

---

[103] XDN 38-1-34-2 Beijingshi Erlonglu gongshe gongye jiben qingkuang.
[104] BMA 112-001-00782-4 Guanyu xian jieduan chengshi renmin gongshe ruogan wenti de guiding (cao'an).
[105] BMA 001-006-01864-1 Chengshi renmin gongshe diaocha cailiao zhiyi – dui chengshi renmin gongshe xingzhi, renwu, he suoyou youzhi wenti de yijian. "Forcing the implementation of QMSYZ, will only increase the burden on the state without any benefit."

had developed at an increasingly fast pace, so that by June 1961 they had a capital of ¥3,990,000, of which ¥1,032,000 was fixed capital, and the rest was circulating capital. By then, they had repaid almost the entirety of the initial funding, and 92.5 percent of the means of production belonged to the commune. Looking back at that history, commune authorities argued, strangely, that commune industries belonged to QMZSYZ, because they all stemmed from the initial (state-provided) capital and relied on (state-guaranteed) tax exemptions. That analysis notwithstanding, the commune authorities nonetheless concluded that the commune should be administered as if it were under collective ownership. This was because it was indispensable to maintain and continuously reaffirm a separation and a radical distinction between SOE workers and commune employees, who were once again described as "housewives," with low productivity and low consciousness. A 1961 report concluded:

> The experience of the Erlonglu Commune over the past few years has proved that while ownership by the whole people occupies the dominant position, the commune adopts the form of collective ownership (not announced to the masses) in management and distribution, and it can thus avoid aligning with state-run enterprises in terms of wages and welfare, which they would require the state to guarantee. It can also adopt some management systems and organizational forms of production different from those of state-run enterprises but conforming to the characteristics of street industries.[106]

Another report from the same year rearticulated the entire ownership system of the commune in four levels, allowing for the more low-tech, dispersed, and flexible kinds of production. Besides "commune-level collective ownership," which included the larger and more technologically advanced factories, there was collective ownership at the level of factory and production team, and finally there was individual ownership (*geti suoyouzhi* 个体所有制) for those artisans or providers who wanted to work independently.[107] The process of collectivization I have described for the previous years, aimed at eliminating every form of noncollective work, was here completely reversed, in what was essentially a rapid and directly mandated *decollectivization*.

## 5.4    End of a Promise

The process of decollectivization massively affected the side of the urban commune enterprise that more clearly embodied the promise of

---

[106] BMA 112-001-00783-3 Guanyu Erlonglu gongshe suoyouzhi wenti de baogao.
[107] XDN 11-4-63-7 Guanyu Erlonglu renmingongshe gongye guihua (cangao) 关于二龙路人民公社工业规划（草稿）[Industrial planning for the Erlonglu people's commune (draft)].

liberation and of a revolutionized everyday. This was precisely the side that had already revealed itself to be the most problematic to manage: welfare and social services. As a report from Erlonglu commune pithily summarized, "they were needed but they had problems."[108]

As already discussed, the first problem the reports identified and kept highlighting was that many of those enterprises registered substantial economic losses. A 1961 survey of canteens and childcare centers remarked how all the services were run at a deficit, with the commune making up for those shortfalls with the revenue coming from the productive sector. For example, the Xinjiekou commune had an overall surplus of ¥1,280,000 but had to transfer ¥24,9000 to the service sector; at Erlonglu, 20 percent and at Chunshu 29.8 percent of the annual profit went to subsidize welfare. The twenty-eight canteens at the Xichang'an commune were all operating in the red, so the commune subsidized them at the rate of about ¥2 per customer (1,800 of them on average). At Erlonglu, the subsidies amounted to about ¥11 per employee per month, equivalent to 55 percent of the average salary of ¥20.6, while childcare subsidies were at about 40 percent. The Chunshu commune provided support for childcare to the tune of ¥4.3 per child on average. These estimates do not seem particularly dire, as these communes were sacrificing only a portion of their revenue to subsidize those social services on which women's participation in "productive" labor – and, with it, the very promise of women's liberation and the transformation of social relations – depended. Yet commune and city authorities perceived this situation as presenting a grave financial liability. They stressed that, while it had been necessary and good to have subsidized services in the initial phase of collectivization, it had later turned into a "continuously flowing water" or a "bottomless pit" approach ("changliushui" "wudidong" de banfa "长流水" "无底洞" 的办法).[109]

Another 1961 report from Erlonglu provided slightly different numbers and a darker financial picture. There, in 1960, canteen workers had received on average ¥14.38 yuan of subsidies, equal to 69.8 percent of their average salary (¥20.6), and the reason was identified in the low productivity and high cost of service enterprises. In canteens, the employee to customer ratio was 1:17, and it was even higher in childcare (1:7.5 children). There was also reported waste of capital and resources:

---

[108] BMA 002-020-01135-1 Youguan chengshi renmin gongshe yixie qingkuang de huizhai.
[109] BMA 084-003-00072-4 Chengshi gongshe tuo'ersuo, shitang gongye, dongyuan huanxiang deng gongzuo de diaocha cailiao 城市公社托儿所、食堂工业、动员还乡等工作的调查材料 [Survey materials on urban communes' operations: Nurseries, communal eating, and mobilization to return people to the countryside], June 30, 1961.

Commune authorities calculated that of the ¥445,000 disbursed for welfare (27.6 percent for infrastructure, 39.8 percent for salaries and subsidies, 32.6 percent for other expenses), ¥44,400 had been "irrationally" spent. For example, the staple food processing plant had originally planned to serve 10,000 customers but found itself with only 2,000 and thus was left with a giant empty building and unused, expensive machinery. Similarly, the commune bought a large number of children's beds, and, even after distributing them to all the centers, they still had 215 left; the service centers had purchased several boilers, but many remained unused; and the newly opened photography store had so far sold only one camera.[110]

Such overestimations of commune members' potential use of welfare services look less surprising – and much less "irrational" – if put in the context of the rapid decline in attendance that affected them almost uniformly in this period. This decline exemplifies the continuation and the final exacerbation of some of those fundamental contradictions that, as we have seen, had plagued the service sector since its inception. At Niujie, the commune's twelve canteens registered a drop in 1961, with an average of about 700 customers, only 300 of them commune members. More worryingly, cadres estimated that, given the relatively low participation among commune members, there was not much room for growth, and that they only needed four or five canteens and thirty to thirty-five workers to satisfy the much reduced demand.[111] At Erlonglu, while reports reiterated how crucial canteens were in the effort to ease women's double burden (especially for those who were taking care of weak or elderly relatives), they could not but register the desultory and much diminished attendance. Commune employees constituted only 34.5 percent of canteen patrons and they did not come regularly, thus making the ratio of canteen workers to customers unstable and financially unsustainable. If that situation did not improve, three of the seven existing canteens needed to be shut down, following in the footsteps of Dongcheng district, where all communal eating had been eliminated.[112]

Chongwen district, facing a 40 percent collapse in canteen attendance, surveyed over a thousand of the Qianmen commune employees. Despite the fact that, as the survey registered, many more clearly *needed* communal eating, only 19 percent of employees ate regularly at the eight

---

[110] XDN 11-4-57-3 Guanyu Erlonglu renmin gongshe jilei yu fenpei qingkuang de diaocha baogao.

[111] XDS 31-3-73-10 Guanyu hebing shitang de qingkuang baogao 关于合并食堂的情况报告 [Report on the consolidation of canteens], July 27, 1961.

[112] BMA 002-020-01135-1 Youguan chengshi renmin gongshe yixie qingkuang de huizhai.

canteens (five managed by factories, three by neighborhoods). Among those, there were a few workers who had just moved from the countryside and whose families resided in the suburban districts. More significantly, 862 employees had no one at home who could cook for them, yet only 227 took advantage of communal mess halls, most of them cadres and activists with a busy schedule of work, study, and meetings. The remaining 635, other than a small group of people with stomach issues or chronic diseases and some better-off residents who preferred to eat their own food, were women with several children who could not all be (or simply were not) placed under collective childcare. Among those who took advantage of the canteens, some did it for practical reasons – they lived too far from work to commute back for meals – some were canteen workers themselves, and others did not get along with their mothers-in-law and preferred to avoid fights during meals. There was also a subset of the ideologically motivated, who saw eating at a canteen as a political duty or an expression of activism. For example, Chen Lihua, who could easily go home to eat, used to go to the canteen because she thought party members should be an example; when she found (during the survey) that it was indeed voluntary, she stopped attending. Another case was that of Li Guizhen, a commune factory worker, whose father-in-law was a labeled a capitalist; so as to draw a clear line between them, and because she refused to act as a devoted daughter and serve her politically questionable in-laws, she ate all her meals at the canteen even though her home was very close by. The fact that what was supposed to be a crucial element in both women's liberation and the very possibility of industrial development became a manifestation of individual political conscious-ness gives a sense of the crisis in welfare services. Most people did not want to eat at the canteen because the food was better at home, was more convenient, and, more importantly, was cheaper. Commune workers, the report concluded, condescendingly, were still "housewives," so they were used to cooking, which constituted just a part of a larger set of domestic tasks: "In winter you need to heat the house, and in summer you need hot water to wash in the evenings, so once there is a fire, you can cook on it. In winter, you can prep the next day's lunch when you make dinner, and in summer, with a long break at noon, you can come home in time to cook."[113] This assessment was based once again on the naturalized evaluation of domestic labor as something valueless, some-thing that women did naturally, almost as an effortless side product of

---

[113] BMA 001-006-01864-4 Chengshi renmin gongshe diaocha cailiao zhisi – guanyu shitang wenti 城市人民公社调查材料之四 – 关于食堂问题 [Survey documents on the urban people's communes No. 4 – Problems concerning canteens], August 24, 1961.

their position in the home. And of course, it was grounded on the seemingly fixed characterization as "housewives" that remained attached to commune women even after years of tireless work in factories, canteens, and nurseries. As long as they remained "housewives," they could not separate themselves from their valueless and naturalized domesticity, and they carried that lack of value even to the factory.

Collective childcare was deep into a similar declining spiral. As the Xuanwu district *fulian* noted in 1961, 40 percent of the communal childcare centers could not be financially self-sufficient, as the number of participating children had dropped.[114] The same problem was recorded at the Qianmen commune, where there were over 200 children eligible for childcare who did not attend: Their families preferred to leave them with neighbors or lock them in a room. Now, this is not too surprising given the reportedly infamous quality of care: Caregivers, who were often illiterate and untrained, were known to "lose" children at times, to forget to feed them, or, worse, to curse the children and eat their food; hygiene was questionable and infectious diseases spread widely.[115]

In the end, however, the low quality of some of the service enterprises was more a consequence of than a reason behind the fundamental issue that made those services unsustainable. "Why is it not possible to achieve socialization of domestic work at present?" The answer provided in a 1961 city-wide report was that "at present, the level of development of social productive forces is not high, so it is impossible for everyone to participate in production and labor; at the same time, the accumulation from social production is not yet enough to provide the money necessary to organize these welfare undertakings." Barring a disbursal from state coffers, there was not enough capital to fund commune collective services as welfare (i.e., gratis), nor to improve their quality; on the other hand, the programmatically designed paucity of commune salaries made it impossible for workers to pay for those services at the individual level. As the report concluded, "income levels were not high enough to demand collectivization at once."[116]

---

[114] XDS 1-11-5-9 Guanyu gongshe xitong tuo'ersuo, you'eryuan shixing dandu hesuan zifuyingkui de gongzuo qingkuang baogao.
[115] BMA 001-006-01864-5 Zhonggong Chongwenqu bangongshi zhengli 中共崇文区办公室整理 [Compiled by the office of the CCP Chongwen district committee], "Chengshi renmin gongshe diaocha cailiao zhwu – guanyu gongshe tuo'er zuzhi" 城市人民公社调查材料之五 – 关于公社托儿组织 [Survey documents on the urban people's communes No. 5 – On communal childcare organizations], August 29, 1961.
[116] BMA 001-028-00029-8 Chengshi gongshe jiti shenghuo fuli shiye jinianlai de fazhan qingkuang he wenti 城市公社集体生活福利事业几年来的发展情况和问题 [Development and challenges of collective welfare enterprises in urban communes over the past few years]. This assessment echoed earlier arguments against the expansion of the supply

This presented a seemingly unsolvable conundrum: At the very practical level, the development of productive forces was functional to participation in industrial labor, which was impossible without socialization of domestic labor. That does not mean that solutions were not offered, and remedies not proposed. The most obvious and purely "economic" one was to reduce expenses and increase prices. At the Xuandimiao canteen in the Qianmen commune, for example, which had been subsidized through 1960 to the tune of ¥2,800, they cut expenses by 50 percent – including a reduction of personnel – and increased prices; as a consequences, they lost further customers (30 out of about 200), but they balanced the books.[117] At Erlonglu, once the commune had stopped subsidizing poor families' access to welfare, they cut personnel and increased nurseries' fees from ¥0.2 to ¥0.5 and the canteen's from ¥1 to ¥1.2.[118] At Dashilar, financially troubled canteens were merged, and fees could be raised after consultation with customers.[119] But making collective services more expensive for commune members clearly also made them even more inaccessible for the poorest among them, the ones who needed those services most. In response, authorities suggested the establishment of facilities with basic services and lower fees, and encouraged coordination with residents' committees and women's organizations so that the masses could themselves create their own "simple childcare organizations based on neighborhood mutual-aid" (*linli huzhu xingzhi de jianyi tuo'er zuzhi* 邻里互助性质的简易托儿组织).[120] Here we have an almost seamless reversion to the reaffirmation of the continuous reproduction of class differences *within collective services*. And, in a very practical sense, if quality was an issue with the existing services, one can only imagine what a "simpler" and even more poorly funded welfare enterprise would look like. In addition, the displacement of accountability for such services onto the lowest possible

---

system, which stated the need to first develop the forces of production and increase individual income. See Liqun Xu, "Have We Already Reached the Stage of Communism?," in Robert R. Bowie and John K. Fairbanks, eds., *Communist China, 1955–1959: Policy Documents with Analysis* (Cambridge, MA: Harvard University Press, 1962): 479–483. Originally published in *Hongqi*, November 1958.

[117] BMA 001-006-01864-4 Chengshi renmin gongshe diaocha cailiao zhisi – guanyu shitang wenti.

[118] BMA 112-001-00783-6 Guanyu Erlonglu gongshe shitang, tuo'er zuzhi shixing ziji zizu wenti de baogao.

[119] XDS 13-1-37-2 Guanyu xian jieduan chengshi renmin gongshe ruogan zhengce wenti de yijian (cao'an).

[120] XDS 13-1-37-2 Guanyu xian jieduan chengshi renmin gongshe ruogan zhengce wenti de yijian (cao'an). See also BMA 112-001-00783-6 Guanyu Erlonglu gongshe shitang, tuo'er zuzhi shixing ziji zizu wenti de baogao.

unit – the neighborhood – allowed the state and possibly even the city to abdicate all responsibility for social services.

The issue of the financial viability of communal services led to the more fundamental question of what kind of organizations they were and whom they were supposed to be serving. At a more theoretical level, there was a split among those who considered childcare centers, canteens, and service centers as collective service enterprises serving both the commune and society at large and those who regarded them as providing welfare mainly for commune members, with the option of opening them up for others if resources allowed.[121] Or, in other words, were they supposed to be service enterprises (*fuwuxing qiye* 服务性企业) or organizations for collective welfare (*jiti fuli shiye* 集体福利事业)?[122] Commune sources seem to register an almost universal agreement that these services had been established to provide for the needs of newly recruited commune workers and their families; they were welfare organizations and should therefore be reserved primarily for commune members, accepting non-commune customers (students, shopkeepers, local residents) only once the needs of the former had been satisfied.[123] It was precisely because they were communal welfare organizations that they had been heavily subsidized in the previous years by the commune. Yet this principled agreement had become practically moot since it had been decided that nurseries, kindergartens, and canteens had to operate as much as possible as financially independent units of accounting, solely responsible for their own profits and losses. The seventy-seven canteens in Xicheng district were registering a loss of over ¥3,000, but that was not equally distributed; commune employees did not pay any fees, while cadres and non-commune members paid ¥1 for adults and ¥0.5 for children under fourteen, and that obviously generated a financial incentive to accept people from outside the commune and created discrepancies among canteens depending on the composition of their clientele.

---

[121] BMA 001-028-00029-3 Shiwei chengshi gongshe gongzuozu 市委城市公社工作组 [Municipal Party committee task force on urban communes], Guanyu chengshi gongshe tuoyou zuzhi zuotanhui de qingkuang fanying 关于城市公社托幼组织座谈会的情况反映 [Summary report on the symposium about childcare organizations in urban communes], September 16, 1961.

[122] BMA 001-006-01864-6 Zhonggong Chongwenqu bangongshi zhengli 中共崇文区办公室整理 [Compiled by the office of the Chongwen district party committee], Chengshi renmin gongshe diaocha cailiao zhiliu – guanyu gongshe de fuwu shiye 城市人民公社调查材料之六 – 关于公社的服务事业 [Survey documents on the urban people's commune No. 6 – About the communes' service sector], August 28, 1961.

[123] BMA 112-001-00783-6 Guanyu Erlonglu gongshe shitang, tuo'er zuzhi shixing ziji zizu wenti de baogao; BMA 112-001-00782-4 Guanyu xian jieduan chengshi renmin gongshe ruogan wenti de guiding (cao'an); BMA 001-028-00029-3 Guanyu chengshi gongshe tuoyou zuzhi zuotanhui de qingkuang fanying.

In this case, the district advocated for an expansion of subsidies and opposed the transformation of canteens into independent units of accounting.[124] A year later, that position became much less defensible, and subsidies were largely eliminated. Chongwen district authorities accepted the practical reality that, if communal services had to be run in a financially sustainable fashion, they could only be run as "enterprises," open to anybody willing to pay the required fees.[125]

A city-wide survey clarified the way ahead by pitting successful and unsuccessful service units against each other. The Chaoyangmen commune's thirteen canteens had lost ¥1,292 in February 1961, which required the commune to subsidize ¥1 yuan per customer. In March they implemented independent accounting, reduced the number of employees, and instituted fees for non-commune members (¥0.5 for students, ¥1.5 for workers), and they thus turned a profit. For childcare, the city survey extolled the case of Donghuamen, which had fixed fees, and criticized Chunshu, which had much lower fees, especially for commune members, and relied too much on subsidies. The service centers at Jiaodaokou were very profitable, while Xinjiekou's had registered massive losses – ¥63,000 in 1960 and ¥25,000 already in April 1961. The reason, the report argued, was that the former focused on "productive" tasks, like washing, mending, repairing, for which one could ask a relatively substantial fee, while the latter did mostly "unproductive" work, like selling stamps, transferring phone calls, delivering newspapers, and helping with domestic chores.[126] In line with the slide into pure "economism" that marked the end of the Great Leap, "productive" work is here reduced to work that can engender profit, in the narrowest understanding of what economic profit could be. Repair services, for example, were singled out as exemplary "productive," while the services that were deemed most "unproductive" were those more directly aimed at socializing and replacing some of the intimate and often hidden aspects of social reproduction: the minute acts of service and care that constituted the texture of the residents' everyday subsumed under terms as "*xiahu fuwu*" 下户服务 (door-to-door services) or "*shenghuo fuwu*" 生活服务 (services for everyday life), tasks that were invisible when performed in the home, and, because of that, assumed to be valueless. This

[124] XDN 7-1-812-3 Guanyu jiedao shitang buzhu banfa deng fangmian de jiejue yijian 关于街道食堂补助办法等方面的解决意见 [Proposed solution for neighborhood canteens subsidy methods and related issues].
[125] BMA 001-006-01864-6 Chengshi renmin gongshe diaocha cailiao zhiliu – guanyu gongshe de fuwu shiye.
[126] BMA 084-003-00072-4 Chengshi gongshe tuo'ersuo, shitang gongye, dongyuan huanxiang deng gongzuo de diaocha cailiao.

in turn meant that the success of communal services was no longer measured by how they responded to the needs of the people, and not even by how they helped the production drive of the Great Leap, but simply by their basic profitability as "normal" enterprises. This was an evident and politically determined reversal of the original drive toward collectivization. Not surprisingly, when communal laundries in Xuanwu district hiked prices and introduced a fee for storing clothes, customers complained loudly, one of them calling them "a capitalist operation, charging for processing and adding storage fees" (*Nimen jiushi zibenzhuyi jingying, shoule jiagongfei, hai jia baoguanfei* 你们就是资本主义经营, 收了加工费, 还加保管费).[127]

Overall, in 1961–1962, Beijing communes experienced the collapse of anything that had resembled a "supply system," including the elimination of any form of subsidy and the dissolution of entire sectors of communal services; this was the counterpart of the precarization and delocalization of labor described earlier. As in other cases, Erlonglu and Chunshu led the way. In 1961, Erlonglu abolished marriage, funeral, and sickness pay as well as subsidies for nurseries and canteen usage. As for the 2 percent of families who were in seriously dire straits, they were invited to rely on the husband's *danwei* for support; the commune would step in to help only if the wife was the sole earner in the family.[128] At Chunshu, in 1962, the authorities discussed subsidies and incentives in a way that sounded more fitting for Reaganite libertarians than to Chinese socialists. They singled out as excessive the case of one worker with four children who received a subsidy of ¥12 in addition to her salary, and they decided to do away with any financial support for nurseries, canteens, and laundry services. Conversely, they celebrated the case of another worker, previously quite slow, who had learned to be faster once they refused to increase her salary.[129] In 1962, city authorities

---

[127] XDS 22-2-133-17 Xuanwuqu fuwu gongsi guanyu xiranye tiaojia hou de qingkuang huibao 宜武区服务公司关于洗染业调价后的情况汇报 [Report by the Xuanwu District Service Company on the situation after price adjustments in the washing and dyeing industry], August 16, 1961. See also XDS 22-2-133-19 Xuanwuqu fuwu gongsi guanyu xiranye zhixing 'yuqi buqu, jiashou baoguanfei' qingkuang huibao 宜武区服务公司关于洗染业执行 '逾期不取, 加收保管费' 情况汇报 [Report by the Xuanwu District Service Company on the implementation of "late pick-up storage fees" in the laundry/dyeing industry], September 11, 1961.

[128] BMA 112-001-00783-7 Erlonglu gongshe diaochazu 二龙路公社调查组 [Erlonglu commune survey group], Guanyu Erlonglu gongshe gongzi, fuli, jiangli wenti de baogao 关于二龙路公社工资、福利、奖励问题的报告 [Report on the issue of wages, benefits, and bonuses at the Erlonglu commune], August 17, 1961.

[129] BMA 112-001-00848-5 Chunshu gongshe gongye zhengdun diaozheng qingkuang 椿树公社工业整顿调整情况 [Rectification and reorganization of the industrial sector at the Chunshu commune], February 15, 1962.

anticipated that they were very likely going to completely eliminate subsidies and time off (for funerals, weddings, or illness), while stressing once again how wages for commune labor had to remain low.[130]

The consequences of this rapid elimination of subsidies were significant. By summer 1962, childcare centers registered a drop of 42.3 percent in the number of employees, 61.7 percent in the number of children, and 76.1 percent in the overall number of centers. More than half of the children under communal care were sons and daughters of employees of SOEs, schools, and agencies, with only 40 percent coming from commune families. Beijing communal canteens recorded a 90 percent decrease in all aspects compared with 1960, and five communes had already shut down all their canteens. Between April 1960 and March 1961, the number of the city's service centers had decreased by 84.5 percent and their employees by 56 percent; in line with what I singled out earlier, this had affected primarily services for "everyday life," while "repair services" had been expanded.[131]

With the almost complete disappearance of communal welfare, it is not surprising that many more of those women who continued to work in factories (or participated in "scattered" production) were now fully shouldering the burden of industrial and domestic labor. At Beixinqiao, as of September 1962, over 50 percent of commune workers had more than two children who required care; 68.7 percent had to go home every day to cook lunch and dinner; and 75.3 percent carried the entire responsibility for cleaning, washing, grocery shopping, and other chores.[132] Two months later, another report from Beixinqiao stated that 90 percent of all commune workers, who had an average of 2.6 children per worker, were also fully responsible for housekeeping and childcare. Under those conditions, not only could people not devote any time to after-work classes, thus erasing any possibility for personal or career

[130] BMA 001-028-00036-12 Guanyu chengshi renmin gongshe de jiben qingkuang.
[131] BMA 001-028-00036-12 Guanyu chengshi renmin gongshe de jiben qingkuang. The collapse of services corresponded to a similar "restructuring" of the commune industrial sector. In 1960, Beijing commune industries had employed 140,000 people; in 1961, 100,000; in 1962, 83,000. The output value dropped even more drastically from ¥505,000,000 to ¥252,000,000 to ¥90,000,000. BMA 112-001-00849 Beijingshi shougongyeju dangzu 北京市手工业局党组 [Party group of the Beijing municipal handicraft industry bureau], Guanty chengshi renmin gongshe gongye fazhan qingkuang he jinhou yijian de qingshi (chugao) 关于城市人民公社工业发展情况和今后意见的请示(初稿) [Request for instructions on the current status and future development of the industries in urban people's communes (preliminary draft)], September 12, 1962.
[132] BMA 001-028-00036-17 Chengshi renmin gongshe gongye bu neng yifeng chui – guanyu Beixinqiaorenmin gongshe gongye de qingluang diaocha.

improvement, but there were also alarming reports of workers/mothers exhausting themselves and eventually falling ill.[133]

The dismantling of communal functions and the irreversible crisis of the commune structure provoked the outward expression of resentments and dissatisfaction by commune members, who sometimes addressed specific issues as well as long-term grievances. For example, in Yuetan and Dewai, both with large Muslim communities, when the communes were created, local mosques had been handed over to the commune authorities to be used as places to shower, childcare centers, and factories. While this had allegedly been done "at the request of the local Muslim population," in 1962, hundreds of residents signed petitions to have the mosques revert to their original roles, citing, among other reasons, dissatisfaction with the communes.[134] In the same year, residents of Fusuijing asked for the commune to finally replace household items that had been collected during the 1958 industrial "anti-drought campaign." Among these items were iron bed frames, and the source highlights the case of one "capitalist" who had purchased a Simmons bed for his son's wedding. Surveyed residents complained vociferously: They did not believe that those bed frames had ever been used for industrial production, and assumed they had gone to hotels.[135]

But it was the demise of collective welfare and subsidies which was more harshly criticized by commune members. Sources record the persisting need for those services and the often-vocal protests against their elimination. A city-wide report from 1961 noted that there was massive opposition among workers to the elimination of paid maternity leave as

---

[133] BMA 001-028-00036-8 Beixinqiao gongshe gongye de laodongli qiangkuang fenxi (Beixinqiao gongshe gongye diaocha cailiao zhisi) 北新桥公社工业的劳动力情况分析 (北新桥公社工业调查材料之四) [Analysis of the labor force in the Beixinqiao commune industry (Beixinqiao Commune Industry Survey Document No. 4)], November 19, 1962.

[134] BMA 001-028-00036-4 Dewai, Yuetan gongshe Huimin qunzhong lianming xiexin yaoqiu tuihui bei gongshe zhanyong de qingzhensi 德外、月坛公社回民群众联名写信要求退回被公社占用的清真寺 [The Muslims of Dewai and Yuetan communes write a joint letter demanding the return of the mosque occupied by the communes], July 21, 1962.

[135] BMA 001-028-00029-7 Zhonggong Beijing shiwei chengshi gongshe gongzuo xiaozu 中共北京市委城市公社工作小组 [Urban commune work group of the Beijing Municipal Party Committee], Fusuijingrenmin gongshe yuan Zhongxiang xia jumin weiyuanhui bufen jingjifenzi dui yijiuwuba nian jiedao zhiyuan gongye kanghan yundong de yijian 福绥境人民公社原中乡下居民委员会部分积极分子对一九五八年街道支援工业抗旱运动的意见 [Opinions of some activists of the former Zhongxiang residents' committee of the Fusuijing people's commune on the 1958 urban campaign to support industrial drought relief], December 2, 1961.

well as to the closure of canteens and nurseries.[136] The suburban commune of Jiuxianqiao, which by 1962 was left with no canteen and only four childcare centers and five service centers, conducted a survey of its members, who expressed a renewed request for welfare and specifically those "everyday" services that had been eliminated because they were deemed "unproductive." Commune workers were on average young and with children, so the remaining nurseries were overflowing. Some 64.6 percent of the elementary students in the commune were on a two-shift system, and that was a huge problem for families where both parents worked. When the children left school every day and there was no one home, they ended up running around, fighting, stealing, trampling crops, and damaging flowers and trees. The surveyed parents complained that there was no place to send them. They did not want to lock them in the house, and letting them run around was not good either, especially in the winter. They asked the commune to coordinate with schools and the ACFTU to set up an after-school program. The closure of commune canteens was problematic for people who lived far away, and cooking at home cut into the time needed for rest and study. Workers complained that if they prepped their meals the day before they ended up eating cold food in the winter and spoiled food in the summer, damaging their health. One cadre's nine-year-old child, while attempting to make himself lunch, added pesticide (666 powder, hexachlorocyclohexane) to his congee; luckily, the neighbors found out and stopped him before he ended up poisoning himself. The workers agreed that the canteens were necessary and had to be restored.[137]

A city-wide report similarly commented on the hastened dismantling of services and of its social effects. Some 95 percent of commune canteens had been shut down since the heyday of 1960, and that process seems to have been conducted indiscriminately and quite brutally. While most canteens had been folded up because of financial losses, profitable ones had been closed as well, as was the case at the Jiaodaokou commune. This was also often done without any forewarning: It was announced one day,

---

[136] BMA 001-028-00029-4 Shiwei chengshi gongshe gongzuo xiaozu [Urban commune work group of the Municipal Party Committee] 市委城市公社工作小组, Guanyu chengshi gongshe gongzi, fuli, jiangli wenti zuotanhui qingkuang fanying 关于城市公社工资、福利、奖励问题座谈会情况反映 [Summary report on the symposium on wages, benefits, and bonuses in urban communes], September 23, 1961.

[137] BMA 001-028-00036-11 Jiuxianqiao diqu xiuli he shenghuo fuwu de qingkuang he jinhou gongshe xiuli he shenghuo fuwu fazhan de fangxiang (caogao). Fujian: er 酒仙桥地区修理和生活服务的情况和今后公社修理和生活服务发展的方向（草稿）。附件：二 [Current status of repair and domestic services in the Jiuxianqiao area and directions of future development for commune-based services (draft). Appendix: II], January 18, 1962.

and the following day the canteen was gone, creating huge problems for customers and employees. At Jiaodaokou, after one canteen that catered specifically to elementary school students was shut down, the children kept lining up in front of its barricaded door, crying for days. In another case, once the local canteen closed, factory workers who found themselves with nowhere to eat petitioned to get the cooking equipment so that the factory could create a canteen on its own.[138]

At the Chunshu commune, two school-aged brothers, whose mother had died, had been eating at the local canteen for four years; when it suddenly closed, they found that they had nowhere to eat, and their uncle had to ask the commune administration for help with their plight.[139] Canteen workers also protested, finding themselves suddenly without a salary. One source reported that there was a loss of faith in the Communist Party among laid-off welfare workers, and that the commune was forced to rehire them, even if there was nothing for them to do.[140] Factory workers were equally disheartened by closures and the reduction in personnel or hours. In one commune in the city of Shenyang, female workers who had been fired cried and begged to be let inside their factory, "the factory we left home for, and that we built with our bare hands."[141] In similar cases taking place in Beijing, the reactions were harsher, as in the firewood factory at the Dahongmen commune (Fengtai district), whose forty-one employees were not even informed of the decision to close their plant. The two factory leaders remonstrated with the commune administration: "You gave us this responsibility, and then you treat us like outsiders, you say that the factory should close, and just like that, it's

---

[138] BMA 001-028-00036-15 Shiwei chengshi renmin gongshe gongzuo xiaozu 市委城市人民公社工作小组 [Urban people's commune work group of the Municipal Party Committee], Guanyu shaoshu chengshi renmin gongshe qiang xing jiesan shitang wenti de baogao 关于少数城市人民公社强行解散食堂问题的报告 [Report on the forced dissolution of communal canteens in a few urban people's communes], June 11, 1962.

[139] BMA 001-028-00036-14, Shiwei chengshi gongshe gongzuo xiaozu 市委城市公社工作小组 [Urban commune work group of the Municipal Party Committee], Chunshu renmin gongshe guanbi shitang hou de qunzhong fanyin 椿树人民公社关闭食堂后的群众反映 [Popular reactions to the closure of the canteens in the Chunshu people's commune] (May 30, 1962).

[140] BMA 001-028-00036-14, Chunshu renmin gongshe guanbi shitang hou de qunzhong fanyin.

[141] BMA 001-028-00036-3, Guanyu canjia guojia jiwei, quanzong dangzu chengshi gongshe bangongshi lianhe zhaokai de chengshi gongshe gongye tiaozheng wenti zuotahui qingkuang huibao 关于参加国家计委、全总党组城市公社办公室联合召开的城市公社工业调整问题座谈会情况汇报 [Report on the forum about the problem of restructuring the industrial sector of the urban communes convened by the national planning commission and the urban commune office of the CCP group in the All-China Federation of Trade Unions], July 1962.

closed. You don't even say one word to us. This is really intolerable."
When the workers went to collect their last pay, they were told it was not
ready yet. Tired and angry, they lodged a protest with the commune
leaders, but they were told to disperse and come back another time; the
person responsible was taking his nap. They asked for the accumulated
capital of the factory to be redistributed and for severance pay; when both
requests were summarily declined, they directly addressed the Municipal
Committee of the CCP.[142]

The resentment over elimination of services, which represented the
(only partially fulfilled) promise of women's liberation and the very
foundation of women's participation in collective labor, compounded
the already existing exasperation for the profound inequalities that
marked gendered labor in the commune. The sources recorded their
loud, passionate remonstrances. Facing chronically low salaries and
rapidly disappearing welfare, commune workers at Beixinqiao highlighted the disparity between their circumstances and those of SOE
employees: They suffered from the "three lows" (low salary, low services,
and low rations) and "two misfortunes" (could not find a partner, could
not raise a family).[143] In another case, the casus belli was the reduced
amount of cloth rations allotted to commune workers. "We are commune members," one worker argued, "but as far as our welfare, we are
housewives. We and the SOE factory workers both labor, we both create
wealth for the country; how come we are not at all equal when it comes to
cloth rations?" Even party members joined in, remarking how, despite
the fact that they went through their clothing faster than anybody because
of their work, they were given the same rations of the average city
resident; with that meager amount of cloth, they would end up going
around bare-bottomed. Another worker reverted to cursing: "Fuck you!
You just give us four *chi* of cloth, what can we do with that? Better not
give us anything!" And finally, one woman registered the difference
between the commune and the SOE workers in clearly gendered terms:
"They [the SOE employees] are workers, we are just whores."[144]

---

[142] BMA 001-028-00036-16 Zhonggong Beijing shiwei chengshi gongshe gongzuo xiaozu
中共北京市委城市公社工作小组 [Urban commune work group of the Municipal Party
Committee], Dahongmen gongshe yuejin pichai chang shengchan renyuan jiti qingyuan
de qingkuang 大红门公社跃进劈柴厂生产人员集体请愿的情况 [On the collective
petition by production staff of the Leap Forward firewood factory at Dahongmen
commune], June 1962. The sources do not mention what happened after they
pleaded with the municipal committee.

[143] BMA 001-028-00036-18 Guanyu chengshi renmin gongshe gongye de qingkuang he
jinhou yijian de baogao.

[144] BMA 001-028-00029-5 Shiwei chengshi gongshe gongzuo xiaozu 市委城市公社工作小
组 [Urban commune work group of the Municipal Party Committee], Guanyu chengshi
gongshe xitong shengchan fuwu renyuan dui fa bupiao de fanying 关于城市公社系统生

These voices reclaimed the promises of urban collectivization and reacted harshly to the betrayal of those promises under the post-GFL Thermidorean reaction. But they also clearly identified the inherent assumption concerning productive and valued labor – that is, factory work, work that produces an economic profit – which in turn made "housewives" and the domestic labor they performed invisible. "Housewives" could only appear, partially and temporarily, as subjects when they were recruited into "real" work, thus indirectly reinforcing their political invisibility as women and neutralizing any relevance of domestic labor and social reproduction in political negotiations.[145] These conditions help to explain women's "willingness" to accept "extra-domestic employment at wages far below those of men," but, more importantly, they justify the very definition of women's labor outside the home as always supplementary to men's waged labor and domestic work: As the latter was the indispensable element in the cycle of production and reproduction, the former was always inherently flexible and disposable.[146] The extreme "flexibility" that gendered commune labor assumed in the last phase of the movement was therefore a logical consequence of the social relationships defining production and repro-duction. The Great Leap was configured as a radical, yet perhaps still insufficient, attempt to transform those relationships, but that attempt was cut short by the political retrenchment of the early 1960s.

Without a radical transformation of the entire mode of production, the radical inequality embodied in the figure of the "housewife" cannot be amended, and liberation cannot be achieved. In the Great Leap, this was briefly but significantly recognized, and it is not by chance that collectiv-ization coincided with the debate over "bourgeois right," which was a discussion of the how the socialist system of production – and, one should add, of social reproduction – continued to reproduce fundamen-tal inequalities. Without revolutionizing that system, the inclusion of women in the process of production itself – the generator of inequalities – even with the proviso of certain welfare services, was always destined to fail. As Mariarosa Dalla Costa argued, "to demand a communal canteen in the neighborhood without integrating this demand into a practice of struggle against the organization of labor, against labor time, risks giving the impetus for a new leap that, on the community level, would regiment

---

产服务人员对发布票的反映 [Reactions by service and production workers in the urban commune system to the distribution of cloth rations], November 28, 1961. The term used is *poxie* 破鞋 "broken shoes." A *chi* is about one third of a meter, or one foot.

[145]  Picchio, *Social Reproduction*: 109–110.
[146]  Fortunati, *The Arcana of Reproduction*: 99.

none other than women in some alluring work so that we will then have the possibility at lunchtime of eating shit collectively in the canteen."[147] That, at best, could result in the *self-management of one's own poverty*, a continuous limitation of the laborers' needs under conditions of intensification of their labor, which is exactly what the urban communes were made to devolve into.[148]

To take stock of that experience, I could not find a better conclusion than the trenchant, unequivocable, fighting words, once again, of Mariarosa Dalla Costa:

Let us sum up. The role of housewife, behind whose isolation is hidden social labor, must be destroyed. But our alternatives are strictly defined. Up to now, the myth of female incapacity, rooted in this isolated woman dependent on someone else's wage and therefore shaped by someone else's consciousness, has been broken by only one action: the woman getting her own wage, breaking the back of personal economic dependence, making her own independent experience with the world outside the home, performing social labor in a socialized structure, whether the factory or the office, and initiating there her own forms of social rebellion along with the traditional forms of the class. *The advent of the women's movement is a rejection of this alternative....* For we have worked enough. We have chopped billions of tons of cotton, washed billions of dishes, scrubbed billions of floors, typed billions of words, wired billions of radio sets, washed billions of nappies, by hand and in machines. Every time they have "let us in" to some traditionally male enclave, it was to find for us a new level of exploitation.[149]

---

[147] Dalla Costa, "Women and the Subversion of the Community": 23–24.

[148] Comitato per il Salario al Lavoro Domestico di Padova, "Le operaie della casa" (1977), *Viewpoint Magazine* (October 31, 2015), https://viewpointmag.com/2015/10/31/excerpts-from-le-operaie-della-casa/.

[149] Dalla Costa, "Women and the Subversion of the Community": 34.

# Epilogue
## Urban Collectivization and Its Afterlives

In this short epilogue, I want first to revisit the questions I borrowed from Henri Lefebvre and that marked the intellectual and political origins of this project: Did the Maoist revolution create a space of its own, alternative and different from that of capitalist societies? Did it shape a new everyday for all or at least some of the people in the PRC? Given how central the issues related to social reproduction and women's liberation were to that search, these questions substantially overlap with the one Gail Hershatter asked in her *The Gender of Memory*: Did Chinese women have a revolution?[1] The answer Hershatter provides in her masterful book is a complex and nuanced one, and she carefully avoids the binary choice between a yes and a no. In the previous pages, I tried to replicate such nuance and attention to details, while dealing with the much narrower and much chronologically limited case of urban collectivization during the Great Leap Forward. I have described the complexity of that effort, the promises it held for leaders and participants, and the far-reaching social transformations it intended to produce. Contrary to descriptions that reduce the Leap to a foolish and failed "economic" experiment, the history of urban communes shows that the campaign programmatically transcended the sphere of the economic and aimed at a sweeping redefinition of social and productive relationships, from the factory to the family. The Great Leap Forward then aimed at instantiating the promise to "transform existence, not merely the state and the distribution of property," which are not ends, but only means to a revolutionary end. And that transformation was supposed to be produced not through state imposition, but through mass mobilization, urban communes being the expression of "a collectivity assuming the responsibility of its own social function and destiny," of self-administration.[2]

The radical nature of the Great Leap was therefore not in its supposed inherent irrationality or utopian hubris. As I have shown, urban

---

[1] Hershatter, *The Gender of Memory*: 31.
[2] Lefebvre, *Everyday Life in the Modern World*: 204.

collectivization responded to actual needs of large sectors of city residents and aimed at bringing closer a revolutionary future that early Soviet-style modernization seemed to preclude. It strove to achieve that goal by following a path that was in many ways eminently rational, labor being the only abundant resource available at the time. Rather, the deep revolutionary character of the Great Leap Forward and specifically of urban collectivization lay in the fact that it eschewed the economic-centered paradigm of the priority of productive forces and targeted directly and purposefully the social space perhaps most resilient to change, that between the economic base and the ideological superstructure, the level of social relations, the everyday, an area that "drags itself along in the wake of change. More than that: it resists change." Once again, I borrow Lefebvre's words:

> The masses come together to make revolution because they are no longer willing to live as hitherto. If revolution fails to bring them the new life they hoped for (and which perhaps can be expressed in Utopian terms: revolution, communism), if the revolution only changes representations, these masses seek refuge in an everyday which is an extension of the previous one: private life, life based upon the close relations of neighborhood and friendships. Could not these facts be responsible for one of the inner contradictions of the world socialist and communist movement? On one hand, an officialized ethic encourages this withdrawal, which makes it possible to distinguish between work and life beyond work, and thus to devote the maximum energy to productive labor. On the other hand, is it not sometimes necessary to shatter the stability of the everyday and the obscure resistance it puts up through the structures it re-establishes at times of important change?[3]

I contend that Mao and others who were most dissatisfied with the state of the revolutionary society after the FFYP had a clear sense that for their revolutionary enterprise to survive they had to challenge that "obscure resistance." The acquired stability of the socialist everyday needed to be shattered. This urgency was expressed theoretically in the debate on bourgeois right and practically in the lived experimentation of collectivization, in the very daily struggle of millions of urban residents to alter basic praxes such as cooking, eating, caring, rearing, and laboring, praxes that in turn determined the structure of family, the definition of worker and labor, and the processes of social reproduction. What is usually considered to be the "utopian" élan of the Great Leap should instead be interpreted as the very realistic assessment of where the obstacles to revolutionary change lay hidden.

---

[3] Lefebvre, *Critique of Everyday Life, vol. 2*: 34–35.

Given the extent and depth of the social change it aimed to produce, it is not surprising that urban collectivization could not achieve success. The campaign was limited from the beginning by economic scarcity, and was marred by problems due to excessive haste and lack of coordination in its implementation. But, more significantly, some of the very goals collectivization aimed to achieve – women's liberation and the remaking of urban social relationships – were impeded by the methods it adopted, first and foremost the expansion of exploitative forms of labor, and by the persistence of profound gendered social distinctions. To borrow Kristin Ross's recent formulation, Beijing's communes never became the "space where labor time has ceased to be the dominant social time and the time of cooperation fills the void."[4] Quite the contrary. The interrupted time-line of the Great Leap prevented any possibility to find solutions to those problems; the Thermidorean reaction and the political reversal that took place after 1960 halted any search of adjustments or alternatives. Yet, through the experience of urban communes, even in their compressed duration, activists and leaders unearthed crucial issues that defined socialist politics and revealed some of the profound contradictions that entangled the transitional temporality of socialism. In that, urban collectivization during the Great Leap is indicative of the promises of both the revolution and its deepest ambiguities and limitations.

## E.1 Communal Legacies

After the Great Leap, and perhaps because of the horrendous famine it contributed to create, there were no experiments of a similar magnitude and depth in the rest of the Maoist era. As Wang Zheng documents, the issue of women's liberation was pushed away from the center of the CCP agenda, even during moments of high revolutionary activism, such as the Cultural Revolution.[5] In the cities, urban collectivization remained unparalleled as an intervention that affected all social relations, in the factory, in the street, in the family.

Urban communes, however, left significant traces in Chinese cities, even after their administrative structures were emptied out and then dismantled. Beijing, as mentioned in Chapter 5, was unique in that its communes survived into the Cultural Revolution. But even in other cities, the collective manufacturing sector spearheaded by the Great Leap outlasted that effort. Lu Hanchao documents the longer history of Shanghai's neighborhood production units – Alleyway Production Teams (APTs, *lilong shengchangzu*) – well past the early 1960s. Even

---

[4] Ross, *The Commune Form*: 72.    [5] Wang, *Finding Women in the State*.

after the demise of the Leap, over 100,000 residents remained employed in Shanghai's neighborhood workshops. The best and more profitable among them were elevated to the category of "street factories" (*jiedao gongchang* 街道工厂) and were run by the industrial bureaus within the municipal government. "These factories were known as 'big collectives' and the level of compensation for their employees was second only to state-owned enterprises in China's industrial hierarchy. Employees received a monthly salary (rather than daily wages) as well as fringe benefits, including medical care and a pension."[6] Other smaller APTs were categorized as "small collectives," and employees received daily wages and no benefits.[7] These workshops survived and, to a certain extent, thrived precisely because of the form and conditions of labor they required. In 1968, the Shanghai government surveyed the city's APTs (ten years after their creation) and its assessment echoed some of the language I cited throughout this book: The APTs cost nothing to the state, they did not need large buildings or high-end equipment, and they were "small, dispersed, and flexible in their operations" and used recycled materials. The marked difference from the language of the Great Leap was the complete disappearance of any reference to "women's liberation" or the transformation of social relations. "The report concluded that 'APTs are different from [state-run] factories and enterprises; they should not be detached from urban neighborhood organizations and take a so-called path to gradual elevation to become full-fledged work units.' This policy continued for the next ten years."[8] In suburban districts, which were largely rural, communes were often not disbanded. The anthropologist Norman Chance visited one of those outside Beijing and noted the existence of "sideline industries, small factories and service agencies that comprise a rising secondary layer of the economy characteristic of suburban communes located near cities."[9] But the commune also hosted a large chemical factory, state-owned and commune-run, which had evolved into a highly modernized and profitable enterprise from its scrappy beginnings in 1958.[10]

The other legacy of urban collectivization was the massive expansion in women's participation in labor outside the home that the Leap had initiated. While I would not go as far as saying that liberating the women's labor force "turned out to be a win-win situation for both the

---

[6] Lu, *Shanghai Tai Chi*: 144.    [7] Lu, *Shanghai Tai Chi*: 144.
[8] Lu, *Shanghai Tai Chi*: 151.
[9] Norman A. Chance, *China's Urban Villagers. Life in a Beijing Commune* (New York: Holt, Rinehart and Winston, 1984): 29.
[10] Chance, *China's Urban Villagers*: 52–53.

state and society,"[11] it is widely recognized that it was the year 1958 that gave rise to the new norm in urban China that practically all working-age women should work outside the home.[12] An extra inducement to women's employment was also the fact that, as Kam Wing Chan noted, the average wage for workers in the state sector was kept low – or even declined – between 1957 and 1977, making women's contribution even more valuable.[13] Overall, through the 1960s and the 1970s, the benefits associated with the *danwei* system were expanded to an increasing number of urban residents, male and female, so that by the end of the Mao era, an overwhelming majority enjoyed the guarantees and norms of what Joel Andreas has called "workplace citizenship," among them secure job tenure and a varying amount of *fuli*.[14] Yet despite all this progress, there were still plenty of city residents who continued to live outside or at the very margins of the *danwei* system well into the Reform era, constantly deprived of the advantages that system conferred. Harriet Evans has described the lives of some of those residents in the case of Beijing, people who inhabited the very same city space where urban communes had flourished years earlier.[15]

## E.2    Value's Vengeance

While the overall expansion of the "supply system" in the last two decades of the Mao era configured a reduction and a restriction of commodity exchange as part of the practical functioning of the socialist economy, there was no further *mass* movement aimed at tackling the issues that collectivization had brought to the fore, such as the permanence of bourgeois right, the centrality of the wage system, and the relation between production and social reproduction (among others). Some of these issues, specifically the continued role of the bourgeois right and the law of value, reemerged at the center of the theoretical discussion during the Cultural Revolution, in particular, in the debates surrounding the compilation of various versions of a textbook on the political economy, an effort spearheaded by Zhang Chunqiao.[16] In the last ten years of the Mao era, the "economists" who had prevailed in the 1959 debate on the law of value and the socialist economy were forced to retreat, and

---

[11] Lu, *Shanghai Tai Chi*: 165.       [12] Lu, *Shanghai Tai Chi*: 139.
[13] Chan, *Cities with Invisible Walls*: 73.
[14] Andreas, *Disenfranchised*. According to Lu Duanfang, "By 1978, around 95 per cent of urban workers belonged to a work unit of one kind or another." Lu, *Remaking Chinese Urban Form*: 47.
[15] Evans, *Beijing from Below*.
[16] Christensen and Delman, "A Theory of Transitional Society."

their political influence was temporarily and forcibly limited.[17] The reversal of verdicts at the beginning of the Deng era returned them to positions of authority. Looking at some of their writings from 1978–1979, I was surprised at how large the shadow of the Great Leap loomed in their analysis, as if it was necessary to exorcise that experience and restate even more forcefully the normative rationality of the economic, at the precise moment in which the PRC was moving toward embracing a full-blown commodity economy. That embrace could only be predicated by the "total negation" of the search for any socialist alternative and the reaffirmation of "the economic" as an independent ontological realm.[18]

At the beginning of the Deng era, prominent economists such as Sun Yefang and Xue Muqiao rehashed positions they had stated in 1959, and they strongly restated the absolute need to follow the law of value even under the planned economy. In 1978, Sun Yefang, in stressing the centrality of the law of value for socialist accounting and statistics and its use as a tool in the hands of the people, made direct reference to the Great Leap, whose "communist winds" he described as "a form of naked dispossession without remuneration" (*nazhong chiluoluo de wuchang boduo* 那种赤裸裸的无偿剥夺).[19] The same year, Song Yangtan wrote how the revival of the law of value was necessarily connected to the reprisal of material incentives, as its operation depended mainly on "economic factors" "to mobilize socialist enterprises and workers' enthusiasm for production." In a sleight of hand that prefigures the Reform-era use of Marxist verbiage to justify capitalist measures, Song concluded that, "according to Marxism, economic or material interests are one of the most tangible interests for the people, and therefore people are very concerned about them. The so-called regulating effect of the law of value is, in the final analysis, the dominating effect on people's actions of the economic interests of the masses embodied in value as a relation of production."[20]

---

[17] Xue Muqiao was sent to the countryside in 1969, while Sun Yefang was imprisoned.

[18] Alessandro Russo has argued how the post-1978 period was constituted as the total negation (*chedi fouding*) of the experience of the Cultural Revolution. Russo, "How Did the Cultural Revolution End? The Last Dispute between Mao Zedong and Deng Xiaoping, 1975," *Modern China* 39:3 (May 2013): 239–279.

[19] Sun Yefang 孙冶方, "Yao quanmian tihui Mao Zhuxi guanyu jiazhi guilü wenti de lunshu" 要全面体会毛主席关于价值规律问题的论述 [We must fully understand Chairman Mao's exposition on the question of the law of value], *Jingji yanjiu* 经济研究 [Economic research] 11 (1978): 10. The essay had been originally written in 1964–1965.

[20] Song Yangtan宋养琰, "Jiazji guilü zai shehuizhuyi zong laodong fenpei he shangchan zhong de tiaojie zuoyong" 价值规律在社会主义总劳动分配和生产中的调节作用 [The regulating role of the law of value in the socialist distribution of total labor and production], *Jingji yanjiu* 经济研究 [Economic research] 11 (1978): 24.

A year later, in 1979, Xue Muqiao depicted the law of value almost as a vengeful force, which had punished the Soviet Union and was now punishing the PRC for having had the hubris to neglect or ignore its functioning. Here Xue moved further from the position more generally held at the time of the Great Leap, when the permanence of the law of value under socialism was justified mainly for its role in coordinating planning. Xue held instead that it was to be deployed in determining profit and loss in SOEs, but also, and more alarmingly, he praised the functioning of the law of value within capitalism, where it automatically regulated prices and made them correspond to values, according to the balance of supply and demand.[21] We see here how, by 1979, those very capitalist forms (or vestiges of capitalism) that in the 1959 debate appeared to have been tamed enough that they could be deployed within the socialist planned economy were being accepted and extolled precisely because of their explicit capitalist character and functioning. An essay by Zhuo Jiong in the same year criticized the long-standing conception of the law of value and commodity production as relics of capitalism, and embraced instead their wholehearted adoption, precisely because in them lay the secret of capitalist countries' superior developmental speed.[22] The law of value's vengeance on the legacy of the Great Leap was then practically instantiated in the economic path undertaken in the reform era.

## E.3    Rescuing Neoliberalism from the Leap

In terms of historiography, the 1981 "Resolution on Certain Questions in the History of Our Party since the Founding of the People's Republic of China" sanctioned the official evaluation of the experience of collectivization, and did so by restoring "productive force determinism." Collectivization had been a "leftist" mistake, grounded on profound ignorance of the development of the productive forces, with very negative consequence: "To maintain as advanced a system that has been established under specific historical conditions and is not in line with the requirements of the development of the productive forces, and to tie the most advanced relations of production to an extremely backward productive force, will, of course, destroy the productive forces of

---

[21]  Xue Muqiao 薛暮桥, "Liyong jiazhi guilü wei jingji jianshe shiye fuwu" 利用价值规律为经济建设事业服务 [Use the law of value to serve the cause of economic construction], 红旗 [Red flag] 1 (1979): 18 and 20.

[22]  Zhuo Jiong 卓炯, "Jiazhi guilü yu sige xiandaihua" 价值规律与四个现代化 [The law of value and the four modernizations], *Xueshu yuekan* 学术月刊 [Academic monthly] 2 (1979): 29.

society."[23] This was, and I think still officially is, the "correct" political line for any history of the Great Leap. However, in recent years, new historical interpretations have surfaced that, often pushing past the limits of sense and logic, frame the experience of the Leap, and specifically of urban communes, in completely different terms. In that, they configure a strange attempt to rescue a completely different political meaning from that experience, one that better fit the political trends of the 2010s. I close this long exploration with a few words on these new readings of the Leap.

A piece by historians Li Duanxiang and Wang Qianzhen, for example, criticizes how women's liberation was pursued under urban collectivization. While the Leap achieved a certain amount of emancipation, they argue, that was not the product of a bottom-up feminist movement, but "the result of direct intervention by state power."[24] It was therefore a passive emancipation, which ignored women's subjective consciousness. That's not an unfounded critique, and it echoes some of the criticism voiced by women workers at the time. However, Li and Wang cannot push that critique any further, because that would inevitably lead them to support the notion of an autonomous feminist movement, something that is basically intolerable – and de facto illegal – in today's China. Instead, in the rest of the piece, they point out at the harsh labor conditions in commune factories, which exposed women to health risks (especially affecting their reproductive health), and the essay ends by incongruously reiterating the role of the state in "guiding" women and reproducing official code words such as "harmony" and "Chinese characteristics":

[W]hile mobilizing and organizing women to participate in economic construction through a Marxist perspective on women, it is also necessary to guide and educate them – based on social conditions – to establish their own identity, find their rightful place, and play a unique role in revitalizing the economy and promoting social progress, thereby seeking their comprehensive development and true liberation. Moreover, this path must align with China's national conditions, forging a distinctive Chinese approach to women's liberation, one that harmonizes the development of both genders, balances women's growth with societal progress, and integrates women's advancement with the nation's harmonious development.[25]

Another, seemingly minoritarian but quite astonishing take on urban communes focuses instead strictly on their nature as an "economic" phenomenon. According to this interpretation, urban communes were

---

[23] Liu Zhenqing, "Chengshi renmin gongshe shulun": 99.
[24] Li and Wang, "Chengshi renmin gongshe yu funü jiefang": 84.
[25] Li and Wang, "Chengshi renmin gongshe yu funü jiefang": 86.

created not by following the initiative and guidance of the CCP leadership, but through a "spontaneous act" by urban residents. The result of an unplanned, popular effort, urban collectivization then confronted the Party with a new economic system, which the Party was not ready to accept.[26] In the most extreme version of such a view, neighborhood and commune enterprises are described as presenting an existential challenge to the planned economy, and in turn, it was "the management model of the planned economy, especially the policy of unified purchasing and marketing," which "limited the dynamism" of these enterprises.[27] In what seems almost a neoliberal fever dream worthy of Milton Friedman, collective enterprises here become the expression of the entrepreneurial nature of the people, developing quickly due to their "flexible and diversified nature." But, in their development, they exposed the defects and limitations of the planned economy, and if they had been allowed to continue to operate freely, they would have eventually disrupted it. Then, to save the very model of socialist planning, collective enterprises had to be sacrificed.[28]

In light of what I described in the previous pages, it should be clear that this view is untenable or, rather, absurd. But what is perhaps most galling is how it aims to produce a radical historical flattening, by shaping a past in which the logic of neoliberal self-interest was always already dominant, thus erasing the very possibility of any collective, revolutionary alternative. The Great Leap is rightfully associated with tragedy. It is perhaps not tragic, but it is certainly darkly ironic, that in twenty-first-century China, its legacy can be summoned not to remember or reimagine the revolutionary aspirations of those who toiled, perhaps foolishly or fruitlessly, to create a society where each and everybody's needs could be satisfied, but to reinvent that past as a precursor of the neoliberal present.

---

[26] Guo Xiuping, "Woguo chengshi renmin gongshehua yundong weigaocheng juda zainan de yuanyin": 44.

[27] Lin Chaochao, "'Dayuejin' shiqi Shanghai jiedao gongye de dingwei yu zhuanxing": 44.

[28] Lin Chaochao, "'Dayuejin' shiqi Shanghai jiedao gongye de dingwei yu zhuanxing": 48. A similar, but less starkly neoliberal argument is made in Huang Lixin 黄利新 and Zhang Xuhua 张栩华, "Dayuejin shiqi Guangzhoushijiedao gongye yanjiu" 大跃进时期广州市街道工业研究 [Neighborhood industries in Guangzhou at the time of the Great Leap Forward], *Guangdong dangshi yu wenxiang yanjiu* 广东党史与文献研究 [Guangdong Party history and document research] 3 (2019): 48–59. Here the authors mainly extol the dynamism of collective enterprises and their incompatibility with the planned economy.

# Bibliography

Andors, Phyllis. "Social Revolution and Woman's Emancipation: China during the Great Leap Forward." Bulletin of Concerned Asian Scholars 7:1 (1975): 33–42.

Bachman, David. Bureaucracy, Economy, and Leadership in China: The Institutional Origins of the Great Leap Forward. Cambridge: Cambridge University Press, 1991.

Bao Chang 鲍昌. "Lifa yougan" 理发有感 [Reflections on a Haircut]. RMRB, January 13, 1957.

Baomu shouce 保姆手册 [Manual for children caregivers]. 山西省卫生厅编印, 1958.

Benston, Margaret. "The Political Economy of Women's Liberation." Monthly Review 41:7 (December 1989). https://monthlyreview.org/2019/09/01/the-political-economy-of-womens-liberation/.

Bettelheim, Charles. The Transition to Socialist Economy. Translated from the French by Brian Pearce. Sussex: Harvester Press, 1975.

Bhattacharya, Tithi. "How Not to Skip Class: Social Reproduction of Labor and the Global Working Class." Viewpoint Magazine (October 31, 2015). https://viewpointmag.com/2015/10/31/how-not-to-skip-class-social-reproduction-of-labor-and-the-global-working-class/

Bingham, Charles, and Gert J. J. Biesta, with Jacques Rancière. Jacques Rancière: Education, Truth, Emancipation. London: Continuum, 2010.

Bray, David. Social Space and Governance in Urban China: The Danwei System from Origins to Reform. Stanford, CA: Stanford University Press, 2005.

Bray, Francesca. Technology and Gender: Fabrics of Power in Late Imperial China. Berkeley: University of California Press, 1997.

Brown, Jeremy. City versus Countryside in Mao's China: Negotiating the Divide. Cambridge: Cambridge University Press, 2012.

Brown, Jeremy, and Matthew D. Johnson, eds. Maoism at the Grassroots: Everyday Life in China's Era of High Socialism. Cambridge, MA: Harvard University Press, 2015.

Bubeck, Diemut Elisabet. Care, Gender, and Justice. Oxford: Clarendon Press, 1995.

Caldwell, Peter C. Dictatorship, State Planning, and Social Theory in the German Democratic Republic. Cambridge: Cambridge University Press, 2003.

Chan, Alfred L. Mao's Crusade: Politics and Policy Implementation in China's Great Leap Forward. New York: Oxford University Press, 2001.

Chan, Kam Wing. Cities with Invisible Walls: Reinterpreting Urbanization in Post-1949 China. Oxford: Oxford University Press, 1994.

Chance, Norman A. China's Urban Villagers: Life in a Beijing Commune. New York: Holt, Rinehart and Winston, 1984.

Chen Ming 陈明. "Bu gai tuichu gongjizhi de chendi" 不该退出供给制的阵地 [We should not retreat from the battlefield of the supply system]. RMRB, October 30, 1958.

Chen, Nai-Ruenn. The Chinese Economy under Maoism: The Early Years, 1949–1969. London: Routledge, 2017.

Chen Zhengren 陈正人. "Lun renmin gongshe de suoyouzhi he fenpei zhidu" 论人民公社的所有制和分配制度 [About people's communes' ownership and distribution system]. RMRB, October 18, 1959.

Chen, Tina Mai. "Dressing for the Party: Clothing, Citizenship, and Gender-Formation in Mao's China." Fashion Theory 5:2 (2001): 143–171.

   "Proletarian White and Working Bodies in Mao's China." positions: east asia cultures critique 11:2 (Fall 2003): 361–393.

Cheng Zhaosheng 程钊生. "Fenqing liangzhing bupingdeng" 分清两种不平等 [Distinguish between two kinds of inequality]. RMRB, December 3, 1958.

"Chengshi gongshe gongye yao an yu xiao, jing yu xiao (shelun)" 城市公社工业要安于小、精于小（社论）[Urban commune industries should be content with small, proficient at small (editorial)]. Beijing Ribao 北京日报, February 21, 1961. Reprinted in Li, ed., Chenghsi renmin gongshe yanjiu ziliao xuanbian, vol. 7: 117–118.

Christensen, Peer Moller, and Jorgen Delman. "A Theory of Transitional Society: Mao Zedong and the Shanghai School." Bulletin of Concerned Asian Scholars 13:2 (1981): 2–15.

Chu Hongdao 初宏道. "Cong sheban gongye de gongchanxiao qingkuang kanlai, sheban qiye shi shu quanminsuoyouzhi xingzhide" 从社办工业的供产销情况看来，社办企业是属全民所有制性质的 [Judging from the conditions of supply, production, and marketing in commune industries, they belong to ownership of the whole people]. Zhongguo jingji wenti 中国经济问题 (Economic Issues in China), no. 8 (1960): 14.

Chuang. "Sorghum and Steel: The Socialist Developmental State and the Forging of China." Chuang, no. 1 (2016). https://chuangcn.org/journal/one/sorghum-and-steel/

Comitato per il Salario al Lavoro Domestico di Padova. "Le operaie della casa" (1977). Viewpoint Magazine (October 31, 2015). https://viewpointmag.com/2015/10/31/excerpts-from-le-operaie-della-casa.

Connery, Christopher Leigh. "Introduction: Worlded Pedagogy in Santa Cruz." In Rob Wilson and Christopher Leigh Connery, eds., The Worlding Project. Doing Cultural Studies in the Era of Globalization. Santa Cruz, CA: New Pacific Press, 2007: 1–12.

Dalla Costa, Mariarosa. "Women and the Subversion of the Community." In Mariarosa Dalla Costa and Selma James, The Power of Women and The Subversion of the Community (1972). https://libcom.org/library/power-women-subversion-community-della-costa-selma-james.

Davin, Delia. Woman Work: Women and the Party in Revolutionary China. Oxford: Oxford University Press, 1976.

Day, Alexander F. "Breaking with the Family Form: Historical Categories, Social Reproduction, and Everyday Life in Late 1950s Rural China." positions: asia critique 29:4 (2021): 879–894.

"Diaohui fuwuyuan, huifu fuwudian. Guangzhou dali jiaqiang lifa, xiran, yinshi, sheying deng fuwu hangye. Jishu zhiliang he fuwu taidu shoudai qunzhong huanying" 调回服务员 恢复服务点 广州大力加强理发、洗染、饮食、摄影等服务行业 技术质量和服务态度受到群众欢迎 [Redeployment of attendants; restoration of service points. Guangzhou vigorously strengthens service industries such as hairdressing, washing and dyeing, catering, photography, etc. Technical quality and service attitude are welcomed by the public]. RMRB, June 18, 1959.

Dillon, Nara. Radical Inequalities: China's Revolutionary Welfare State in Comparative Perspective. Cambridge, MA: Harvard University Press, 2015.

Ding Ran 丁然., dir. Nülifashi 女理发师 [Female hairdresser]. 1962. https://youtu.be/v8kAC_xWGpM.

Dong, Madeleine Yue. Republican Beijing: The City and Its Histories. Berkeley: University of California Press, 2003.

Dong, Yige. "'Red Housekeeping' in a Socialist Factory: Jiashu and Transforming Reproductive Labor in Urban China (1949–1962)." International Review of Social History (January 18, 2024): 1–24.

Donnithorne, Audrey. China's Economic System. New York: Praeger, 1967.

Dutton, Micheal, Hsiu-ju Stacy Lo, and Dong Dong Wu. Beijing Time. Cambridge, MA: Harvard University Press, 2008.

Engels, Frederick. The Origin of the Family, Private Property, and the State (1884). www.marxists.org/archive/marx/works/1884/origin-family/index.htm.

Evans, Harriet. Beijing from Below: Stories of Marginal Lives in the Capital's Center. Durham, NC: Duke University Press, 2020.

  The Subject of Gender: Daughters and Mothers in Urban China. Lanham, MD: Rowman and Littlefield, 2007.

Federici, Silvia. Caliban and the Witch: Women, the Body, and Primitive Accumulation. New York: Autonomedia, 2004.

"Fengtaiqu ge lifadian bangzhu jiedao peiyang lifa renyuan" 丰台区各理发店帮助街道培养理发人员 [Barbershops in Fengtai help train neighborhood barbers]. RMRB, August 12, 1959.

Fortunati, Leopoldina. L'Arcano della riproduzione: Casalinghe, prostitute, operai e capitale. Venice: Marsilio, 1981. English version, The Arcana of Reproduction: Housewives, Prostitutes, Workers and Capital, translated by Arlen Austin and Sara Colantuono. London, Verso, 2025.

Frost, Adam K., and Zeren Li. "Markets under Mao: Measuring Underground Activity in the Early PRC." China Quarterly 258 (June 2024): 309–328.

Gao, Yuan. "Peasant Cooperation and Agricultural Growth in Historical Perspective: Southeastern Shanxi in the 1950s." Modern China 45:5 (2019): 537–563.

Gerth, Karl. Unending Capitalism: State Consumerism and the Negation of the Chinese Socialist Revolution. Cambridge: Cambridge University Press, 2020.

Goldstein, Joshua. Remains of the Everyday: A Century of Recycling in Beijing. Berkeley: University of California Press, 2020.

Guan Feng 关锋. "Lüeyu renmin gongshe de weida lishi yiyi" 略諭人民公社的伟大历史意义 [Brief discussion of the huge historical meaning of people's communes]. *Zhexue yanjiu* 哲学研究 (Philosophical research), no. 5 (1958): 1–8.

"Xiang gongchanzhuyi guoshe de zuihao de fenpei xingzshi: Shilun bufen gongji he bufen gongzi xiangjiehe de fenpei zhidu" 向共产主义过渡的最好的分配形式 试论部分供给和部分工资相结合的分配制度 [The best form of distribution for the transition to communism: Experimenting with a distribution system combining partial supply and partial wages]. *RMRB*, October 22, 1958.

"Guanyu renmin gongshe ruogan wenti de jueyi. Zhongguo gongchandang dibajie Zhongyang weiyuanhui diliuci quanti huiyi tongguo" 关于人民公社若干问题的决议. 中国共产党第八届中央委员会第六次全体会议通过 [Resolution on Several Issues Concerning People's Communes. Adopted by the Sixth Plenary Session of the Eighth Central Committee of the Communist Party of China]. *RMRB*, December 19, 1958.

"Guke you jishi, tangfa zhi yong yixiaoshi" 顾客有急事 烫发只用一小时 [The customer is in a hurry, the perm takes only one hour]. Beijing ribao 北京日报, December 27, 1959: 2.

Guo Xiuping 郭秀平. "Woguo chengshi renmin gongshehua yundong weigaocheng juda zainan de yuanyin" 我 国城市人 民公社化运动 未造成 巨 大灾难 的原 因 [Reasons why the urban commune movement did not produce a huge catastrophe]. *Dangshi yanjiu yu jiaoxue* 党史研究与教学 [Research and Teaching in Party History], no. 3 (2006): 41–49.

Guojia tongjiju shehui tongjisi bian 国家统计局社会统计司编. Zhongguo laodong gongzi tongji ziliao 中国劳动工资统计资料1949–1985 [China's Labor Wage Statistics 1949–1985]. Beijing: China Statistic Press, 1987.

"Guoshe dao gongchanzhuyi de jige tiaojian: Shaoqi tongzhi zai Henan shichashi juti chanshu" 过渡到共产主义的几个条件: 少奇同志在河南视察时具体阐述 [Some conditions for the transition to communism: Comrade Liu Shaoqi's concrete suggestions during his inspection tour of Henan]. *RMRB*, September 24, 1958.

He Tianzhong 贺天中. "Anlaofuchou shi woguo muqian fenpei zhidu de jichu" 按劳付酬是我国目前分配制度的基础 [Remuneration according to labor is the foundation of the current distribution system of our country]. *RMRB*, November 28, 1958.

Hershatter, Gail. The Gender of Memory: Rural Women and China's Collective Past. Berkeley: University of California Press, 2011.

Hoffmann, Charles. "Work Incentive Policy in Communist China." *China Quarterly*, no. 17 (January–March 1964): 95–96.

Hou Mingfang 侯明方. "Zichan jieji faquan canyu bushi zichanjiejie faquan" 资产阶级法权残余不是资产阶级法权 [The remnants of bourgeois right are not bourgeois right]. *RMRB*, January 3, 1959.

Hsue Mu-chiao, Su Hsing, and Lin Tse-li. The Socialist Transformation of the National Economy in China. Beijing: Foreign Language Press, 1960.

Hu Sheng 胡绳. "Cong gongjizhi shuoqi" 从供给制说起 [Bringing up the supply system]. *RMRB*, November 13, 1958.

"Jiawu laodong de jitihua, shehuihua" 家务劳动的集体化、社会化 [The collectivization and socialization of household labor]. *Hongqi* 红旗 [Red Flag], no. 7 (July 1958): 24–30.

Huang Lixin 黄利新 and Zhang Xuhua 张栩华. "Dayuejin shiqi Guangzhoushi jiedao gongye yanjiu" 大跃进时期广州市街道工业研究 [Neighborhood industries in Guangzhou at the time of the Great Leap Forward]. *Guangdong dangshi wenxian yanjiu* 广东党史与文献研究 [Guangdong Party History and Document Research], no. 3 (2019): 48–59.

Ji Xichao 池曦朝. "'Anlao quchou' bushi zichanjieji faquan" '按劳取酬'不是资产阶级法权 ["Remuneration according to labor" is not bourgeois right]. *RMRB*, November 22, 1958.

Jiang Chunze 江春泽. "Gaixing gongzizhi bing mei you cuo" 改行工资制并没有错 [There is nothing wrong with switching to a salary system]. *RMRB*, November 19, 1958.

"Jiedao gongzuozhong de yimian hongqi – ji Tianjin shi Hongshunli zuzhi qilai hou de xin qixiang" 街道工作中的一面红旗－记天津市鸿顺里组织起来后的新气象 [A red flag in neighborhood work – Remembering the new atmosphere after the reorganization of Hongshunli in Tianjin]. *RMRB*, August 19, 1958.

"Jinyibu zhankai jingsai, tigao fuwu zhiliang (Biejing shi fuwu shiyea guanliju fuzhang Ding Tiefeng)" 进一步展开竞赛，提高服务质量 (北京市服务事业管理局副局长 丁铁峰) [Further develop the competition to improve the quality of services (Ding Tiefeng, Deputy Director of Beijing Municipal Service Administration)]. *Beijing Ribao*北京日报, August 2, 1959: 2.

Joseph, William A. "A Tragedy of Good Intentions: Post-Mao Views of the Great Leap Forward." Modern China 12:4 (October 1986): 419–457.

Karl, Rebecca E. "Culture, Revolution, and the Times of History: Mao and 20th-Century China." *China Quarterly*, no. 187 (September 2006): 697–698.

The Magic of Concepts: History and the Economic in Twentieth-Century China. Durham, NC: Duke University Press, 2017.

"Serve the People." In Christian Sorace, Ivan Franceschini, and Nicholar Loubere, eds., Afterlives of Chinese Communism. Political Concepts from Mao to Xi. Canberra: ANU Press, 2019: 247–250.

Kelly, Jason M. Market Maoists: The Communist Origins of China's Capitalist Ascent. Cambridge, MA: Harvard University Press, 2021.

Kim Yong-uk. "Workers in Mao's China: Labour and Capital under Chinese State Capitalism, 1949–62." In Owen Miller, ed., State Capitalism and Development in East Asia since 1945. Leiden: Brill, 2023: 84–148.

Kindler, Benjamin. Writing to the Rhythm of Labor: Cultural Politics of the Chinese Revolution, 1942–1976. New York: Columbia University Press, 2025.

Lanza, Fabio. "A City of Workers, a City for Workers? Remaking Beijing Urban Space in the Early PRC." In Ding Yannan, Maurizio Marinelli, and Zhang Ziaohong, eds., China: A Historical Geography of the Urban. London: Palgrave Macmillan, 2018: 41–66.

"Introduction: The Politics of (Maoist) History." positions: asia critique 29:4 (2021): 675–688.

ed. "PRC History Roundtable: Karl Gerth, *Unending Capitalism: How Consumerism Negated China's Communist Revolution* (Cambridge University Press, 2020)," PRC History Review 5:1 (October 2020). https://networks.h-net.org/volume-5-number-1-october-2020.

"The Search for a Socialist Everyday: The Urban Communes." In Alan Baumler, ed., The Routledge Handbook of Revolutionary China. London: Routledge, 2019: 74–88.

Lefebvre, Henri. Critique of Everyday Life, vol. 1: Introduction. Translated by John Moore. London: Verso, 1991.

Critique of Everyday Life, vol. 2: Foundations for a Sociology of the Everyday. Translated by John Moore. London: Verso, 2002.

Everyday Life in the Modern World. New York: Transaction, 1984.

The Production of Space. Translated by Donald Nicholson-Smith. Oxford: Blackwell, 1991.

Lei Yaoling 雷尧玲. "Chengshi renmin gongshe suoyouzhi jibenshang shi quanmin xingzhide" 城市人民公社所有制基本上是全民性质的 [The form of ownership in urban people's communes is essentially universal in nature]. *Zhongguo jingji wenti* 中国经济问题 (Economic Issues in China), no. 8 (1960): 11.

Lenin, V. I. "A Great Beginning: Heroism of the Workers in the Rear 'Communist Subbotniks'" (June 28, 1919). In *Collected Works*, vol. 29: 408–434. www.marxists.org/archive/lenin/works/1919/jun/19.htm.

"The Immediate Tasks of the Soviet Government" (March–April 1918). In Collected Works, 4th English edition, vol. 27. Moscow: Progress Publishers, 1972: 235–377. www.marxists.org/archive/lenin/works/1918/mar/x03.htm.

"International Working Women's Day" (March 4, 1921). www.marxists.org/archive/lenin/works/1921/mar/04.htm.

Li Chengzong 李成宗. "Wo dui chengshi renmin gongshe suoyouzhi xingzhi de kanfa" 我对城市人民公社所有制性質的看法 [My opinion on the ownership in urban communes]. *Zhongguo jingji wenti*中国经济问题 (*Economic Issues in China*), no. 8 (1960): 12–14.

Li Duanxiang 李端祥 ed. *Chengshi renmin gongshe yanjiu ziliao xuanbian* 城市人民公社研究资料选编 [Selected research materials on urban people's communes]. 8 vols. 人民出版社, 2021.

Li Duanxiang 李端祥. Chengshi renmin gongshe yundong yanjiu 城市人民公社运动研究 [Studies on the Urban People's Commune Movement]. Changsha: Hunan Renmin Chubanshe, 2006.

"Chengshi renmin gongshehua yundong de xingwang yu lishi jiaoxun" 城市人民公社化运动的兴亡与历史教训 [The rise and fall of the urban people's commune movement and its lessons for history]. *Qiusuo* 求索 [Explore], no. 7 (2004engshi renmin gongshe yanjiu ziliao xuan): 232–234.

"Duiyu Beijing chengshi renmin gongshe lishi de kaocha" 对于北京城市人民公社历史的考察 [An examination of the history of urban people's communes in Beijing]. In Li Duanxiang, ed., *Chengshi renmin gongshe yanjiu ziliao xuanbian*, vol. 1: 16–26. Originally published in *Beijing dangshi* 北京党史, 2005, no. 1.

Li Duanxiang 李端祥 and Wang Qianzhen 汪前珍. "Chengshi renmin gongshe yu funü jiefang" 城市人民公社与妇女解放 [Urban people's commune and women's liberation]. *Dangshi yanjiu yu jiaoxue* 党史研究与教学 [Research and teaching of Party history], no. 3 (2014): 78–86.

Li Duanxiang 李端祥 and Xiao Chuchu 肖楚楚. "Chengshi renmin gongshe gonggong shitang chengyin tanxi" 城市人民公社公共食堂成因探析 [An analysis of the causes for the formation of public canteens in urban people's communes]. Hunan keji daxue xuebao 湖南科技大学学报 (社会科学版) Journal of the Hunan University of Science and Technology (Social Science Edition)] 17:6 (November 2014): 102–106.

Li, Hou. Building for Oil: Daqing and the Formation of the Chinese Socialist State. Cambridge, MA: Harvard University Press, 2018.

Li Huaiyin. The Master in Bondage: Factory Workers in China, 1949–2019. Stanford, CA: Stanford University Press, 2023.

*Lifaye gongzuo renyuan yewu shouce: Zhuangong ge lifadian gong zuo renyuan xuexi yewu zhi yong* 理发业工作人员业务手册: 专供各理发店工作人员学习业务之用 [Manual for employees of the haircutting industry: To be used for study by personnel in every barbershop]. 上海市福利事业公司编印, January 1958.

Lin Chaochao 林超超. "'Dayuejin' shiqi Shanghai jiedao gongye de dingwei yu zhuanxing '大跃进' 时期上海街道工业的定位与转型 [The orientation and transformation of Shanghai street industry at the time of the Great Leap Forward]. *Zhonggong dangshi yanjiu* 中共党史研究 [CCP history research], no. 8 (2018): 43–54.

Lin, Cyril Chihren. "The Reinstatement of Economics in China Today." China Quarterly 1 (1981): 1–48.

Lin Wei 林韦. "Saochu zichanjieji dengjizhi de canji" 扫除资产阶级等级制的残迹 [Let's remove the vestiges of bourgeois hierarchy]. *RMRB*, November 3, 1958.

Liu Jing 刘竞. "Ruguo ni xiang lifa ..." 如果你想理发 ... [If you think about becoming a barber ...]. *RMRB*, May 4, 1960.

Liu Yong 刘勇. "Cong zuzhi shengchan rushou, shengchan shenghuo yiqi zhua" 从组织生产入手, 生产生活一起抓 [Start from organizing production, grasp production and life together]. *Beijing Ribao*, April 18, 1960. Reprinted in Li, ed., Chengshi renmin gongshe yanjiu ziliao xuanbian, vol. 7: 95–97.

Liu Zhenqing 刘振清. "Chengshi renmin gongshe shulun" 城市人民公社述论 [A discussion of urban people's communes]. *Changbai xuekan* 长白学刊 [Changbai journal], (February 10, 2006): 96–99.

Liu, Joyce C. H., and Viren Murthy, eds. East-Asian Marxisms and Their Trajectories. London: Routledge, 2017.

Liu, Song 刘松. "Guanyu jiawu laodong de jitihua, shehuihu" 关于家务劳动的集体化, 社会化 [Concerning the collectivization and socialization of household labor]. *Qingnian gongchanzhuyizhe congkan* Qingnian gongchanzhuyizhe congkan 青年共产主义者丛刊 [Youth Communist] (November 1958): 89–96.

Lu Duanfang. Remaking Chinese Urban Form: Modernity, Scarcity and Space, 1949–2005. London: Routledge, 2006.

Lu Hanchao. Shanghai Tai Chi: The Art of Being Ruled in Mao's China. Cambridge: Cambridge University Press, 2023.

Lu Ren 鲁韧, dir. *Jintian wo xiuxi* 今天我休息 [Today is my day off]. 1959. www.virtualshanghai.net/Films/Collection?ID=109.

Luard, D. E. T. "The Urban Communes." *China Quarterly*, no. 3 (July–September 1960): 74–79.

Luo Gengmo 骆耕漠. "Gongzishi he gongjizhi dou you liangzhongxing" 工资制和供给制都有两重性 [Both wage and supply systems have a dual nature]. *RMRB*, November 12, 1958.

MacFarquhar, Roderick. The Origins of the Cultural Revolution, vol. 2: The Great Leap Forward 1958–1960. New York: Columbia University Press, 1983.

MacFarquhar, Roderick, Timothy Cheek, and Eugene Wu, eds. The Secret Speeches of Chairman Mao: From the Hundred Flowers to the Great Leap Forward. Cambridge, MA: Harvard University Press, 1989.

Manning, Kimberley Ens. "Making a Great Leap Forward? The Politics of Women's Liberation in Maoist China." Gender & History 18:3 (November 2006): 574–593.

Mao Zedong [Tsetung]. A Critique of the Soviet Economics. Translated by Moss Roberts, annotated by Richard Levy. With an introduction by James Peck. New York: Monthly Review Press, 1977.

Mao Zedong. "Dui 'Zhengzhou huiyi guanyu renmin gongshe ruogan wenti de jueyi' de xiugai he xinjian" 对 '郑州会议关于人民公社若干问题的决议'的修改和信件 [Letter and amendments on the 'Resolution of the Zhengzhou Conference on Certain Issues of the People's Commune']. In Zhonggong zhongyang wenxian yanjiushi, ed., Jianguo yilai Mao Zedong wengao 建国以来毛泽东文稿 [Mao Zedong's manuscripts since the founding of the PRC]. Vol. 7. Beijing: Zhongyang wenxian chubanshe, 1993: 513–521 (November 11–12, 1958).

"On the Correct Handling of Contradictions among the People" (February 27, 1957). www.marxists.org/reference/archive/mao/selected-works/volume-5/mswv5_58.htm.

"On the Ten Major Relationships" (April 25, 1956). www.marxists.org/reference/archive/mao/selected-works/volume-5/mswv5_51.htm.

"Strengthen Party Unity and Carry Forward Party Traditions" (August 30, 1956). www.marxists.org/reference/archive/mao/selected-works/volume-5/mswv5_53.htm.

Marx, Karl. Capital, a Critique of Political Economy, Volume 1. London: Penguin Classics, 1992.

*Critique of the Gotha Program* (1875). www.marxists.org/archive/marx/works/1875/gotha/.

Grundrisse: Foundations of the Critique of Political Economy. London: Penguin Books, 1973.

Mau, Søren. Mute Compulsion: A Marxist Theory of the Economic Power of Capital. London: Verso, 2023.

Meisner, Maurice. Mao's China and After: A History of the People's Republic. 3rd ed. New York: Free Press, 1999.

Meyskens, Covell F. "Rethinking the Political Economy of Development in Mao's China." positions: asia critique 29:4 (November 2021): 809–834.

Mezzadri, Alessandra. "On the Value of Social Reproduction: Informal Labour, the Majority World and the Need for Inclusive Theories and Politics." Radical Philosophy 2:4 (Spring 2019): 33–41.

    "A Value Theory of Inclusion: Informal Labour, the Homeworker, and the Social Reproduction of Value." Antipode 53:4 (2021): 33–41.

Mies, Maria. Patriarchy and Accumulation on a World Scale: Women in the International Division of Labour. London: Bloomsbury Academic; Reprint edition: 2022.

Nongcun baoyuyuan shouce 农村保育员手册 [Manual for children caregivers in the countryside]. 上海市卫生局, 1958.

Perry, Elizabeth J. "The Promise of PRC History." Journal of Modern Chinese History 10:1 (2016): 113–117.

Piazzaroli Longobardi, Andrea. "What Does a Socialist Factory Produce? Workers in the Chinese Cultural Revolution." PRC History Review 6:1 (February 2021): 1–13. https://networks.h-net.org/volume-6-number-1-february-2021.

Picchio, Antonella. Social Reproduction: The Political Economy of the Labour Market. Cambridge: Cambridge University Press, 1992.

Postone, Moishe. "Rethinking Marx in a Postmarxist World." In Charles Camic, ed., Reclaiming the Sociological Classics. Cambridge, MA: Blackwell, 1998: 45–80.

"Quanguo zonggonghui zhishi gonghui geji zuzhi fadong qunzhong canjia he jiandu gongzi gaige gongzuo" 全国总工会指示工会各级组织 发动群众参加和监督工资改革工作 [The All-China Federation of Trade Unions instructs trade union organizations at all levels to mobilize the masses to participate in and supervise the wage reform process]. RMRB, July 6, 1956.

Ren Baige 任白戈. "Zuzhi chengshi renmin de jingji shenghuo shi jianshe shehuizhuyi xin chengshi de yige zhongyao fangmian" 组织城市人民的经济生活是建设社会主义新城市的一个重要方面 [Organizing the economic life of urban people is an important aspect of building new socialist cities] Hongqi 红旗 5 (1960). Reprinted in Li Duanxiang 李端祥, ed., Chengshi renmin gongshe yanjiu ziliao xuanbian 城市人民公社研究资料选编 [Selected research materials on urban people's communes]. 人民出版社, vol. 8 (2021): 186–197.

Ren Zhongping 任仲平. "'Anlao fen pei' bushi zichanjieji faquan canyu" '按劳分配' 不是资产阶级法权残余 [Remuneration according to labor is not a remnant of bourgeois right]. RMRB, February 12, 1959.

"Renren canjia shehui laodong, jiajia dou guo jitishenghuo. Hongshunli jumin shenghuo dageming. Chengli shengchan fusu hezuoshe, shuli le wo wei renren, renren weiwo de xinfengge" 人人参加社会劳动 家家都过集体生活 鸿顺里居民生活大革命 成立生产服务合作社，树立了我为人人、人人为我的新风格 [Everyone participates in social work, and every family lives collectively. A revolution in the life of the residents of Hongshunli. The establishment of production and service cooperatives has created a new style of "I for everyone and everyone for me"]. *RMRB*, August 19, 1958.

Ross, Kristin. Communal Luxury: The Political Imaginary of the Paris Commune. London: Verso Books, 2015.

The Commune Form: The Transformation of Everyday Life. London: Verso Books, 2024.

Rubin, I. I. Essays on Marx's Theory of Value. Montreal: Black Rose Books, 1973.

Russo, Alessandro. Cultural Revolution and Revolutionary Culture. Durham, NC: Duke University Press, 2020.

"How Did the Cultural Revolution End? The Last Dispute between Mao Zedong and Deng Xiaoping, 1975." Modern China 39:3 (May 2013): 239–279.

Sa Renxing 撒仁兴. "'Anlao fenpei' shi shehuizhuyi de yuance" '按劳分配' 是社会主义的原则 ["Remuneration according to labor" is a socialist principle]. *RMRB*, February 19, 1959.

Salaff, Janet. "The Urban Communes and Anti-City Experiment in Communist China." *China Quarterly*, no. 29 (January–March 1967): 82–110.

Schoenhals, Michael. "Elite Information in China." *Problems of Communism*, no. 34 (September–October 1985): 65–71.

"Saltationist Socialism: Mao Zedong and the Great Leap Forward 1958." Doctoral dissertation, University of Stockholm, 1987.

Schurman, Franz. Ideology and Organization in Communist China. 2nd ed. Berkeley: University of California Press, 1968.

Shen Lizhu 沈丽珠. "Guangwai gongshe guanche zhixing qinjian fangzhen" 广外公社贯彻执行勤俭方针 [The Guangwai Commune carries out the policy of diligence and thrift]. *Beijing Ribao*, August 10, 1960. Reprinted in Li, ed., *Chengshi renmin gongshe yanjiu ziliao xuanbian*, vol. 7: 105–106.

Shields, Rob. Lefebvre Love & Struggle: Spatial Dialectics. London: Routledge, 1999.

Shih Ch'eng-chih. Urban Commune Experiments in Communist China. Communist China Problem Research Series. Hong Kong: Union Research Institute, 1962.

Siegelbaum, Lewis H. "Production Collectives and Communes and the 'Imperatives' of Soviet Industrialization, 1929–1931." Slavic Review 45:1 (Spring 1986): 65–84.

Sloin, Andrew. "Theorizing Soviet Antisemitism: Value, Crisis, and Stalinist 'Modernity.'" Critical Historical Studies 3:2 (Fall 2016): 249–281.

Smith, Aminda M. "Long Live the Mass Line! Errant Cadres and Post-Disillusionment PRC History." positions: asia critique 29:4 (November 2021): 783–807.

Thought Reform and China's Dangerous Classes: Reeducation, Resistance, and the People. Lanham, MD: Rowman and Littlefield, 2012.

Song Shaopeng. "The State Discourse on Housewives and Housework in the 1950s in China." In Mechthild Leutner, ed., Rethinking China in the 1950s. Münster: LIT Verlag, 2007: 49–63.

Song Yangtan 宋养琰. "Jiazji guilü zai shehuizhuyi zong laodong fenpei he shangchan zhong de tiaojie zuoyong" 价值规律在社会主义总劳动分配和生产中的调节作用 [The regulating role of the law of value in the socialist distribution of total labor and production]. *Jingji yanjiu* 经济研究 [Economic Research], no. 11 (1978): 20–27.

Spufford, Francis. Red Plenty. London: Faber and Faber, 2010.

Stalin, J. V. Economic Problems of Socialism in the U.S.S.R. Peking: Foreign Language Press, 1972.

"New Conditions – New Tasks in Economic Construction" (June 23, 1931). www.marxists.org/reference/archive/stalin/works/1931/06/23.htm.

"Report to the Seventeenth Party Congress on the Work of the Central Committee of the C.P.S.U.(B.)" (January 26, 1934). www.marxists.org/reference/archive/stalin/works/1934/01/26.htm.

Su Shucheng 苏树澄. "Guanyu chengshi renmin gongshe suoyouzhi xingzhi wenti de shangque" 关于城市人民公社所有制性質問題的商榷 [Discussing the issue of the nature of ownership in urban communes]. *Zhongguo jingji wenti* 中国经济问题 (Economic Issues in China), no. 8 (1960): 14–17.

Sun, Lung-kee. "The Politics of Hair and the Issue of the Bob in Modern China." Fashion Theory 1:4 (1997): 353–366.

Sun Piqi 孙丕祺. "Yao gongchanzhuyi, buyao jijian gongzi. Wei gongchanzhuyi, bushi wei qian" 要共产主义，不要计件工资 为共产主义，不是为钱 [We want communism, not piece-rate wages. For communism, not for money]. *RMRB*, October 23, 1958.

Sun Yefang 孙冶方. "Ba jihua he tongji fangzai jiazhi guilü de jichushang" 把计划和统计放在价值规律的基础上 [Place planning and statistical work on the basis of the law of value]. *Jingji Yanjiu* 经济研究 [*Economic Research*], no. 6 (1956): 30–38.

Sun Yefang 孙方冶. "Qian guilü, wan guilü, jiazhi guilüdiyitiao" 千规律，万规律，价值规律第一条 [There are a thousand laws, but the first is the law of value]. *Guangming ribao* 光明日报, October 28, 1978.

Sun Yefang 孙冶方. "Yao quanmian tihui Mao Zhuxi guanyu jiazhi guilü wenti de lunshu" 要全面体会毛主席关于价值规律问题的论述 [We must fully understand Chairman Mao's exposition on the question of the law of value]. *Jingji yanjiu* 经济研究 [Economic Research], no. 11 (1978): 8–19.

Teiwes, Frederick C., and Warren Sun. China's Road to Disaster: Mao, Central Politicians and Provincial Leaders in the Great Leap Forward, 1955–59. Armonk, NY: M. E. Sharpe, 1999.

Toscano, Alberto. "Transition Deprogrammed." South Atlantic Quarterly 113:4 (Fall 2014): 761–775.

Varela, Paula. "Social Reproduction in Dispute: A Debate between Autonomists and Marxists." *Spectre* (December 10, 2021). https://spectrejournal.com/social-reproduction-in-dispute/.

Vora, Kalindi. "After the Housewife: Surrogacy, Labour and Human Reproduction." Radical Philosophy 2:4 (Spring 2019): 42–46.

Wang Chunying and Y. Yvon Wang. "Gray Markets in the Great Leap: Prosecuting 'Profiteering' in Liangshan County, Shandong, 1958–1960." Modern China 48:5 (2022): 948–981.

Wang Congchao 王丛超. "Cong guojia caizheng jiaodu laikan, chengshi renmin gongshe suoyouzhi jibenshang shi jitixingzhi de" 从国家财政角度来看，城市人民公社所有制基本上是集体性质的 [From the point of view of state finance ownership in urban communes is essentially collective in nature]. Zhongguo jingji wenti 中国经济问题 [Economic Issues in China), no. 8 (1960): 9–11.

Wang Pu 王璞. "Bu neng fouding wuzhi liyi yuance" 不能否定物质利益原则 [We cannot deny the principle of material benefits]. *RMRB*, January 20, 1959.

Wang Xianming 王先明. "Cong jumin dao sheyuan: chengshi renmin gongshe chengyuan de shenfen renting – Yi Tianjin chengshi renmin gongshe wei li" 从居民到社员:城市人民公社成员的身份认同 – 以天津城市人民公社为例 [From residents to members: The identity of urban people's commune members—The case of Tianjin urban people's commune]. *Shehui kexue yanjiu* 社会科学研究 [Social sciences research], no. 4 (2020): 142–150.

Wang Yongxi 王永錫, Zhao Guoliang 趙国良, Wang Fangtian 王方田, Guo Shaoxiang 郭紹湘, Li Bicheng 李必成, and Xiao Deyu 肖德愚. "Guanyu chengshi renmin gongshe suoyouzhi wenti de chubu tantao" 关于城市人民公社所有制問題的初步探討 [A preliminary study on the ownership of urban people's communes]. *Caijing kexue* 财经科学 [Finance and economics], no. 4 (1960): 21–33.

Wang Zheng. Finding Women in the State: A Socialist Feminist Revolution in the People's Republic of China, 1949–1964. Berkeley: University of California Press, 2016.

Wemhauer, Felix. Famine Politics in Maoist China and the Soviet Union. New Haven, CT: Yale University Press, 2014.

Willimott, Andy. Living the Revolution: Urban Communes & Soviet Socialism, 1917–1932. Oxford University Press, 2017.

Wu Chuanqi 吴传启. "Cong renmin gongshe kan gongchanzhuyi" 从人民公社看共产主义 [Looking at communism from the people's communes]. *RMRB*, October 1, 1958.

Wu Dingqiu 吴定求. "Yao quanmian gujia 'anlaoquchou'" 要全面估价 '按劳取酬' [We have to fully appraise "remuneration according to labor"]. *RMRB*, November 19, 1958.

Wu Hung. Remaking Beijing: Tiananmen Square and the Creation of a Political Space. Chicago: University of Chicago Press, 2005.

"Xiang zichanjieji faquan guannian xuanzhan" 向资产阶级法权观念宣战 [Declaring war on bourgeois right]. *RMRB*, November 1, 1958.

Xin Zhongguo liushinian Tongji ziliao huibian 新中国六十年统计资料汇编 (China Compendium of Statistics 1949–2008). Compiled by the Department of Comprehensive Statistics of National Bureau of Statistics. Beijing: China Statistics Press, 2009.

Xiong Fu 熊复. "Tongxiang gongchanzhuyi de daolu dakaile" 通向共产主义的道路打开了 [The road to communism is open]. *RMRB*, November 7, 1958.

Xu Hongzhong 徐红中. "Dakai zichanjieji faquan de fangkongdong" 打开资产阶级法权的防空洞 [Break open the bomb shelter of bourgeois right]. *RMRB*, October 30, 1958.

Xu, Liqun. "Have We Already Reached the Stage of Communism?" In Robert R. Bowie and John K. Fairbank, eds., Communist China, 1955–1959: Policy

Documents with Analysis. Cambridge, MA: Harvard University Press, 1962: 479–483. Originally published in *Hongqi* (Red Flag), November 16, 1958.

Xue Muqiao 薛暮桥. "Liyong jiazhi guilü wei jingji jianshe shiye fuwu" 利用价值规律为经济建设事业服务 [Use the law of value to serve the cause of economic construction]. *Hongqi* 红旗 [Red flag], no. 1 (1979): 15–27.

"Shehuizhuyi shehui de anlaofenpei zhidu" 社会主义社会的按劳分配制度 [The remuneration according to labor system of socialist society]. *RMRB*, October 23, 1959.

Yang, Dali L. Calamity and Reform in China: State, Rural Society, and Institutional Change since the Great Leap Famine. Stanford, CA: Stanford University Press, 1996.

Yao Ertao 姚二涛. "Chengshi renmin gongshe 'gongchanfeng' tanwei" 城市人民公社'共产风'探微 [Exploring the 'communist winds' in urban people's communes]. *Guangdong dangshi yu wenxian yanju* 广东党史与文献研究 [Guangdong Party History and Literature Research], no. 1 (2022): 85–95.

"Yiding yao jixu yuejin, yiding neng jixu yuejin" 一定要继续跃进, 一定能继续跃进 [We definitely must continue to leap forward, we definitely can continue to leap forward]. *RMRB*, March 31, 1960.

Yin Jianqing 尹剑青. "Gai gongzizhi shi yie lishi jiaoxun" 改工资制是一个历史教训 [Reforming the wage system is a history lesson]. *RMRB*, October 27, 1958.

"Yong gongchanzhuyi guandian kan fenpei zhidu. Gedi taolun zichanjieji faquan wenti" 用共产主义观点看分配制度 各地讨论资产阶级法权问题 [Looking at the distribution system using the concept of communism. Discussions on bourgeois legal rights in various places]. *RMRB*, November 3, 1958.

Yu Yingshi 于英士. "Zhoumo lifaji" 周末理发记 [Weekend haircut]. *RMRB*, June 26, 1963.

Zhang Chengxian 张承先. "Jiaqiang gongchanzhuyi jiaoyu, jiasu shehuizhuyi jianshe" 加强共产主义教育 加速社会主义建设 [Strengthen communist education, speed up socialist construction]. *RMRB*, January 22, 1959.

Zhang Chunqiao 张春桥. "Pochu zichanjieji de faquan sixiang" 破除资产阶级的法权思想 [Do away with the ideology of bourgeois right]. *RMRB*, October 13, 1958. English translation at http://marxistphilosophy.org/BourgeoisRightWeb .pdf.

Zhang, Kevin H. "The Evolution of China's Urban Transformation: 1949–2000." In Chen Aimin, Gordon G. Liu, and Kevin H. Zhang, eds., Urban Transformation in China. London: Routledge, 2016 (Kindle edition).

Zhang Minzhi 张民植 and Cui Chengshan 崔成善. "Jianshe shehuizhuyi shehui yao you gongchanzhuyi sixiang – Ji Taiyuan suliaochang chengpin chejian-gongren de yichang da bianlun" 建设社会主义社会要有共产主义思想 – 记太原塑料厂成品车间工人的一场大辩论 [To build a socialist society we need communist ideology – A record of the debate among workers at the finished product workshop in the Taiyuan plastic factory]. *RMRB*, November 5, 1958.

Zhang, Zhuoyuan, ed. Historical Perspectives on Chinese Economics (1949–2011). Translated by Xiaotong Zhang. Singapore: China Social Sciences Press/Springer, 2020.

Zheng Jiqiao 郑季翘. "Tantan xiaochu zichanjieji faquan" 谈谈削除资产阶级法权 [Talking about the eradication of bourgeois right]. *RMRB*, October 18, 1958.

"Zaitan xiaochu zichanjieji faquan" 再谈削除除资产阶级法权 [Discussing again the elimination of bourgeois right]. *RMRB*, January 27, 1959.

"Zhonggong Beijing, Shanghai, Tianjin, Wuhan, Guangzhou wushi shiwei shuji zai rendahui shang lianhe fayan dachengshi bixu zhubu fenpi shixian gong-shehua" 中共北京、上海、天津、武汉、广州五市市委书记 在人大会上联合发言 大城市必须逐步分批实现公社化 [The municipal party committee secretaries of Beijing, Shanghai, Tianjin, Wuhan, and Guangzhou spoke jointly at the National People's Congress]. *RMRB*, April 10, 1960.

Zhonggong Zhongyang dangshi he wenxian yanjiuyuan 中共中央党史和文献研究院, ed. Jianguo yilai Mao Zedong wengao 建国以来毛泽东文稿 [Mao Zedong's writing since the founding of the country]. 20 vols. Beijing: Zhongyang wenxian chubanshe, 2024.

Zhongguo kexueyuan jingji yanjiusuo bian 中国科学院经济研究所编. *Guanyu shehuizhuyi zhiduxia shangpin shengchan he jiazhi guilüwenti. 1959 nian 4 yue taolunhui lunwen* 关于社会主义制度下商品生产和价值规律问题。1959 年4月讨论会论文、资料汇编 [A compilation of papers and materials from the April 1959 conference on commodity production and the law of value under the socialist system]. 科学出版社, 1959.

Zhuo Jiong 卓炯. "Jiazhi guilü yu sige xiandaihua" 价值规律与四个现代化 [The law of value and the four modernizations]. *Xueshu yuekan* 学术月刊 [Academic monthly], no. 2 (1979): 29–32.

# Index

For EU product safety concerns, contact us at Calle de José Abascal, 56–1°, 28003 Madrid, Spain or eugpsr@cambridge.org.

www.ingramcontent.com/pod-product-compliance
Ingram Content Group UK Ltd.
Pitfield, Milton Keynes, MK11 3LW, UK
UKHW022136120526
471007UK00012B/1079